THE KEY

STUDENT STUDY GUIDE

Math 10 Academic

THE KEY student study guide is designed to help students achieve success in school. The content in each study guide is 100% curriculum aligned and serves as an excellent source of material for review and practice. To create this book, teachers, curriculum specialists, and assessment experts have worked closely to develop the instructional pieces that explain each of the key concepts for the course. The practice questions and sample tests have detailed solutions that show problem-solving methods, highlight concepts that are likely to be tested, and point out potential sources of errors. ***THE KEY*** is a complete guide to be used by students throughout the school year for reviewing and understanding course content, and to prepare for assessments.

Rao, Gautam, 1961 –
THE KEY –Math 10 Academic
Ontario

1. Mathematics – Juvenile Literature. I. Title

Published by
Castle Rock Research Corp.
2340 Manulife Place
10180 – 101 Street
Edmonton, AB T5J 3S4

2 3 4 FP 13 12 11

Publisher
Gautam Rao

Contributors
Renee Nutt
Ted Whyte

CASTLE ROCK
RESEARCH CORP

Dedicated to the memory of Dr. V. S. Rao

THE KEY–Grade 10 Academic Mathematics

THE KEY consists of the following sections:

KEY Tips for Being Successful at School gives examples of study and review strategies. It includes information about learning styles, study schedules, and note taking for test preparation.

Class Focus includes a unit on each area of the curriculum. Units are divided into sections, each focusing on one of the specific expectations, or main ideas, that students must learn about in that unit. Examples, definitions, and visuals help to explain each main idea. Practice questions on the main ideas are also included. At the end of each unit is a test on the important ideas covered. The practice questions and unit tests help students identify areas they know and those they need to study more. They can also be used as preparation for tests and quizzes. Most questions are of average difficulty, though some are easy and some are hard—the harder questions are called *Challenger Questions*. Each unit is prefaced by a ***Table of Correlations***, which correlates questions in the unit (and in the practice tests at the end of the book) to the specific curriculum expectations. Answers and solutions are found at the end of each unit.

KEY Strategies for Success on Tests helps students get ready for tests. It shows students different types of questions they might see, word clues to look for when reading them, and hints for answering them.

Practice Tests includes one to three tests based on the entire course. They are very similar to the format and level of difficulty that students may encounter on final tests. In some regions, these tests may be reprinted versions of official tests, or reflect the same difficulty levels and formats as official versions. This gives students the chance to practice using real-world examples. Answers and complete solutions are provided at the end of the section.

For the complete curriculum document (including specific expectations along with examples and sample problems), visit www.edu.gov.on.ca/eng/curriculum/secondary.

THE KEY *Study Guides* are available for many courses.
Check www.castlerockresearch.com for a complete listing of books available for your area.

For information about any of our resources or services, please call Castle Rock Research at 905.625.3332 or visit our website at http://www.castlerockresearch.com.

At Castle Rock Research, we strive to produce an error-free resource. If you should find an error, please contact us so that future editions can be corrected.

CONTENTS

KEY Tips for Being Successful at School

KEY FACTORS CONTRIBUTING TO SCHOOL SUCCESS

In addition to learning the contents of your courses, there are some other things that you can do to help you do your best at school. Some of these strategies are listed below.

- **ATTEND SCHOOL REGULARLY** so you do not miss any classes, notes, or important activities that will help you learn.
- **KEEP A POSITIVE ATTITUDE.** Always reflect on what you can already do and what you already know.
- **BE PREPARED TO LEARN.** Have the necessary materials (pencils, pens, notebooks, and other required materials) with you in class.
- **COMPLETE ALL OF YOUR ASSIGNMENTS.** Do your best to finish all of your assignments. Even if you know the material well, practice will reinforce your knowledge. If an assignment or question is difficult for you, work through it as far as you can so your teacher can see exactly where you are having difficulty.
- **SET SMALL GOALS** for yourself when you are learning new material. For example, when learning formulas, do not try to learn everything in one night. Work on only one formula each study session. When you understand one particular formula and have memorized it, move on to another one. Continue this process until you have learned and memorized all of the required formulas.
- **REVIEW YOUR CLASSROOM WORK** regularly at home to be sure you understand the material you learned in class.
- **ASK YOUR TEACHER FOR HELP** when you do not understand something or when you are having difficulty completing your assignments.
- **GET PLENTY OF REST AND EXERCISE.** Concentrating in class is hard work. It is important to be well-rested and have time to relax and socialize with your friends. This helps you to keep a positive attitude about your school work.
- **EAT HEALTHY MEALS.** A balanced diet keeps you healthy and gives you the energy you need for studying at school and at home.

HOW TO FIND YOUR LEARNING STYLE

Every student has a certain manner in which it seems easier for him or her to learn. The manner in which you learn best is called your learning style. By knowing your learning style, you can increase your success at school. Most students use a combination of learning styles.

Do you know what type of learner you are? Read the following descriptions. Which of these common learning styles do you use most often?

- **Do you need to say things out loud?** You may learn best by saying, hearing, and seeing words. You are probably really good at memorizing dates, places, names, and facts. To learn the steps in a process, a formula, or the actions that lead up to a significant event, you may need **to write them and then read them out loud**.

- **Do you need to read or see things?** You may learn best by looking at and working with pictures. You are probably really good at puzzles, imagining things, and reading maps and charts. You may need to use strategies like **mind mapping and webbing** to organize your information and study notes.

- **Do you need to draw or write things down?** You may learn best by touching, moving, and figuring things out using manipulatives. You are probably really good at physical activities and learning through movement. You may need to **draw your finger over a diagram** to remember it, ***tap out*** **the steps** needed to solve a problem, or ***feel*** **yourself writing** or typing a formula.

SCHEDULING STUDY TIME

You should review your class notes regularly to be sure you have a clear understanding of all the new material you learned. Reviewing your lessons on a regular basis helps you to learn and remember ideas and concepts. It also reduces the quantity of material you need to study prior to a test. Creating a study schedule will help you to make the best use of your time.

Regardless of the type of study schedule you use, you may want to consider the following strategies for making the most of your study time and effort:

- Organize your work so you begin with the most challenging material first.
- Divide the subject content into small, manageable chunks.
- Alternate regularly between your different subjects and types of study activities in order to maintain your interest and motivation.
- Make a daily list with the headings *must do*, *should do*, and *could do*.
- Begin each study session by quickly reviewing what you studied the day before.
- Maintain your usual routine of eating, sleeping, and exercising to help you concentrate better for extended periods of time.

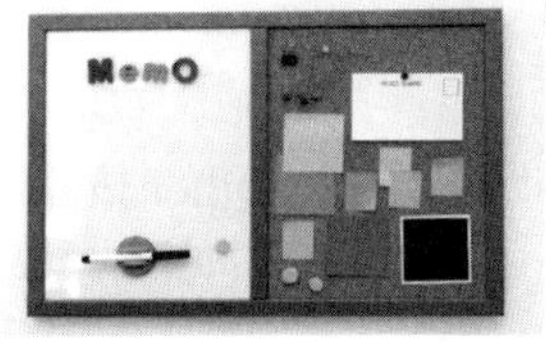

CREATING STUDY NOTES

MIND-MAPPING OR WEBBING

- Use the key words, ideas, or concepts from your class notes to create a *mind map* or *mind web*, which is a diagram or visual representation of the given information. A mind map or web is sometimes referred to as a *knowledge map*.
- Write the key word, concept, theory, or formula in the centre of your page.
- Write down related facts, ideas, events, and information and then link them to the central concept.
- The following examples of a Frayer Model illustrate how this technique can be used to study mathematical vocabulary.

Definition – Perimeter is the distance around a polygon	**Characteristics** – Measured in linear units (e.g., metres, centimetres)
Examples – Fence around a yard – Distance around a circle (circumference)	**Non-examples** – Grass covering a yard – Area of rug covering a floor

Definition A cube is a solid 3-D object that has – 6 square faces, all equal in size – 8 vertices – 12 equal edges	**Visual Presentation** 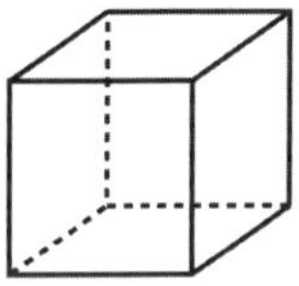
Characteristics or Properties – 6 square faces – 8 vertices – 12 edges – 6 flat faces	**Examples** 

Index Cards

To use index cards while studying, follow these steps:

- Write a key word or question on one side of an index card.
- On the other side, write the definition of the word, answer to the question, or any other important information you want to remember.

What is a prime number?

What is a prime number?

A prime number is a number that has exactly 2 factors. A prime number can be divided evenly only by itself and one. E.g., 2, 3, 5, 7, 17, 19. The number 1 is not a prime number.

Symbols and Sticky Notes—Identifying Important Information

- Use symbols to mark your class notes. For example, an exclamation mark (!) might be used to point out something that must be learned well because it is a very important idea. A question mark (?) may highlight something you are not certain about, and a diamond (◊) or asterisk (*) could mark interesting information you want to remember.
- Use sticky notes to mark a page in a book that contains an important diagram, formula, or explanation.

KEY STRATEGIES FOR REVIEWING

Reviewing textbook material, class notes, and handouts should be an ongoing activity. Spending time reviewing becomes more critical when you are preparing for tests. You may find some of the following review strategies useful when studying during your scheduled study time.

- Before reviewing a unit, note the headings, charts, graphs, and chapter questions.
- Highlight mathematical key concepts, vocabulary, definitions, and formulas.
- Carefully read over each step in a procedure.
- Draw a picture or diagram to help make the concept clearer.

KEY STRATEGIES FOR SUCCESS—A CHECKLIST

Review, review, review: that is a huge part of doing well at school and preparing for tests. Below is a checklist for you to keep track of how many suggested strategies for success you use. Read each question and then put a check mark (✓) in the correct column. Look at the questions for which you have checked the *No* column. Think about how you might try using some of these strategies to help you do your best at school.

***KEY* Strategies for Success**	**Yes**	**No**
Do you attend school regularly?		
Do you know your personal learning style—how you learn best?		
Do you spend 15 to 30 minutes each day reviewing your notes?		
Do you study in a quiet place at home?		
Do you clearly mark the most important ideas in your study notes?		
Do you use sticky notes to mark texts and research books?		
Do you practice answering multiple-choice and written-response questions?		
Do you ask your teacher for help when you need it?		
Do you maintain a healthy diet and sleep routine?		
Do you participate in regular physical activity?		

NOTES

Quadratic Functions

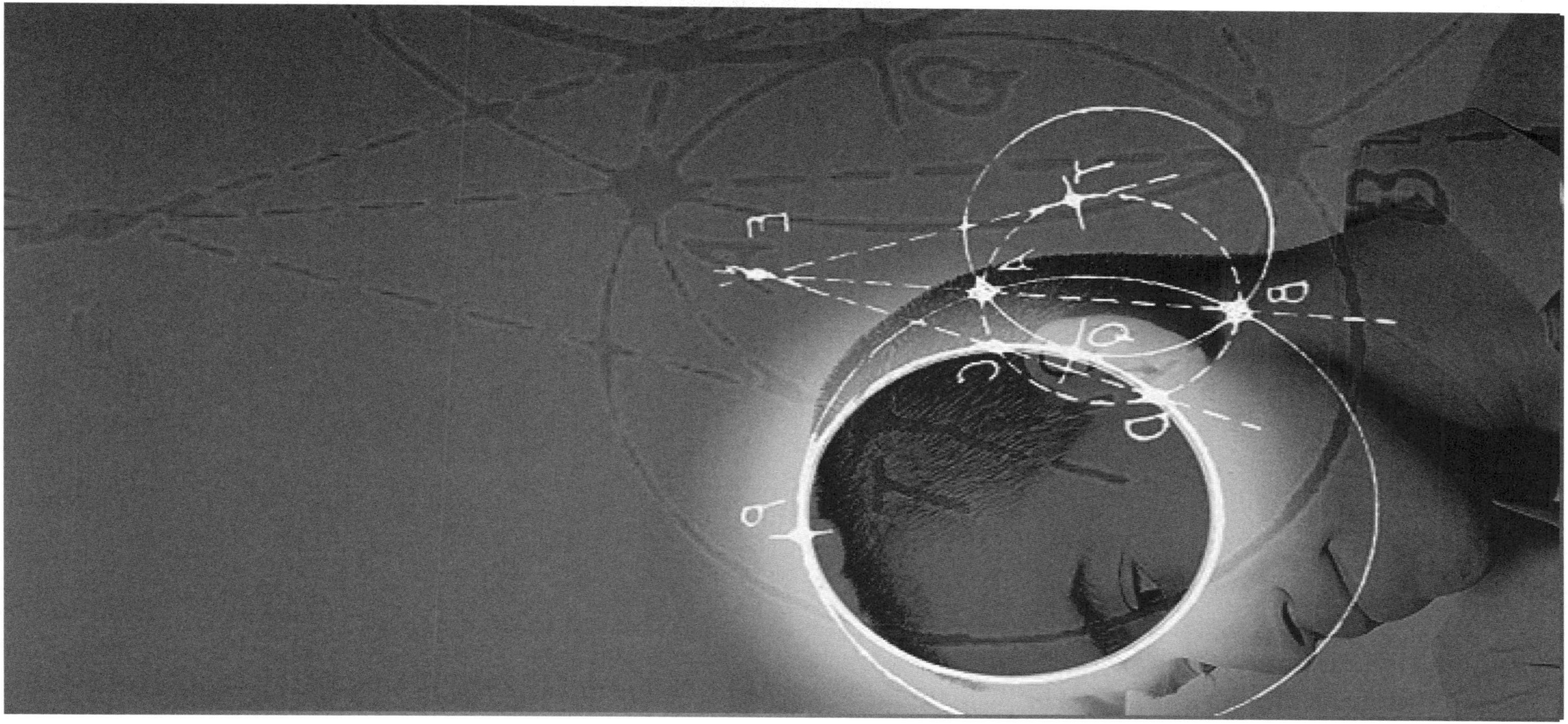

Quadratic Relations

Table of Correlations

Specific Expectation	Practice Questions	Unit Test Questions
QR1 Investigating the Basic Properties of Quadratic Relations		
QR1.1 *collect data that can be represented as a quadratic relation, from experiments using appropriate equipment and technology or from secondary sources ; graph the data and draw a curve of best fit, if appropriate, with or without the use of technology*	1, 2, 3	1
QR1.2 *determine, through investigation with and without the use of technology, that a quadratic relation of the form* $y = ax^2 + bx + c (a \neq 0)$ *can be graphically represented as a parabola, and that the table of values yields a constant second difference*	4, 5, 6	2
QR1.3 *identify the key features of a graph of a parabola, and use the appropriate terminology to describe them*	7, 8, 9	3, 4, 5
QR1.4 *compare, through investigation using technology, the features of the graph of* $y = x^2$ *and the graph of* $y = 2^x$, *and determine the meaning of a negative exponent and of zero as an exponent*	10, 11	6, 7
QR2 Relating the Graph of $y = x^2$ and Its Transformations		
QR2.1 *identify, through investigation using technology, the effect on the graph of* $y = x^2$ *of transformations by considering separately each parameter* a, h, *and* k	12, 13, 14	8, 9
QR2.2 *explain the roles of* a, h, *and* k *in* $y = a(x - h)^2 + k$, *using the appropriate terminology to describe the transformations, and identify the vertex and the equation of the axis of symmetry*	15, 16, 17	10, 11, 12
QR2.3 *sketch, by hand, the graph of* $y = a(x - h)^2 + k$ *by applying transformations to the graph of* $y = x^2$	18, 19, 20	13
QR2.4 *determine the equation, in the form* $y = a(x - h)^2 + k$, *of a given graph of a parabola*	21, 22, 23a, 23b, 23c	14, 15, 16a, 16b, 16c
QR3 Solving Quadratic Equations		
QR3.1 *expand and simplify second-degree polynomial expressions using a variety of tools and strategies*	24, 25	17, 18
QR3.2 *factor polynomial expressions involving common factors, trinomials, and differences of squares using a variety of tools and strategies*	26, 27, 28, 29	19, 20
QR3.3 *determine, through investigation, and describe the connection between the factors of a quadratic expression and the* x*-intercepts of the graph of the corresponding quadratic relation, expressed in the form* $y = a(x - r)(x - s)$	30, 31	21, 22
QR3.4 *interpret real and non-real roots of quadratic equations, through investigation using graphing technology, and relate the roots to the* x*-intercepts of the corresponding relations*	32, 33, 34	23, 24
QR3.5 *express* $y = ax^2 + bx + c$ *in the form* $y = a(x - h)^2 + k$ *by completing the square in situations involving no fractions, using a variety of tools*	35, 36, 37, 38	25, 26, 27
QR3.6 *sketch or graph a quadratic relation whose equation is given in the form* $y = ax^2 + bx + c$, *using a variety of methods*	39, 40, 41	28, 29
QR3.7 *explore the algebraic development of the quadratic formula*	42, 43	30, 31
QR3.8 *solve quadratic equations that have real roots, using a variety of methods*	44, 45, 46, 47a, 47b, 47c	32, 33, 34a, 34b, 34c

Specific Expectation	Practice Questions	Unit Test Questions
QR4 Solving Problems Involving Quadratic Relations		
QR4.1 *determine the zeros and the maximum or minimum value of a quadratic relation from its graph or from its defining equation*	48, 49, 50	35, 36
QR4.2 *solve problems arising from a realistic situation represented by a graph or an equation of a quadratic relation, with and without the use of technology.*	51, 52, 53, 54a, 54b, 54c	37, 38, 39, 40a, 40b, 40c, 40d

QR1.1 *collect data that can be represented as a quadratic relation, from experiments using appropriate equipment and technology or from secondary sources ; graph the data and draw a curve of best fit, if appropriate, with or without the use of technology*

Quadratic Relations That Model Data

Quadratic relations can represent certain types of motion, populations, and other numerical rate problems and can therefore be used to model a specific set of **data**.

Collecting Data

There are several methods in which data can be collected for mathematical analysis. These include:

- Conducting experiments in class involving motion and concrete materials.
- Conducting experiments using technology such as graphing calculators and the CBR™.
  *Note that when collecting data by conducting experiments, several trials should be done to ensure more realistic results.
- Using a secondary source such as the Internet or Statistics Canada.

Graphing the Data

After data is collected, it can be represented by a set of points on a Cartesian plane and may generate a pattern that can be represented by drawing a single curve. This curve is called the **curve of best fit** and can be drawn either by hand or by using technology.

Example

Number of Registered Apprentices in Building Construction Trades in Canada, from 1991 to 2003

Year	Year Number	Number (Thousands)
1991	1	46 925
1992	2	43 703
1993	3	40 996
1994	4	36 679
1995	5	34 786
1996	6	33 394
1997	7	32 957
1998	8	33 395
1999	9	36 496
2000	10	39 090
2001	11	42 109
2002	12	47 545
2003	13	53 606

Source: Statistics Canada, Registered Apprenticeship Information System.

Draw, by hand as well as by using technology, the curve of best fit that represents the data. Assume that the data represents a quadratic relation.

Plot the points and sketch a curve that best represents the points, as illustrated below.

Using Graph Paper:

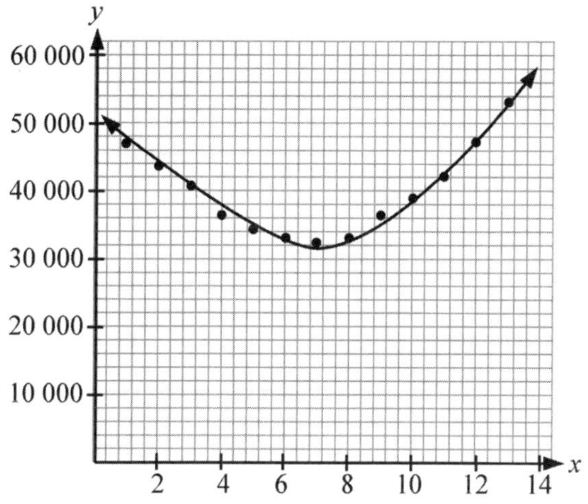

Note: the curve of best fit should be similar to the curve shown but may not be exactly the same.

Using a TI-83 Plus Graphing Calculator:

1. Enter the lists into the list editor.

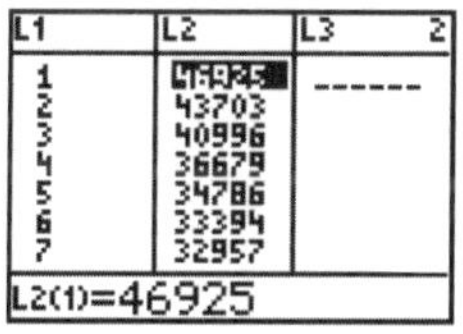

2. Perform a **quadratic regression**, and then enter the resulting equation in [Y =] in order to plot the curve of best fit.

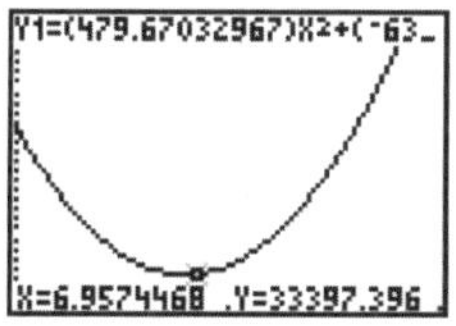

Practice

Numerical Response

Use the following information to answer the next two questions.

The owner of a 300-seat theatre sells tickets for $20 each. He believes that for every dollar he increases the price of a ticket, he will lose 10 customers. He has charted his research as follows:

Increase in Price ($)	Revenue ($)
0	6 000
1	6 090
2	6 160
3	6 210
4	6 240
5	6 250
6	6 240

1. If the owner's revenue is $5 760, then he is charging $____ per ticket.

2. Which of the following equations **best** models the given data?

   A. $y = -10x^2 + 93x + 6\ 036$

   B. $y = -10x^2 + 110x + 5\ 990$

   C. $y = -9x^2 + 107x + 6\ 000$

   D. $y = -10x^2 + 100x + 6\ 000$

Use the following information to answer the next question.

One of the factors that determines the cost of car insurance is the age of the driver. It has been found that drivers under the age of 25 and drivers over the age of 70 are statistically more likely to have accidents compared to drivers between the ages of 25 and 70. The data in the table shows the percentage of accidents reported to a particular insurance company by their clients for various age groups.

Age Group (in years)	Group Number	Percent of Accidents
Under 20	1	20
20–30	2	16
30–40	3	12
40–50	4	10
50–60	5	11
60–70	6	14
Over 70	7	17

3. Which of the following graphs **best** displays the information given in the table shown?

A.

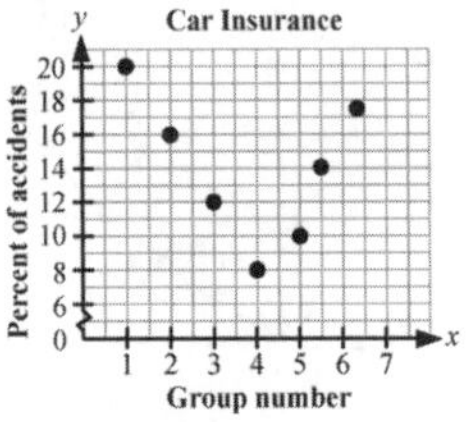

B.

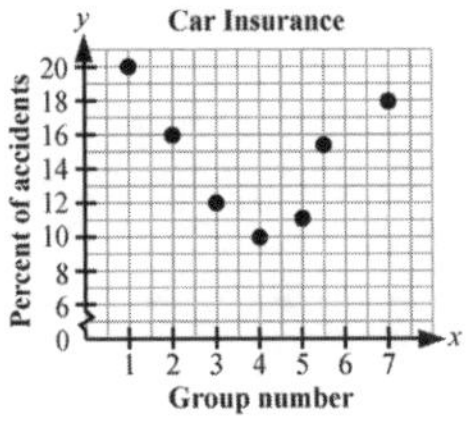

C.

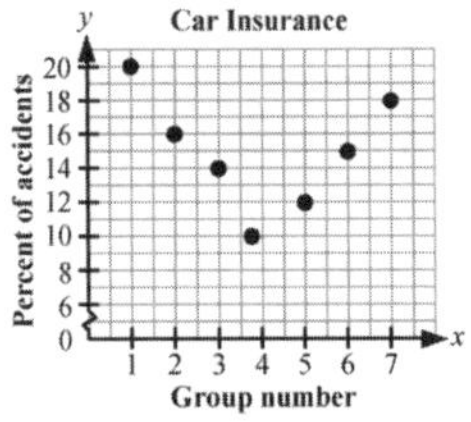

D.

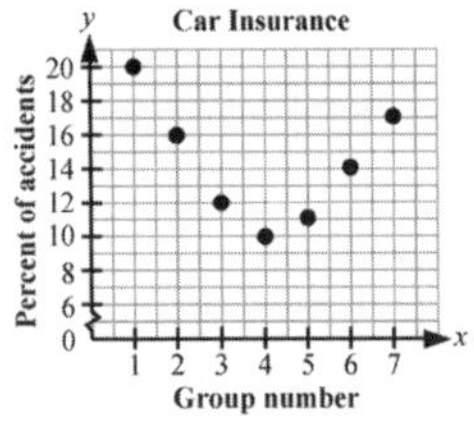

QR1.2 *determine, through investigation with and without the use of technology, that a quadratic relation of the form* $y = ax^2 + bx + c \, (a \neq 0)$ *can be graphically represented as a parabola, and that the table of values yields a constant second difference*

Parabolas and Second Differences

A relation of the form $y = ax^2 + bx + c, (a \neq 0)$ will yield a U-shaped graph that either opens upward or downward. This graph is called a **parabola**. Also, when the second differences from a table of values for a relation of the form $y = ax^2 + bx + c$, $(a \neq 0)$ are constant, the relation is quadratic.

Example

Using the second difference, determine if the given data represents a quadratic relation.

x	−1	0	1	2	3	4
y	−1	0	1	8	27	81

One possible partial table of values is shown

Constant increment of 1

x	y	1st diff	2nd diff
−1	−1		
		1	
0	0		0
		1	
1	1		6
		7	
2	8		12
		19	
3	27		35
		54	
4	81		

Since the second differences for this set of data are not constant, this function does not represent a quadratic relation of the form $y = ax^2 + bx + c$, $(a \neq 0)$.

Example

Determine the direction of opening and the second difference for the quadratic function $h = 5.5 + 6t - 3.2t^2$.

Begin by entering $h = 5.5 + 6t - 3.2t^2$ into a TI-83 Plus graphing calculator.

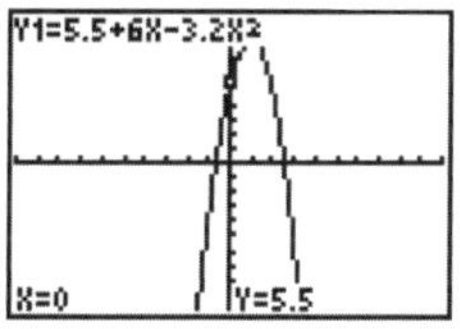

The graph shows a parabola opening downward.

Now, use the table feature from the TI-83 Plus graphing calculator. One possible table of values is shown below.

Constant increment of 1

x	y	1st diff	2nd diff
0	5.5		
		2.8	
1	8.3		−6.4
		−3.6	
2	4.7		−6.4
		−10	
3	−5.3		−6.4
		−16.4	
4	−21.7		−6.4
		−22.8	
5	−44.5		−6.4
		−29.2	
6	−73.7		

Using the table of values and calculating the second differences, there is a constant difference of −6.4. Therefore, $h = 5.5 + 6t - 3.2t^2$ is a parabola that opens downward, and the function has a second difference of −6.4.

Practice

4. Which of the following graphs could represent the graph of $y = ax^2$?

A.
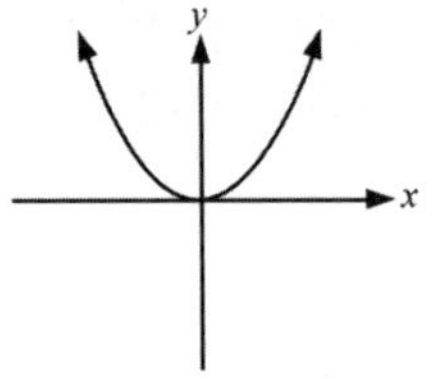

B.
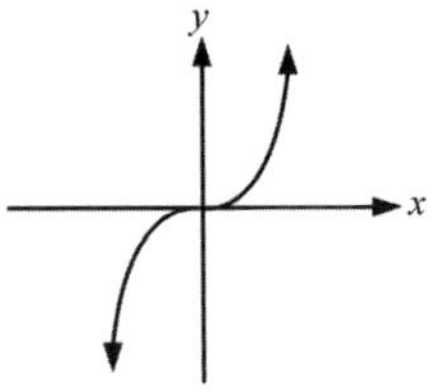

C.
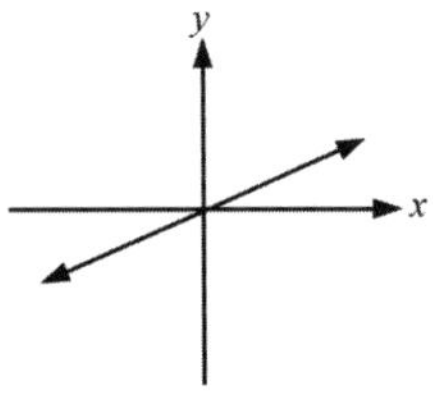

D.
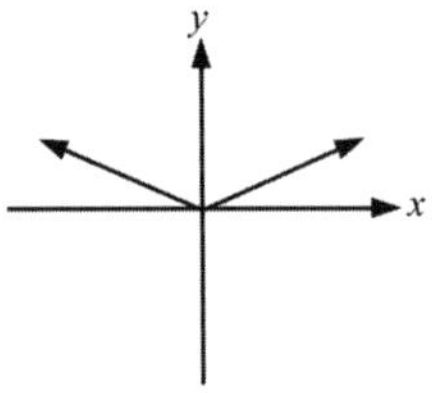

5. The equation of a quadratic function that opens upward and has a second difference of 5 could be

A. $y = -0.8x^2 - 5.5x + 23.8$

B. $y = -2.5x^2 + 6x + 5$

C. $y = 5x^2 + 4x - 3$

D. $y = 2.5x^2 - 3x - 8$

6. Which of the following partial tables of values could represent a table of values for a quadratic function?

A.

x	y	First Difference
1	8	}3
2		}3
3		}3
4		}3
5		}3
6		

B.

x	y	First Difference
1	4	}9
2		}15
3		}21
4		}27
5		}33
6		

C.

x	y	First Difference
1	4	}2
2		}5
3		}9
4		}14
5		}20
6		

D.

x	y	First Difference
1	0	}1
2		}4
3		}9
4		}16
5		}25
6		

QR1.3 *identify the key features of a graph of a parabola, and use the appropriate terminology to describe them*

Identifying Key Features of a Parabola

From QR 1.2, recall that the graph of a quadratic function is a U-shaped curve opening either upward or downward. This U-shaped curve is called a parabola. The key features of a parabola are the maximum and minimum values, the vertex, the axis of symmetry, zeros, and the y-intercept.

Maximum or Minimum Values

A **maximum value** occurs when the parabola opens downward. The maximum value is the y-coordinate of the highest point on the curve.

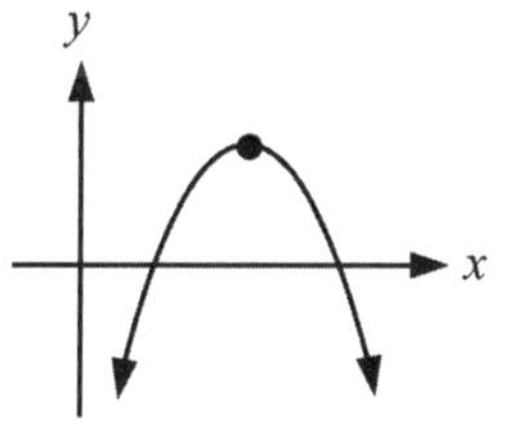

A **minimum value** occurs when the parabola opens upward. The minimum value is the y-coordinate of the lowest point on the curve.

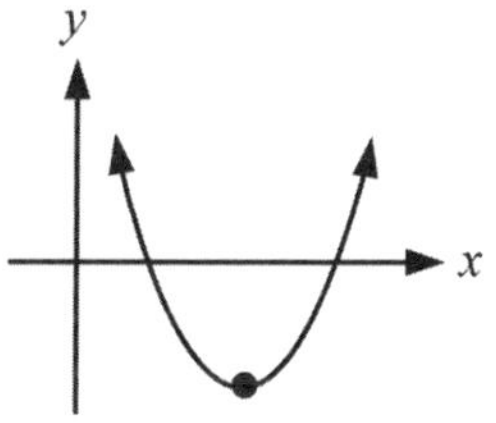

Vertex

The **vertex** is the ordered pair where the maximum or minimum value of y occurs.

The parabola shown below has a maximum value of 1 when $x = 0$. The vertex is $(0, 1)$.

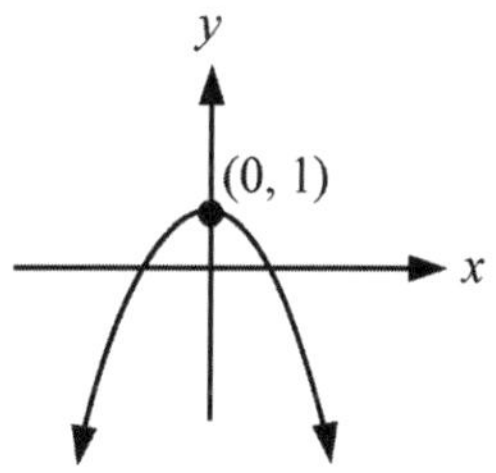

Axis of Symmetry

The **axis of symmetry** is a vertical line that passes through the vertex of the parabola and divides the parabola into two equal halves each of which is the mirror image of the other. The axis of symmetry also passes through the midpoint of any horizontal segment that connects two points on the parabola.

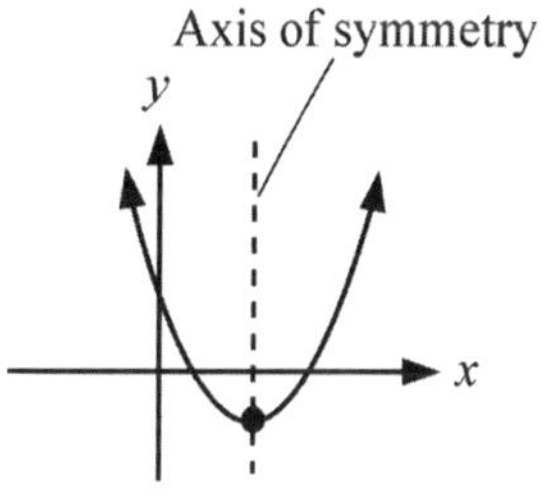

ZEROS

The **zeros** of a quadratic relation of the form $y = ax^2 + bx + c, (a \neq 0)$ are the value(s) of x that make the quadratic relation equal to zero. Thus, the zeros (also called the x-intercepts) are the x-coordinates of each ordered pair where the parabola touches or intersects the x-axis. For a quadratic function, there can either be 0, 1 or 2 real zeros.

y-INTERCEPT

The **y-intercept** of a quadratic relation of the form $y = ax^2 + bx + c, (a \neq 0)$ is the y-coordinate of the ordered pair where the parabola intersects the y-axis.

Example

Determine the following features of the parabola shown.

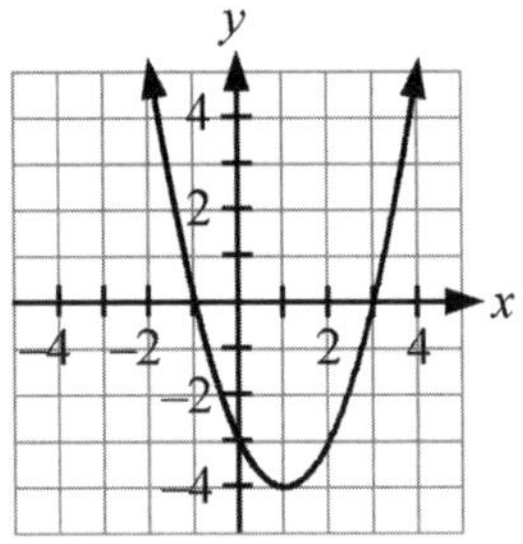

- Vertex
- Maximum or minimum value
- Zeros
- y-intercept
- Axis of symmetry

The vertex of the parabola is $(1, -4)$, the ordered pair where the minimum value of y occurs.

The minimum value is $y = -4$, (-4 is the y-coordinate of the vertex).

The zeros are $x = -1$ or $x = 3$, the x-coordinate of each ordered pair where the parabola intersects the x-axis.

The parabola passes through the y-axis at the ordered pair $(0, -3)$ so the y-intercept is -3.

The axis of symmetry is the vertical line $x = 1$ (1 is the x-coordinate of the vertex).

EXTRA INFORMATION

Domain – The **domain** of a relation is the permissible x-values. These are the x-values for which the relation is defined.

The domain of the quadratic relation $y = ax^2 + bx + c, (a \neq 0)$ will always be $x \in \mathbf{R}$.

Range – The **range** of a relation is the permissible y-values. These are the y-values for which the relation is defined. In the previous example, the range is $y \geq -4$.

Practice

Use the following information to answer the next question.

The partial graph of the quadratic function $y = f(x)$ is shown.

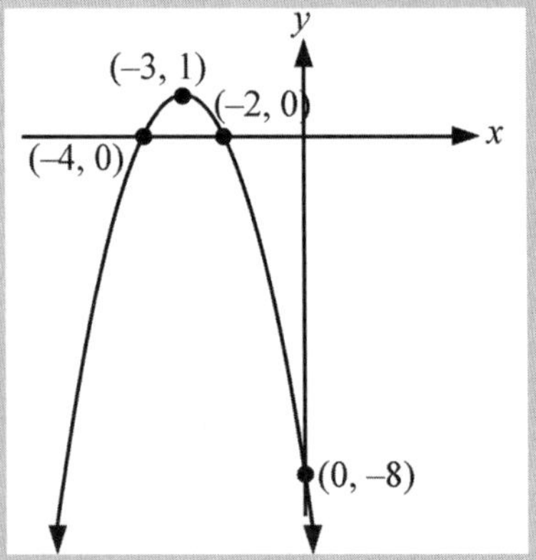

7. Which of the following statements about the graph of $y = f(x)$ is **false**?

A. The domain is $x \in \mathbf{R}$.

B. The coordinates of the vertex are $(3, -1)$.

C. The equation of the axis of symmetry is $x + 3 = 0$.

D. The y-intercept is located at the ordered pair $(0, -8)$.

Use the following information to answer the next question.

The partial graph of a parabola is shown.

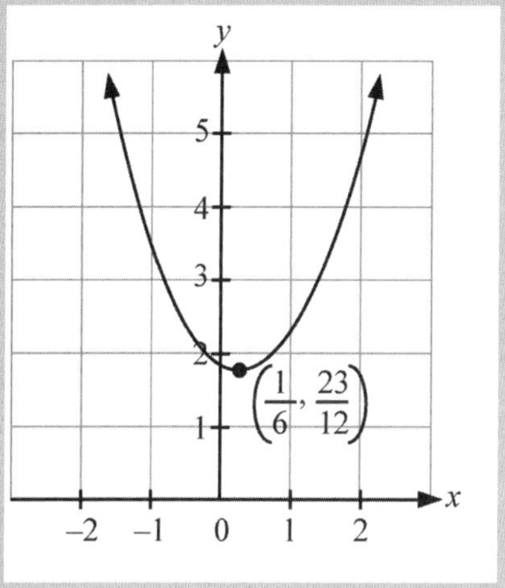

8. Which of the following statements about the graph of the parabola shown is **true**?

A. The minimum value is $y = \frac{1}{6}$, and the equation of the axis of symmetry is $x = \frac{23}{16}$.

B. The maximum value is $y = \frac{23}{16}$, and the equation of the axis of symmetry is $x = \frac{1}{6}$.

C. The minimum value is $y = \frac{23}{12}$, and the equation of the axis of symmetry is $x = \frac{1}{6}$.

D. The maximum value is $y = \frac{1}{6}$, and the equation of the axis of symmetry is $x = \frac{23}{16}$.

Numerical Response

9. The y-intercept of the graph of the quadratic relation $y = -2(x + 3)^2 - 4$ is located at the ordered pair $(0, -K)$. What is the value of K? ____

QR1.4 *compare, through investigation using technology, the features of the graph of $y = x^2$ and the graph of $y = 2^x$, and determine the meaning of a negative exponent and of zero as an exponent*

Comparing Quadratic Functions and the Exponential Function $y = 2^x$

A **quadratic function** of the form $y = ax^2 + bx + c$, $(a \neq 0)$ differs in several ways when compared to an **exponential function** of the form $y = ab^x$.

Comparing the Features of $y = x^2$ and $y = 2^x$

The graphs

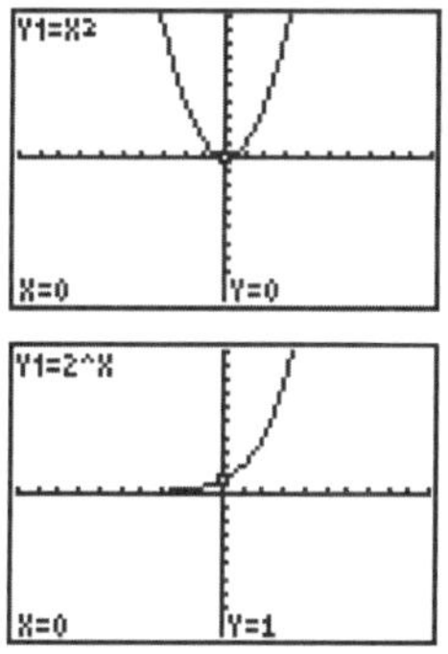

Vertex, Maximum Value, Minimum Value, and Axis of Symmetry

The graph of the function $y = x^2$ is a parabola opening upward. The vertex is located at (0, 0). The minimum value is 0, and the equation of the axis of symmetry is $x = 0$.

The graph of the exponential function $y = 2^x$ is a continuous curve that rises from the left to the right. The graph is asymmetrical and does not have a maximum or a minimum value; therefore, it does not have a vertex.

Second Difference

One possible table of values for $y = x^2$ is shown.

$y = x^2$

x	y	1st diff	2nd diff
−3	9	} −5	} 2
−2	4	} −3	} 2
−1	1	} −1	} 2
0	0	} 1	} 2
1	1	} 3	} 2
2	4	} 5	
3	9		

Because this is a quadratic function, the second difference is a constant. In this case, the second difference is 2.

One possible table of values for $y = 2^x$ is shown.

$y = 2^x$

x	y	1st diff	2nd diff
−3	0.125	} 0.125	} 0.125
−2	0.25	} 0.25	} 0.25
−1	0.5	} 0.5	} 0.5
0	1	} 1	} 1
1	2	} 2	} 2
2	4	} 4	
3	8		

For this function, neither the first nor second difference has a constant value; therefore, it is not linear, or quadratic.

x-Intercept

The x-intercept for the graph of the function $y = x^2$ is $x = 0$.

The function $y = 2^x$ does not cross or touch the x-axis; thus, the graph of $y = 2^x$ has no x-intercept.

y-Intercept

The y-intercept for the graph of the function $y = x^2$ is $y = 0$.

For the function $y = 2^x$, the graph crosses the y-axis at (0, 1); therefore, the intercept is $y = 1$.

The Negative Exponent

When a number or variable has a negative exponent in the numerator, the expression can be rewritten with a positive exponent in the denominator;

$$x^{-n} = \frac{1}{x^n}.$$

Example

Using the negative exponent rule, evaluate 3^{-3}.

$$3^{-3} = \frac{1}{3^3} = \frac{1}{27}$$

Zero as an Exponent

Any number (except 0) or variable with an exponent of zero is equal to 1; $x^0 = 1$.

For example, evaluate the expression $3^2 \times 3^{-2}$ using the negative exponent rule as well as the product rule for exponents to show that $3^0 = 1$.

Apply the negative exponent rule.

$$3^2 \times 3^{-2} = 3^2 \times \frac{1}{3^2} = 9 \times \frac{1}{9} = 1$$

Apply the product rule for exponents.

$$3^2 \times 3^{-2} = 3^{2+(-2)} = 3^0$$

Thus, $3^0 = 1$

Practice

10. The graph of $y = x^0$, where $x \neq 0$, is the same as the graph of

A. $y = 1$ **B.** $y = 2$

C. $y = 3$ **D.** $y = 4$

11. The graph of $y = x^2$ and the graph of $y = 2^x$ will both have

A. the same x-intercept

B. the same y-intercept

C. an undefined maximum value

D. an undefined minimum value

QR2.1 *identify, through investigation using technology, the effect on the graph of $y = x^2$ of transformations by considering separately each parameter a, h, and k*

Transformations of a Quadratic Function

The Effect of a in $y = ax^2$

- Regardless of the a-value, each point (x_1, y_1) on the original graph becomes (x_1, ay_1).
- a causes a **vertical stretch** or **vertical compression** as shown below.

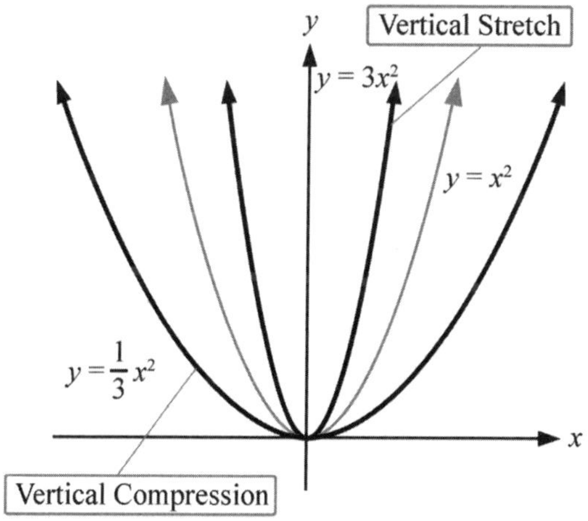

- when a is negative, it causes a **reflection in the x-axis**, which creates a graph that is a mirror image of the original graph in the x-axis as shown below.

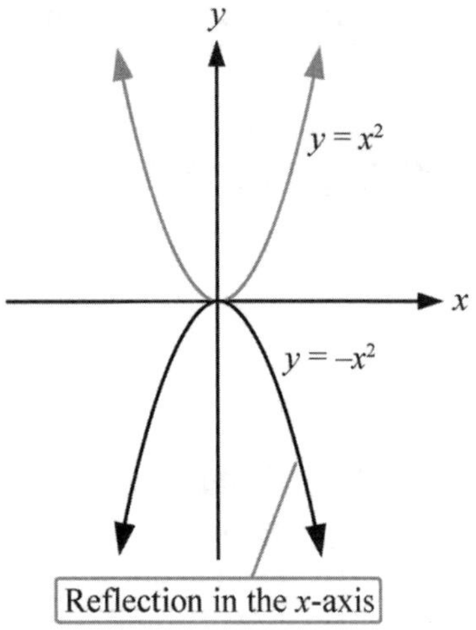

- Generally, the value of a does not have an effect upon the domain, vertex, axis of symmetry, x-intercept of the parabola.

The Effect of h in $y = (x - h)^2$

The h-value causes a **horizontal translation** (shifting the parabola left or right) and affects the following:

- the vertex, $(h, 0)$
- the axis of symmetry, defined as $x = h$

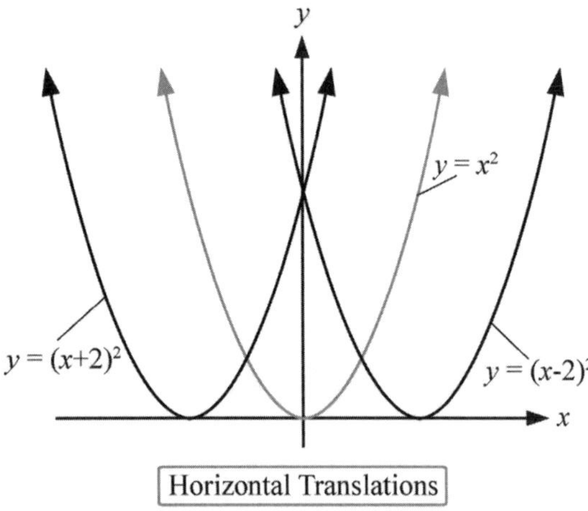

The Effect of k in $y = x^2 + k$

The k-value causes a **vertical translation** (shifting the parabola upward or downward) and affects the following:

- the vertex, $(0, k)$
- the range, $y \geq k$
- the minimum or maximum value, which is k

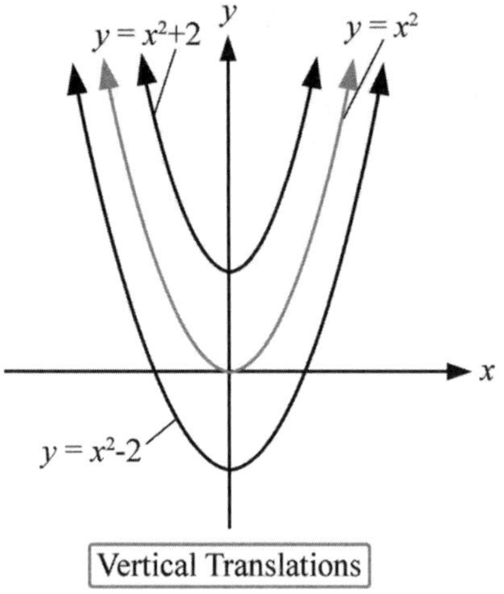

Example

Two transformations were applied to the graph of $y = x^2$ to obtain the second graph. Describe these transformations.

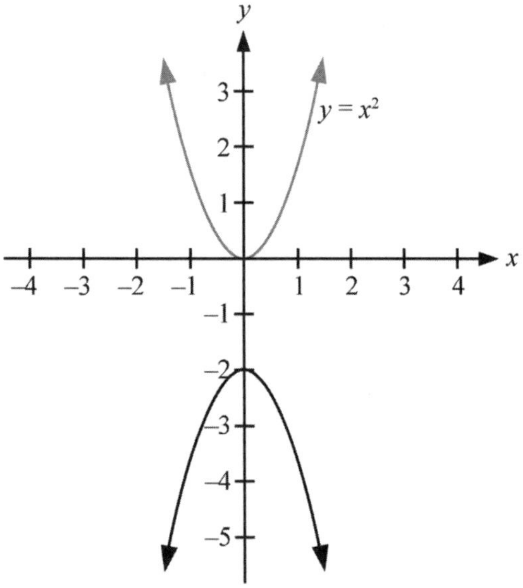

Because the transformed graph has a maximum value and opens downward, there is a reflection in the x-axis.
The transformed graph has also been translated vertically downward 2 units since the vertex is at $(0, -2)$.
There is no vertical stretch or compression, since the original graph and the transformed graph have the same basic shape and size.

Practice

12. Which of the following graphs could be the graph of the quadratic function $y = ax^2 + k$, where $a > 0$?

A.
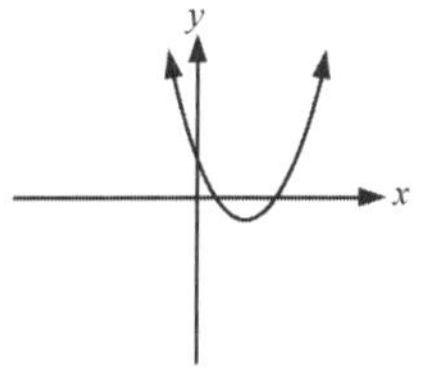

B.
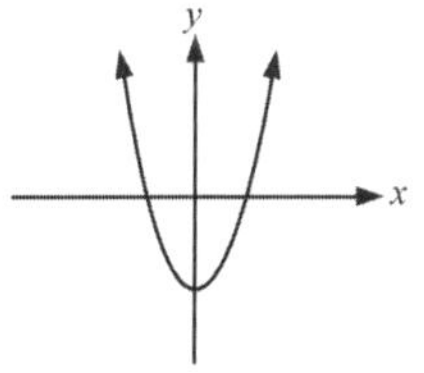

C.
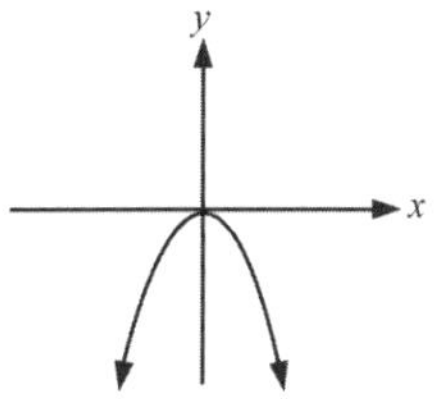

D.
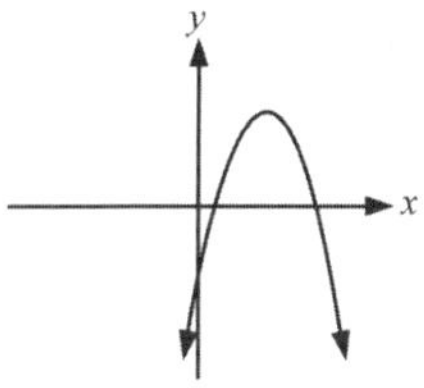

13. If the value of k increases in the equation $y = x^2 + k$, then the graph is shifted

A. left **B.** right

C. upward **D.** downward

Numerical Response

14. The graph of the function $y = x^2$ can be transformed to the graph of the function $y = 2(x + 3)^2 - 5$ by performing the following transformations:

a vertical stretch about the x-axis by a factor of ____, a horizontal translation of ____ unit(s) to the left, and a vertical translation downward by ____ unit(s).

QR2.2 *explain the roles of a, h, and k in $y = a(x - h)^2 + k$, using the appropriate terminology to describe the transformations, and identify the vertex and the equation of the axis of symmetry*

Describing Transformations of a Parabola

For the quadratic function $y = a(x - h)^2 + k$, the parameters a, h, and k as well as the vertex and equation of the axis of symmetry reveal important information about the transformations of a parabola.

The Role of *a*

- a is responsible for vertical stretches and compressions, as well as the reflection in the x-axis
- If $a > 1$, there is a vertical stretch by a factor of a.
- If $0 < a < 1$, there is a vertical compression by a factor of a.

When $a > 0$:

- The parabola opens upward.
- The function has a minimum value of k.
- The range of the function is $y \geq k$.

When $a < 0$:

- The parabola opens downward, and there is a reflection in the x-axis.
- The function has a maximum value of k.
- The range of the function is $y \leq k$.

THE ROLE OF h

- h represents a horizontal translation of h units:
  - left if $h < 0$.
  - right if $h > 0$.

THE ROLE OF k

- k represents a vertical translation of k units
  - downward if $k < 0$.
  - upward if $k > 0$.

VERTEX, AXIS OF SYMMETRY, AND DOMAIN

- The vertex is (h, k).
- The equation of the axis of symmetry is $x = h$.
- The domain of the function is the set of real numbers, which can be written as $x \in \mathbf{R}$.

Example

Write the equation of the transformed function if the graph of the quadratic function $y = x^2$ is reflected in the x-axis and then translated 7 units to the right and 9 units down.

A reflection in the x-axis will change the a-value from 1 to -1.
Translations of 7 right and 9 down give h- and k-values of 7 and -9, respectively.
The equation of the transformed graph is $y = -1(x - (7))^2 - 9$ or $y = -(x - 7)^2 - 9$.

Example

For the quadratic function $y = 2(x + 3)^2 - 5$, determine the following:

1. The values of a, h, and k, and describe the transformations of this graph when compared to the graph of $y = x^2$.

The equation $y = 2(x + 3)^2 - 5$ can be written as $y = 2(x - (-3))^2 - 5$.
Therefore, $a = 2$, $h = -3$, and $k = -5$.
Compared with the graph of the function $y = x^2$, the graph of the function $y = 2(x + 3)^2 - 5$ has been vertically stretched by a factor of $2(|a| = 2)$ about the x-axis and then translated 3 units to the left $(h = -3)$ and 5 units downward $(k = -5)$.

2. The vertex and the equation of the axis of symmetry.

Since $h = -3$ and $k = -5$, the vertex is $(-3, -5)$, and the axis of symmetry is the vertical line $x = -3$.

Practice

15. The graph of the parabola $y = -2(x - 1)^2 + 3$ is symmetric about a line. What is the equation of that line?

A. $x = -1$ **B.** $x = 1$

C. $y = 1$ **D.** $y = 3$

16. The parabola $y = x^2$ is vertically stretched by a factor of 4, reflected in the x-axis, and translated 7 units to the left and 6 units up. If the equation of the transformed function is in the form $y = a(x - h)^2 + k$, then the respective values of a, h, and k are

A. 4, −7, and 6

B. −4, 7, and 6

C. −4, −7, and 6

D. −4, −7, and −6

17. If a quadratic function has a minimum value of k and its graph has an axis of symmetry of $x - 5 = 0$, then the function could be

A. $y = (x - 5)^2 + k$

B. $y = (x + 5)^2 + k$

C. $y = -(x + 5)^2 + k$

D. $y = -(x - 5)^2 + k$

QR2.3 *sketch, by hand, the graph of $y = a(x - h)^2 + k$ by applying transformations to the graph of $y = x^2$*

Sketching the Graph of $y = x^2$

In order to sketch the graph of $y = a(x - h)^2 + k$ by hand, transformations can be applied to the graph of $y = x^2$. All points on the transformed graph must satisfy the given transformations.

For example, consider the following graphs:

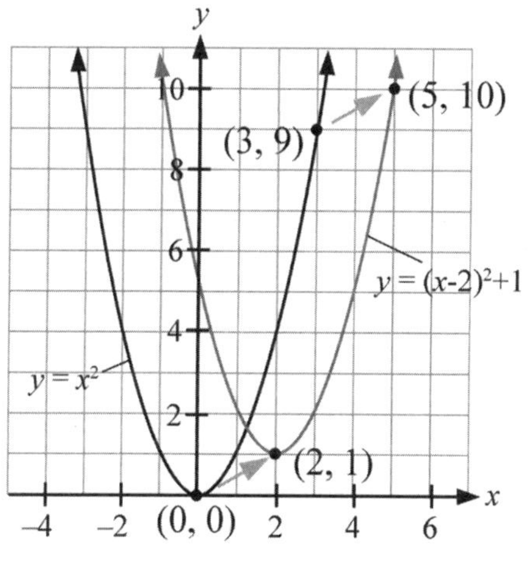

Compared to the graph of $y = x^2$, the graph of the function $y = (x - 2)^2 + 1$ has been translated 2 units right and 1 unit up and has a vertex of (2, 1) rather than (0, 0). Similarly, the point (3, 9), which is on the graph of $y = x^2$, will become the point (5, 10) on the graph of $y = (x - 2)^2 + 1$, since 5 is 2 units right of 3 and 10 is 1 unit up from 9.

Order of Transformations

When sketching the graph of $y = a(x - h)^2 + k$ by applying transformations to the graph of $y = x^2$, the order of transformations should be as follows:

1. Vertical stretch or compression
2. Reflection in the x-axis
   (Note: Steps 1 and 2 can be reversed.)
3. Vertical and/or horizontal translations (in either order)

Example

Sketch the graph of $y = 3(x - 1)^2 + 4$ by applying transformations to the graph of $y = x^2$, and verify using technology.

To sketch the graph by hand:

Compared to the graph of $y = x^2$, the graph of $y = 3(x - 1)^2 + 4$ has the following transformations applied:

1. Vertical stretch by a factor of 3
2. Vertical translation 4 units up
3. Horizontal translation 1 unit right

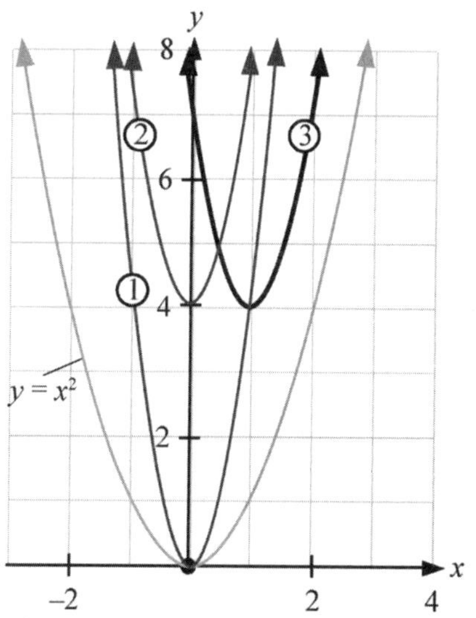

To verify with technology:

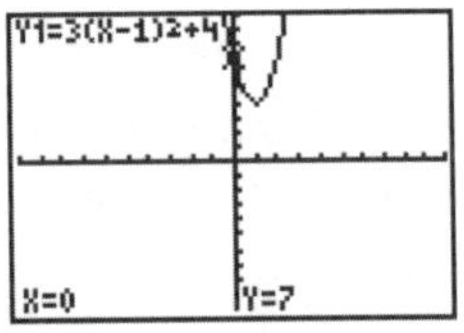

Practice

CHALLENGER QUESTION

Use the following information to answer the next question.

The following four transformations are applied, in order, to the graph of $y = x^2$.

- a reflection about the x-axis
- a vertical stretch about the x-axis by a factor of 2
- a horizontal translation 5 units to the left
- a vertical translation 4 units upward

18. Point (4, 16) on the graph of $y = x^2$ becomes point $(-1, y)$ on the transformed graph. The value of y is

A. −12 **B.** −28

C. −68 **D.** −72

Use the following information to answer the next question.

A student performed a series of transformations on the graph of $y = x^2$ to produce the graph shown.

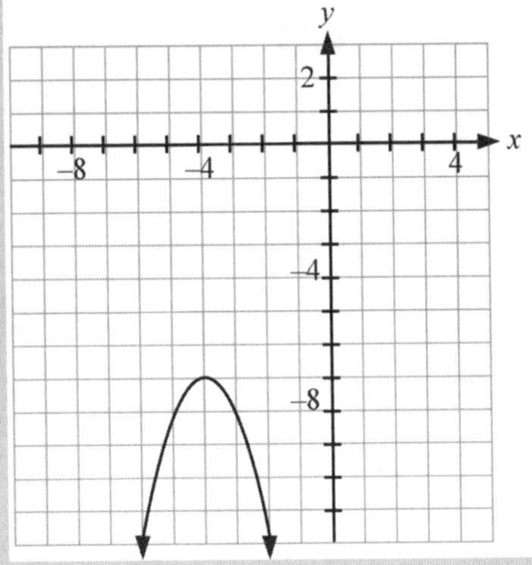

19. If the first transformation was a reflection in the x-axis, then the next two transformations were a horizontal translation

A. 4 units left and a vertical translation 7 units down

B. 4 units right and a vertical translation 7 units down

C. 4 units right and a vertical translation 7 units up

D. 4 units left and a vertical translation 7 units up

20. Which of the following graphs **best** illustrates the equation $y = -x^2 + \frac{7}{2}$?

A.

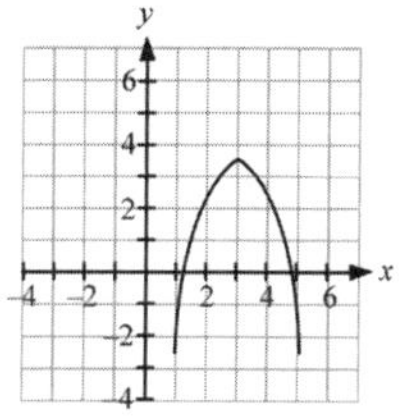

B.

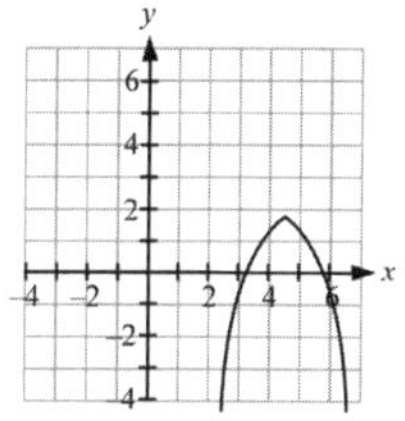

C.

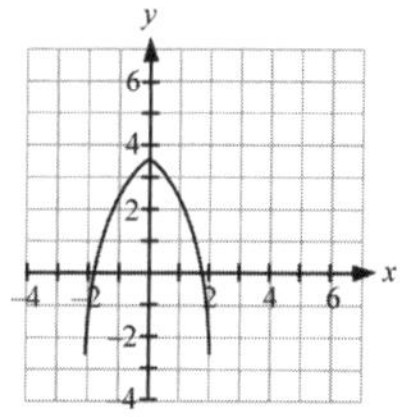

D.

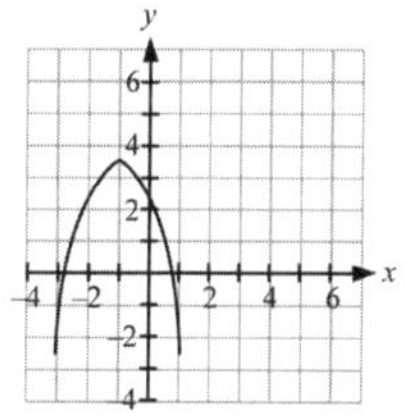

QR2.4 *determine the equation, in the form* $y = a(x - h)^2 + k$*, of a given graph of a parabola*

The Equation of a Parabola

From the graph of a parabola, follow these steps to determine the equation in the form $y = a(x - h)^2 + k$:

1. Identify the coordinates of the vertex (h, k).
2. Substitute the respective values for h and k into the formula $y = a(x - h)^2 + k$.

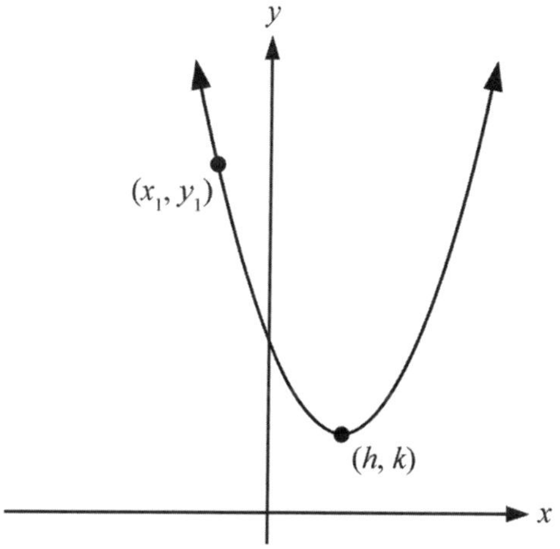

3. From the graph, choose any point (x_1, y_1) that has coordinates that can be identified.
4. Substitute the respective values of x_1, y_1 into the equation created in step 2.
5. Solve for a.
6. Rewrite the equation $y = a(x - h)^2 + k$, substituting the values of a, h, and k.

Note: Although steps 1 to 4 can be done in a single step, it is often easier to do items in separate steps.

Example

The graph of a quadratic function with a y-intercept of -3 is shown below.

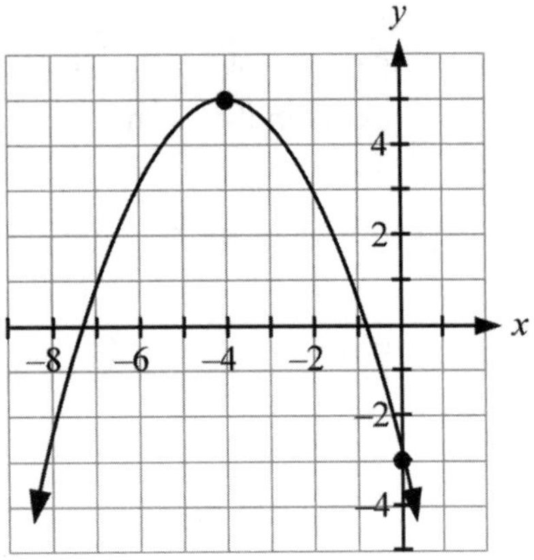

If the y-intercept of the parabola shown is -3, then determine the equation of the quadratic function in the form of $y = a(x - h)^2 + k$.

Step 1: The vertex is $(-4, 5)$.
Step 2: $y = a(x + 4)^2 + 5$
Step 3: The y-intercept is -3, so the corresponding ordered pair is $(0, -3)$.
Steps 4 and 5: Substitute and solve for a.

$-3 = a(0 + 4)^2 + 5$

$-3 = a(16) + 5$

$-8 = 16a$

$-\frac{1}{2} = a$

Step 6: The equation for this parabola is

$y = -\frac{1}{2}(x + 4)^2 + 5.$

Practice

Use the following information to answer the next question.

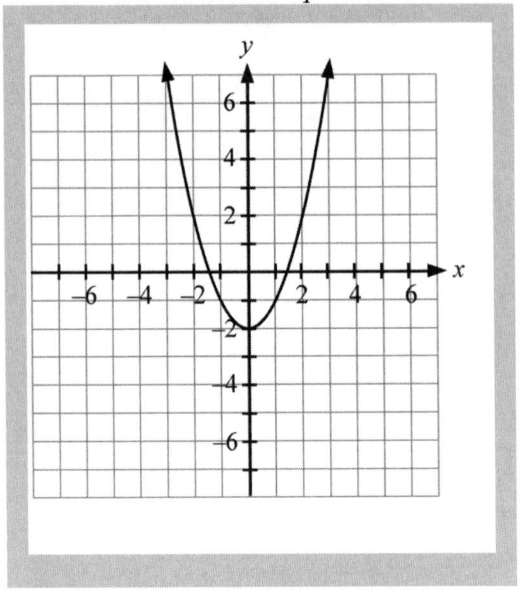

21. The graph shown can be represented by the equation

A. $y = (x + 2)^2$

B. $y = 2x^2$

C. $y = (x - 2)^2$

D. $y = x^2 - 2$

CHALLENGER QUESTION

Numerical Response

Use the following information to answer the next question.

The graph of a particular quadratic function is shown.

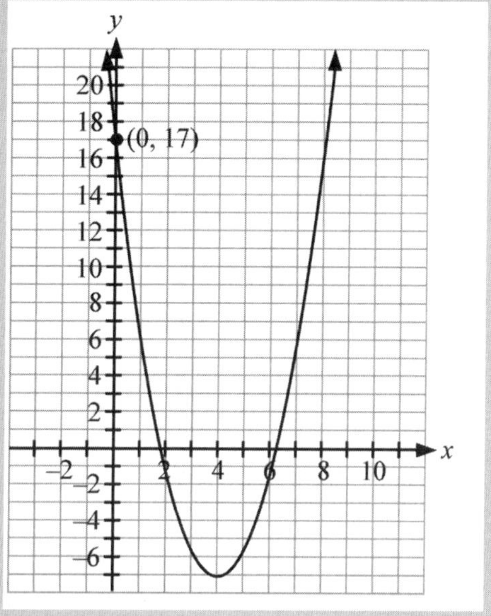

22. If the equation of the parabola shown is $y = a(x - 4)^2 - 7$, $a \in \mathbf{R}$, then the value of a, to one decimal place, is ____.

Use the following information to answer the next multipart question.

23. The graph of a quadratic function is shown.

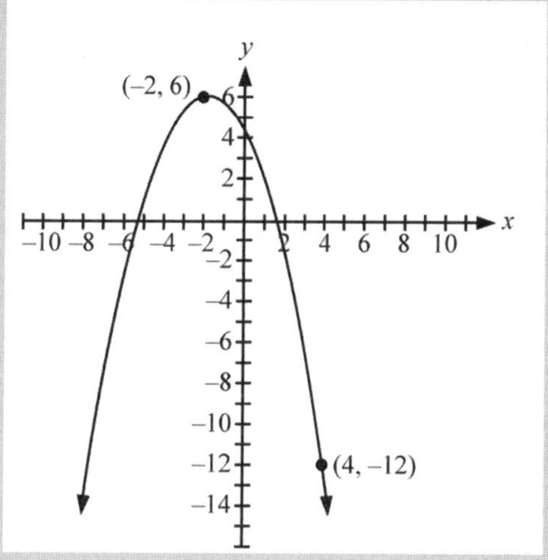

Part A

Open Response

Determine the equation of the quadratic function of the graph shown. Write your answer in the form of $y = a(x - h)^2 + k$.

Show your work.

Part B

Open Response

What is the y-intercept of the graph of the given quadratic equation?

Show your work.

Part C

Open Response

Is the ordered pair $(-8, -12)$ on the graph of the given quadratic function?

Justify your answer.

QR3.1 *expand and simplify second-degree polynomial expressions using a variety of tools and strategies*

Expanding and Simplifying Polynomials

Before getting started, there are some key terms to review. Recall that a **monomial** is a single term expression; i.e., 5, $5x$, $5xy$.
A **binomial** is the sum or difference of two monomials; i.e., $2x + 9y$, $2x - 9y$, $3x^2 - 5x$.

Expanding and Simplifying Using Algebra Tiles

Algebra tiles can be used to model several types of operations relating to polynomial expressions. For these purposes, the positive x^2, x, and constants are shaded, and the negative x^2, x, and constants are white.

To represent the product of $2x(x + 3)$, make a rectangle that is two x-tiles wide and x + 3-tiles long, and then form the resulting rectangle.

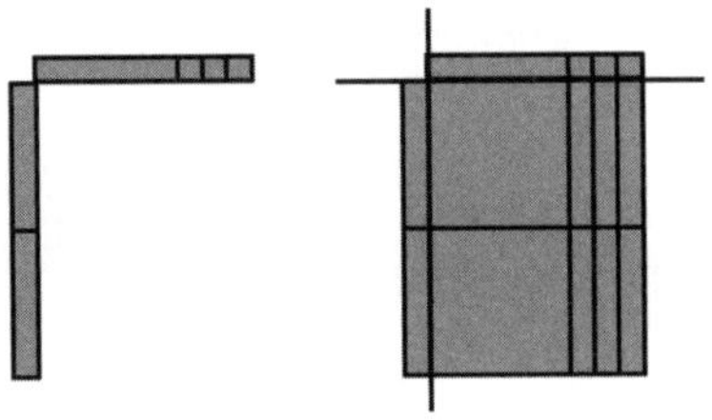

The tiles show that the product is $2x^2 + 6x$.

Expanding and Simplifying Using an Algebraic Approach

When expanding and simplifying polynomial expressions algebraically, these main mathematical processes are used:

- Distributive property: $a(x + y) = ax + ay$
- Product law of exponents: $x^a \cdot x^b = x^{a+b}$
- Collecting and simplifying all like terms

Example

Simplify $2xy(3x - 1)$.

$$(2xy)(3x - 1)$$

$$= 2xy(3x) + 2xy(-1)$$
$$= 6x^2y - 2xy$$

Multiplying Two Binomials

FOIL is a *mnemonic* device used to help remember how to multiply two binomials.
F: multiply the first term in each binomial together
O: multiply the two outside terms together
I: multiply the two inside terms together
L: multiply the last two terms together
After multiplying the terms together, gather like terms.

Example

Expand and simplify $(2x + 1)(x - 3)$.

$$(2x + 1)(x - 3)$$

$$= 2x(x) + 2x(-3) + 1(x) + 1(-3)$$

F O I L

$$= 2x^2 - 6x + x - 3$$

F O I L

$$= 2x^2 - 5x - 3$$

Expanding Perfect Square Binomials

A perfect square binomial is a binomial of the form $(a+b)^2$. The following formulas can be used to expand a perfect square binomial.

$$(a+b)^2 = a^2 + 2ab + b^2$$
$$(a-b)^2 = a^2 - 2ab + b^2$$

Example

Expand and simplify $(2x+5)^2$.
This perfect square will follow the formula
$(a+b)^2 = a^2 + 2ab + b^2$
In this case, $a = 2x$ and $b = 5$.
Substitute these values into the formula, as follows.
$(2x)^2 + 2(2x)(5) + (5)^2$
$= 4x^2 + 20x + 25$

Practice

24. The coefficient of x in the expanded form of the expression $(x-5)(4x+5)$ is

A. -25 **B.** -15
C. 1 **D.** 4

25. If $(3x-4)(4x-1) = 12x^2 + bx + 4$, then the value of b is

A. -16 **B.** -19
C. -27 **D.** -33

QR3.2 *factor polynomial expressions involving common factors, trinomials, and differences of squares using a variety of tools and strategies*

Factoring Polynomials

Factoring is the process of expressing polynomials as a product of polynomials of lesser degree.

Factoring out a Greatest Common Factor (GCF)

When factoring out the GCF (the largest factor common to two or more terms), look at what is common in each term of the polynomial expression. Once the greatest common factor has been identified, divide it out of each term in the polynomial.

For example, to factor the binomial $6x^2 + 8x$, note that 2 and x are common to both $6x^2$ and $8x$. Therefore, $2x$ can be factored out of each term as shown below.
$6x^2 + 8x$
$= (2x)(3x+4)$

Factoring by Grouping

Factoring by grouping involves rewriting a polynomial with an even number of terms into smaller groups that contain a common factor. Remove the GCF from each group. Then, factor out the common binomial.

For example, to factor the expression $x^2 + 2x + x + 2$, use grouping as shown in the following steps:
Step 1: Group the terms $(x^2 + 2x) + (x+2)$.
Step 2: Remove the GCF from each group $x(x+2) + 1(x+2)$.
Step 3: Factor out the common binomial $(x+2)(x+1)$.

FACTORING $x^2 + bx + c$ USING ALGEBRA TILES

To factor a polynomial, begin by arranging the algebra tiles into a rectangle, and then add algebra tiles to the outside of the rectangle.

The tiles representing $x^2 + 5x + 6$ can be arranged into the following rectangle:

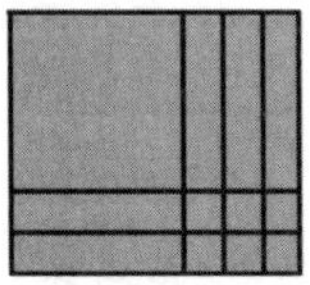

Now, add algebra tiles to the left and upper sides of the rectangle to form the two factors.

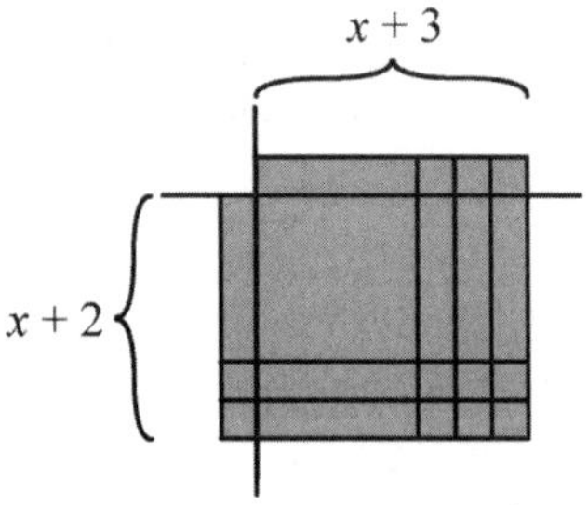

The factors are $(x + 2)(x + 3)$.

FACTORING TRINOMIALS OF THE FORM $ax^2 + bx + c$

One commonly used procedure for factoring trinomials of this form is **decomposition**. Decomposition starts by taking the middle term (bx) of the trinomial and splitting it into two separate monomials such that the resulting expression can be factored by grouping.

In order to factor $2x^2 - 5x - 3$:

1. Find two numbers that have a product of −6 $(a \times c)$ and a sum of −5 (the b-value). In this case, the numbers are −6 and 1.
2. Rewrite the expression by replacing the term $-5x$ with $-6x$ and x.
3. Group using brackets.
4. Remove the GCF from each group.
5. Factor out the common binomial.

$$\begin{aligned}2x^2 - 5x - 3 &= 2x^2 - 6x + x - 3\\ &= (2x^2 - 6x) + 1(x - 3)\\ &= 2x(x - 3) + 1(x - 3)\\ &= (2x + 1)(x - 3)\end{aligned}$$

FACTORING A DIFFERENCE OF SQUARES

In factoring a difference of squares, use the following formula:
$a^2 - b^2 = (a - b)(a + b)$

Example

Factor $4x^2 - 9$.
This is a difference of squares where $a^2 = 4x^2$, so $a = 2x$, and $b^2 = 9$, so $b = 3$.
Since $a^2 - b^2 = (a - b)(a + b)$,
$4x^2 - 9 = (2x)^2 - (3)^2 = (2x - 3)(2x + 3)$.

Practice

26. One of the factors of the binomial $16a^2b^2 - 9c^2$ is

A. $8ab - 3c$ **B.** $8ab - 9c$
C. $4ab + 3c$ **D.** $4ab - 9c$

27. One of the factors of the trinomial $2x^2 + x - 28$ is

A. $2x + 1$ **B.** $2x - 7$
C. $x + 7$ **D.** $x - 4$

Use the following information to answer the next question.

A student is asked to factor four different polynomials. The given table shows the four polynomials and the student's solutions.

	Polynomial	Student's Solution
I	$8x^3 + 4x^2$	$4x^2(2x + 1)$
II	$25a^2 - 4b^2c^2$	$(5a + 2bc)(5a - 2bc)$
III	$2x^2 - 18y^2$	$2(x + 3y)(x - 3y)$
IV	$4a^3 - a$	$a(2a - 1)^2$

28. Which polynomial did the student factor **incorrectly**?

A. Polynomial I **B.** Polynomial II

C. Polynomial III **D.** Polynomial IV

Numerical Response

29. The polynomial expression $x^2 - 3x - 4$ is factored as $(x - m)(x + n)$.
The value of $m + n$ is ___.

QR3.3 *determine, through investigation, and describe the connection between the factors of a quadratic expression and the x-intercepts of the graph of the corresponding quadratic relation, expressed in the form $y = a(x - r)(x - s)$*

The Factors and x-Intercepts of a Quadratic Relation

Recall the following:

- The x-intercepts of a graph are located at the points where the graph touches or crosses the x-axis.
- The x-intercepts of the graph of a quadratic function can be used to determine the zeros of the quadratic function.

Making Connections between Factors and the Zeros of Quadratic Expressions

Through investigation, you will observe that when a quadratic function is expressed in the factored form $y = a(x - r)(x - s)$, the x-intercepts (the zeros) of the graph of the quadratic function are $x = r$ and $x = s$.

Example

Determine the x-intercepts for the graph of the function $y = (x + 6)(x - 2)$.

Since the function $y = (x + 6)(x - 2)$ is expressed in the factored form $y = a(x - r)(x - s)$, $a = 1$, $r = -6$, $s = 2$.

Therefore, the x-intercepts are $x = -6$ and $x = 2$.

It is possible to assemble a quadratic function from given information such as the x-intercepts and another given point.

Example

The graph of a particular quadratic relation is shown below.

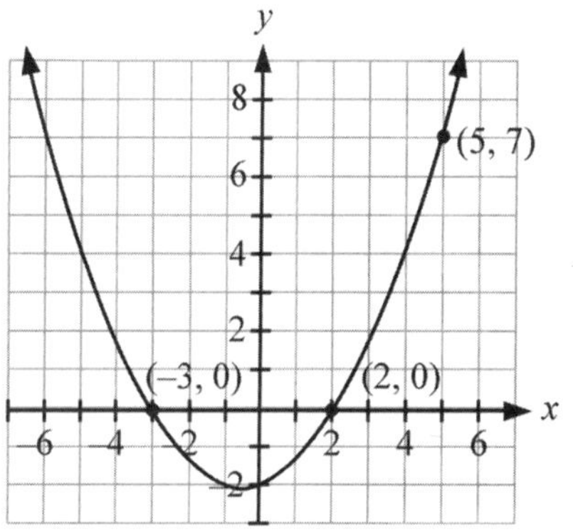

Write the equation of the quadratic relation in the form $y = a(x - r)(x - s)$.

The x-intercepts of the graph shown are -3 and 2. Therefore, substitute -3 for r and 2 for s in the equation $y = a(x - r)(x - s)$ as follows:

$y = a(x - (-3))(x - 2)$

$y = a(x + 3)(x - 2)$

The ordered pair $(5, 7)$ is a point on the graph shown. Solve for a in the equation $y = a(x + 3)(x - 2)$ by substituting 5 for x and 7 for y as follows:

$7 = a((5) + 3)((5) - 2)$

$7 = a(8)(3)$

$7 = 24a$

$a = \frac{7}{24}$

The equation of the quadratic relation in the form $y = a(x - r)(x - s)$ is $y = \frac{7}{24}(x + 3)(x - 2)$.

Practice

30. The quadratic equation $6x^2 + 13x - 28 = 0$ can be written in factored form as $(3x - 4)(2x + 7) = 0$. The roots of the quadratic equation $6x^2 + 13x - 28 = 0$ are

A. $\frac{4}{3}$ and $\frac{-7}{2}$

B. $\frac{-4}{3}$ and $\frac{7}{2}$

C. $\frac{3}{4}$ and $\frac{-2}{7}$

D. $\frac{-3}{4}$ and $\frac{2}{7}$

Use the following information to answer the next question.

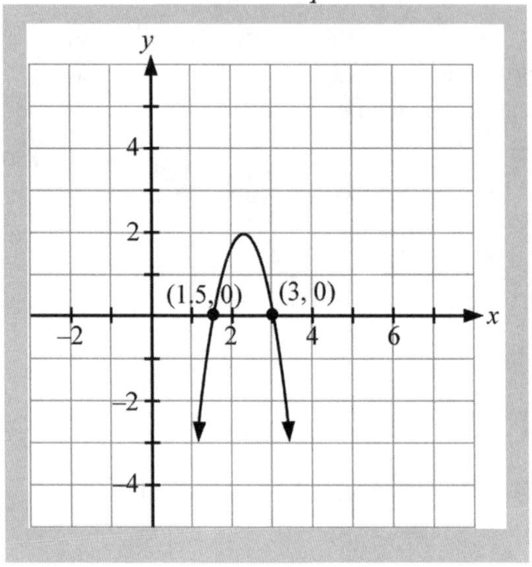

31. Which of the following equations **best** represents the graph shown?

A. $y = 2x^2 + 9x - 9$

B. $y = -2x^2 + 9x - 9$

C. $y = -2x^2 + 4.5x - 4.5$

D. $y = 2x^2 + 4.5x + 4.5$

QR3.4 *interpret real and non-real roots of quadratic equations, through investigation using graphing technology, and relate the roots to the x-intercepts of the corresponding relations*

Interpreting the Roots of a Quadratic Equation

When the value of y in the quadratic function $y = ax^2 + bx + c$ is set equal to zero, the resulting equation $ax^2 + bx + c = 0$ is called a **quadratic equation**.

The **roots** of a quadratic equation are the value(s) of the variable (in most cases, the variable chosen is "x") that satisfy the given quadratic equation (make the equation equal to zero).

Through investigation, you will find that there are three possible scenarios that can occur when discussing the roots of a quadratic equation. These include:

1. Two real and different roots

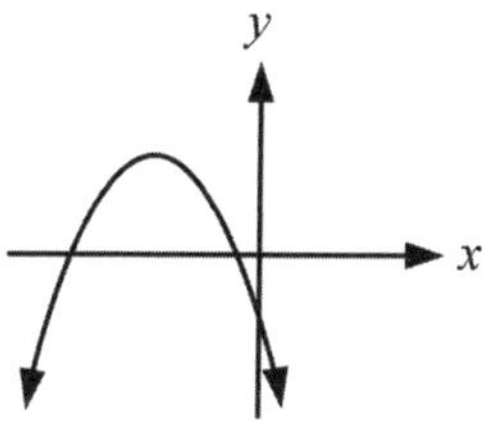

Two x-intercepts

2. One real root
   (Two real and equal roots)

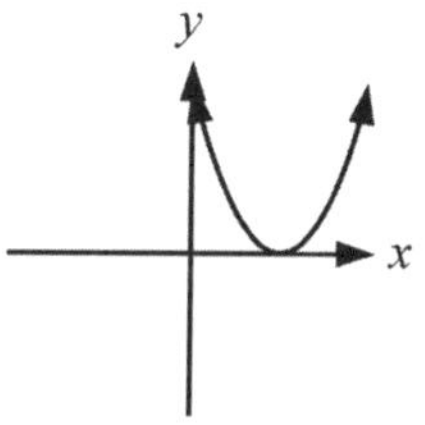

One x-intercept

3. Non-real roots
   (values such as $\sqrt{-5}$, $\sqrt{-16}$, $6 \div 0$, etc.).

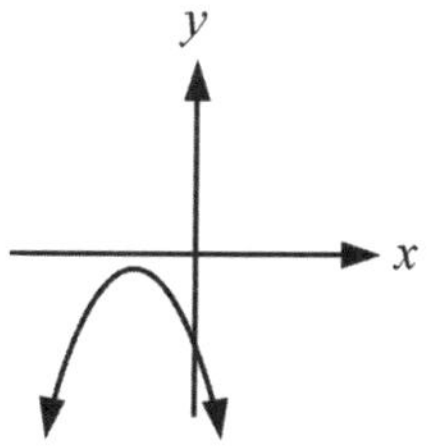

No x-intercepts

Example

Using technology, graph the function $y = -3x^2 - 2x + 10$, and then describe and state the roots to the quadratic equation $-3x^2 - 2x + 10 = 0$ to the nearest hundredth.

Graphing the function $y = -3x^2 - 2x + 10$ gives the following image:

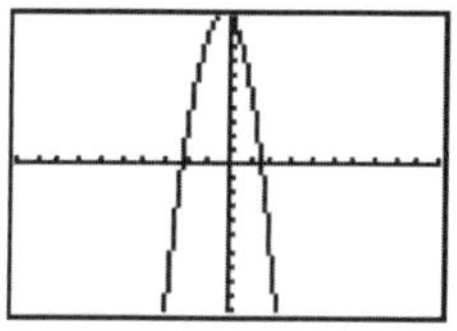

Since there are two x-intercepts, this means there are two real and different roots.
Using the **CALCULATE** feature and the **ZERO** option on the TI-83 Plus calculator, obtain the following:

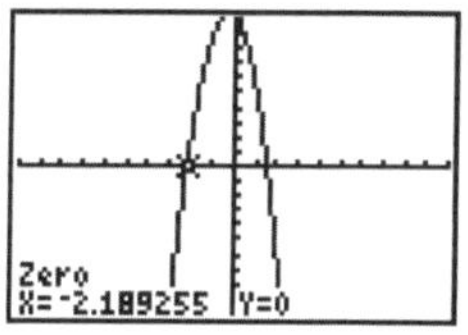

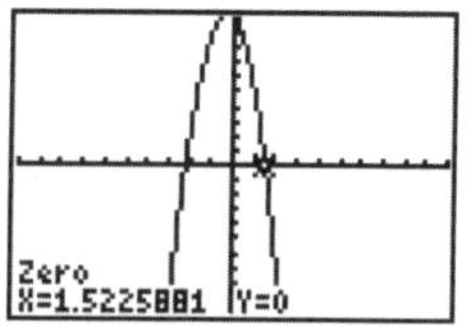

Therefore, to the nearest hundredth, the roots of $-3x^2 - 2x + 10 = 0$ are -2.19 and 1.52.

Practice

Use the following information to answer the next question.

The roots of the equation $2x^2 + 9x - 5 = 0$ can be found using technology. The first step of each of two possible procedures is shown.

Procedure A	Procedure B
Step 1: Graph the equation $y = 2x^2 + 9x - 5$	**Step 1:** Graph the equations $y = 2x^2$ and $y = 5 - 9x$

32. Which of the following statements regarding the two possible procedures for determining the roots of the quadratic equation using technology is **false**?

A. With procedure A, the solution is found by determining the x-intercepts of the graph of the given function.

B. Two distinct roots of the equation $2x^2 + 9x - 5 = 0$ will be obtained regardless of whether procedure A or procedure B is used.

C. With procedure B, the solution is found by determining the x-coordinate of each of the points of intersection of the graphs of the two given functions.

D. The zeros in procedure A will be exactly the same as the y-coordinates of the points of intersection of the graphs of the two given functions in procedure B.

33. Which of the following quadratic equations has real roots?

A. $y = \frac{1}{3}x^2 - \frac{4}{3}x + \frac{5}{3}$

B. $x^2 - 5x + 6 = 0$

C. $3x^2 - 18x + 29 = 0$

D. $-\frac{1}{2}x^2 + 2x - 3 = 0$

34. The respective roots of the quadratic equations $x^2 + x + 1 = 0$ and $x^2 + 5x + 3 = 0$ are

A. real and real

B. real and non-real

C. non-real and real

D. non-real and non-real

QR3.5 *express $y = ax^2 + bx + c$ in the form $y = a(x - h)^2 + k$ by completing the square in situations involving no fractions, using a variety of tools*

COMPLETING THE SQUARE

Completing the square is the mathematical process used to change the form of a quadratic function from the general form $y = ax^2 + bx + c$ to the standard form $y = a(x - h)^2 + k$.

Completing the Square Using Algebra Tiles

When using algebra tiles to complete the square, the focus needs to be on creating a figure that represents a perfect square trinomial.

Example

Using algebra tiles, create a perfect square trinomial for $x^2 + 6x + c = (x + ?)^2$.

Step 1: Create a partial square with algebra tiles to represent $x^2 + 6x$. Start with the x^2-tile, and arrange the x-tiles around x^2 to create a square.

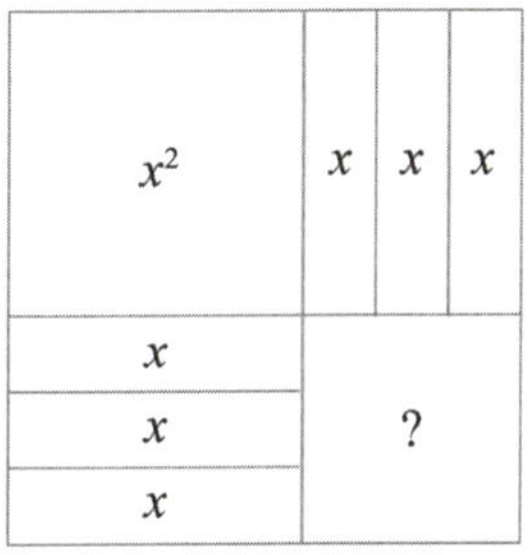

Step 2: Determine how many unit tiles are needed to complete the square.

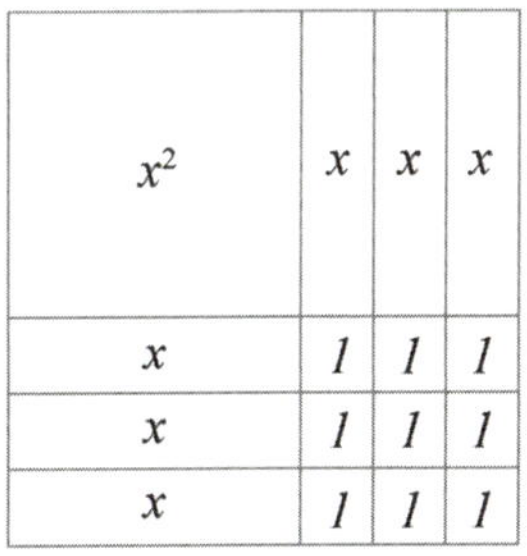

In this case, 9 unit tiles are needed to completely fill this square.

Step 3: Determine the dimensions of the completed square.

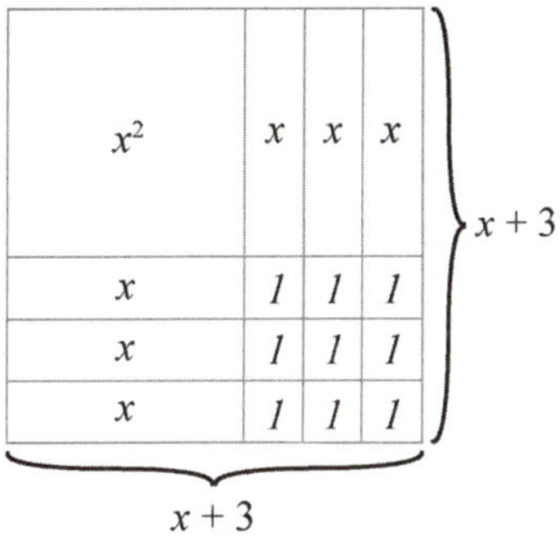

Therefore,

$(x + 3)(x + 3) = (x + 3)^2 = x^2 + 6x + 9$

Completing the Square Using Algebra

The following example shows the steps to algebraically complete the square.

Example

Complete the square for $y = -2x^2 + 8x + 3$.

1. Identify and remove the common factor from the x^2- and x-terms of the expression. In this example, the common factor is -2.

   $y = -2(x^2 - 4x) + 3$

2. Notice the coefficient of the x-term. Divide this value by 2, and then square it.

   $y = -2(x^2 - 4x) + 3 \qquad \left(\frac{-4}{2}\right)^2 = 4$

3. Both add and subtract this value (4) inside the brackets in order to keep the value of the expression the same.

   $y = -2(x^2 - 4x + \underline{4 - 4}) + 3$

4. Move the value that will not contribute to a perfect square trinomial outside the brackets.

$$y = -2(x^2 - 4x + 4 - 4) + 3$$

$$y = -2(x^2 - 4x + 4) + 8 + 3$$

5. Factor the trinomial inside the brackets to form a perfect square, and collect like terms outside the bracket.

$$y = -2(x - 2)^2 + 11$$

Practice

Use the following information to answer the next question.

> To convert the quadratic function $y = -3x^2 + 24x + 5$ into the completed square form $y = a(x - h)^2 + k$, a student performed the following steps:
> **Step 1:** $y = 3(x^2 + 8x) + 5$
> **Step 2:** $y = 3(x^2 + 8x + 12) + 5 - 36$
> **Step 3:** $y = 3(x^2 + 8x + 12) - 31$
> **Step 4:** $y = 3(x + 4)^2 - 31$

35. In which step did the student's first error occur?

A. Step 1 **B.** Step 2

C. Step 3 **D.** Step 4

36. The equation $y = 4x^2 + 32x + 59$ can be expressed in the form $y = a(x - h)^2 + k$ as

A. $y = 4(x + 4)^2 - 5$

B. $y = 4(x + 5)^2 - 4$

C. $y = 4(x + 4)^2 + 5$

D. $y = 4(x + 5)^2 + 4$

37. The quadratic function $y = x^2 - 8x + 23$ can be expressed in the form $y = a(x - h)^2 + k$ as

A. $y = (x - 7)^2 + 4$

B. $y = (x - 4)^2 + 7$

C. $y = (x - 8)^2 + 23$

D. $y = (x - 4)^2 + 23$

CHALLENGER QUESTION

Numerical Response

38. If the equation $y = -2x^2 + 12x + \frac{1}{3}$ is written in the completed square form $y = a(x - h)^2 + k$, then the value of k, correct to the nearest tenth, is ____.

QR3.6 *sketch or graph a quadratic relation whose equation is given in the form $y = ax^2 + bx + c$, using a variety of methods*

METHODS OF GRAPHING A QUADRATIC RELATION

There are three main methods of graphing a quadratic relation: by using intercepts and symmetry, completing the square, and using technology.

Graph Sketching Using Intercepts and Symmetry

To use this sketching method, begin by determining the x-intercept(s) and the y-intercept of the graph of the quadratic relation. Then, use symmetry and the vertex of the graph to complete the sketch. For example, graph the function $y = -x^2 + x + 6$, as follows:

Step 1: Find the x-intercepts.

$0 = -x^2 + x + 6$

$0 = -(x - 3)(x + 2)$

$x = 3$

$x = -2$

Step 2: Find the y-intercept.

$y = -(0)^2 + 0 + 6$

$y = 6$

Step 3: Find the **midpoint** of the x-intercepts in order to find the equation of the axis of symmetry.

$$M = \left(\frac{x_1 + x_2}{2}\right), \left(\frac{y_1 + y_2}{2}\right)$$

$$= \left(\frac{3 + (-2)}{2}\right), \left(\frac{0 + 0}{2}\right)$$

$$= \left(\frac{1}{2}, 0\right)$$

The equation of the axis of symmetry is $x = \frac{1}{2}$.

Step 4: Find the vertex (substitute $\frac{1}{2}$ for x).

$$y = -\left(\frac{1}{2}\right)^2 + \left(\frac{1}{2}\right) + 6$$

$$y = \frac{25}{4} \text{ or } y = 6.25$$

The vertex is at point $\left(\frac{1}{2}, \frac{25}{4}\right)$ or (0.5, 6.25).

Step 5: Using the information from steps 1, 2, 3, and 4, sketch the graph of $y = -x^2 + x + 6$.

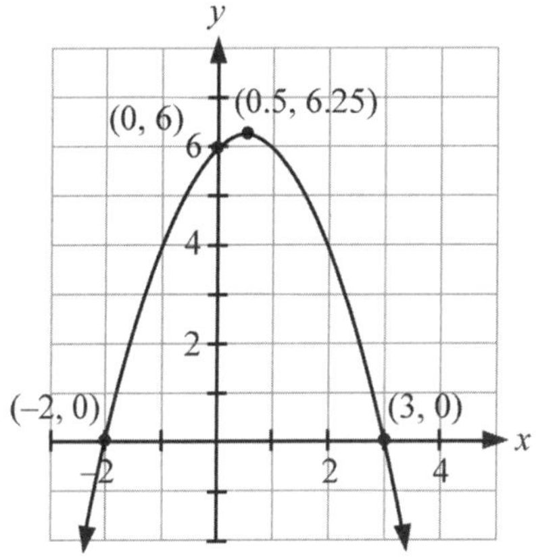

GRAPH SKETCHING BY COMPLETING THE SQUARE AND APPLYING TRANSFORMATIONS

This method involves changing the quadratic function from the general form $y = ax^2 + bx + c$ to the completed square form $y = a(x - h)^2 + k$. Transformations are then applied to the graph of $y = x^2$.

Consider the function $y = 4x^2 - 8x + 1$. Recall the steps for completing the square from previous lessons.

Step 1: $y = 4(x^2 - 2x) + 1$

Step 2: $y = 4(x^2 - 2x) + 1 \quad \left(\frac{-2}{2}\right)^2 = 1$

Step 3: $y = 4(x^2 - 2x + 1 - 1) + 1$

Step 4: $y = 4(x^2 - 2x + 1 - 1) + 1$

Step 5: $y = 4(x - 1)^2 - 3$

Thus, the function $y = 4x^2 - 8x + 1$ can be written in completed square form as $y = 4(x - 1)^2 - 3$.

Now, sketch the graph of $y = 4(x - 1)^2 - 3$ by applying transformations to the graph of $y = x^2$.

The transformations are as follows:

1. Vertical stretch by a factor of 4 about the x-axis.
2. Horizontal translation 1 unit to the right.
3. Vertical translation 3 units downward.

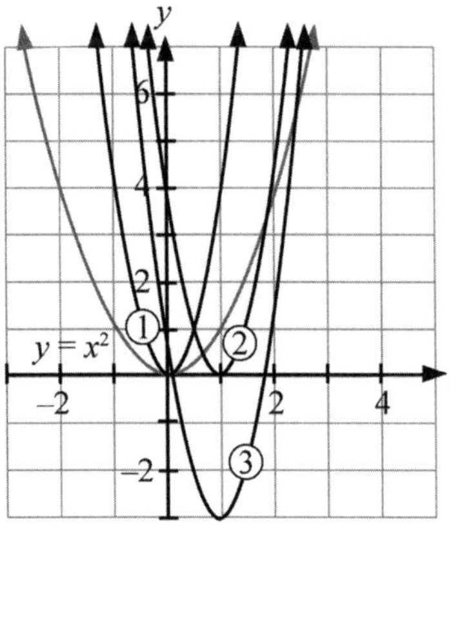

GRAPHING USING TECHNOLOGY

Using technology, such as a TI-83 Plus calculator, to graph a quadratic function requires the use of proper window settings and scale and following the appropriate steps.

Example

Graph the function $P = -25s^2 + 1\,010s - 3\,253$ using technology.

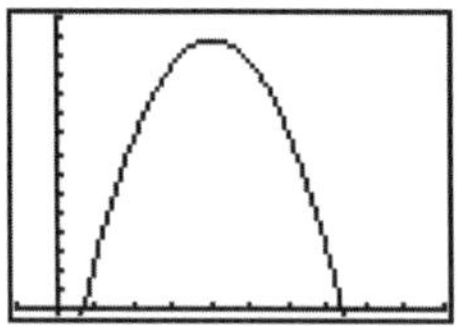

This graph uses the window setting $x{:}[-5,\ 50,\ 5]\,y{:}[-100,\ 7\,500,\ 500]$

Practice

39. John is attempting to sketch the graph of a given quadratic function. He correctly determines that the x-intercepts of the graph are $\frac{1}{2}$ and -4. The equation of the axis of symmetry of this graph is

A. $x = -\frac{7}{4}$ **B.** $x = -\frac{9}{4}$

C. $x = -\frac{7}{2}$ **D.** $x = -\frac{9}{2}$

40. The sketch of the graph of $y = x^2 - 6x + 4$ is completed by applying transformations to the graph of $y = x^2$. The vertex of the graph of $y = x^2 - 6x + 4$ is located

A. 3 units right and 5 units down from the vertex of the graph of $y = x^2$

B. 3 units left and 5 units down from the vertex of the graph of $y = x^2$

C. 6 units left and 4 units up from the vertex of the graph of $y = x^2$

D. 6 units right and 4 units up from the vertex of the graph of $y = x^2$

CHALLENGER QUESTION

Use the following information to answer the next question.

Gladys would like to graph the quadratic function $y = -4.9x^2 + 30x + 1$ using her graphing calculator. Four possible window settings are given.

	Window Setting			
	I	II	III	IV
x_{min}	−10	−20	−15	−10
x_{max}	10	20	15	10
x_{scl}	1	2	2	1
y_{min}	−10	−30	−10	−20
y_{max}	10	30	40	60
y_{scl}	1	3	2	4
x_{res}	1	1	1	1

41. The window setting Gladys must use in order to display the graph with its vertex is

A. I **B.** II **C.** III **D.** IV

QR3.7 *explore the algebraic development of the quadratic formula*

The Quadratic Formula

Since not all quadratic equations can be factored, using technology to find the roots will only give an approximate answer.
In order to obtain the exact roots of a quadratic equation, a formula (called the **quadratic formula**) can be developed by completing the square of the general form of a quadratic equation $ax^2 + bx + c = 0$.

Development of The Quadratic Formula

Isolating x in the equation $ax^2 + bx + c = 0$ is accomplished by completing the square.

$$ax^2 + bx + c = 0$$

$$a\left(x^2 + \frac{b}{a}x\right) + c = 0$$

$$a\left(x^2 + \frac{b}{a}x + \frac{b^2}{4a^2} - \frac{b^2}{4a^2}\right) + c = 0$$

$$a\left(x + \frac{b}{2a}\right)^2 - \frac{b^2}{4a} + c = 0$$

$$a\left(x + \frac{b}{2a}\right)^2 = \frac{b^2}{4a} - c$$

$$\left(x + \frac{b}{2a}\right)^2 = \frac{b^2}{4a^2} - \frac{c}{a}$$

$$\left(x + \frac{b}{2a}\right)^2 = \frac{b^2}{4a^2} - \frac{4ac}{4a^2}$$

$$\left(x + \frac{b}{2a}\right)^2 = \frac{b^2 - 4ac}{4a^2}$$

$$\sqrt{\left(x + \frac{b}{2a}\right)^2} = \pm\sqrt{\frac{b^2 - 4ac}{4a^2}}$$

$$x + \frac{b}{2a} = \pm\frac{\sqrt{b^2 - 4ac}}{2a}$$

$$x = -\frac{b}{2a} \pm \frac{\sqrt{b^2 - 4ac}}{2a}$$

$$x = \frac{-b \pm \sqrt{b^2 - 4ac}}{2a}$$

The roots of the quadratic equation $ax^2 + bx + c = 0$, where $a \neq 0$, can be expressed in terms of a, b, and c by using the quadratic formula:

$$x = \frac{-b \pm \sqrt{b^2 - 4ac}}{2a}$$

Example

Find the exact roots to the equation $0 = x^2 - 8x + 5$ by applying the quadratic formula.

Step 1: Identify the values of a, b, and c.

$a = 1 \qquad b = -8 \qquad c = 5$

Step 2: Substitute these values into the quadratic formula.

$$\begin{aligned} x &= \frac{-b \pm \sqrt{b^2 - 4ac}}{2a} \\ &= \frac{-(-8) \pm \sqrt{(-8)^2 - 4(1)(5)}}{2(1)} \\ &= \frac{8 \pm \sqrt{64 - 20}}{2} \\ &= \frac{8 \pm \sqrt{44}}{2} \\ &= \frac{8 \pm \sqrt{4 \times 11}}{2} \\ &= \frac{2(4 \pm \sqrt{11})}{2} \\ &= 4 \pm \sqrt{11} \end{aligned}$$

The roots of the given equation are $4 + \sqrt{11}$ or $4 - \sqrt{11}$.

Practice

Use the following information to answer the next question.

Marianne has chosen to use the quadratic formula to solve the equation $2x^2 - 3x - 1 = 0$. The steps she used to arrive at a solution are given.

Step 1	$x = \frac{-3 \pm \sqrt{(-3)^2 - 4(2)(-1)}}{2(2)}$
Step 2	$x = \frac{-3 \pm \sqrt{9 + 8}}{4}$
Step 3	$x = \frac{-3 \pm \sqrt{17}}{4}$
Step 4	$x = -1.78x = 0.28$

42. In which step did Marianne's first error occur?

A. Step 1 **B.** Step 2

C. Step 3 **D.** Step 4

Use the following information to answer the next question.

The first three steps in the algebraic development of the quadratic formula are shown.

$ax^2 + bx + c = 0$

Step 1: $a\left(x^2 + \frac{b}{a}x\right) + c = 0$

Step 2: $a\left(x^2 + \frac{b}{a}x + \frac{b^2}{4a^2} - \frac{b^2}{4a^2}\right) + c = 0$

Step 3: $a(x + K)^2 - \frac{b^2}{4a} + c = 0$

43. The variable K represents the expression

A. $\frac{b^2}{4a^2}$ **B.** $\frac{b^2}{2a^2}$

C. $\frac{b}{4a}$ **D.** $\frac{b}{2a}$

QR3.8 *solve quadratic equations that have real roots, using a variety of methods*

Solving Quadratic Equations

Quadratic equations can be solved using methods such as factoring, using the quadratic formula, and graphing. In general, unless otherwise specified in the question, the following tips are recommended for solving a quadratic equation of the form $ax^2 + bx + c = 0$:

1. Attempt to solve the equation by factoring.
2. If the equation cannot be solved by factoring or is difficult to factor, use the quadratic formula.
3. Use a graphical procedure to solve the equation or verify your solution.
4. Simplify the roots (solution values), if necessary, and clearly state the solution(s) using "$x =$ ".

Example

Solve the equation $0 = x^2 + 4x - 21$.

Method 1—Factoring

$0 = x^2 + 4x - 21$

$0 = (x - 3)(x + 7)$

$0 = (x - 3)$ or $0 = (x + 7)$

$x = 3$ or $x = -7$

Method 2—Using the Quadratic Formula

$a = 1$, $b = 4$, and $c = -21$

$$x = \frac{-b \pm \sqrt{b^2 - 4ac}}{2a}$$

$$x = \frac{-(4) \pm \sqrt{(4)^2 - 4(1)(-21)}}{2(1)}$$

$$x = \frac{-4 \pm \sqrt{16 + 84}}{2}$$

$$x = \frac{-4 \pm \sqrt{100}}{2}$$

$$x = \frac{-4 \pm 10}{2}$$

Either:

$$x = \frac{-4 + 10}{2} \text{ or } x = \frac{-4 - 10}{2}$$

$$x = \frac{6}{2} \text{ or } x = \frac{-14}{2}$$

$x = 3$ or $x = -7$

Method 3—Graphing

From the ZERO feature, you should see that the x-intercepts or zeros are $x = 3$ and $x = -7$.

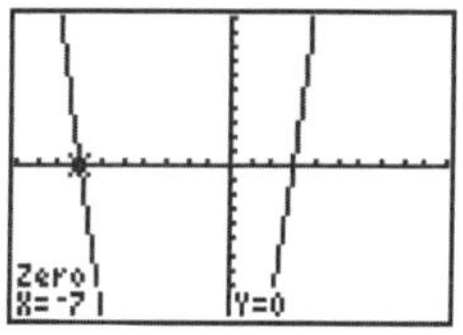

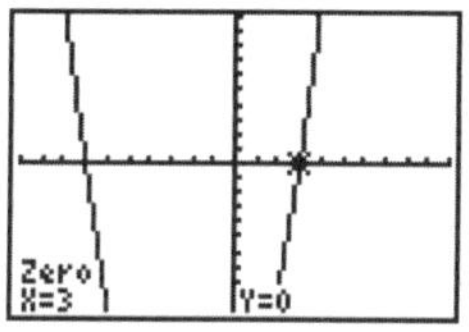

Thus, the solution to the equation $0 = x^2 + 4x - 21$ is $x = 3$ or $x = -7$.

Practice

Use the following information to answer the next question.

A math teacher asks her class to solve the quadratic equation $8x^2 - 2x = 3$. The partial solution of each of two students is given.

Tayla
$8x^2 - 2x = 3$
$8x^2 - 2x - 3 = 0$
$8x^2 - 6x + 4x - 3 = 0$
$2x(4x - 3) + 1(4x - 3) = 0$
$(4x - 3)(2x + 1) = 0$
Honoria
$8x^2 - 2x = 3$
$8x^2 - 2x - 3 = 0$
$x = \dfrac{-(-2) \pm \sqrt{(-2)^2 - 4(8)(-3)}}{2(8)}$
$x = \dfrac{2 \pm \sqrt{4 + 96}}{16}$
$x = \dfrac{2 \pm \sqrt{100}}{16}$

44. Which of the following statements is **true**?

A. Tayla's work and Honoria's work will each lead to a correct solution.

B. Tayla's work and Honoria's work will each lead to an incorrect solution.

C. Tayla's work will lead to an incorrect solution, and Honoria's work will lead to a correct solution.

D. Tayla's work will lead to a correct solution, and Honoria's work will lead to an incorrect solution.

45. The solutions to the quadratic equation $10x + 3 = 7x^2$ are

A. $x = \dfrac{3 + \sqrt{46}}{7}$ or $x = \dfrac{3 - \sqrt{46}}{7}$

B. $x = \dfrac{4 + \sqrt{46}}{7}$ or $x = \dfrac{4 - \sqrt{46}}{7}$

C. $x = \dfrac{5 + \sqrt{46}}{7}$ or $x = \dfrac{5 - \sqrt{46}}{7}$

D. $x = \dfrac{7 + \sqrt{46}}{7}$ or $x = \dfrac{7 - \sqrt{46}}{7}$

46. The solutions to the quadratic equation $7x^2 + 2x - 5 = 11x^2 - 6x - 4$ are

A. $x = \dfrac{2 \pm \sqrt{3}}{2}$

B. $x = 1 \pm 4\sqrt{3}$

C. $x = \dfrac{2 \pm \sqrt{5}}{2}$

D. $x = 1 \pm 4\sqrt{5}$

Use the following information to answer the next multipart question.

47. The graph of the quadratic function $y = 2x^2 - x - 15$ is shown.

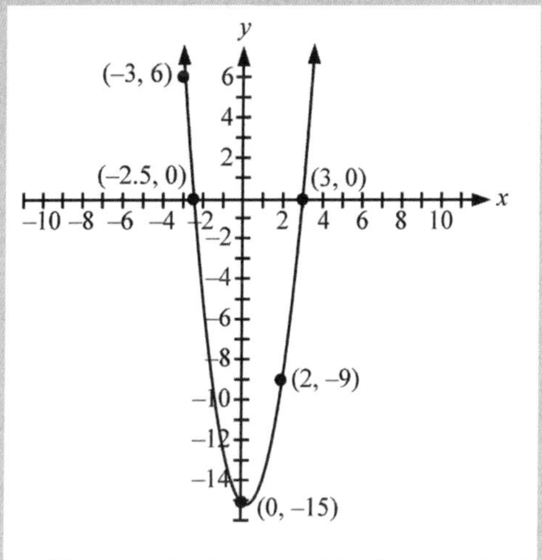

Part A

Open Response

What are the roots of the quadratic equation $2x^2 - x - 15 = 0$?

Part B

Open Response

Algebraically, solve the quadratic equation $2x^2 - x - 15 = 30$.

Part C

Open Response

If a student were to solve the equation $2x^2 - x - 15 = 0$ by using the quadratic formula, would the value of $b^2 - 4ac$ be a number that is a perfect square?

Justify your answer.

QR4.1 *determine the zeros and the maximum or minimum value of a quadratic relation from its graph or from its defining equation*

Determining the Zeros and the Maximum or Minimum Value of a Parabola

Using a Graphical Approach

Recall the following from previous lessons:

- The zero(s) of a function are the x-coordinates where the curve crosses or touches the x-axis.
- The maximum value is the y-coordinate of the highest point on the graph of the quadratic relation and occurs when the graph opens downward.
- The minimum value is the y-coordinate of the lowest point on the graph of the quadratic relation and occurs when the graph opens upward.

Consider the function $y = x^2 + 6x - 11$. Using the ZERO feature on a TI-83 Plus calculator, determine the zeros of the function.

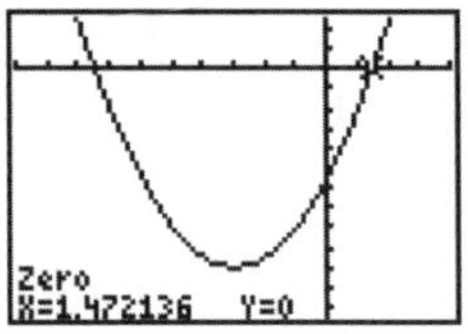

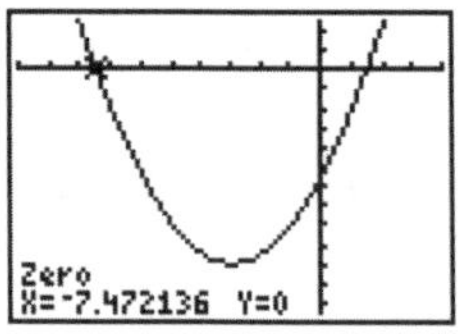

Window setting used: x:[−10, 4, 1] y:[−25, 5, 2]. To the nearest hundredth, the zeros of the function $y = x^2 + 6x - 11$ are $x = 1.47$ and $x = -7.47$.

Since this graph opens upward, use the MINIMUM feature on the graphing calculator to determine the minimum value of the function $y = x^2 + 6x - 11$.

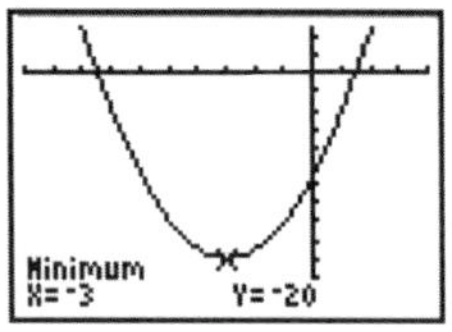

The y-coordinate from this screen indicates the minimum value. Therefore, the minimum value of the function $y = x^2 + 6x - 11$ is −20.

Using an Algebraic Approach

Recall that when using an algebraic approach:

- The zero(s) of a function can be determined by substituting 0 for y into the equation $y = ax^2 + bx + c, a \neq 0$ and then solving for x.
- The maximum or minimum value can be determined when the function is written in the form $y = a(x - h)^2 + k$.
- The maximum value is k when $a < 0$.
- The minimum value is k when $a > 0$.

Example

Determine the zero(s) and the maximum or minimum value for the function $y = -2(x + 6)^2 + 5$.

To determine the zero(s) of the function, substitute 0 for y, and solve for x.

$$0 = -2(x + 6)^2 + 5$$

$$-5 = -2(x + 6)^2$$

$$\frac{5}{2} = (x + 6)^2$$

$$\pm\sqrt{\frac{5}{2}} = \sqrt{(x + 6)^2}$$

$$\pm\sqrt{\frac{5}{2}} = x + 6$$

$$\pm\sqrt{\frac{5}{2}} - 6 = x$$

Thus, either $x = -6 + \sqrt{\frac{5}{2}}$ or $x = -6 - \sqrt{\frac{5}{2}}$

$x = -4.4$ and $x = -7.6$

To the nearest tenth, the zeros for the function $y = -2(x + 6)^2 + 5$ are $x = -4.4$ or $x = -7.6$.

The function $y = -2(x + 6)^2 + 5$ is written in the form $y = a(x - h)^2 + k$. Since $a < 0$, the graph of the function opens downward. Therefore, a maximum value occurs at k. For the function $y = -2(x + 6)^2 + 5$, the maximum value is 5.

Practice

48. Megan was given a math problem requiring her to design a pigpen with maximum area given a fixed amount of fencing. She was able to generate a quadratic function expressed in the completed square form $y = a(x - h)^2 + k$ to help her determine the maximum area of the pigpen. Megan wants to confirm that the pigpen has a maximum area rather than a minimum area. From the completed square form $y = a(x - h)^2 + k$, Megan needs to examine the value of

A. only the variable a

B. only the variable k

C. both variables k and h

D. both variables a and k

CHALLENGER QUESTION

49. The minimum value of the function $y = ax^2 + bx + c$ is -1. If the zeros of the function are 1 and 2, then the value of c is

A. 5 **B.** 6 **C.** 8 **D.** 9

Numerical Response

50. The minimum value of the function $y = 40 - 12x + x^2$ is ____.

(Correct to the nearest whole number.)

QR4.2 *solve problems arising from a realistic situation represented by a graph or an equation of a quadratic relation, with and without the use of technology.*

Quadratic Functions and Problem Solving

Quadratic functions can be used to model real-world situations that are represented by a graph or an equation.

Example

The trajectory of a baseball is represented by the graph shown below.

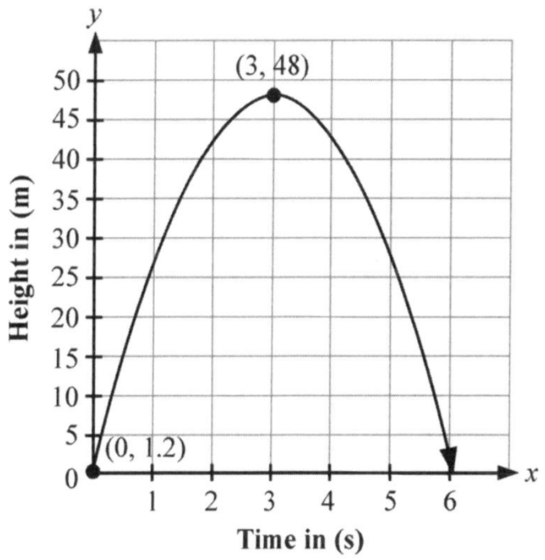

a. What is the maximum height of the baseball?

The given parabola opens downward and has a vertex of (3, 48).
Therefore, the maximum height of the baseball is 48 m (the y-coordinate of the vertex).

b. From what height was the baseball initially hit?

At the initial height, the time will equal 0 s. This corresponds to the ordered pair (0, 1.2) on the graph. Thus, the baseball was hit from an initial height of 1.2 m.

c. How long does the baseball remain in the air?

The ball remains in the air until it hits the ground. This occurs where the graph intersects the x-axis after it has reached its maximum height. Since the graph intersects the x-axis at 6, the ball remains in the air for 6 s.

Example

A city's population can fluctuate. A small Ontario city that has a declining population is expecting the population to begin increasing in the near future because of the introduction of several industrial development initiatives. The city planners predict that the city's population can be modelled by the function $P = 150t^2 - 1\,200t + 14\,900$, $t \geq 0$, where t is the time in years since January 1, 2007 and P is the population. Use technology, where appropriate, to answer the following questions.

a. What was the city's population on January 1, 2008?

On January 1, 2008, exactly one year will have passed since January 1, 2007. Therefore, substitute 1 for t into the equation $P = 150t^2 - 1\,200t + 14\,900$, and solve for P.

$P = 150(1)^2 - 1\,200(1) + 14\,900$

$P = 150 - 1\,200 + 14\,900$

$P = 13\,850$

The population on January 1, 2008 was 13 850.

b. At the beginning of what year will the city's population be at its lowest point?

Use the MINIMUM feature of a TI-83 Plus graphing calculator and a window setting such as $x{:}[-5,\ 12,\ 2]$ $y{:}[7\,500,\ 20\,000,\ 2\,500]$

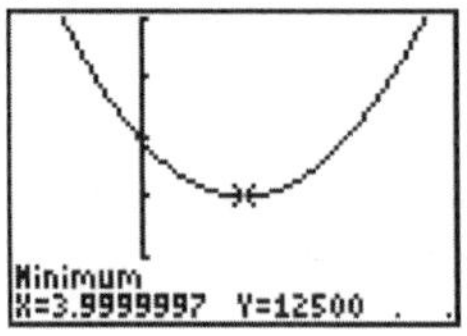

The function's minimum value occurs when $x = 4$; therefore, at the beginning of the year 2011, the city's population will be at its lowest point.

c. What is the first year that the city's population will be more than 24 000?

This problem requires you to use a TI-83Plus graphing calculator to graph the line $y = 24\,000$ and use the INTERSECTION feature to find the first positive intersection point with the function $y = 150x^2 - 1\,200x + 14\,900$.

d. The first positive intersection point is:

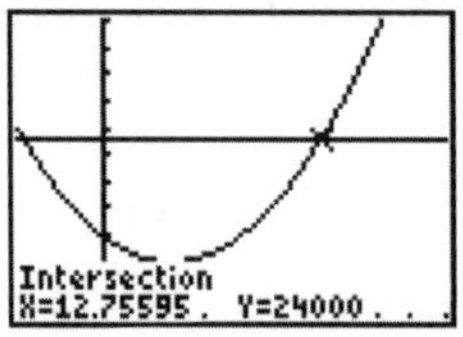

Since $x = 12.76$, the first year that the population will be more than 24 000 is at the end of 2019.

Practice

51. Ben observed that an arrow shot from a bow followed a parabolic path for which the height is approximated by the quadratic function $h = -4.9(t - 1.5)^2 + 12, t \geq 0$, where h is the height in metres and t is the time in seconds. Which of the following graphs **best** represents this quadratic function?

A.
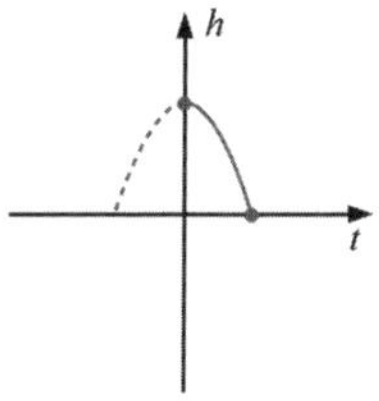

B.
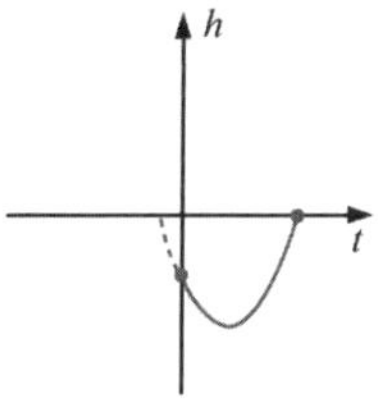

C.
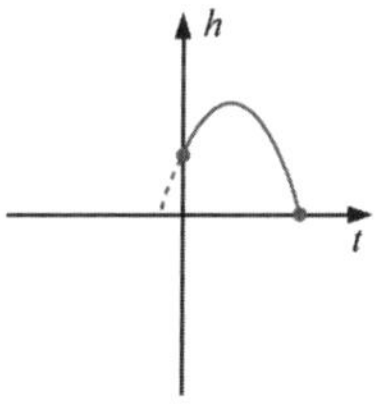

D.
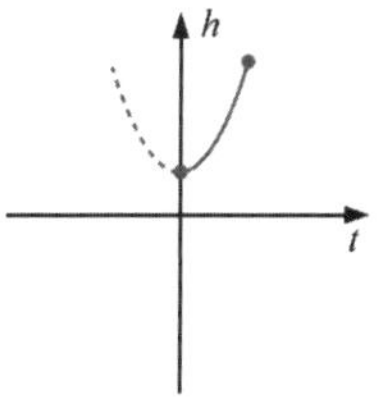

CHALLENGER QUESTION

Use the following information to answer the next question.

A rectangular lot is bordered on one side by a river and on the other three sides by a total of 60 m of fencing, as shown in the diagram.

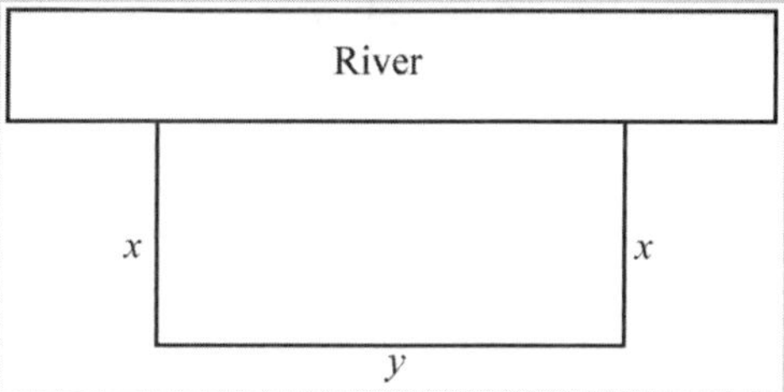

52. If x represents the width of the lot and y represents the length of the lot, then the equation $2x + y = 60$ represents the total amount of fencing expressed in terms of x and y. The maximum area, A, of the lot in terms of x is given by the equation $A = -2x^2 + 60x$. The length of the lot is

A. 15 m **B.** 25 m

C. 30 m **D.** 40 m

Use the following information to answer the next question.

The path of a roller coaster car can be modelled by the function $h = -7t^2 + 61t + 98$ for the section of the ride, where $1 \leq t \leq 10$. For this function, h is the height of the car above the ground in feet and t is the time in seconds elapsed since the beginning of the ride.

53. To the nearest tenth, the maximum height reached by the roller coaster car in the interval $1 \leq t \leq 10$ is

A. 61.0 ft **B.** 98.0 ft

C. 115.5 ft **D.** 230.9 ft

CHALLENGER QUESTION

Use the following information to answer the next multipart question.

54. The daily profit, P, in dollars of a hot dog vendor in Toronto is described by the equation $P = -40x^2 + 240x - 75$, where x dollars is the selling price per hot dog.

Part A

Open Response

Describe the financial impact if the hot dog vendor does not sell any hot dogs.

Part B

Open Response

What should the selling price per hot dog be in order for the vendor to maximize his daily profit?

Justify your answer algebraically.

Part C

Open Response

What is the maximum daily profit for the hot dog vendor?

Solutions–Quadratic Relations

1. 32	**13. C**	Part C- **OR**	**35. A**	**47.** Part A- **OR**
2. D	**14. 2, 3, 5**	**24. B**	**36. A**	Part B- **OR**
3. D	**15. B**	**25. B**	**37. B**	Part C- **OR**
4. A	**16. C**	**26. C**	**38. 18.3**	**48. A**
5. D	**17. A**	**27. B**	**39. A**	**49. C**
6. B	**18. B**	**28. D**	**40. A**	**50. 4**
7. B	**19. A**	**29. 5**	**41. D**	**51. C**
8. C	**20. C**	**30. A**	**42. A**	**52. C**
9. 22	**21. D**	**31. B**	**43. D**	**53. D**
10. A	**22. 1.5**	**32. D**	**44. A**	**54.** Part A- **OR**
11. C	**23.** Part A- **OR**	**33. B**	**45. C**	Part B- **OR**
12. B	Part B- **OR**	**34. C**	**46. A**	Part C- **OR**

1. 32

Graph the function obtained from the quadratic regression, $y = -10x^2 + 100x + 6\,000$, in the calculator and graph the line $y = 5\,760$. Find the point of intersection between the two graphs. The x-coordinate of the point of intersection is the number of dollar increases in price that correspond to a revenue of \$5 760.

From this, the owner needs to increase his price by \$12 to generate a revenue of \$5 760, and this corresponds to a ticket price of \$32. (\$20 + \$12).

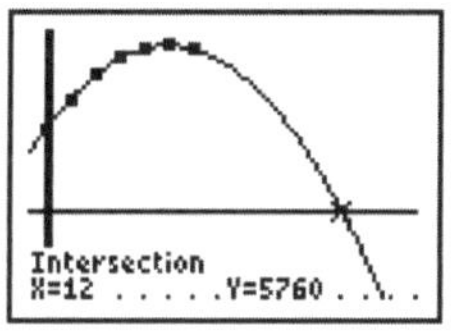

2. D

Enter the data into the calculator, and perform a quadratic regression.

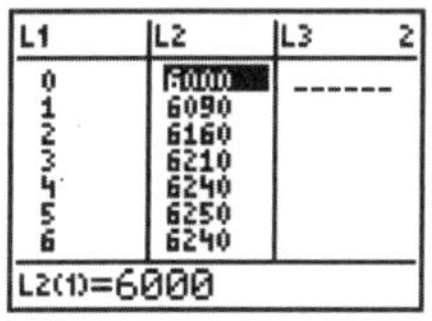

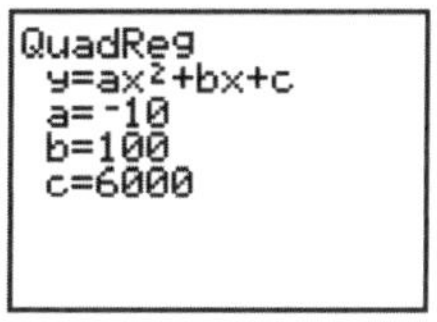

The formula $y = -10x^2 + 100x + 6\,000$ will result.

3. D

Sketch the specified ordered pairs, by hand to get the following graph:

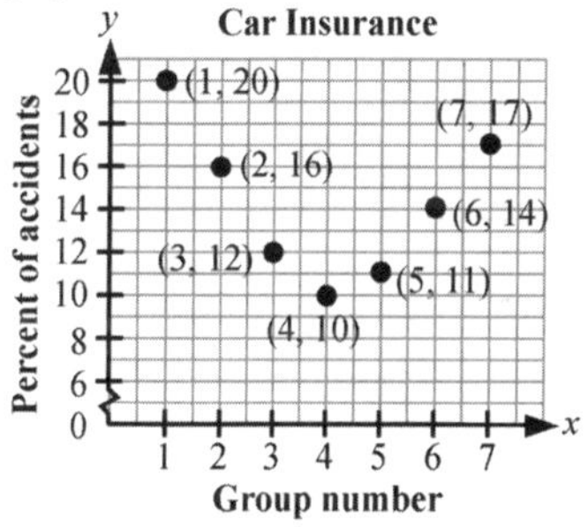

Therefore, graph D is the best display of information given in the table.

4. A

The graph of any quadratic function $y = ax^2$ is a parabola. Choice B is the shape of a third degree or cubic function of the form, $y = ax^3$. Choice C is the graph of a linear function of the form, $y = ax$, and choice D is the V-shaped graph of an absolute value function of the form, $y = a|x|$.

5. D

If $a > 0$ in the equation $y = ax^2 + bx + c$, the parabola opens upward. Therefore, $y = 5x^2 + 4x - 3$ and $y = 2.5x^2 - 3x - 8$ are two possible equations.
From the table of values, calculate the second difference for each equation.

$y = 5x^2 + 4x - 3$:

x	y	1st diff	2nd diff
1	6	} 19	
2	25	} 29	} 10
3	54	} 39	} 10
4	93	} 49	} 10
5	142	} 59	} 10
6	201		

$y = 2.5x^2 - 3x - 8$:

x	y	1st diff	2nd diff
1	–8.5	} 4.5	
2	–4	} 9.5	} 5
3	5.5	} 14.5	} 5
4	20	} 19.5	} 5
5	39.5	} 24.5	} 5
6	64		

Therefore, the equation of a quadratic function that opens upward and has a second difference of 5 is $y = 2.5x^2 - 3x - 8$.

6. B

In order for a relation to be quadratic, the second differences from a table of values are constant and not equal to zero.
Examine the second differences for each of the table of values.

A

x	y	1st diff	2nd diff
1	8	} 3	
2		} 3	} 0
3		} 3	} 0
4		} 3	} 0
5		} 3	} 0
6			

B

x	y	1st diff	2nd diff
1	4	} 9	
2		} 15	} 6
3		} 21	} 6
4		} 27	} 6
5		} 33	} 6
6			

C

x	y	1st diff	2nd diff
1	1	} 2	
2		} 5	} 3
3		} 9	} 4
4		} 14	} 5
5		} 20	} 6
6			

D

x	y	1st diff	2nd diff
1	0	} 1	
2		} 4	} 3
3		} 9	} 5
4		} 16	} 7
5		} 25	} 9
6			

Since table B has a constant second difference of 6, it represents a quadratic function.

7. B

The graph of the function shown is a parabola that opens downward and has the following features:
The vertex of the parabola is $(-3,\ 1)$, the ordered pair where the maximum value of y occurs.
The maximum value is $y = 1$ (1 is the y-coordinate of the vertex).
The zeros are $x = -4$ or $x = -2$, the x-coordinate of each ordered pairs where the parabola intersects the x-axis.
The parabola passes through the y-axis at the ordered pair $(0,\ -8)$, so the y-intercept is -8.
The axis of symmetry is the vertical line $x = -3$ (-3 is the x-coordinate of the vertex).
The domain of the quadratic function is $x \in \mathbf{R}$.
Therefore, the false statement is B since the vertex is $(-3,\ 1)$, not $(3,\ -1)$.

8. C

The graph shown is of a parabola that opens upward; therefore, a minimum value occurs at the vertex $\left(\frac{1}{6}, \frac{23}{12}\right)$.

The minimum value is $y = \frac{23}{12}$ (the y-coordinate of the vertex).

The axis of symmetry is the vertical line $x = \frac{1}{6}$ (the x-coordinate of the vertex).

9. 22

The y-intercept of the graph of the quadratic relation $y = -2(x+3)^2 - 4$ can be found by substituting 0 for x into the relation $y = -2(x+3)^2 - 4$.

$y = -2(0+3)^2 - 4$
$y = -2(9) - 4$
$y = -18 - 4$
$y = -22$

Therefore, the value of K in the ordered pair $(0,\ -K)$ is 22.

10. A

Recall that any number (except 0) or variable with an exponent of zero is equal to 1: $x^0 = 1$.

The graphs of $y = x^0$ and $y = 1$ are shown below.

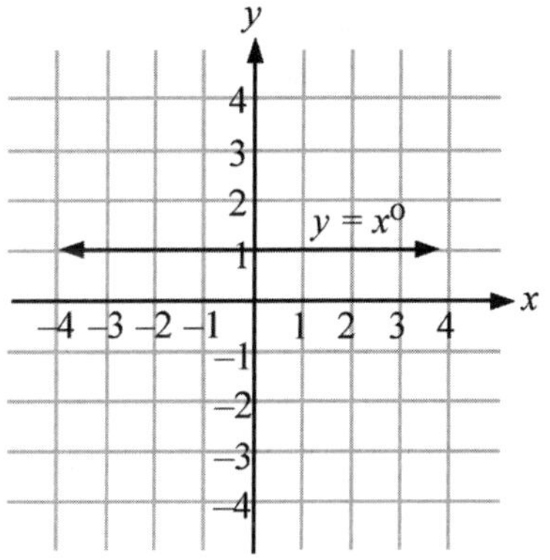

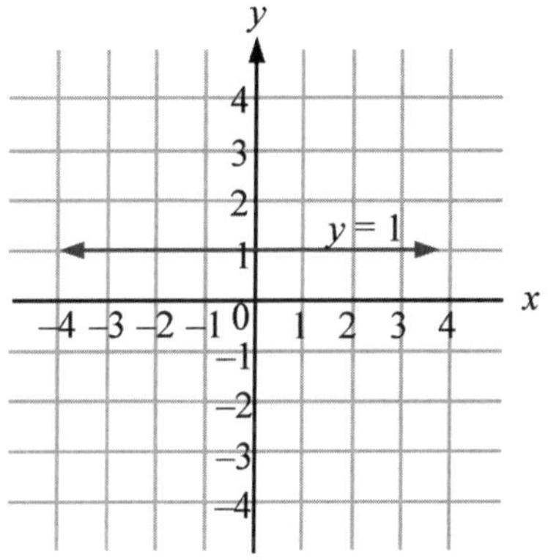

Therefore, the graph of $y = x^0$, where $x \neq 0$, is the same as the graph of $y = 1$.

11. C

Compare the graph of $y = x^2$ and the graph of $y = 2^x$.

The x-intercept for the graph of the function $y = x^2$ is $x = 0$.

The function $y = 2^x$ does not cross or touch the x-axis; thus, the graph of $y = 2^x$ has no x-intercept.

The y-intercept for the graph of the function $y = x^2$ is $y = 0$.

For the function $y = 2^x$, the graph crosses the y-axis at $(0,\ 1)$; therefore, the y-intercept is $y = 1$.

The minimum value of the graph of $y = x^2$ is 0 and has an undefined maximum value.

The graph of the exponential function $y = 2^x$ has an undefined maximum and an undefined minimum value. Both graphs have an undefined maximum value.

12. B

Since $a > 0$, the graph of the quadratic function $y = ax^2 + k$ must open upward.
Also, the k-value causes a vertical translation (shifting the parabola upward or downward). Since the only parameters are a and k, there is no horizontal translation. Therefore, the following graph best models the quadratic function $y = ax^2 + k$.

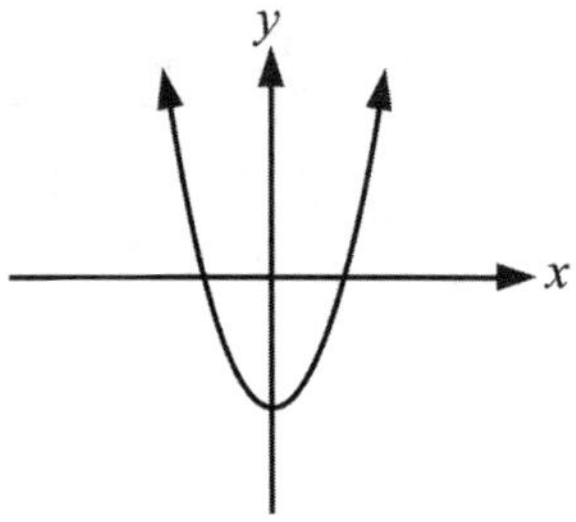

13. C

If the value of k increases in the equation $y = x^2 + k$, the graph is shifted up.
The k-value causes a vertical translation (shifting the parabola upward or downward).

14. 2, 3, 5

For the graph of the function $y = 2(x + 3)^2 - 5$, it follows that
$a = 2$, $h = -3$ and $k = -5$.

- Since $a = 2$, there is a vertical stretch about the x-axis by a factor of 2.
- Since $h = -3$ there is a horizontal translation of 3 units to the left.
- Since $k = -5$ there is a vertical translation downward by 5 units.

15. B

In the equation $y = -2(x - 1)^2 + 3$, it follows that $a = -2$, $h = 1$, and $k = 3$.
The equation of the axis of symmetry is $x = h$; therefore, the graph of the parabola
$y = -2(x - 1)^2 + 3$ is symmetric about the line $x = 1$.

16. C

A vertical stretch by a factor of 4 will change the a-value from 1 to 4.
A reflection in the x-axis will change the a value from 4 to -4.
A translation of 7 units to the left means h is -7.
A translation of 6 units up means k is 6.
The values are $a = -4$, $h = -7$, and $k = 6$.

17. A

Since the equation of the axis of symmetry for a quadratic function is $x = h$ and for this quadratic function, the axis of symmetry is $x - 5 = 0$ or $x = 5$, it follows that $h = 5$.
Also, since the quadratic function has a minimum value, the graph opens upward, which means that $a > 0$.
Substitute 5 for h into the equation $y = a(x - h)^2 + k$, where $a > 0$ to get $y = (x - 5)^2 + k$.

18. B

All points on the transformed graph must satisfy the given transformations.
A reflection about the x-axis will change (4, 16) to (4, −16)
A vertical stretch about the x-axis by a factor of 2 will change (4, −16) to (4, −32).
A horizontal translation 5 units to the left changes (4, −32) to (−1, −32).
A vertical translation 4 units upward changes (−1, −32) to (−1, −28).
The value of y is −28.

19. A

Begin with the graph of $y = x^2$.

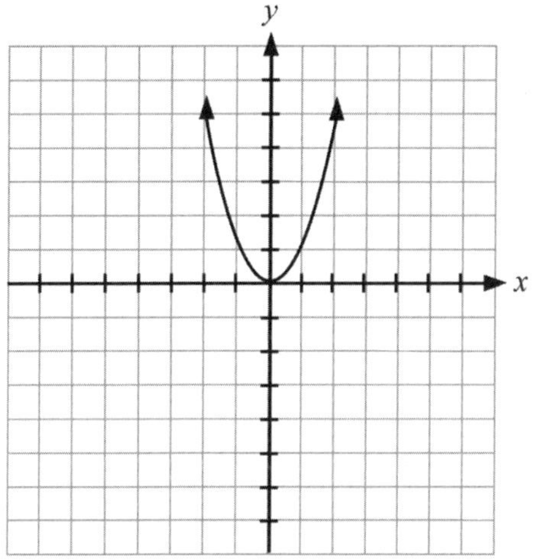

Perform a reflection in the x-axis.

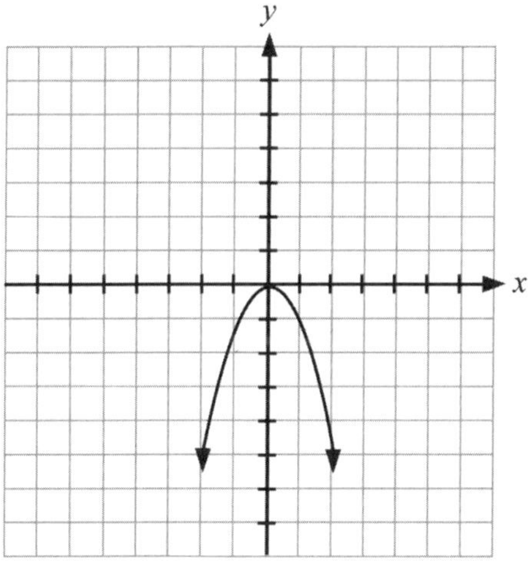

The vertex is at $(-4, -7)$ in the original graph, so after the reflection, the graph was translated left 4 units and down 7 units.

20. C

The equation is $y = -x^2 + \frac{7}{2} = -x^2 + 3.5$.

Comparing this with the equation $y = a(x-h)^2 + k$, $a = -1, h = 0$, and $y = 3.5$.
Since $a = -1$ and $-1 < 0$, the parabola will open downward.

The graph of $y = -x^2 + \frac{7}{2}$ can be obtained by reflecting the graph of $y = x^2$ in the x-axis and then translating the graph 3.5 units upward.
Therefore, the graph is as shown:

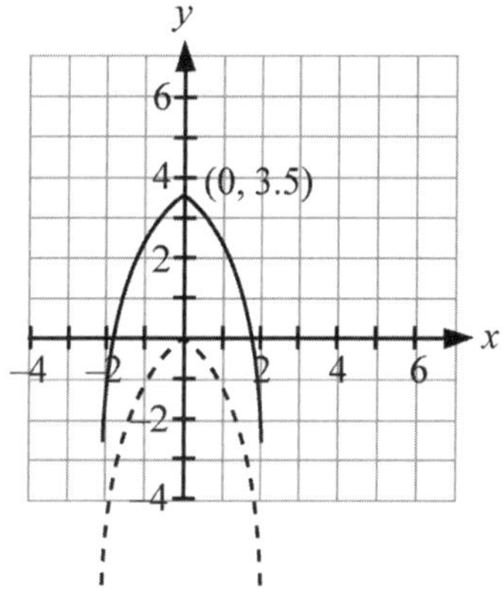

21. D

The parabola shown can have an equation of the form $y = a(x-h)^2 + k$, where (h, k) is the vertex. Since the vertex is at $(0, -2)$, $h = 0$ and $k = -2$.
Substitute 0 for h and -2 for k into the equation $y = a(x-h)^2 + k$ to get $y = ax^2 - 2$.
Since the equation passes through the point (2, 2), $x = 2$ and $y = 2$.

$y = ax^2 - 2$

Substitute 2 for x and 2 for y. Solve for a.

$2 = a(2)^2 - 2$

$2 = 4a - 2$

$4 = 4a$

$1 = a$

Substitute 1 for a into the equation $y = ax^2 - 2$ to get $y = x^2 - 2$.

Thus, the equation for this parabola is $y = x^2 - 2$.

22. 1.5

In order to solve for a, substitute 0 for x and 17 for y into the equation $y = a(x-4)^2 - 7$.

$17 = a(0-4)^2 - 7$

$17 = a(16) - 7$

$24 = 16a$

$\frac{3}{2} = a = 1.5$

Thus, the value of a, to one decimal place, is 1.5.

23. **Part A – Open Response**

Begin by locating the vertex of the parabola shown. This ordered pair is $(-2, 6)$.

Now, make use of equation $y = a(x-h)^2 + k$.
Substitute -2 for h and 6 for k.

$y = a(x-(-2))^2 + 6$

$y = a(x+2)^2 + 6$

Since the parabola passes through the ordered pair $(4, -12)$, solve for a as follows:

$y = a(x+2)^2 + 6$

Substitute 4 for x and -12 for y.

$-12 = a(4+2)^2 + 6$

$-12 = a(6)^2 + 6$

$-12 = 36a + 6$

$-18 = 36a$

$\frac{-18}{36} = a$

$-\frac{1}{2} = a$

Thus, the equation of the quadratic function of the graph shown is $y = -\frac{1}{2}(x+2)^2 + 6$.

Part B – Open Response

In order to determine the y-intercept of the given parabola, substitute 0 for x in the equation $y = -\frac{1}{2}(x+2)^2 + 6$, and solve for y as shown:

$y = -\frac{1}{2}(0+2)^2 + 6$ Substitute 0 for x.

$y = -\frac{1}{2}(2)^2 + 6$

$y = -\frac{1}{2}(4) + 6$

$y = -2 + 6$

$y = 4$

The y-intercept of the parabola shown is 4.

Part C – Open Response

If the ordered pair $(-8, -12)$ is on the graph of the quadratic function, then the ordered pair $(-8, -12)$ must satisfy the equation $y = -\frac{1}{2}(x+2)^2 + 6$. Determine this as follows:

Substitute -8 for x and -12 for y.

$-12 = -\frac{1}{2}(-8+2)^2 + 6$

$-12 = -\frac{1}{2}(-6)^2 + 6$

$-12 = -\frac{1}{2}(36) + 6$

$-12 = -18 + 6$

$-12 = -12$

Since $-12 = -12$, the ordered pair $(-8, -12)$ is on the graph of the given quadratic function.

24. B

$(x-5)(4x+5)$

Use the FOIL strategy to multiply each term within the first set of brackets by each term within the second set of brackets.

$x(4x) + x(5) - 5(4x) - 5(5)$

$4x^2 + 5x - 20x - 25$

Collect like terms.

$4x^2 - 15x - 25$

Thus, the coefficient of x is -15.

25. B

$(3x-4)(4x-1)$

Use the FOIL strategy to multiply each term within the first set of brackets by each term within the second set of brackets.

$3x(4x) + 3x(-1) - 4(4x) - 4(-1)$

$12x^2 - 3x - 16x + 4$

Collect like terms.

$12x^2 - 19x + 4$

Compare the expression $12x^2 - 19x + 4$ to the expression $12x^2 + bx + 4$. In order for the expressions to be equal $b = -19$.

26. C

Apply the difference of squares factoring procedure where $a^2 = 16a^2b^2$, so $a = 4ab$ and $b^2 = 9c^2$ so $b = 3c$.

Since $a^2 - b^2 = (a-b)(a+b)$,

$16a^2b^2 - 9c^2 = (4ab)^2 - (3c)^2 = (4ab - 3c)(4ab + 3c)$.

Therefore, one factor is $4ab + 3c$.

27. B

In order to factor $2x^2 + x - 28$, find two numbers that have a product of -56 $(a \times c = 2 \times -28)$ and a sum of 1 (the b-value).
In this case, 8 and -7.
Rewrite the expression by replacing the term x with $8x - 7x$.
$= 2x^2 + 8x - 7x - 28$
Group using brackets.
$= (2x^2 + 8x) + (-7x - 28)$
Remove the GCF from each group.
$= 2x(x + 4) - 7(x + 4)$
Factor out the common binomial.
$= (2x - 7)(x + 4)$
Therefore, one factor is $2x - 7$.

28. D

Polynomial IV should be factored as $a(2a + 1)(2a - 1)$. Therefore, polynomial IV has an incorrect student solution.

29. 5

The factored form of $x^2 - 3x - 4$ is $(x - 4)(x + 1)$. Therefore, $m = 4$ and $n = 1$, so $m + n = 4 + 1 = 5$.

30. A

The quadratic equation $(3x - 4)(2x + 7) = 0$ can be re-written as follows:
Factor out the coefficient of x from each set of brackets.
$3\left(x - \frac{4}{3}\right)2\left(x + \frac{7}{2}\right) = 0$
Simplify.
$6\left(x - \frac{4}{3}\right)\left(x + \frac{7}{2}\right) = 0$
When a quadratic function is expressed in the factored form $y = a(x - r)(x - s)$, the x-intercepts (the zeros) of the graph of the quadratic function are $x = r$ and $x = s$.
Since the quadratic equation $6x^2 + 13x - 28 = 0$ can be expressed in the form $6\left(x - \frac{4}{3}\right)\left(x + \frac{7}{2}\right) = 0$,
the zeros are $x = \frac{4}{3}$ and $x = -\frac{7}{2}$.

31. B

The x-intercepts of the graph shown are 1.5 and 3. Therefore, substitute 1.5 for r and 3 for s in the equation $y = a(x - r)(x - s)$ as follows:
$y = a(x - 1.5)(x - 3)$
$y = a(x^2 - 4.5x + 4.5)$
Since the graph of the parabola shown opens downward, $a < 0$.
$y = -a(x^2 - 4.5x + 4.5)$
$y = -ax^2 + 4.5ax - 4.5a$
Therefore, the equation that best models the parabola is $y = -2x^2 + 9x - 9$ since it can be arrived at by substituting 2 for a into the equation
$y = -ax^2 + 4.5ax - 4.5a$.
$y = -(2)x^2 + 4.5(2)x - 4.5(2)$
$y = -2x^2 + 9x - 9$

32. D

Procedure A	Procedure B
Step 1: Graph the equation $y = 2x^2 + 9x - 5$	Step 1: Graph the equations $y = 2x^2$ and $y = 5 - 9x$
Step 2: Using the calculate feature and the zero option, determine the x-intercepts of the graph.  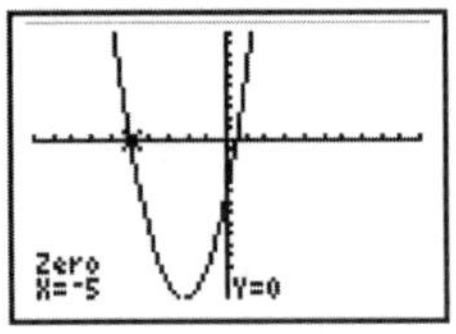 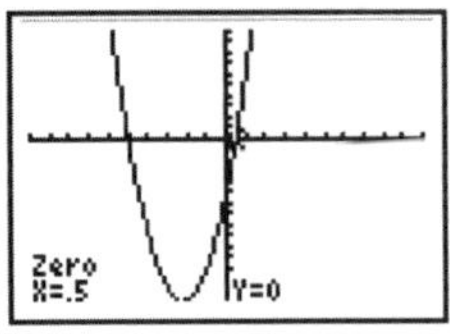 The zeros are displayed as the x-coordinate, when $y = 0$.	Step 2: Using the calculate feature and the intersect option, determine the x-coordinate of each of the points of intersection of the graphs of the two given functions.  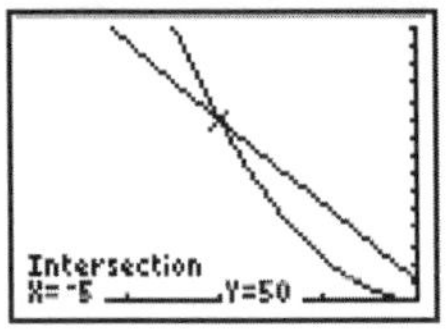 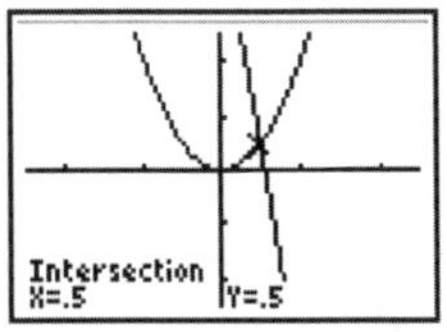 The zeros are displayed as the x-coordinate of the points of intersection of the two graphs.

Two distinct roots of the equation $2x^2 + 9x - 5 = 0$ will be obtained regardless of whether procedure A or procedure B is used.
Therefore, statement D is false, since the zeros in procedure A will be exactly the same as the x-coordinates (not the y-coordinates) of the points of intersection of the graphs of the two given functions in procedure B.

33. B

$y = 3x^2 - 18x + 29$ (1)

$y = -\frac{1}{2}x^2 + 2x - 3$ (2)

$y = x^2 - 5x + 6$ (3)

$y = \frac{1}{3}x^2 - \frac{4}{3}x + \frac{5}{3}$ (4)

These quadratic relations are plotted:

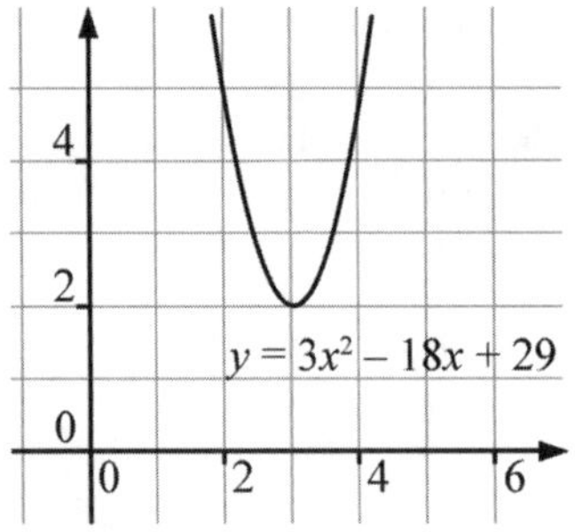

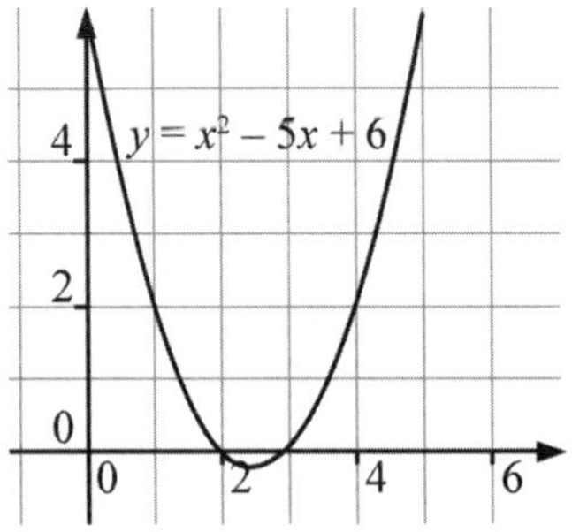

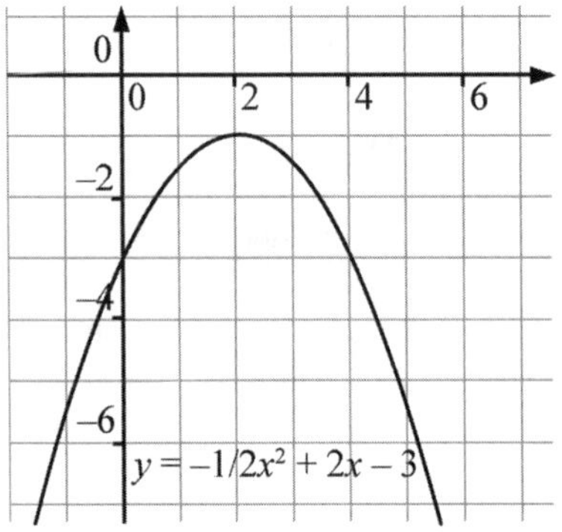

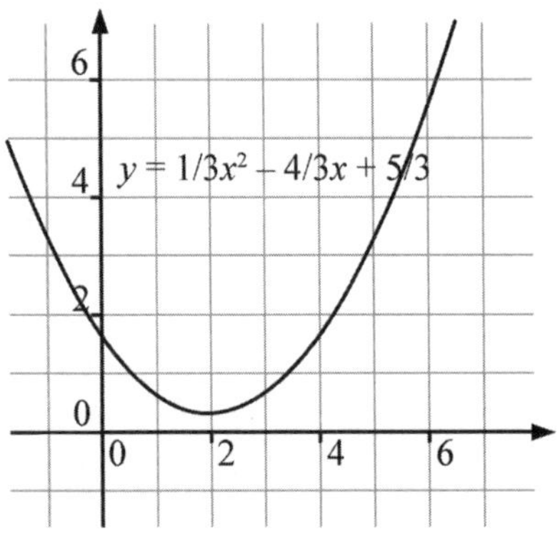

If roots of a quadratic equation $ax^2 + bx + c = 0$ are non-real, its graph does not intersect the x-axis. The equation $y = x^2 - 5x + 6$ has real roots since it forms x-intercepts at points with coordinates (2, 0) and (3, 0).

34. C

The graph of $y = x^2 + x + 1$ can be plotted as shown:

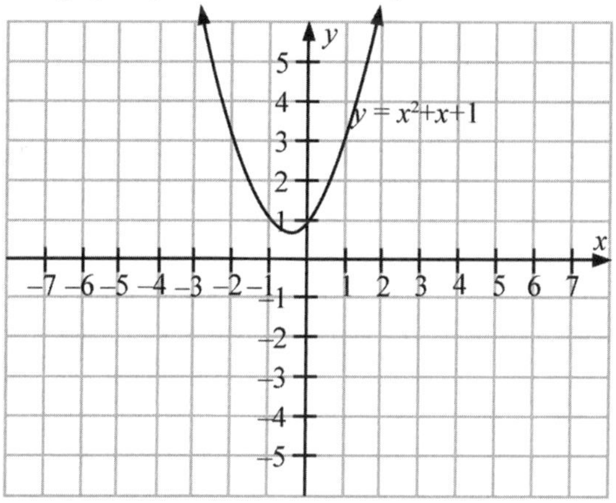

Since the graph of $y = x^2 + x + 1$ has no x-intercepts, the equation $x^2 + x + 1 = 0$ has non-real roots.
The graph of $y = x^2 + 5x + 3 = 0$ can be plotted as shown:

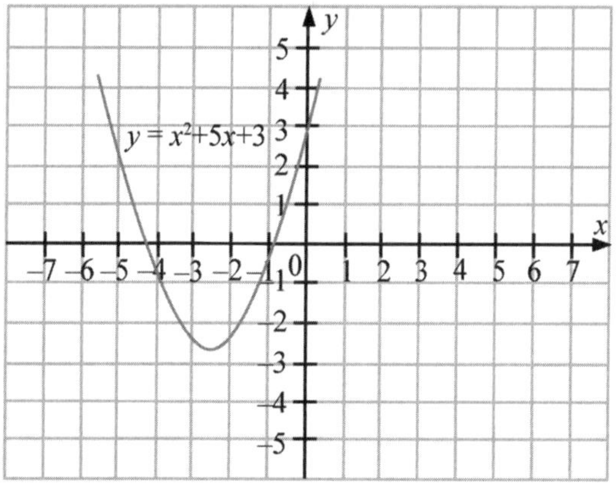

Since the curve of $y = x^2 + 5x + 3 = 0$ has two distinct x-intercepts, it has real roots.

Equations $x^2 + x + 1 = 0$ and $x^2 + 5x + 3 = 0$ have non-real and real roots, respectively.

35. A

The student's first error occurred in step 1. The student incorrectly removed the common factor of 3, and should have removed the common factor of −3. Step 1 should be as follows:

Step 1: $y = -3(x^2 - 8x) + 5$	Identify and remove the common factor from the x^2 and x term of the expression. In this case, the common factor is −3.

36. A

$y = 4(x^2 + 8x) + 59$	Identify and remove the common factor from the x^2 and x term of the expression. In this case, the common factor is 4.
$y = 4(x^2 + \underline{8x}) + 59$ $\left(\frac{8}{2}\right)^2 = 16$	Notice the resulting coefficient for the x-term. Divide this value by 2, and then square it.
$y = 4(x^2 + 8x + \underline{16 - 16}) + 59$	Both add and subtract this value inside the brackets.
$y = \underline{4}(x^2 + 8x + 16 \underline{- 16}) + 59$ $y = 4(x^2 + 8x + 16) \underline{- 64} + 59$	Move the value that will not contribute to a perfect square outside the brackets. [**Note**: With the distributive property, you have really added −64 and +64 to the function, since $4(16) = 64$ and $4(-16) = -64$. To move −16 outside the brackets, it becomes −64.]
$y = 4(x + 4)^2 - 5$	Factor the trinomial inside the brackets to form a perfect square, and collect like terms outside the bracket.

The equation can be expressed as $y = 4(x + 4)^2 - 5$.

37. B

$y = (x^2 - 8x) + 23$	Identify and remove the common factor from the x^2 and x term of the expression. In this case, the common factor is 1.
$y = (x^2 - \underline{8x}) + 23$ $\left(\frac{-8}{2}\right)^2 = 16$	Notice the resulting coefficient for the x-term. Divide this value by 2, and then square it.
$y = (x^2 - 8x + \underline{16 - 16}) + 23$	Both add and subtract this value inside the brackets.
$y = (x^2 - 8x + 16\underline{- 16}) + 23$ $y = (x^2 - 8x + 16)\underline{- 16} + 23$	Move the value that will not contribute to a perfect square outside the brackets.
$y = (x - 4)^2 + 7$	Factor the trinomial inside the brackets to form a perfect square, and collect like terms outside the bracket.

The equation can be expressed as $y = (x - 4)^2 + 7$.

38. 18.3

$y = -2(x^2 - 6x) + \frac{1}{3}$	Identify and remove the common factor from the x^2 and x term of the expression. In this case, the common factor is -2.
$y = -2(x^2 - \underline{6x}) + \frac{1}{3}$ $\left(\frac{-6}{2}\right)^2 = 9$	Notice the resulting coefficient for the x-term. Divide this value by 2, and then square it.
$y = -2(x^2 - 6x + \underline{9 - 9}) + \frac{1}{3}$	Both add and subtract this value inside the brackets.
$y = \underline{-2}(x^2 - 6x + 9\underline{- 9}) + \frac{1}{3}$ $y = -2(x^2 - 6x + 9)\underline{+18} + \frac{1}{3}$	Move the value that will not contribute to a perfect square outside the brackets. [**Note**: With the distributive property, you have really added -18 and $+18$ to the function, since $-2(9) = -18$ and $-2(-9) = 18$. To move -9 outside the brackets, it becomes $+18$.]
$y = -2(x - 3)^2 + \frac{55}{3}$	Factor the trinomial inside the brackets to form a perfect square, and collect like terms outside the bracket.

When the equation $y = -2x^2 + 12x + \frac{1}{3}$ is written in the completed square form $y = a(x - h)^2 + k$, it becomes $y = -2(x - 3)^2 + \frac{55}{3}$. The k value is $\frac{55}{3}$ and when written as a decimal value, to the nearest tenth, is 18.3.

39. A

Find the midpoint of the x-intercepts in order to find the equation of the axis of symmetry.

$$M = \left(\frac{x_1 + x_2}{2}\right), \left(\frac{y_1 + y_2}{2}\right)$$
$$= \left(\frac{\frac{1}{2} + (-4)}{2}\right), \left(\frac{0 + 0}{2}\right)$$
$$= \left(-\frac{7}{4}, 0\right)$$

The equation of the axis of symmetry is $x = -\frac{7}{4}$.

40. A

To determine the vertex of the graph of $y = x^2 - 6x + 4$, complete the square.

$y = \left(x^2 - 6x\right) + 4$

$y = \left(x^2 - \underline{6x}\right) + 4$

$\left(\frac{-6}{2}\right)^2 = 9$

$y = \left(x^2 - 6x + \underline{9 - 9}\right) + 4$

$y = \left(x^2 - 6x + 9\right)\underline{- 9} + 4$

$y = (x - 3)^2 - 5$

When written in this form, you can see that the vertex is at the point $(3, -5)$. Therefore, the vertex of the graph of $y = x^2 - 6x + 4$ is located 3 units right and 5 units down from the vertex of the graph of $y = x^2$.

41. D

The graph of the quadratic function $y = -4.9x^2 + 30x + 1$ is displayed with each of the given window settings.

I.

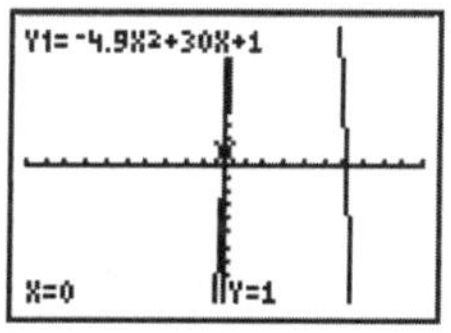

II.

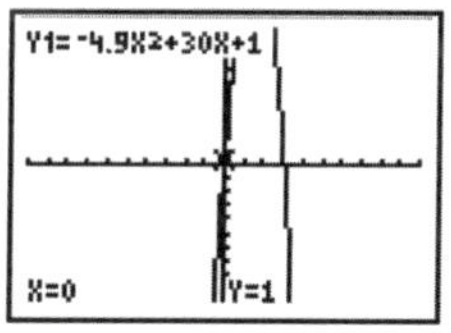

III.

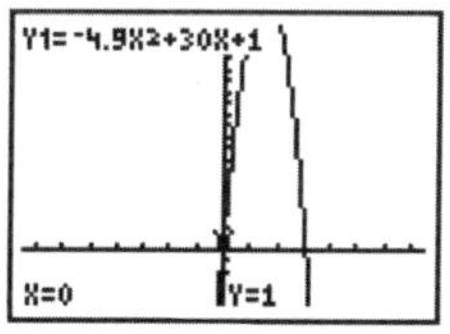

IV.

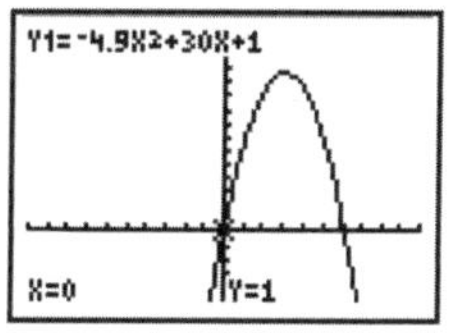

Graph IV uses a window setting that displays the graph with its vertex.

42. A

Apply the quadratic formula $x = \frac{-b \pm \sqrt{b^2 - 4ac}}{2a}$

Substitute 2 for a, -3 for b, and -1 for c into the quadratic formula.

$= \frac{-(-3) \pm \sqrt{(-3)^2 - 4(2)(-1)}}{2(2)}$

$= \frac{3 \pm \sqrt{9 + 8}}{4}$

$= \frac{3 \pm \sqrt{17}}{4}$

The roots of the given equation are approximately -0.28 or 1.78.

The error occurred in step 1, as the student did not correctly substitute -3 for b.

43. D

In step 3, the value that will not contribute to a perfect square is moved outside the brackets. Applying the distributive property, multiply $\frac{b^2}{4a^2}$ by the a in front of the brackets, so the value outside the brackets becomes $\frac{b^2}{4a}$.

Now, factor the trinomial inside the brackets to form a perfect square, thus, making step 3 $a\left(x + \frac{b}{2a}\right)^2 - \frac{b^2}{4a} + c = 0$. Therefore, the value of K represents the expression $\frac{b}{2a}$.

44. A

To solve by factoring (Tayla's procedure), begin by rearranging the equation $8x^2 - 2x = 3$ to $8x^2 - 2x - 3 = 0$.

Factor by decomposition by finding two numbers that have a product of -24 $(a \times c = 8 \times -3)$ and a sum of -2 (b-value). In this case, these numbers are 4 and -6.

$8x^2 - 2x - 3 = 0$

$8x^2 + 4x - 6x - 3 = 0$

$4x(2x + 1) - 3(2x + 1) = 0$

$(4x - 3)(2x + 1) = 0$

$x = \frac{3}{4}$ or $x = -\frac{1}{2}$

To solve using the quadratic formula (Honoria's solution), begin by rearranging the equation $8x^2 - 2x = 3$ to $8x^2 - 2x - 3 = 0$.

$$x = \frac{-b \pm \sqrt{b^2 - 4ac}}{2a}$$

Substitute 8 for a, -2 for b, and -3 for c into the quadratic formula.

$$x = \frac{-(-2) \pm \sqrt{(-2)^2 - 4(8)(-3)}}{2(8)}$$

$$x = \frac{2 \pm \sqrt{4 + 96}}{16}$$

$$x = \frac{2 \pm \sqrt{100}}{16}$$

$$x = \frac{2 \pm 10}{16}$$

$$x = \frac{2 + 10}{16} = \frac{12}{16} = \frac{3}{4} \text{ or } x = \frac{2 - 10}{16} = \frac{-8}{16} = -\frac{1}{2}$$

Tayla's work will lead to a correct solution, and Honoria's work will lead to correct solution as well.

45. C

To solve using the quadratic formula, begin by rearranging the equation $10x + 3 = 7x^2$ to $0 = 7x^2 - 10x - 3$.

Apply the quadratic formula $x = \frac{-b \pm \sqrt{b^2 - 4ac}}{2a}$

Substitute 7 for a, -10 for b, and -3 for c into the quadratic formula.

$$x = \frac{-(-10) \pm \sqrt{(-10)^2 - 4(7)(-3)}}{2(7)}$$

$$x = \frac{10 \pm \sqrt{100 + 84}}{14}$$

$$x = \frac{10 \pm \sqrt{184}}{14}$$

$$x = \frac{10 \pm \sqrt{4 \times 46}}{14}$$

$$x = \frac{10 \pm 2\sqrt{46}}{14}$$

$$x = \frac{2(5 \pm \sqrt{46})}{14}$$

$$x = \frac{5 \pm \sqrt{46}}{7}$$

46. A

Begin by collecting like terms to form a quadratic equation equal to 0.

$7x^2 + 2x - 5 = 11x^2 - 6x - 4$

$0 = 4x^2 - 8x + 1$

Now, solve using the quadratic formula.

$$x = \frac{-b \pm \sqrt{b^2 - 4ac}}{2a}$$

Substitute 4 for a, -8 for b, and 1 for c into the quadratic formula.

$$x = \frac{-(-8) \pm \sqrt{(-8)^2 - 4(4)(1)}}{2(4)}$$

$$x = \frac{8 \pm \sqrt{64 - 16}}{8}$$

$$x = \frac{8 \pm \sqrt{48}}{8}$$

$$x = \frac{8 \pm \sqrt{16 \times 3}}{8}$$

$$x = \frac{8 \pm 4\sqrt{3}}{8}$$

$$x = \frac{4(2 \pm \sqrt{3})}{8}$$

$$x = \frac{2 \pm \sqrt{3}}{2}$$

47. Part A – Open Response

The roots of the quadratic equation $2x^2 - x - 15 = 0$ can be determined by locating the x-intercepts of the graph of $y = 2x^2 - x - 15$. Since the x-intercepts of the graph of $y = 2x^2 - x - 15$ are located at the ordered pairs $(-2.5, 0)$ and $(3,0)$, the roots of the quadratic equation $2x^2 - x - 15 = 0$ are $x = -2.5$ or $x = 3$.

Part B – Open Response

In order to solve the quadratic equation $2x^2 - x - 15 = 30$, set the equation equal to 0, and if possible, solve by factoring. If the equation is not factorable, solve by applying the quadratic formula.

$2x^2 - x - 15 = 30$

$2x^2 - x - 45 = 0$

The two numbers that have a product of $-90[2 \times (-45)]$ and a sum of -1 (the coefficient of x) are -10 and 9.

$2x^2 - 10x + 9x - 45 = 0$

Remove a common factor of $2x$ from $2x^2 - 10x$ and 5 from $9x - 45$.

$2x(x-5) + 9(x-5) = 0$

$(x-5)(2x+9) = 0$

$x - 5 = 0$ or $2x + 9 = 0$

$x = 5$ $\quad$ $2x = -9$

$x = \frac{-9}{2}$

Part C – Open Response

If $2x^2 - x - 15$ is factorable, then the roots of the equation $2x^2 - x - 15 = 0$ can be expressed as exact values. In order for an equation to have exact roots, the value of $b^2 - 4ac$ in the quadratic formula $x = \frac{-b \pm \sqrt{b^2 - 4ac}}{2a}$ must be a number that is a perfect square. Otherwise, the equation will only have approximate roots. Now, check to see if $2x^2 - x - 15$ is factorable.

The two numbers that have a product of $-30\,[2 \times (-15)]$ and a sum of -1(the coefficient of x) are -6 and 5.

$2x^2 - x - 15 = 2x^2 - 6x + 5x - 15$

Remove a common factor of $2x$ from $2x^2 - 6x$ and 5 from $5x - 15$.

$= 2x(x-3) + 5(x-3)$

$= (x-3)(2x+5)$

Since $2x^2 - x - 15$ is factorable, the value of $b^2 - 4ac$ in the quadratic formula $x = \frac{-b \pm \sqrt{b^2 - 4ac}}{2a}$ must be a number that is a perfect square.

48. A

- The maximum or minimum value can be determined when the function is written in the form $y = a(x-h)^2 + k$.
- The maximum value is k when $a < 0$.
- The minimum value is k when $a > 0$.

Therefore, Megan only needs to examine the a-variable.

49. C

The zeros of the function $ax^2 + bx + c$ are 1 and 2. Thus,

$y = a(x-1)(x-2)$

$y = a(x^2 - 3x + 2)$

$y = ax^2 - 3ax + 2a$

The x-coordinate of the vertex can be determined by calculating the midpoint of the two zeros of the given function. Thus, $x = \frac{1+2}{2} = 1.5$.

Substitute 1.5 for x and -1 (the minimum value) for y in the equation $y = ax^2 - 3ax + 2a$.

$-1 = a(1.5)^2 - 3a(1.5) + 2(1.5)$

$-1 = 2.25a - 4.5a + 2a$

$-1 = -0.25a$

$4 = a$

Finally, compare the equation $y = ax^2 - 3ax + 2a$ to the equation $y = ax^2 + bx + c$. Observe $c = 2a$. Thus, $c = 2(4) = 8$.

50. 4

Since the coefficient of x^2 is positive, the minimum value of the given function is equal to the y-coordinate of the vertex of the graph of the function.

To find the coordinate of the vertex, rewrite the given function in completed square form.

$y = x^2 - 12x + 40$

$y = x^2 - 12x + 36 - 36 + 40$

$y = (x^2 - 12x + 36) + 4$

$y = (x-6)^2 + 4$

The vertex of this parabola, is (6, 4).

Therefore, the minimum value of the given function is 4.

51. C

Since the quadratic function $h = -4.9(t - 1.5)^2 + 12$, $t \geq 0$ is given in the form $y = a(x - h)^2 + k$, it follows that $a = -4.9$, $h = 1.5$, and $k = 12$.
Since $a = -4.9$ and $-4.9 < 0$, the graph of the function opens downward. Since $h = 1.5$ and $k = 12$, the graph of the function has been shifted right 1.5 units and 12 units upward, when compared to the graph of $y = x^2$. The graph shown best illustrates the graph of
$h = -4.9(t - 1.5)^2 + 12$.

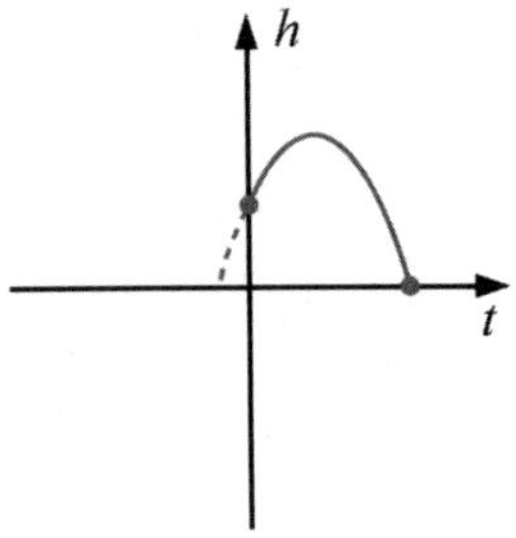

52. C

To begin, write the equation $A = -2x^2 + 60x$ in completed square form.

$A = -2x^2 + 60x$

$A = -2(x^2 - \underline{30x})$

$\left(\frac{-30}{2}\right)^2 = 225$

$A = -2(x^2 - 30x + \underline{225 - 225})$

$A = -\underline{2}(x^2 - 30x + 225 \underline{- 225})$

$A = -2(x^2 - 30x + 225)\underline{+450}$

$A = -2(x - 15)^2 + 450$

In this form, the equation models a parabola with a vertex of (15, 450).
Thus, the area of the lot reaches a maximum when $x = 15$.
Substitute 15 for x into the equation $2x + y = 60$.

$2(15) + y = 60$

$30 + y = 60$

$y = 30$

Therefore, the length of the lot is 30 m.

53. D

Using technology, graph the equation
$y = -7t^2 + 61t + 98$.
Then, use the MAXIMUM feature of a TI-83 Plus graphing calculator and a window setting such as $x:[1, 10, 1]y:[0, 300, 20]$.

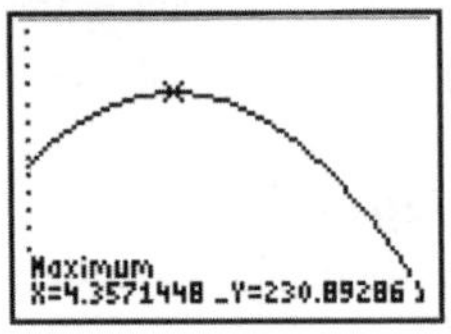

The function's maximum value occurs when $x = 4.35$.
The maximum height reached by the roller coaster car in the interval $1 \leq t \leq 10$, to the nearest tenth, is 230.9 ft.

54. Part A – Open Response

If the vendor does not sell any hot dogs, the value of x in the equation
$P = -40x^2 + 240x - 75$ is zero. If 0 is substituted for x, then $P = -40(0)^2 + 240(0) - 75 = -75$.
Thus, if the vendor does not sell any hot dogs, he will lose $75.

Part B – Open Response

In order to determine the selling price per hot dog to maximize the vendor's daily profit, complete the square of the equation $P = -40x^2 + 240x - 75$ as follows:

$P = -40x^2 + 240x - 75$

$P = -40(x^2 - 6x) - 75$

$P = -40(x^2 - 6x + 9 - 9) - 75$

$\rightarrow \frac{-6}{2} = -3, (-3)^2 = 9$

$P = -40(x^2 - 6x + 9) + 360 - 75$

$P = -40(x - 3)^2 + 285$

The maximum value of P is 285 when $x = 3$.
A selling price of $3 per hot dog will maximize the vendor's daily profit.

Part C – Open Response

The maximum daily profit for the hot dog vendor is $285.

Unit Test

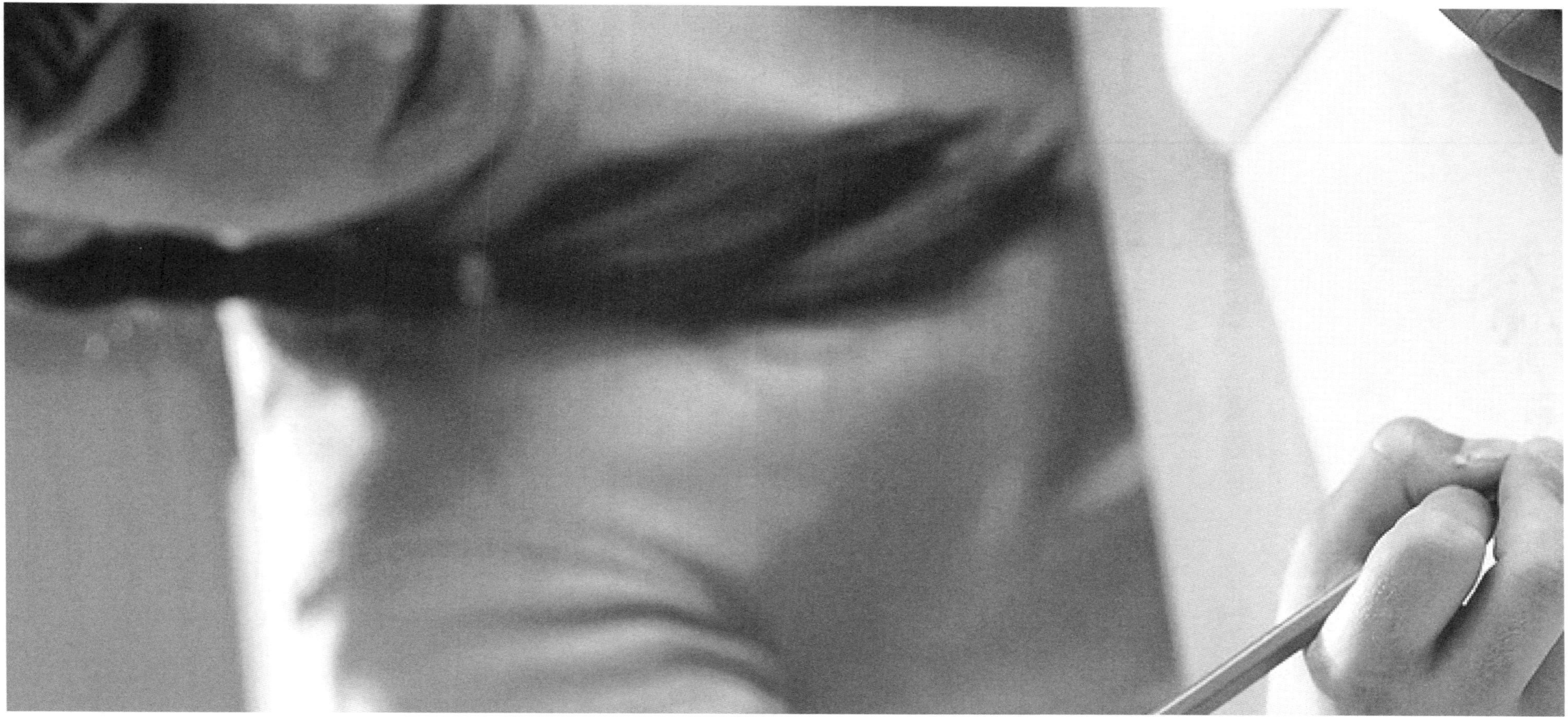

Use the following information to answer the next question.

The owner of a 300-seat theatre sells tickets for $20 a piece. He believes that for every dollar he increases the price of a ticket, he will lose 10 customers. He has charted his research as follows:

Increase in Price ($)	Revenue ($)
0	6 000
1	6 090
2	6 160
3	6 210
4	6 240
5	6 250
6	6 240

1. What increase in price value will yield a revenue of $6 120?

A. $1.29 **B.** $8.61

C. $8.61 **D.** $9.55

CHALLENGER QUESTION

Use the following information to answer the next question.

A partial table of values for a particular function is shown below

x	y	First Difference
−2	−3	
		}5
−1		
		}3
0		
		}1
1		
		}−1
2		
		}−3
3		

2. The equation of the function is

A. $y = x^2 - 2x - 5$

B. $y = x^2 - 2x - 11$

C. $y = -2x + 5$

D. $y = -2x - 3$

3. The graph of a particular quadratic function passes through the ordered pairs $(-2, 6)$ and $(8, 6)$. The equation of the axis of symmetry of this graph is

A. $x = 3$ **B.** $x = 4$

C. $x = 5$ **D.** $x = 6$

Use the following information to answer the next question.

The graph of a particular parabola is shown.

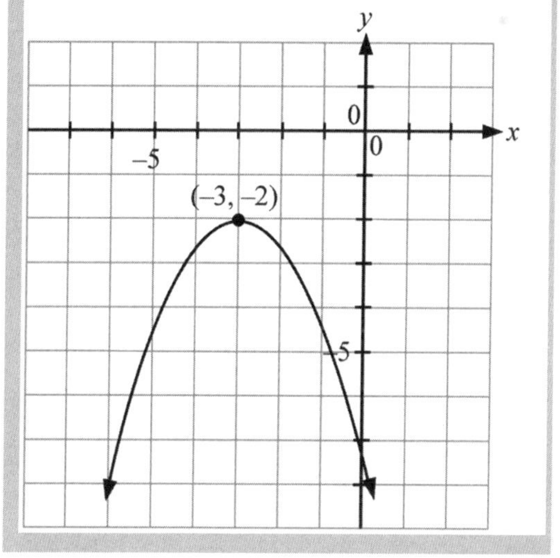

4. Which of the following statements is **true** with respect to the graph of the parabola shown?

   A. The minimum value is −2.

   B. The parabola does not have any zeros.

   C. The equation of the axis of symmetry is $x - 3 = 0$.

   D. The y-intercept of the parabola could be located at the ordered pair $(-8, 0)$.

Numerical Response

Use the following information to answer the next question.

The graph of a parabola with a vertex of $(0, 5)$ is shown.

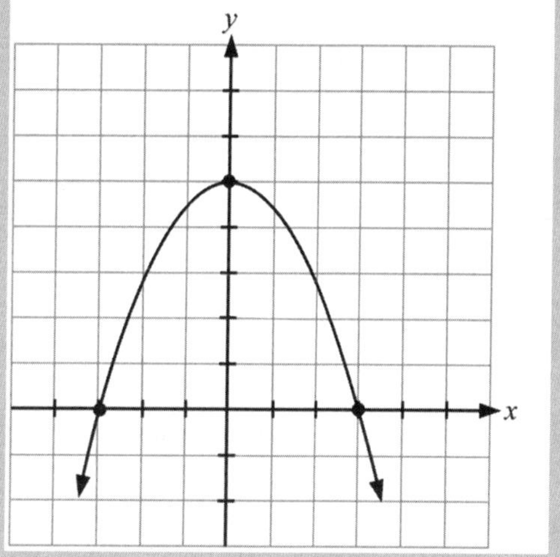

5. The y-intercept of the graph of this parabola is ____.

6. The expression 2^{-x} is equivalent to the expression

   A. -2^x **B.** $(-2)^x$

   C. $\frac{-1}{2^x}$ **D.** $\frac{1}{2^x}$

7. The y-intercept of the graph of $y = 2^x$ is
   A. the same as the y-intercept of the graph of $y = x^2$
   B. one more than the y-intercept of the graph of $y = x^2$
   C. one less than the y-intercept of the graph of $y = x^2$
   D. two more than the y-intercept of the graph of $y = x^2$

8. Which of the following aspects of the graph of $y = ax^2$ could be affected when the value of a is changed?
   A. Only the direction of opening of the parabola
   B. Only the vertical stretch that the parabola experiences
   C. Only the direction of opening and the vertical stretch that the parabola experiences
   D. Only the direction of opening, the x-intercepts and the vertical stretch that the parabola experiences

Use the following information to answer the next question.

The partial graph of the quadratic function $y = a(x - 2)^2 + K$ is shown.

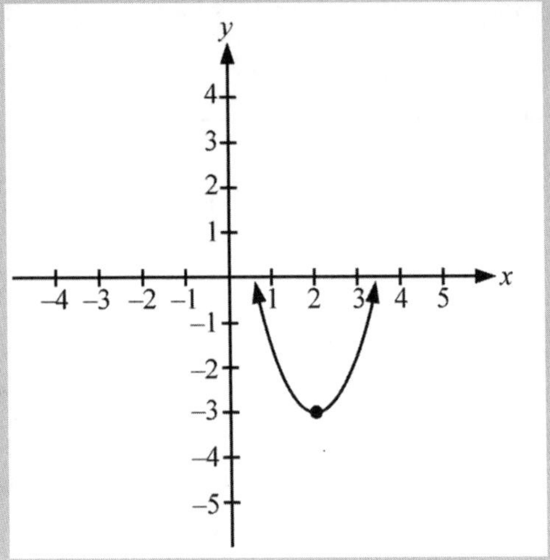

9. The values of a and K in the function $y = a(x - 2)^2 + K$ must be such that
   A. $a < 0$ and $K < 0$
   B. $a < 0$ and $K > 0$
   C. $a > 0$ and $K > 0$
   D. $a > 0$ and $K < 0$

10. The graph of the function $y = x^2$ is vertically stretched by a factor of 4 about the x-axis and then translated such that the vertex of the transformed graph is at $(-2, 51)$. The equation of the transformed function is
   A. $y = 4(x - 2)^2 - 51$
   B. $y = 4(x - 51)^2 - 2$
   C. $y = 4(x + 2)^2 + 51$
   D. $y = -4(x + 2)^2 - 51$

CHALLENGER QUESTION

Use the following information to answer the next question.

The graph of a quadratic function of the form $y = a(x - h)^2 + k$ is shown.

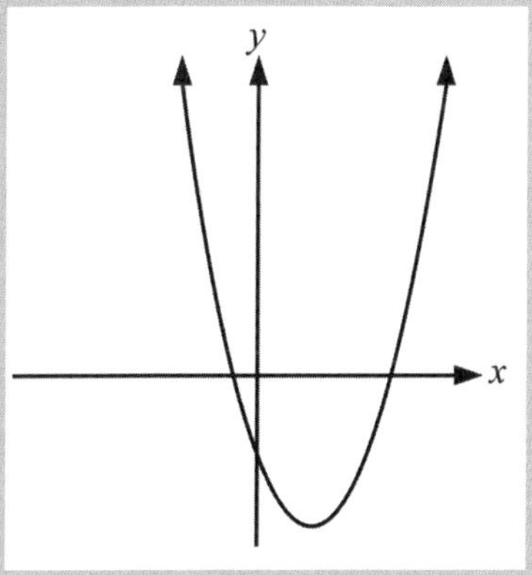

11. Which of the following conditions with respect to the variables, a, h, and k is correct?

A. $a > 0, h > 0$, and $k < 0$

B. $a \geq 0, h > 0$, and $k > 0$

C. $a < 0, h > 0$, and $k > 0$

D. $a \geq 0, h < 0$, and $k < 0$

Numerical Response

12. The equation for the axis of symmetry of the graph of the function $y = -3(x + 2)^2 - 5$ is $x + B = 0$. The value of B is ___.

13. Which of the following partial graphs **best** illustrates the graph of the equation $y = (x + 3)^2 + 2.5$?

A.

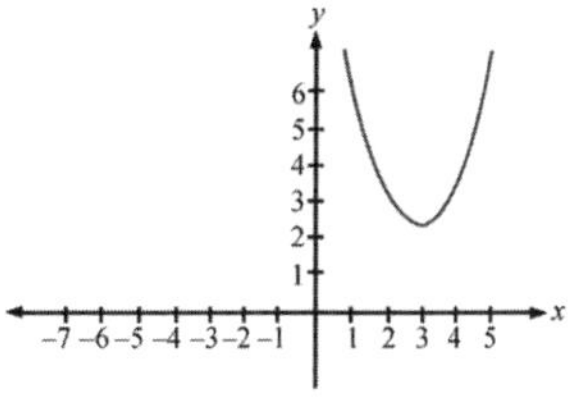

B.

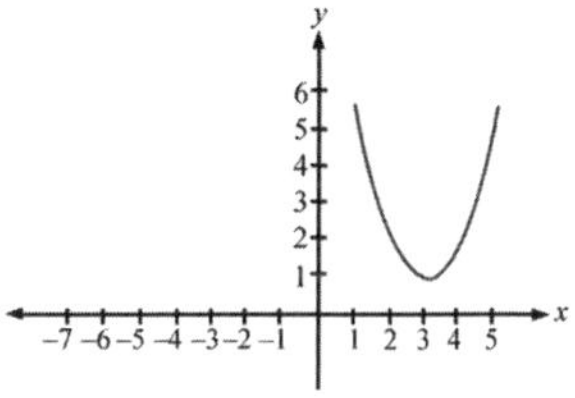

C.

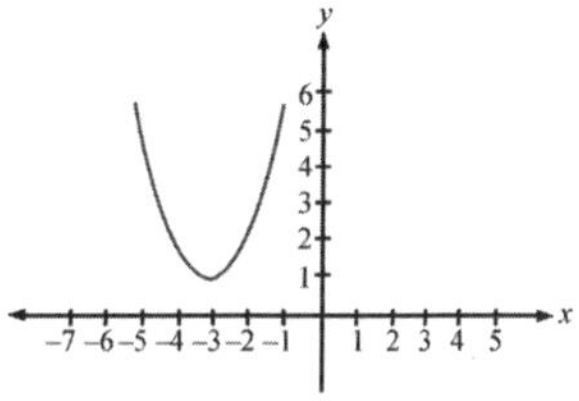

D.

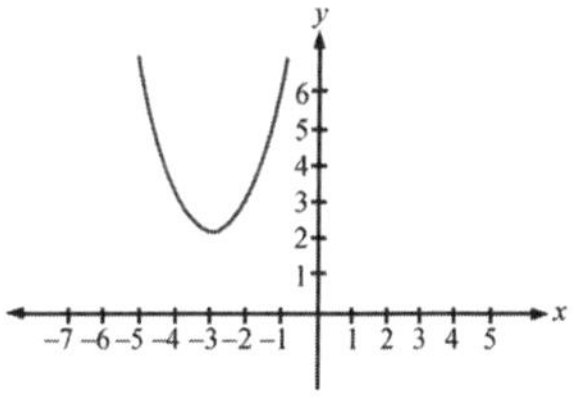

Use the following information to answer the next question.

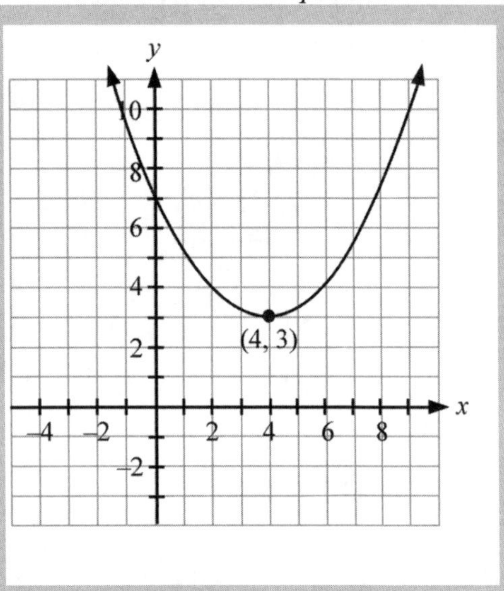

A partial graph of a quadratic function is shown in the diagram.

14. What is the equation of this partial graph?

A. $y = (x - 4)^2 + 3$

B. $y = (x - 4)^2 - 3$

C. $y = \frac{1}{4}(x - 4)^2 - 3$

D. $y = \frac{1}{4}(x - 4)^2 + 3$

Use the following information to answer the next question.

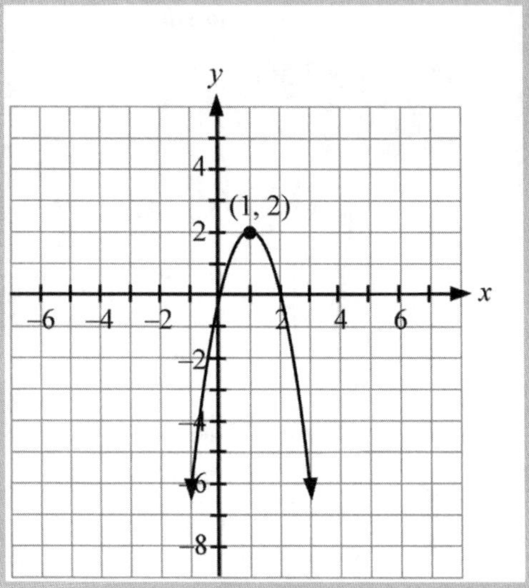

15. The equation of the parabola shown is

A. $y = 2(x + 1)^2 + 2$

B. $y = 2(x - 1)^2 + 2$

C. $y = -2(x + 1)^2 + 2$

D. $y = -2(x - 1)^2 + 2$

Use the following information to answer the next multipart question.

16. The graph of a particular quadratic function is shown.

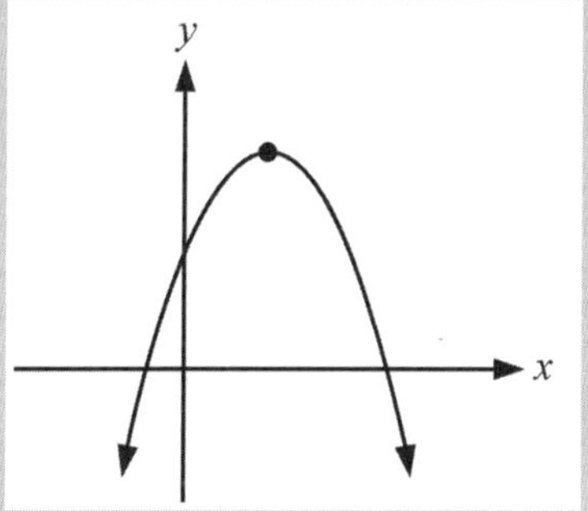

Part A

Open Response

If the equation of the axis of symmetry of the graph of this quadratic function is $x = 2$ and an x-intercept is defined by the ordered pair $(-1,\ 0)$, then what are the coordinates of the other x-intercept?

Show your work.

Part B

Open Response

Write the equation of this quadratic function in the form $y = a(x - r)(x - s)$ given that the y-intercept of the graph is 10.

Show your work.

Part C

Open Response

Write the equation of this quadratic function in the form $y = a(x - h)^2 + k$.

Show your work.

Use the following information to answer the next question.

$(4x-3)(3x-2)-2(3x-2)^2$

17. Which of the following expressions is a simplified form of the given expression?

A. $-6x^2-5x-2$

B. $-6x^2-5x+14$

C. $-6x^2+7x-2$

D. $-6x^2-7x-14$

Numerical Response

18. If $(3x+2)(2x+3)=6x^2+bx+c$, where b and c are real numbers, then the value of $b+c$ is ____.

19. If $5x+k$ is a factor of $10x^2+19x+6$, then the value of k is

A. 1 **B.** 2 **C.** 3 **D.** 6

20. The algebraic expression $2xy-3ay+2xz-3az$ can be written in factored form as

A. $(2x+3a)(y+z)$

B. $(2x-3a)(y-z)$

C. $(2x+3a)(y-z)$

D. $(2x-3a)(y+z)$

21. For the quadratic function $y=x^2-2x-15$, a student let $y=0$ and then wrote the equation $0=x^2-2x-15$. The student then factored this equation to obtain $0=(x+3)(x-5)$. The factored form that the student used leads to the determination of the

A. y-intercepts of the graph of $y=x^2-2x-15$

B. x-intercepts of a parabola the graph of $y=x^2-2x-15$

C. minimum value of a parabola the graph of $y=x^2-2x-15$

D. vertex of the graph of a parabola the graph of $y=x^2-2x-15$

22. The x-intercepts of the graph of $y=a(x-r)(x-s)$ are $(3,0)$ and $(2,0)$. If $r>s$, what are the values of r and s, respectively?

A. 3 and 2 **B.** 2 and 3

C. 6 and 1 **D.** 1 and 6

Use the following information to answer the next question.

Two equations are given.
$2x^2+2.5x-5=0$ (i)
$x^2+0.5x-0.5=0$ (ii)

23. Which of the following statements about the given equations is **true**?

A. Both equations have real roots.

B. Both equations have non-real roots.

C. Equation (i) has non-real roots, and equation (ii) has real roots.

D. Equation (i) has real roots, and equation (ii) has non-real roots.

24. Which of the following graphs illustrates a quadratic function whose corresponding quadratic equation has two real and different roots?

A.

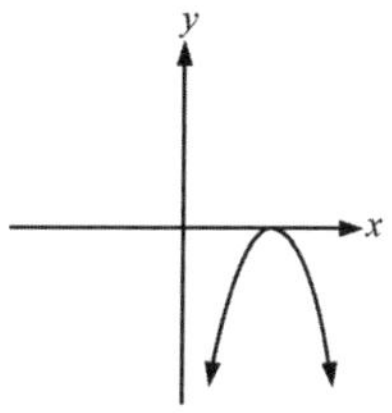

B.

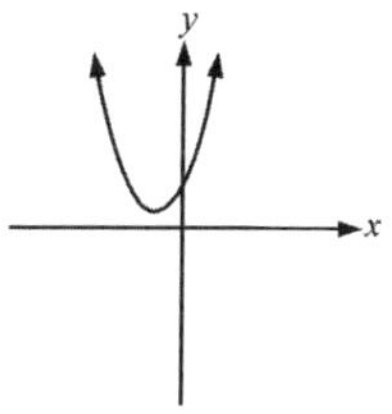

C.

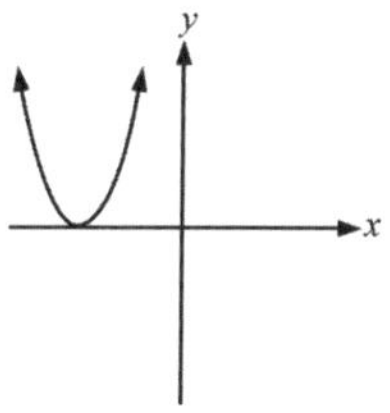

D.

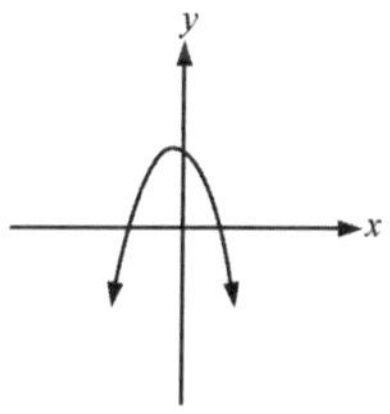

25. If the equation $y = 3x^2 - 24x + \frac{1}{2}$ is written in the completed square form $y = a(x - h)^2 + k$, then the value of k is

A. 97 **B.** $\frac{97}{2}$

C. −95 **D.** $\frac{-95}{2}$

26. Which of the following functions represents the quadratic function $y = 2x^2 + 16x + 26$ when it is changed to its completed square form of $y = a(x - h)^2 + k$?

A. $y = 2(x + 4)^2 - 6$

B. $y = 2(x + 4)^2 - 3$

C. $y = 2(x + 8)^2 + 10$

D. $y = 2(x + 8)^2 - 19$

CHALLENGER QUESTION

Numerical Response

27. When the equation $y = -2x^2 + 16x - 27$ is expressed in the form $y = a(x - h)^2 + k$, the value of h to the nearest hundredth is ____.

28. The x-intercepts of the graph of the quadratic function $y = x^2 - 10x - 24$ are

A. −12 and 2

B. −6 and −4

C. 6 and 4

D. 12 and −2

CHALLENGER QUESTION

29. The equation of the axis of symmetry for the graph of the quadratic equation $y = (2k + 1)x^2 + 3kx + k,\ k \neq -\frac{1}{2},\ k \in \mathbf{R}$ is $x = -1$. The vertex of the graph of the given quadratic function is

A. $(-1, -1)$

B. $(-1, 1)$

C. $(-1, 6k + 1)$

D. $(-1, -4k - 1)$

Use the following information to answer the next question.

Samuel decided to use the quadratic formula to solve a particular quadratic equation. The first step in his solution is given.

$$x = \frac{4 \pm \sqrt{(-4)^2 - 4(7)(-2)}}{2(7)}$$

30. The quadratic equation that Samuel is attempting to solve is

A. $0 = -2x^2 + 4x + 7$

B. $0 = -2x^2 - 4x - 4$

C. $0 = 7x^2 + 4x - 2$

D. $0 = 7x^2 - 4x - 2$

Use the following information to answer the next question.

A student's attempt at developing the quadratic formula is partially shown.

$ax^2 + bx + c = 0$

Step 1: $x^2 + \frac{b}{a}x + \frac{c}{a} = 0$

Step 2: $x^2 + \frac{b}{a}x = -\frac{c}{a}$

Step 3: $x^2 + \frac{b}{a}x + \frac{b^2}{4a^2} - \frac{b^2}{4a^2} = -\frac{c}{a}$

Step 4: $x^2 + \frac{b}{a}x + \frac{b^2}{4a^2} = \frac{b^2}{4a^2} - \frac{c}{a}$

Step 5: $\left(x + \frac{b}{2a}\right)^2 = \frac{b^2}{4a^2} - \frac{c}{a}$

31. If steps 1 to 5 are correct, then a correct step 6 could be

A. $x + \frac{b}{2a} = \frac{b}{2a} - \frac{c}{a}$

B. $x + \frac{b}{2a} = \frac{b}{2a} - \sqrt{\frac{c}{a}}$

C. $\left(x + \frac{b}{2a}\right)^2 = \frac{b^2 - 4ac}{4a^2}$

D. $\left(x + \frac{b}{2a}\right)^2 = \frac{b^2 - 4ac}{2a}$

32. What are the solutions to the quadratic equation $2z^2 + 5z - 3 = 0$?

A. $z = \frac{1}{2}$ or 3

B. $z = \frac{1}{2}$ or -3

C. $z = 2$ or -1

D. $z = 1$ or -1

Numerical Response

33. Expressed to one decimal place, the roots of the quadratic equation $10x^2 - 19x + 14 = 8$ are $x = 1.5$ or $x =$ _____ .

Use the following information to answer the next multipart question.

34. A diver in Acapulco, Mexico dives from a cliff into the sea below. His height y metres above the sea x seconds after diving from the cliff is given by the equation $y = -4.9x^2 + 2x + 40$, where $x \geq 0$.

Part A

Open Response

What is the height of the cliff?

Justify your answer.

Part B

Open Response

Algebraically, determine the number of seconds, to the nearest tenth, that it takes the diver to reach the water.

Show your work.

Part C

Open Response

Explain how a graphical procedure could be used to determine the number of seconds that have elapsed when the diver is 15 m above the water.

CHALLENGER QUESTION

35. If the function represented by the graph of $y = ax^2 + bx + c$, where $a \neq 0$ has a minimum value of -5, then the number of x-intercepts of the graph is

A. 0 **B.** 1 **C.** 2 **D.** 3

36. The maximum value of the graph of the quadratic relation $2x^2 - 8x + y + 19 = 0$ is at the ordered pair

A. $(-11, -2)$

B. $(-2, -11)$

C. $(2, -11)$

D. $(11, -2)$

Use the following information to answer the next question.

The parabolic shape obtained from a quadratic function can be used to design arches. A construction company used the quadratic function $y = a(x - h)^2 + k$ and the resulting graph, as shown, to plan a bridge support for a road.

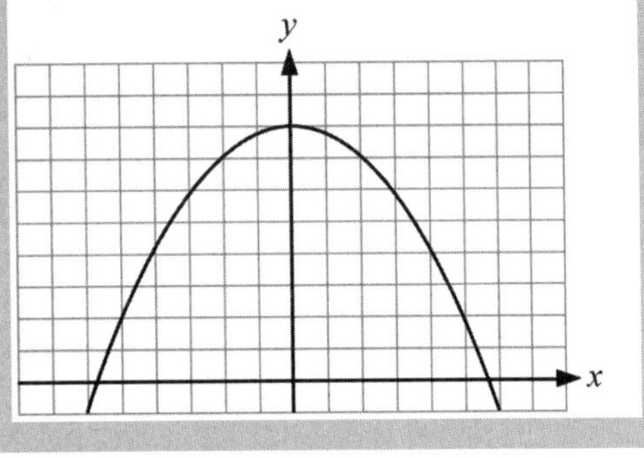

37. Which variable represents the maximum height of the bridge support?

A. h **B.** a **C.** x **D.** k

38. A soccer ball is kicked upward. The height, x, of the ball in metres is given by the function $x = -5t^2 + 30t$, where t is the time in seconds. At what time does the ball reach its maximum height?

A. 2 s **B.** 3 s **C.** 4 s **D.** 5 s

CHALLENGER QUESTION

Numerical Response

Use the following information to answer the next question.

A rocket is launched from a platform. Its height, h, in metres above the ground, is given as a function of the time, t, in seconds by the equation $h = -4.9t^2 + 98t + 5$.

39. What is the maximum height, correct to the nearest tenth, above the ground that can be reached by the rocket? ___.

Use the following information to answer the next multipart question.

40. A rectangular area is to be enclosed by a fence in order to create a playground for kindergarten students. A part of the wall of the school will be used as one side of the rectangular enclosure, as shown.

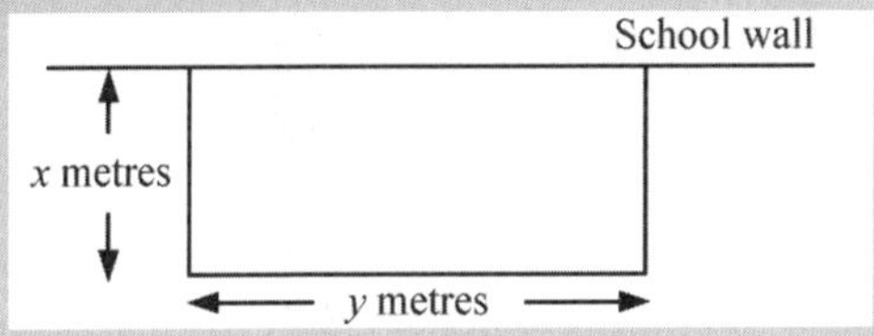

If 300 m of fencing material is to be used, then the table shown illustrates the area, A, in square metres for various values of x.

x (m)	**A (m^2)**
10	2 800
20	5 200
50	10 000
75	11 250
90	10 800
100	10 000
125	6 250
140	2 800

Part A

Open Response

On the grid, draw a graph that illustrates the data given in the table.

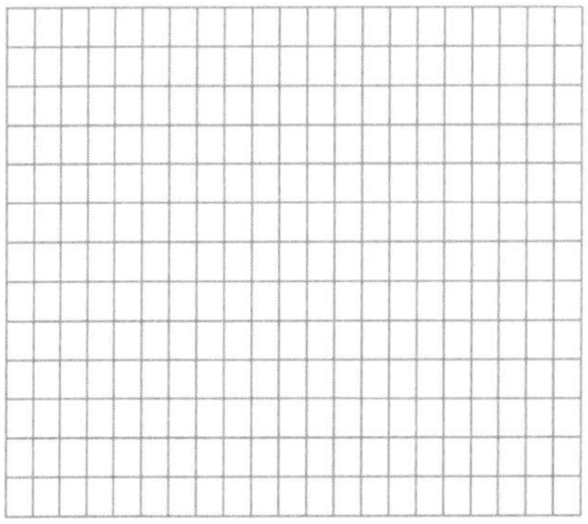

Part B

Open Response

What is the maximum possible area of the rectangular enclosure?

Part C

Open Response

The area, A, in square metres of the playground can be defined by the equation $A = -2x^2 + 300x$, where x is the width of the rectangular enclosure in metres. Using this equation, verify algebraically that your answer in part B is correct.

Part D

Open Response

What will be the dimensions of the playground that produce a maximum area?

SOLUTIONS

1. C	**11. A**	**19. B**	**29. B**	**37. D**
2. B	**12. 2**	**20. D**	**30. D**	**38. B**
3. A	**13. D**	**21. B**	**31. C**	**39. 495.0**
4. B	**14. D**	**22. A**	**32. B**	**40.** Part A- **OR**
5. 5	**15. D**	**23. A**	**33. 0.4**	Part B- **OR**
6. D	**16.** Part A- **OR**	**24. D**	**34.** Part A- **OR**	Part C- **OR**
7. B	Part B- **OR**	**25. D**	Part B- **OR**	Part D- **OR**
8. C	Part C- **OR**	**26. A**	Part C- **OR**	
9. D	**17. C**	**27. 4.00**	**35. C**	
10. C	**18. 19**	**28. D**	**36. C**	

1. C

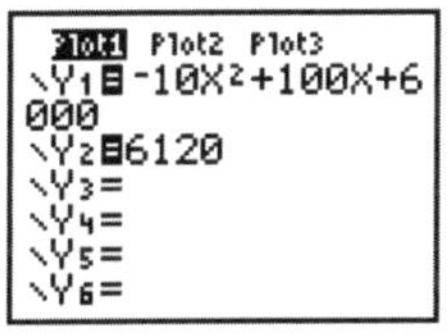

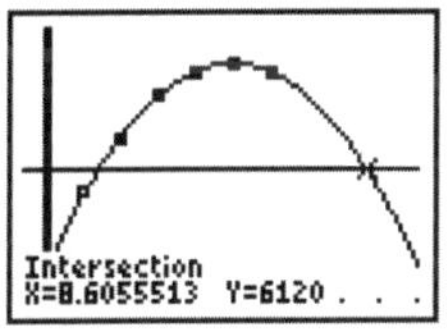

Graph the function obtained from the quadratic regression, $y = -10x^2 + 100x + 6\ 000$ in the calculator and graph the line $y = 6\ 120$. Find the point of intersection between the two graphs. The x-coordinate of the point of intersection is the number of dollar increases in price that correspond to a revenue of \$6 120.

From this we see that the owner needs to increase his price by \$8.61 to generate a revenue of \$6 120.

2. B

Calculate the second difference to determine the nature of the function.

x	y	1st diff	2nd diff
−2	−3		
		−5	
−1			2
		−3	
0			2
		−1	
1			2
		1	
2			2
		3	
3			

Since the table of values yields a constant second difference, this function represents a quadratic relation of the form $y = ax^2 + bx + c$, $(a \neq 0)$.

To determine the exact equation, substitute −2 for x into the two possible equations:

$y = x^2 - 2x - 5$ and $y = x^2 - 2x - 11$, to determine which of the equations has a corresponding y-value of −3.

$$\begin{array}{ll} y = x^2 - 2x - 5 & y = x^2 - 2x - 11 \\ y = (-2)^2 - 2(-2) - 5 & y = (-2)^2 - 2(-2) - 11 \\ y = 4 + 4 - 5 & y = 4 + 4 - 11 \\ y = 3 & y = -3 \end{array}$$

Therefore, the equation of the function is $y = x^2 - 2x - 11$.

3. A

Recall that the axis of symmetry also passes through the midpoint of any horizontal segment that connects two points on the parabola.

Now, find the midpoint of the ordered pairs $(-2, 6)$ and $(8, 6)$ in order to find the equation of the axis of symmetry.

$$M = \left(\frac{x_1 + x_2}{2}\right), \left(\frac{y_1 + y_2}{2}\right)$$
$$= \left(\frac{(-2) + 8}{2}\right), \left(\frac{6 + 6}{2}\right)$$
$$= (3, 6)$$

The equation of the axis of symmetry is $x = 3$.

4. B

The parabola has no zeros since the parabola does not intersect the x-axis.

The vertex of the parabola is $(-3, -2)$.

The axis of symmetry is the vertical line $x = -3$ or $x + 3 = 0$ (-3 is the x-coordinate of the vertex).

Since the parabola opens downward, the maximum value is $y = -2$ (-2 is the y-coordinate of the vertex).

The parabola passes through the y-axis approximately at the ordered pair $(0, -7)$, so the y-intercept is -7.

5. 5

The y-intercept of a quadratic relation of the form $y = ax^2 + bx + c$, $(a \neq 0)$ is the y-coordinate of the ordered pair where the parabola intersects the y-axis. In the graph shown this occurs at the y-value of the vertex, which is 5.

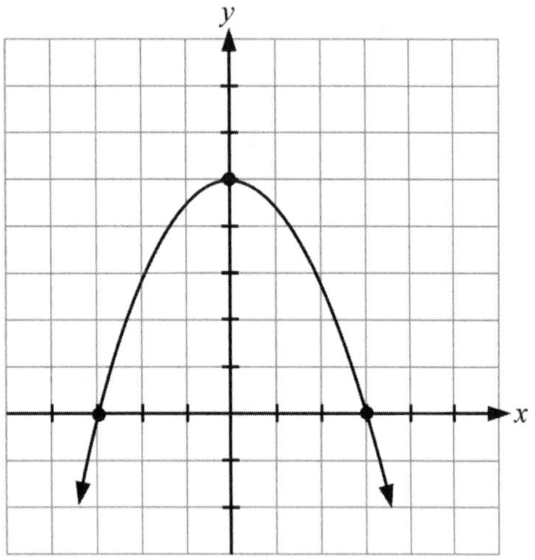

6. D

When a number or variable has a negative exponent in the numerator, the expression can be rewritten with a positive exponent in the denominator. $x^{-n} = \frac{1}{x^n}$

Therefore, the expression 2^{-x} is equivalent to the expression $\frac{1}{2^x}$.

7. B

For the function $y = 2^x$, the graph crosses the y-axis at $(0, 1)$; therefore, the y-intercept is $y = 1$.

The y-intercept for the graph of the function $y = x^2$ is $y = 0$.

Therefore, the y-intercept of the graph of $y = 2^x$ is one more than the y-intercept of the graph of $y = x^2$.

8. C

- Regardless of the a-value, each point (x_1, y_1) on the graph of $y = x^2$ becomes (x_1, ay_1) on the graph of $y = ax^2$.
- a determines the direction of opening of the parabola.
- Changing the value of a results in the graph being vertically stretched by a factor of a.
- Changing the value of a from a positive to a negative or vice-versa results in a reflection of the graph in the x-axis, which creates a graph that is a mirror image of the original graph in the x-axis.
- The value of a in the equation $y = ax^2$ does not have an effect upon the domain, vertex, axis of symmetry, or x-intercept of the parabola.

9. D

Because the partial graph of $y = a(x - 2)^2 + K$ has a minimum value and opens upward, it follows that $a > 0$. Notice that the vertex of the graph is located in quadrant IV. When compared to the graph of $y = x^2$, the graph of $y = a(x - 2)^2 + K$ has been translated vertically downward. Therefore, $K < 0$.

10. C

When the graph of $y = x^2$ is vertically stretched by factor of 4 about the x-axis, the equation of the transformed function is $y = 4x^2$.
In order for the graph of the transformed function to have a vertex of $(-2, 51)$, the graph of $y = 4x^2$ must be translated 2 units left and 51 units up, therefore, $h = -2$ and $k = 51$.
Now, substitute 4 for a, -2 for h, and 51 for k into
$y = a(x - h)^2 + k$.
$y = 4(x + 2)^2 + 51$.
Thus, the equation of the transformed function is
$y = 4(x + 2)^2 + 51$.

11. A

Since the graph opens upward, $a > 0$.
When compared to the graph of $y = x^2$:

- the graph shown has been translated right; therefore, $h > 0$.
- the graph shown has been translated down; therefore, $k < 0$.

12. 2

In the equation $y = -3(x + 2)^2 - 5$, it follows that $a = -3$, $h = -2$, and $k = -5$.
The equation of the axis of symmetry is $x = h$.
Therefore, the graph of the parabola $y = -3(x + 2)^2 - 5$ is symmetric about the line $x = -2$ or $x + 2 = 0$. Thus, the value of B is 2.

13. D

When you compare the given equation $y = (x + 3)^2 + 2.5$ to the equation $y = a(x - h)^2 + k$,
$h = -3$, $a = 1$, and $k = 2.5$.
Therefore, the graph of $y = (x + 3)^2 + 2.5$ can be obtained by translating the graph of $y = x^3$ left 3 units and upward 2.5 units.

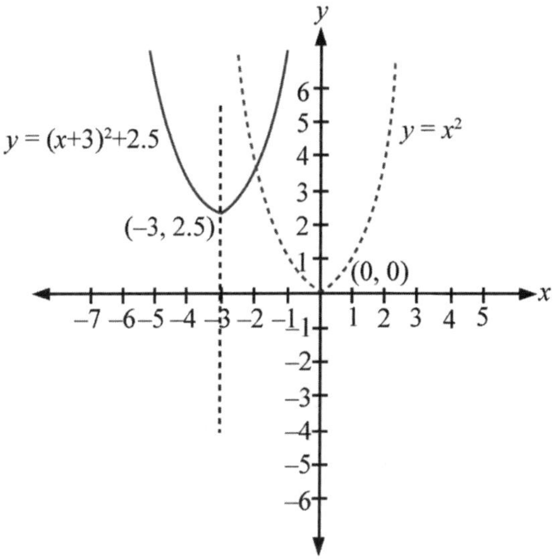

14. D

The parabola shown can have an equation of the form $y = a(x - h)^2 + k$, where (h, k) is the vertex. Since the vertex is at (4, 3), $h = 4$ and $k = 3$.
Substitute 4 for h and 3 for k into the equation
$y = a(x - h)^2 + k$ to get $y = a(x - 4)^2 + 3$.
Since the equation passes through the point (0, 7), $x = 0$ and $y = 7$. Solve for a as follows:
$y = a(x - 4)^2 + 3$
Substitute 0 for x and 7 for y. Solve for a.
$7 = a(0 - 4)^2 + 3$
$7 = a(16) + 3$
$4 = 16a$
$\frac{1}{4} = a$
Substitute $\frac{1}{4}$ for a in the equation $y = a(x - 4)^2 + 3$ to get
$y = \frac{1}{4}(x - 4)^2 + 3$.

Thus, the equation for this parabola is $y = \frac{1}{4}(x - 4)^2 + 3$.

15. D

The parabola shown can have an equation of the form $y = a(x-h)^2 + k$, where (h, k) is the vertex.
Since the vertex is at (1, 2), $h = 1$ and $k = 2$.

Substitute 1 for h and 2 for k into $y = a(x-h)^2 + k$ to get $y = a(x-1)^2 + 2$.
Since the equation passes through the point (0, 0), $x = 0$ and $y = 0$. Solve for a as follows:

$y = a(x-1)^2 + 2$
Substitute 0 for x and 0 for y.
$0 = a(0-1)^2 + 2$
$0 = a + 2$
$a = -2$

Substitute -2 for a in the equation $y = a(x-1)^2 + 2$ to get $y = -2(x-1)^2 + 2$.

Thus, the equation of the graph is $y = -2(x-1)^2 + 2$.

16. Part A – Open Response

Since the equation of the axis of symmetry of the parabola is $x = 2$, the ordered pair $(2, 0)$ must be the midpoint of the two x-intercepts. One x-intercept is given as $(-1, 0)$. This ordered pair is 3 units left of the ordered pair $(2, 0)$. Therefore, the other x-intercept must be 3 units right of the ordered pair $(2, 0)$. Thus, the coordinates of the other x-intercept are $(5, 0)$.

Part B – Open Response

The two x-intercepts of the parabola are $(-1, 0)$ and (5,0). Use the formula $y = a(x-r)(x-s)$.
Substitute -1 for r and 5 for s.
$y = a(x-(-1))(x-5)$
$y = a(x+1))(x-5)$
Since the y-intercept of the parabola is 10, solve for a as follows:
$y = a(x+1))(x-5)$
Substitute 0 for x and 10 for y.
$10 = a(0+1))(0-5)$
$10 = a(1)(-5)$
$10 = -5a$
$\frac{10}{-5} = \frac{-5}{5}a$
$-2 = a$
The equation of the quadratic function in the form $y = a(x-r)(x-s)$ is $y = -2(x+1)(x-5)$.

Part C – Open Response

In order to write the equation of the quadratic function in the form $y = a(x-h)^2 + k$, expand $y = -2(x+1)(x-5)$ and then complete the square of the resulting equation as illustrated:
$y = -2(x+1)(x-5)$
$y = -2(x^2 - 5x + x - 5)$
$y = -2(x^2 - 4x - 5)$
$y = -2x^2 + 8x + 10$
$y = -2(x^2 - 4x) + 10$
$y = -2(x^2 - 4x + 4 - 4) + 10$
$y = -2(x^2 - 4x + 4) + 8 + 10$
$y = -2(x-2)^2 + 18$
The equation of the quadratic function in the form $y = a(x-h)^2 + k$ is $y = -2(x-2)^2 + 18$.

17. C

$(4x-3)(3x-2) - 2(3x-2)^2$
FOIL each group.
$= 12x^2 - 8x - 9x + 6 - 2(9x^2 - 6x - 6x + 4)$
$= 12x^2 - 17x + 6 - 2(9x^2 - 12x + 4)$
Remove the brackets.
$= 12x^2 - 17x + 6 - 18x^2 + 24x - 8$
Collect like terms.
$= -6x^2 + 7x - 2$

18. 19

$(3x+2)(2x+3)$
Use the FOIL procedure to multiply each term within the first set of brackets by each term within the second set of brackets.
$3x(2x) + 3x(3) + 2(2x) + 2(3)$
$6x^2 + 9x + 4x + 6$
Collect like terms.
$6x^2 + 13x + 6$

Compare the expression $6x^2 + 13x + 6$ to the expression $6x^2 + bx + c$. Observe that in order for the expressions to be equal, $b = 13$ and $c = 6$. Thus, the value of $b + c = 13 + 6 = 19$.

19. B

In order to factor $10x^2 + 19x + 6$, find two numbers that have a product of 60 $(a \times c = 10 \times 6)$ and a sum of 19 (the b-value).
In this case, the numbers are 15 and 4.
Rewrite the expression by replacing the term $19x$ with $15x + 4x$.
$= 10x^2 + 15x + 4x + 6$
Group using brackets.
$= (10x^2 + 15x) + (4x + 6)$
Remove the GCF from each group.
$= 5x(2x + 3) + 2(2x + 3)$
Factor out the common binomial.
$= (5x + 2)(2x + 3)$
Since $5x + 2$ is one factor, $k = 2$.

20. D

$2xy - 3ay + 2xz - 3az$
Rewrite expression by grouping terms.
$= 2xy + 2xz - 3ay - 3az$
Remove the GCF. from the first and last two terms.
$= 2x(y + z) - 3a(y + z)$
Factor out the common binomial.
$= (2x - 3a)(y + z)$
The algebraic expression can be written in factor form as $(2x - 3a)(y + z)$.

21. B

When a quadratic function is expressed in the factored form $y = a(x - r)(x - s)$, the x-intercepts of the graph of the quadratic function can be determined.
These x-intercepts are $x = r$ and $x = s$.

22. A

In the equation $y = a(x - r)(x - s)$, $x = r$ and $x = s$ are the x-intercepts.
Hence, when $x = r$, $y = 0$, and when $x = s$, $y = 0$.
In the given question $r > s$ therefore, $r = 3$ and $s = 2$.
The values of r and s are 3 and 2, respectively.

23. A

The graphs of equations $y = 2x^2 + 2.5x - 5$ and $y = x^2 + 0.5x - 0.5$ are shown below:

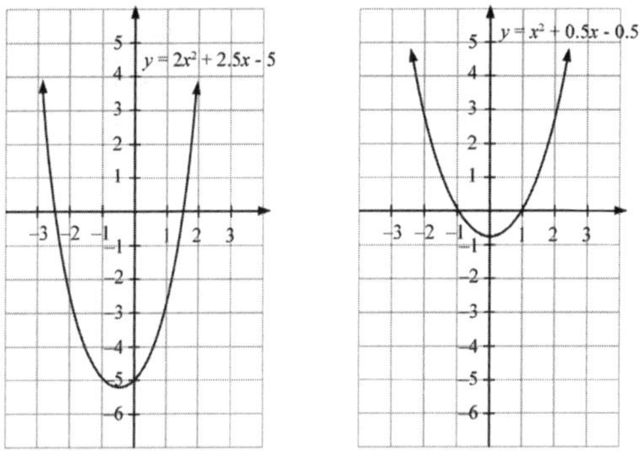

Since the graphs of both the equations have two x-intercepts, both the equations have real roots.

24. D

A quadratic equation with two real and different roots has a corresponding graph that has two distinct x-intercepts. This means the graph of the parabola crosses the x-axis at two different points.

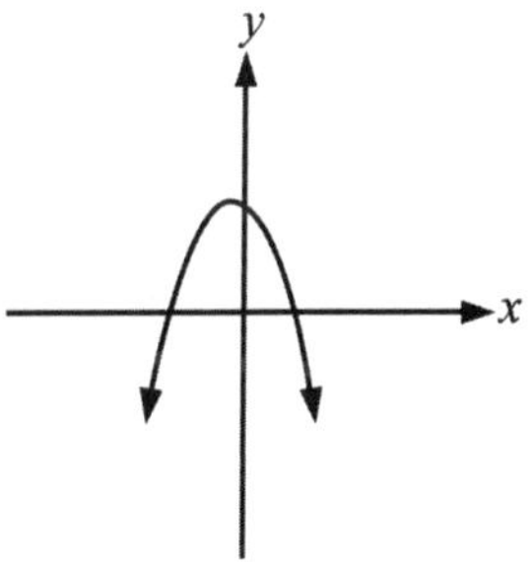

25. D

$y = 3(x^2 - 8x) + \frac{1}{2}$	Identify and remove the common factor from the x^2 and x term of the expression. In this case, the common factor is 3.
$y = 3(x^2 - \underline{8x}) + \frac{1}{2}$ $\left(\frac{-8}{2}\right)^2 = 16$	Notice the resulting coefficient for the x-term. Divide this value by 2, and then square it.
$y = 3(x^2 - 8x + \underline{16 - 16}) + \frac{1}{2}$	Both add and subtract this value inside the brackets.
$y = \underline{3}(x^2 - 8x + 16 \underline{- 16}) + \frac{1}{2}$ $y = 3(x^2 - 8x + 16) \underline{- 48} + \frac{1}{2}$	Move the value that will not contribute to a perfect square outside the brackets. [**Note**: With the distributive property, you have really added -48 and $+48$ to the function, since $3(16) = 48$ and $3(-16) = 48$. To move -16 outside the brackets, it becomes -48.]
$y = 3(x - 4)^2 - \frac{95}{2}$	Factor the trinomial inside the brackets to form a perfect square, and collect like terms outside the bracket.

When the equation $y = 3x^2 - 24x + \frac{1}{2}$ is written in the completed square form $y = a(x - h)^2 + k$, it becomes $y = 3(x - 4)^2 - \frac{95}{2}$. The value of k is $\frac{-95}{2}$.

26. A

$y = 2(x^2 + 8x) + 26$	Identify and remove the common factor from the x^2 and x term of the expression. In this case, the common factor is 2.
$y = 2(x^2 + \underline{8x}) + 26$ $\left(\frac{8}{2}\right)^2 = 16$	Notice the resulting coefficient for the x-term. Divide this value by 2, and then square it.
$y = 2(x^2 + 8x + \underline{16 - 16}) + 26$	Both add and subtract this value inside the brackets.
$y = \underline{2}(x^2 + 8x + 16 \underline{- 16}) + 26$ $y = 2(x^2 + 8x + 16) \underline{- 32} + 26$	Move the value that will not contribute to a perfect square outside the brackets. [**Note**: With the distributive property, you have really added -32 and $+32$ to the function, since $2(-16) = -32$ and $2(16) = 32$. To move -16 outside the brackets, it becomes -32.]
$y = 2(x + 4)^2 - 6$	Factor the trinomial inside the brackets to form a perfect square, and collect like terms outside the bracket.

The equation can be expressed as $y = 2(x + 4)^2 - 6$.

27. 4.00

$y = -2(x^2 - 8x) - 27$	Identify and remove the common factor from the x^2 and x term of the expression. In this case, the common factor is -2.
$y = -2(x^2 - \underline{8x}) - 27$ $\left(\frac{-8}{2}\right)^2 = 16$	Notice the resulting coefficient for the x-term. Divide this value by 2, and then square it.
$y = -2(x^2 - 8x + \underline{16 - 16}) - 27$	Both add and subtract this value inside the brackets.
$y = \underline{-2}(x^2 - 8x + 16\underline{- 16}) - 27$ $y = -2(x^2 - 8x + 16)\underline{+32} - 27$	Move the value that will not contribute to a perfect square outside the brackets. [**Note**: With the distributive property, you have really added -32 and $+32$ to the function, since $-2(16) = -32$ and $-2(-16) = 32$. To move -16 outside the brackets, it becomes $+32$.]
$y = -2(x - 4)^2 + 5$	Factor the trinomial inside the brackets to form a perfect square, and collect like terms outside the bracket.

When the equation $y = -2x^2 + 16x - 27$ is written in the completed square form $y = a(x - h)^2 + k$, it becomes $y = -2(x - 4)^2 + 5$. The h value is 4 or 4.00 to the nearest hundredth.

28. D

Find the x-intercepts by factoring and then solving the equation $0 = x^2 - 10x - 24$.

$0 = x^2 - 10x - 24$
$0 = (x + 2)(x - 12)$
$x = -2$
$x = 12$

The x-intercepts are 12 and -2.

29. B

To find the vertex, substitute -1 for x into the equation $y = (2k + 1)x^2 + 3kx + k, k \neq -\frac{1}{2}, k \in \mathbf{R}$. This will give the y-coordinate of the vertex.

$y = (2k + 1)(-1)^2 + 3k(-1) + k$
$y = 2k + 1 - 3k + k$
$y = 1$

Therefore, the vertex of the graph of the given quadratic function is $(-1, 1)$.

30. D

To arrive at $x = \frac{4 \pm \sqrt{(-4)^2 - 4(7)(-2)}}{2(7)}$, Samuel has substituted 7 for a, -4 for b, and -2 for c into the quadratic formula

$x = \frac{-b \pm \sqrt{b^2 - 4ac}}{2a}$.

Therefore, $a = 7$, $b = -4$, and $c = -2$.
The quadratic formula gives the roots of the quadratic equation $ax^2 + bx + c = 0$, where $a \neq 0$.
Now, substitute 7 for a, -4 for b, and -2 for c into the equation$ax^2 + bx + c = 0$.

$(7)x^2 + (-4)x + (-2) = 0$
$7x^2 - 4x - 2 = 0$

Therefore, the quadratic equation that Samuel is attempting to solve is $0 = 7x^2 - 4x - 2$.

31. C

Step 5 is,

$$\left(x + \frac{b}{2a}\right)^2 = \frac{b^2}{4a^2} - \frac{c}{a}$$

The next correct step involves placing the right side of the equation over the same denominator.

$$\left(x + \frac{b}{2a}\right)^2 = \frac{b^2 - 4ac}{4a^2}$$

32. B

Solve $2z^2 + 5z - 3 = 0$ by using the decomposition procedure.
Begin by finding two numbers that have a product of -6 $(a \times c = 2 \times -3)$ and a sum of 5 (b-value) In this case,
these numbers are -1 and 6. Write $5z$ as $-z + 6z$.

$2z^2 + 5z - 3 = 0$
$2z^2 - z + 6z - 3 = 0$
$z(2z - 1) + 3(2z - 1) = 0$
$(z + 3)(2z - 1) = 0$
$z = -3$ or $z = \frac{1}{2}$

33. 0.4

Write $10x^2 - 19x + 14 = 8$ equal to zero.

$10x^2 - 19x + 6 = 0$

Solve this equation using the quadratic formula,

$x = \frac{-b \pm \sqrt{b^2 - 4ac}}{2a}$.

$a = 10$, $b = -19$, and $c = 6$.

$x = \frac{-(-19) \pm \sqrt{(-19)^2 - 4(10)(6)}}{2(10)}$

$x = \frac{19 \pm \sqrt{361 - 240}}{20}$

$x = \frac{19 \pm \sqrt{121}}{20}$

$x = \frac{19 \pm 11}{20}$

$x = \frac{19 + 11}{20} = \frac{30}{20} = 1.5$ or $x = \frac{19 - 11}{20} = \frac{8}{20} = 0.4$

Note: The equation $10x^2 - 19x + 6 = 0$ could also be solved using the decomposition factoring procedure.

34. Part A – Open Response

The height of the cliff, y metres, can be determined by substituting 0 for x in the equation $y = -4.9x^2 + 2x + 40$ since at time 0 s, the diver is standing at the top of the cliff. Thus, the height of the cliff is 40 m$\left(-4.9(0)^2 + 2(0) + 40\right)$.

Part B – Open Response

When the diver reaches the water, his height above the water will be 0 m. Therefore, to determine the number of seconds it takes the diver to reach the water, substitute 0 for y in the equation $y = -4.9x^2 + 2x + 40$, and solve for x as shown:

$0 = -4.9x^2 + 2x + 40$

Since $-4.9x^2 + 2x + 40$ is not factorable, solve the equation $-4.9x^2 + 2x + 40 = 0$ by applying the quadratic formula.

$x = \frac{-b \pm \sqrt{b^2 - 4ac}}{2a}$

Substitute -4.9 for a, 2 for b, and 40 for c.

$x = \frac{-2 \pm \sqrt{2^2 - 4(-4.9)(40)}}{2(-4.9)}$

$x = \frac{-2 \pm \sqrt{4 + 784}}{-9.8}$

$x = \frac{-2 \pm \sqrt{788}}{-9.8}$

$x = \frac{-2 + \sqrt{788}}{-9.8}$ or $x = \frac{-2 - \sqrt{788}}{-9.8}$

$x \approx -2.66$ $\quad x \approx 3.07$

Since time cannot be negative, it takes the diver 3.1 s to reach the water.

Part C – Open Response

In order to determine the number of seconds that have elapsed when the diver is 15 m above the water by using a graphical approach, the first step is to choose an appropriate window setting. Next, graph $y_1 = -4.9x^2 + 2x + 40$ and $y_2 = 15$. Finally, determine the x-coordinate of the point of intersection of the two graphs.

35. C

Since the graph of the function has a minimum value, the parabola opens upward.

With a minimum value of -5, the y-coordinate of the vertex is -5, which places the vertex 5 units below the x-axis.

The parabola will cross the x-axis at two locations, as shown in the following possible image:

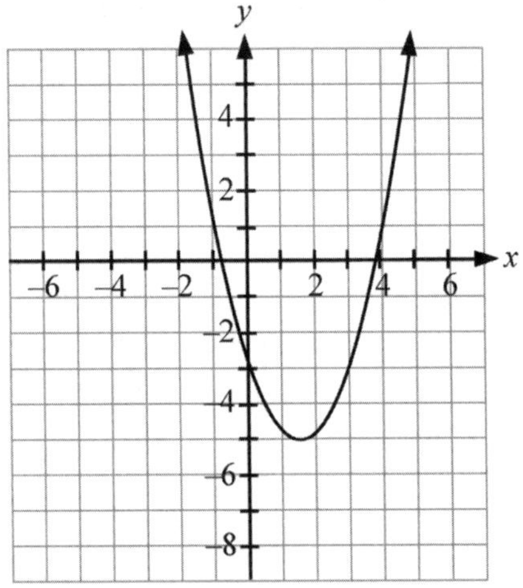

36. C

Begin by rearranging the quadratic relation
$2x^2 - 8x + y + 19 = 0$ to $y = -2x^2 + 8x - 19$.
Now, change the form of the relation by completing the square.

$y = -2(x^2 - 4x) - 19$

$y = -2(x^2 - \underline{4x}) - 19$

$\left(\frac{-4}{2}\right)^2 = 4$

$y = -2(x^2 - 4x + \underline{4 - 4}) - 19$

$y = \underline{-2}(x^2 - 4x + 4 \underline{- 4}) - 19$

$y = -2(x^2 - 4x + 4)\underline{+8} - 19$

$= -2(x - 2)^2 - 11$

This equation is of the form $y = a(x - h)^2 + k$, where $a = -2$, $h = 2$, and $k = -11$.
When the graph is drawn, the vertex of the parabola is $(2, -11)$, and the parabola opens downward since $a < 0$. Thus, the maximum value of the graph of the given quadratic relation is attained at its vertex.
The maximum value is at the ordered pair $(2, -11)$.

37. D

The maximum or minimum value can be determined when the function is written in the form $y = a(x - h)^2 + k$. The maximum value is k when $a < 0$.

38. B

$x = -5t^2 + 30t$

$x = -5(t^2 - 6t)$

$\left(\frac{-6}{2}\right)^2 = 9$

$x = -5(t^2 - 6t + \underline{9 - 9})$

$x = -\underline{5}(t^2 - 6t + 9 \underline{- 9})$

$x = -5(t^2 - 6t + 9)\underline{+45}$

$= -5(t - 3)^2 + 45$

The soccer ball follows a parabolic path with $(3, 45)[t = 3, x = 45]$ as the vertex.
Thus, the ball reaches its maximum height in 3 s.

39. 495.0

Using technology, graph the equation
$y = -4.9t^2 + 98t + 5$.
Then, use the MAXIMUM feature of the TI-83 Plus graphing calculator and a window setting such as $x{:}[0, 20, 1]\,y{:}[-10, 600, 50]$

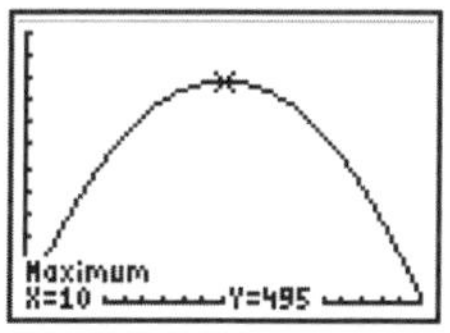

The function's maximum value occurs when $x = 10$. Therefore, the maximum height, correct to the nearest tenth, above the ground that can be reached by the rocket is 495.0 m.

40. Part A – Open Response

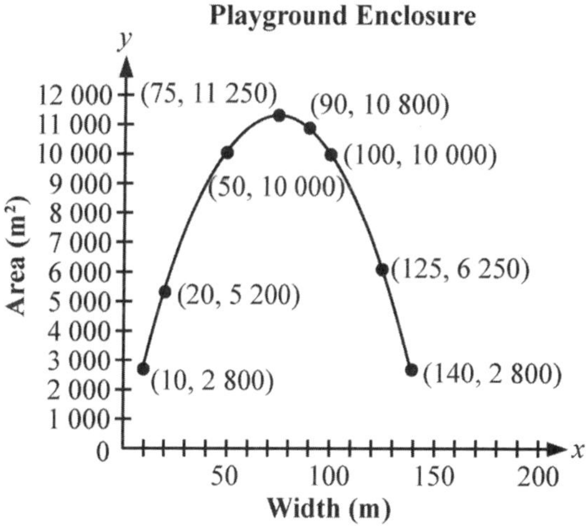

Part B – Open Response

The maximum area of the rectangular enclosure can be determined by evaluating the y-coordinate of the vertex of the parabola. The vertex (the highest point on the parabola) is (75, 11 250). Therefore, the maximum area of the rectangular enclosure is 11 250 m^2.

Part C – Open Response

The maximum area of the rectangular enclosure can be determined by completing the square of the equation as follows:

$A = -2x^2 + 300x$

$A = -2x^2 + 300x$

$A = -2(x^2 - 150x)$

$A = -2(x^2 - 150x + 5\ 625 - 5\ 625)$

$\rightarrow \left(-\frac{150}{2}\right)^2 = 5625$

$A = -2(x^2 - 150x + 5625) + 11250$

$A = -2(x - 75)^2 + 11250$

The maximum value of A is 11 250 m^2 when $x = 75$ m. The value 11 250 m^2 is exactly the same as the value for the maximum area obtained in part B.

Part D – Open Response

Recall $A = LW$ or $A \div W = L$. Since $x = 75$ m, the value of y is 150 m$(11\ 250 \div 75)$. Therefore, the dimensions of the playground that produce a maximum area will have a width (the value of x) of 75 m and a length (the value of y) of 150 m.

Analytic Geometry

Analytic Geometry

Table of Correlations

Specific Expectation	Practice Questions	Unit Test Questions
AG1 Using Linear Systems to Solve Problems		
AG1.1 *solve systems of two linear equations involving two variables, using the algebraic method of substitution or elimination*	1, 2, 3, 4, 5, 6	1, 2, 3, 4, 5
AG1.2 *solve problems that arise from realistic situations described in words or represented by linear systems of two equations involving two variables, by choosing an appropriate algebraic or graphical method*	7, 8, 9, 10, 11a, 11b	6, 7a, 7b, 8, 9
AG2 Solving Problems Involving Properties of Line Segments		
AG2.1 *develop the formula for the midpoint of a line segment, and use this formula to solve problems*	12, 13, 14	10, 11
AG2.2 *develop the formula for the length of a line segment, and use this formula to solve problems*	15, 16, 17, 18	12, 13, 14
AG2.3 *develop the equation for a circle with centre (0, 0) and radius r, by applying the formula for the length of a line segment;*	19, 20	15
AG2.4 *determine the radius of a circle with centre (0, 0), given its equation; write the equation of a circle with centre (0, 0), given the radius; and sketch the circle, given the equation in the form* $x^2 + y^2 = r^2$	21, 22, 23	16, 17, 18
AG2.5 *solve problems involving the slope, length, and midpoint of a line segment.*	24, 25, 26, 27a, 27b, 27c	19, 20, 21a, 21b
AG3 Using Analytic Geometry to Verify Geometric Properties		
AG3.1 *determine, through investigation some characteristics and properties of geometric figures*	28, 29	24
AG3.2 *verify, using algebraic techniques and analytic geometry, some characteristics of geometric figures*	30, 31, 32	23, 25, 26
AG3.3 *plan and implement a multi-step strategy that uses analytic geometry and algebraic techniques to verify a geometric property*	33, 34, 35, 36a, 36b, 36c	22, 27, 28a, 28b, 28c

AG1.1 *solve systems of two linear equations involving two variables, using the algebraic method of substitution or elimination*

Solving Systems of Two Linear Equations

A collection of linear equations involving the same set of variables is called a **system of linear equations**. The solution to a system of linear equations can be found graphically or algebraically and with or without the use of technology.

The Algebraic Method of Substitution

The steps for solving a system of two linear equations using the method of substitution are outlined in the following example.

Example

Solve the following:

$y - 4x + 1 = 0$

$4x - 5y + 3 = 0$

Step 1: Label each equation.

(1) $y - 4x + 1 = 0$

(2) $4x - 5y + 3 = 0$

Step 2: Isolate variable y in the first equation since the coefficient of y is 1.

Thus, equation (1) becomes $y = 4x - 1$.

Step 3: Substitute $4x - 1$ for y into the second equation.

(2) $4x - 5y + 3 = 0$

$4x - 5(4x - 1) + 3 = 0$

Step 4: Solve for the variable x.

$4x - 5(4x - 1) + 3 = 0$

$4x - 20x + 5 + 3 = 0$

$-16x + 8 = 0$

$8 = 16x$

$\frac{8}{16} = x$ or $x = \frac{1}{2}$

Step 5: Substitute $\frac{1}{2}$ for x in either the first or second equation or in the equation $y = 4x - 1$ to determine the value for y.

$y = 4x - 1$

$y = 4\left(\frac{1}{2}\right) - 1$

$y = 2 - 1$

$y = 1$

Step 6: The solution is $x = \frac{1}{2}$ and $y = 1$.

The Algebraic Method of Elimination

This method involves eliminating one of the variables. Some suggested steps for using the method of elimination are outlined in the following example.

Example

Solve the following:

$3x - 4y = 20$

$x + 3y = -2$

Step 1: Label the equations.

(1) $3x - 4y = 20$

(2) $x + 3y = -2$

Step 2: Multiply both sides of equation (2) by 3.

(1) $3x - 4y = 20$

(2) $3x + 9y = -6$

Step 3: Subtract the two equations. Solve for y.

$3x - 4y = 20$

$\underline{3x + 9y = -6}$

$0 - 13y = 26$

$-13y = 26$

$y = -2$

Step 4: Substitute 2 for y in one of the original equations. (In this case, equation 2).

Solve for x.

$x + 3(-2) = -2$

$x - 6 = -2$

$x = 4$

Step 5: The solution is $x = 4$ and $y = -2$.

Practice

1. If the points $(2, -5)$ and $(-5, -2)$ both satisfy the equation $Ax + By = 29$, then the value of A is

A. −7 **B.** −3

C. 3 **D.** 7

2. Which of the following statements about the possible solutions to various linear systems of equations is **false**?

A. A system of parallel lines has no solution.

B. A system of intersecting lines has exactly one solution.

C. A system of coincident lines has infinitely many solutions.

D. A system of intersecting lines where one line is vertical has an undefined solution.

CHALLENGER QUESTION

Use the following information to answer the next question.

A student is asked to solve the following system of linear equations by using a graphical method.

$-9x + 6y = 10$

$Ax - 8y = 15$

After graphing each linear equation, the student observed that the two lines were parallel and concluded that there was no solution to the given system of linear equations.

3. Given that the student's solution is correct, the value of A is

A. 36 **B.** 12

C. −12 **D.** −36

Use the following information to answer the next question.

Rebecca is given the following system of linear equations:

$x + y = 365$

$3x + 2y = 925$

4. In verifying the solution to this system of linear equations, Rebecca must replace

A. x with 170 and y with 195 in both equations

B. x with 195 and y with 170 in both equations

C. x with 170 in the first equation and y with 195 in the second equation

D. x with 195 in the first equation and y with 170 in the second equation

5. If the ordered pair (x, y) is the solution to the system of linear equations $8x + 3y = -41$ and $6x - 5y = -9$, then the value of x is

A. -4 **B.** 4

C. $\frac{-89}{29}$ **D.** $\frac{-159}{29}$

CHALLENGER QUESTION

Numerical Response

6. What is the value of K for which the system of linear equations $12x + Ky = -9$ and $-16x - 20y = 12$ has an infinite number of solutions?___

AG1.2 *solve problems that arise from realistic situations described in words or represented by linear systems of two equations involving two variables, by choosing an appropriate algebraic or graphical method*

Problem Solving Using Systems of Two Linear Equations

When solving problems that arise from realistic situations represented by linear system of two equations, use some of these general hints:

- Assign a different variable to each of the unknown quantities.
- Set up a system of two linear equations, and solve the system using either an algebraic or graphical method.
- Clearly state the solution to the given problem.

Example

Four cabbages and five heads of lettuce cost \$8.40, whereas six cabbages and two heads of lettuce cost \$8.20. Determine the price of one cabbage and of one head of lettuce.

Let the price in dollars of one cabbage = x.

Let the price in dollars of one head of lettuce = y.

Using the information given in the problem, the following system of equations can be formed:

(1)$4x + 5y = 8.40$

(2)$6x + 2y = 8.20$

Multiply equation (1) by 2 and equation (2) by 5 to obtain a common coefficient for y.

(3)$8x + 10y = 16.80$ [2 × (1)]

(4)$\underline{30x + 10y = 41.00}$ [5 × (2)]

Subtract equation (4) from equation (3).

$-22x + 0y = -24.20$

$x = \frac{-24.20}{-22}$

$x = 1.10$

Substitute 1.10 for x into equation (1).

$4(1.10) + 5y = 8.40$

$4.40 + 5y = 8.40$

$5y = 4.00$

$y = 0.80$

The price of a cabbage is \$1.10, and the price of a head of lettuce is \$0.80.

Example

A car rental company offers two plans to rent compact cars at a weekly rate:

Plan A: \$50 plus \$0.05 / km

Plan B: \$80 plus \$0.03 / km

a) For each rental plan, write an equation to represent the total weekly cost in dollars, C, to rent a compact car for x kilometres driven.

Since x = the number of kilometres driven and C = the weekly cost, it follows that:

For Plan A: $C = 50 + 0.05x$

For Plan B: $C = 80 + 0.03x$

b) Determine which plan is more economical if the car is driven 800 km in one week.

To determine which weekly plan is more economical if the car is driven 800 km, substitute 800 for x into each equation.

For Plan A, the cost is $C = 50 + 0.05(800) = \$90$

For Plan B, the cost is $C = 80 + 0.03(800) = \$104$

Therefore, since Plan A costs \$14(\$104 – \$90) less than Plan B, Plan A is more economical.

c) Determine the distance that must be driven for Plan B to be more economical than Plan A.

Plan B will be more economical than plan A after the plans have an equal weekly cost. Recall that graphically, the solution to the system of equations is the intersection point of the two lines.

The graphs displayed with the window setting x:[0,2 000,250], y:[0,200,50] are shown below:

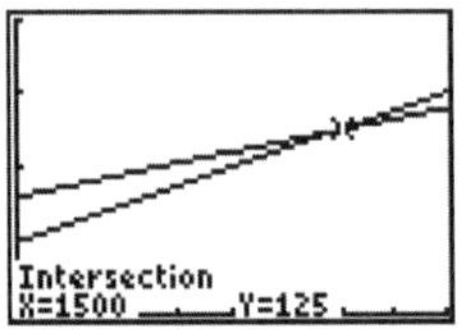

Using the INTERSECTION feature, the intersection point is the ordered pair (1 500, 125). Therefore, Plan B is more economical if the car is driven more than 1 500 km in one week.

Practice

Use the following information to answer the next question.

At a particular theatre, adult tickets cost \$7 each, and student tickets cost \$5 each. For a certain show, three times as many student tickets as adult tickets were sold. The total sales for the show were \$880.

7. If a represents the number of adult tickets sold and b represents the number of student tickets sold, then the system of linear equations that could be solved in order to determine the number of adult and student tickets sold is

A. $7a + 5b = 880$ and $3b = a$

B. $7a + 5b = 880$ and $b = 3a$

C. $a + b = 880$ and $3(5b) = 7a$

D. $a + b = 880$ and $5b = 3(7a)$

Use the following information to answer the next question.

Steve and Noel belong to different fitness gyms. They were comparing the cost of using each gym and were unable to decide who was getting the better deal.

To help them compare, they graphed the cost of using each facility, as shown.

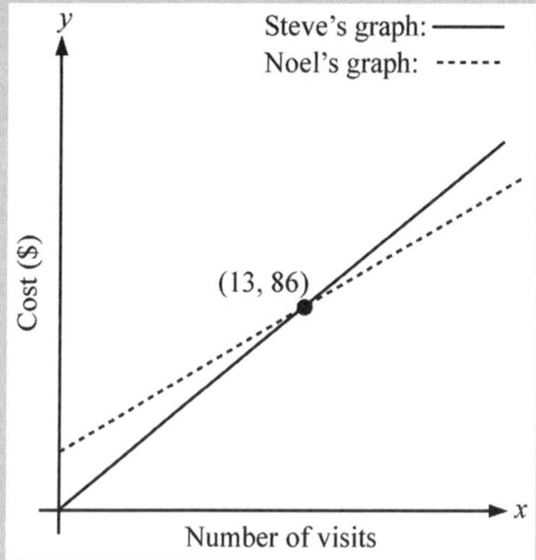

8. Which of the following statements about the information given in the graph is **false**?

A. Noel's gym has an initial membership fee that must be paid even if he never goes to the gym.

B. For a person planning to go to the gym only 8 times, Steve's gym would be the most cost-effective.

C. For a person planning to go to the gym every day for a year, Steve's gym would be the most cost-effective.

D. The point of intersection (13, 86) represents the fact that 13 visits costs \$86 at each facility.

CHALLENGER QUESTION

9. Sally purchased 2 pens and 8 pencils for a total cost of \$5.20. If she had purchased 3 pens and 4 pencils, the total cost would have been \$5.80. The cost of one pen is

A. \$1.20 **B.** \$1.40

C. \$1.50 **D.** \$1.60

Use the following information to answer the next question.

The perimeter of a road marker is in the shape of an isosceles triangle is 71 inches. The base measures 1 inch less than double the length of each of the other two sides.

10. Which of the following systems of linear equations would allow a person to find the dimensions of the road marker?

A. $x + y = 71$
$2x + y = 1$

B. $x + y = 71$
$2x - y = 1$

C. $2x + y = 71$
$2x + y = 1$

D. $2x + y = 71$
$2x - y = 1$

11. Part A

Open Response

Ken invests \$2 500 in an account that pays 4.2% simple interest per year. How much interest will Ken earn at the end of the first year of his investment?

Part B

Open Response

Set up a system of two linear equations showing two variables, and then use this system to solve the following problem.

Ken earned \$6 000 working during July and August. He decided to invest part of the \$6 000 in an account that pays 4% simple interest per year and the remainder of the money in a government bond that pays 3.5% simple interest per year. After one year, the 4% investment earned \$30 more interest than the 3.5% investment. How much interest did Ken earn at each rate?

Show your work.

AG2.1 *develop the formula for the midpoint of a line segment, and use this formula to solve problems*

Midpoint of a Line Segment

The **midpoint** of a line segment is a point on the line segment that is the same distance from either endpoint of the line segment. As shown below, the midpoint of a line segment is often referred to as the middle point of the line segment.

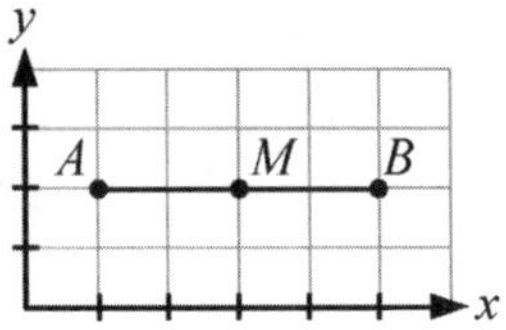

In general, the midpoint of the line segment with endpoints $A(x_1, y_1)$ and $B(x_2, y_2)$ is given by the formula $M_{AB} = \left(\frac{x_1 + x_2}{2}, \frac{y_1 + y_2}{2}\right)$.

Example

Determine the midpoint of each side of the triangle shown below.

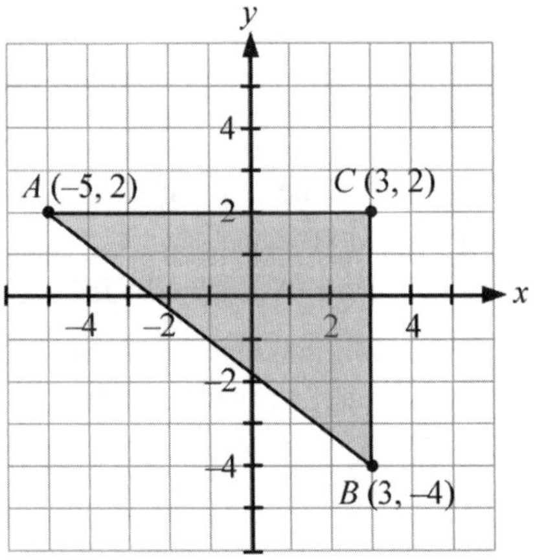

Use the midpoint formula $M = \left(\frac{x_1 + x_2}{2}, \frac{y_1 + y_2}{2}\right)$.

For line segment AB:

$$M_{AB} = \left(\frac{-5+3}{2}, \frac{2+(-4)}{2}\right) = \left(\frac{-2}{2}, \frac{-2}{2}\right)$$

$$M_{AB} = (-1, -1)$$

For line segment BC:

$$M_{BC} = \left(\frac{3+3}{2}, \frac{-4+2}{2}\right) = \left(\frac{6}{2}, \frac{-2}{2}\right)$$

$$M_{BC} = (3, -1)$$

For line segment AC:

$$M_{AC} = \left(\frac{-5+3}{2}, \frac{2+2}{2}\right) = \left(\frac{-2}{2}, \frac{4}{2}\right)$$

$$M_{AC} = (-1, 2)$$

Practice

Use the following information to answer the next question.

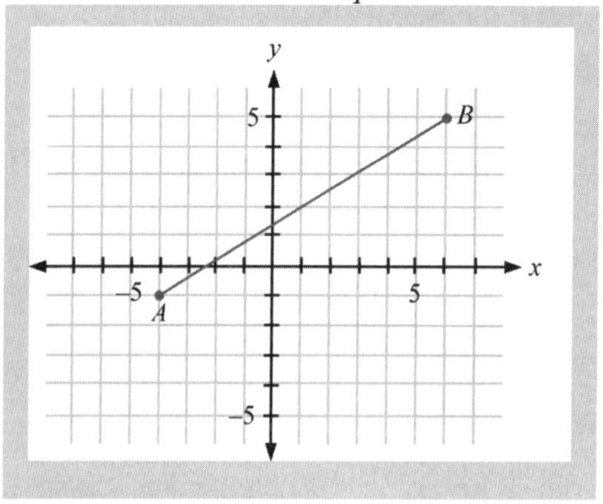

12. The midpoint of line segment AB is

A. (1, 2) **B.** (2, 4)

C. (2, 1) **D.** (4, 2)

13. One endpoint of a line segment is located at point $(6, 5)$. The midpoint of the line segment is located at point $(2, -3)$. The coordinates of the other endpoint are

A. $(4, 1)$

B. $(-2, 3)$

C. $(10, 13)$

D. $(-2, -11)$

CHALLENGER QUESTION

14. If the point $(-1, 2)$ is the midpoint of the line segment with endpoints that are $(a, -4)$ and $(-7, b)$, then the respective values of a and b are

A. 1 and 6 **B.** 3 and 7

C. 5 and 8 **D.** 7 and 9

AG2.2 *develop the formula for the length of a line segment, and use this formula to solve problems*

Finding the Length of a Line Segment

Finding the length of a line segment is useful in many aspects of analytical geometry. In order to determine the distance between points A and B, it is necessary to calculate the length of line segment AB.

Consider the points $A(x_1, y_1)$ and $B(x_2, y_2)$, and build a right triangle as shown below.

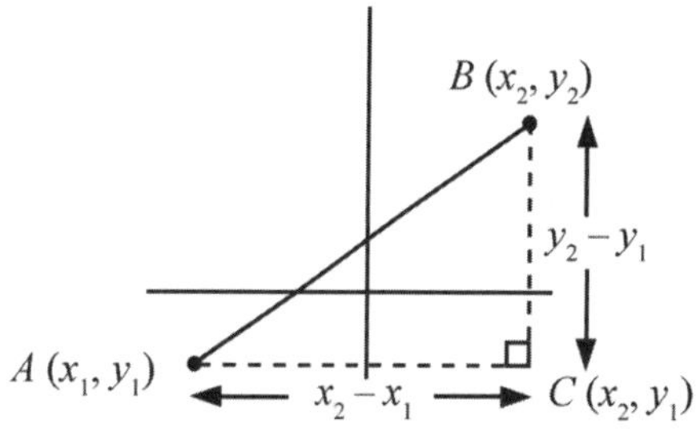

Let d represent the length of line segment AB.

Use the Pythagorean theorem to derive an expression for d.

$$d^2 = (AC)^2 + (BC)^2$$

$$d^2 = (x_2 - x_1)^2 + (y_2 - y_1)^2$$

$$d = \sqrt{(x_2 - x_1)^2 + (y_2 - y_1)^2}$$

Using the Distance Formula

In general, the length of the line segment with endpoints $A(x_1, y_1)$ and $B(x_2, y_2)$ is given by the following formula:

$$d = \sqrt{(x_2 - x_1)^2 + (y_2 - y_1)^2}$$

Example

Determine the length of the line segment with endpoints $A(3, 6)$ and $B(-2, -1)$. Express the answer as an exact value.

Substitute the endpoint values into the distance formula.

$$d = \sqrt{(x_2 - x_1)^2 + (y_2 - y_1)^2}$$

$$= \sqrt{(-2 - 3)^2 + (-1 - 6)^2}$$

$$= \sqrt{(-5)^2 + (-7)^2}$$

$$= \sqrt{25 + 49}$$

$$d = \sqrt{74}$$

The length of the line segment AB is $\sqrt{74}$ units.

Example

A fishing boat sends a distress signal from a location given by the coordinates $(200, 180)$. An ocean freighter at coordinates $(170, 240)$ and a cruise ship at coordinates $(230, 180)$ pick up the distress signal. Which ship is closer to the fishing boat?

In order to determine which of the two ships is closer to the fishing boat, begin by finding the distance from each boat to the fishing boat using the distance formula.

$$d = \sqrt{(x_2 - x_1)^2 + (y_2 - y_1)^2}$$

The distance between the ocean freighter and the fishing boat:

$$= \sqrt{(200 - 170)^2 + (180 - 240)^2}$$
$$= \sqrt{(30)^2 + (-60)^2}$$
$$= \sqrt{900 + 3\,600}$$
$$= \sqrt{4\,500} \approx 67.082$$

The distance between the cruise ship and the fishing boat:

$$= \sqrt{(200 - 230)^2 + (180 - 145)^2}$$
$$= \sqrt{(-30)^2 + (35)^2}$$
$$= \sqrt{900 + 1225}$$
$$= \sqrt{2\,125} \approx 46.098$$

The cruise ship is approximately 21 units closer to the fishing boat than the ocean freighter.

Practice

15. Given two points $A(0, 5)$ and $B(-3, 1)$, what is the length of line segment AB?
    A. 2 **B.** 3 **C.** 4 **D.** 5

16. If the distance between point $(1, 1)$ and point $(a, -3)$ is 5, one possible value of a is
    A. 2 **B.** 3 **C.** 4 **D.** 10

CHALLENGER QUESTION

17. The distance between point A and point B is 10 units on a coordinate grid. If point B lies on the y-axis and point A is at $(-6, 8)$, then two possible sets of coordinates for point B are
    A. (0, 0) and (0, 16)
    B. (0, 0) and (16, 0)
    C. (0, −8) and (0, 8)
    D. (−8, 0) and (8, 0)

Numerical Response

18. Given $A(3, 1)$, $B(5, -2)$, and $C(-3, -5)$, the perimeter of triangle ABC is ____. (correct to one decimal place)

AG2.3 *develop the equation for a circle with centre (0, 0) and radius r, by applying the formula for the length of a line segment;*

Developing the Equation of a Circle

A **circle** is a set of points in a plane equidistant from a given point (the centre).

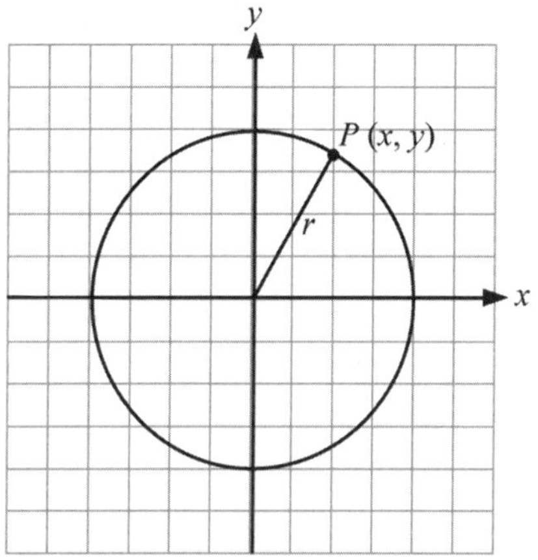

Since any point on the circle can be represented by the ordered pair $P(x, y)$, the distance P to the centre, $(0, 0)$, is the radius, r. Using the distance formula yields the following result:

Length of line segment PO:

$= \sqrt{(x_2 - x_1)^2 + (y_2 - y_1)^2}$

$= \sqrt{(x - 0)^2 + (y - 0)^2}$

$= \sqrt{x^2 + y^2} = r$

Therefore, $x^2 + y^2 = r^2$ when both sides of the equation $\sqrt{x^2 + y^2} = r$ are squared.

The equation of a circle with centre $(0, 0)$ and radius r is $x^2 + y^2 = r^2$.

Example

Using the distance formula, determine the equation of the circle with centre $(0, 0)$ that passes through the point $(-2, 7)$.

$d = \sqrt{(x_2 - x_1)^2 + (y_2 - y_1)^2}$

$= \sqrt{(-2 - 0)^2 + (7 - 0)^2}$

$= \sqrt{4 + 49}$

$= \sqrt{53}$

Recall that $x^2 + y^2 = r^2$.

Thus,

$x^2 + y^2 = (\sqrt{53})^2$

$x^2 + y^2 = 53$

Therefore, the equation $x^2 + y^2 = 53$ describes a circle with centre $(0, 0)$ and passing through the point $(-2, 7)$.

Practice

19. What is the equation of a circle with a radius of 8 units and a centre located at the origin?

A. $x^2 + y^2 = 64$

B. $x^2 - y^2 = 64$

C. $x^2 + y^2 = 8$

D. $x^2 - y^2 = 8$

CHALLENGER QUESTION

20. A circle with centre (0, 0) and a diameter with endpoints (a, b) and (c, d) is shown.

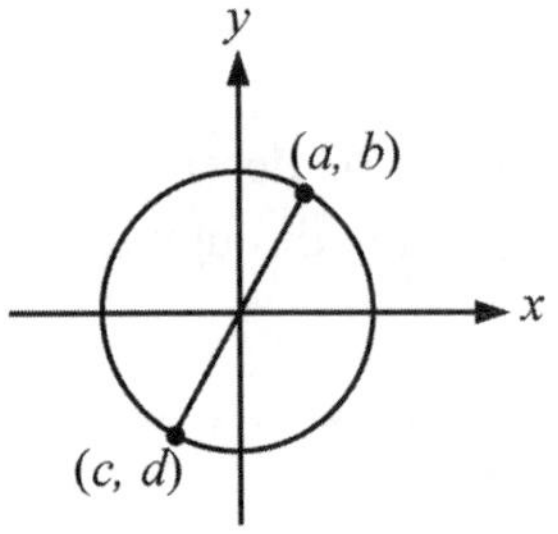

The equation of this circle could be written as

A. $x^2 + y^2 = (a - c)^2 + (b - d)^2$

B. $x^2 + y^2 = \dfrac{(a - c)^2 + (b - d)^2}{2}$

C. $x^2 + y^2 = \dfrac{(a - c)^2 + (b - d)^2}{4}$

D. $x^2 + y^2 = \dfrac{(a - c) + (b - d)}{2}$

AG2.4 *determine the radius of a circle with centre (0, 0), given its equation; write the equation of a circle with centre (0, 0), given the radius; and sketch the circle, given the equation in the form* $x^2 + y^2 = r^2$

Determining the Radius of a Circle

Recall that the equation of a circle with centre (0, 0) and radius r is $x^2 + y^2 = r^2$. Knowing this, you can do the following:

- Determine the radius r of a particular circle written in the form $x^2 + y^2 = r^2$.
- Write the equation of a circle with centre (0, 0), given its radius r.
- On a Cartesian plane, sketch a given circle written in the form $x^2 + y^2 = r^2$.

Example

Determine the radius of the circle defined by the equation $x^2 + y^2 = 81$.

Since the equation $x^2 + y^2 = r^2$ represents a circle with centre (0, 0) and radius r, it follows that:

$r^2 = 81$

$r = \sqrt{81} = 9$

Thus, the radius of the circle $x^2 + y^2 = 81$ is 9 units.

Example

A circle has its centre at (0, 0) and a diameter of 6 units. Write the equation of the circle, and then sketch the circle on a Cartesian plane.

Since the diameter is twice the length of the radius, the radius of the circle is 3 units. In order to write the equation of the circle, substitute 3 for r in the equation $x^2 + y^2 = r^2$.

$x^2 + y^2 = (3)^2$

$x^2 + y^2 = 9$

Thus, the equation of the circle with centre (0, 0) and a diameter of 6 units is $x^2 + y^2 = 9$.

The circle defined by the equation $x^2 + y^2 = 9$ has a centre of (0, 0) and a radius of 3 units. You can choose the ordered pairs (0, 3), (0, −3), (3, 0), and (−3, 0) to help sketch the circle. The circle is sketched below.

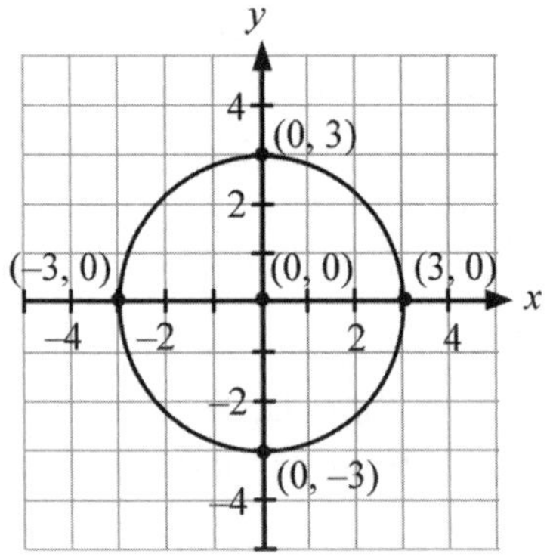

Practice

21. The diagram illustrates a circle sketched on a Cartesian plane.

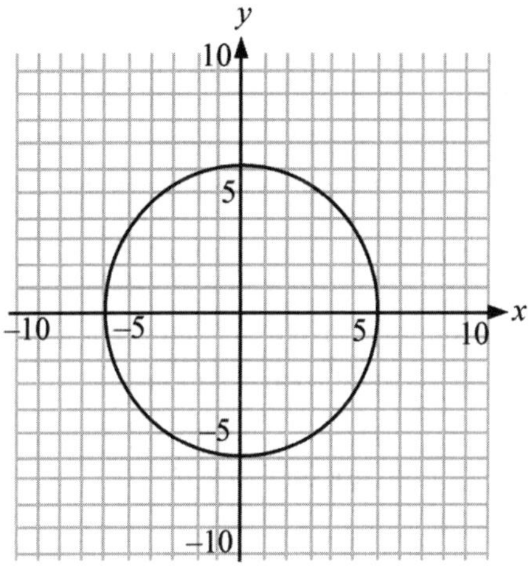

Which of the following equations defines this circle?

A. $x^2 + y^2 = 25$

B. $x^2 + y^2 = 36$

C. $x^2 + y^2 = 100$

D. $x^2 + y^2 = 144$

CHALLENGER QUESTION

22. The diagram illustrates Mrs. Carter's circular flower bed, sketched on a Cartesian plane.

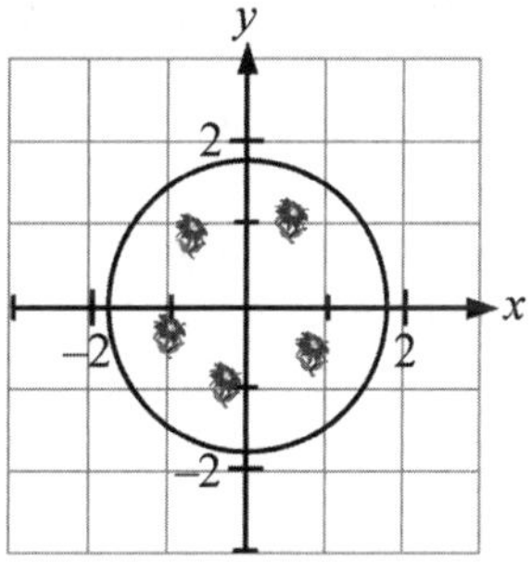

The equation that defines the outside edge of Mrs. Carter's flower bed is $x^2 + y^2 = 2.89$, where the radius is expressed in metres. If Mrs. Carter decides to place a border around her circular flower bed, then the minimum length of the required border material, to the nearest tenth, is

A. 5.3 m **B.** 9.1 m

C. 10.7 m **D.** 18.2 m

Numerical Response

23. A circle is defined by the equation $x^2 + y^2 = 18$. The length of the radius of this circle, to the nearest tenth, is ___units.

AG2.5 *solve problems involving the slope, length, and midpoint of a line segment.*

Solving Slope, Length, and Midpoint Problems

Often, certain analytical geometry problems can be solved using a combination of concepts such as slope, length, and midpoint of a line segment.

Example

Determine the equation of the right bisector of the line segment AB with endpoints $A(-2, 6)$ and $B(4, -3)$.

$$m = \frac{y_2 - y_1}{x_2 - x_1} = \frac{6-(-3)}{-2-4} = \frac{9}{-6} = -\frac{3}{2}$$

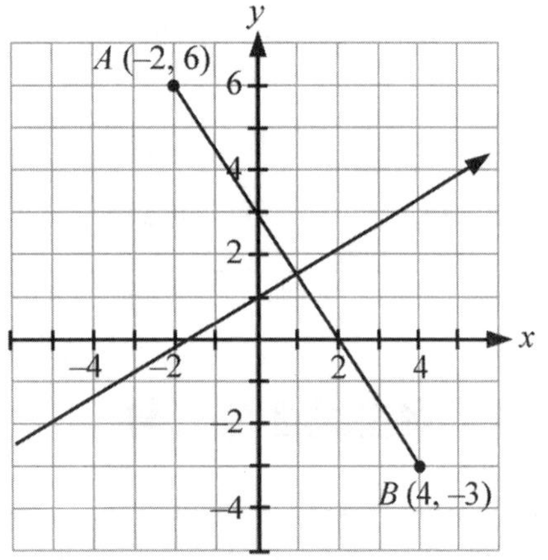

The right bisector of AB has a slope of $\frac{2}{3}$ since it is perpendicular to AB (the negative reciprocal of $-\frac{3}{2}$ is $\frac{2}{3}$).

Now, determine the midpoint of AB.

$$M_{AB} = \left(\frac{x_1 + x_2}{2}, \frac{y_1 + y_2}{2}\right) = \left(\frac{-2+4}{2}, \frac{6+(-3)}{2}\right)$$

$$= \left(\frac{2}{2}, \frac{3}{2}\right)$$

$$M_{AB} = \left(1, \frac{3}{2}\right)$$

Finally, use the point-slope form of the equation of a line to determine the equation of the right bisector.

$$y = m(x - x_1) + y_1$$

$$y = \frac{2}{3}(x-1) + \frac{3}{2}$$

$$y = \frac{2}{3}x - \frac{2}{3} + \frac{3}{2}$$

$$y = \frac{2}{3}x + \frac{5}{6}$$

Example

Determine the shortest distance from the point $(2, 1)$ to the line defined by the equation $y = -x + 7$.

The line AD is perpendicular to $y = -x + 7$.

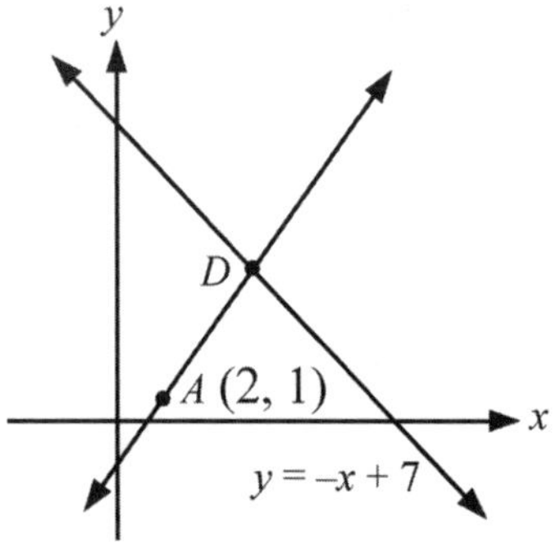

The slope of the line $y = -x + 7$ is -1.

Thus, the slope of AD is 1 (the negative reciprocal of -1).

The equation of line AD can be determined as follows:

$y = m(x - x_1) + y_1$

$y = 1(x - 2) + 1$

$y = x - 2 + 1$

$y = x - 1$

Thus, the equation of line AD is $y = x - 1$.

The intersection point D can be found by solving the following system of two linear equations:

(1) $y = -x + 7$

(2) $y = x - 1$

Solve by substitution.

$x - 1 = -x + 7$

$2x - 1 = 7$

$2x = 8$

$x = 4$

Substitute 4 into equation (2) to find the y-coordinate of point D.

(2) $y = x - 1$

$y = 4 - 1$

$y = 3$

Thus, D is the point $(4,\ 3)$.

The distance from $(2,\ 1)$ to $(4,\ 3)$ can now be determined by applying the distance formula as follows:

$d = \sqrt{(x_2 - x_1)^2 + (y_2 - y_1)^2}$

$d = \sqrt{(4 - 2)^2 + (3 - 1)^2}$

$d = \sqrt{(2)^2 + (2)^2}$

$d = \sqrt{4 + 4}$

$d = \sqrt{8}$

To the nearest hundredth, $d = 2.83$.

Thus, the shortest distance from $(2,\ 1)$ to the line defined by the equation $y = -x + 7$ is approximately 2.83 units.

Practice

24. To the nearest whole number, what is the horizontal distance between the point $(4,\ -7)$ and the line $y = -\frac{1}{3}x + 2$?

A. 5 **B.** 9 **C.** 23 **D.** 34

Use the following information to answer the next question.

The vertices of triangle ABC are $A(-3,\ -4)$, $B(1,\ 4)$, and $C(3,\ 0)$, as shown in the diagram.

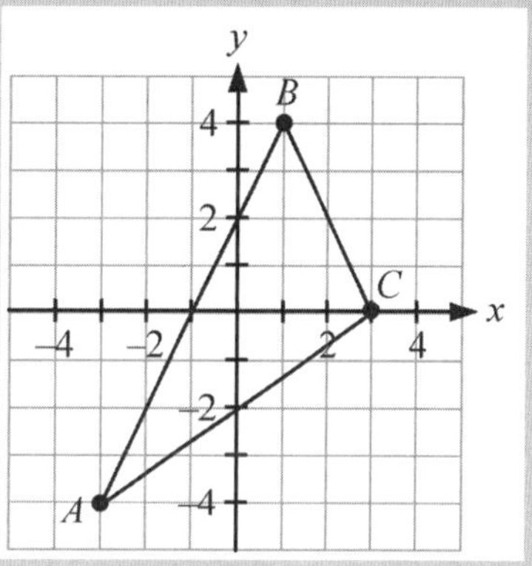

25. To the nearest tenth, the perimeter of the triangle formed by joining the midpoints of each side of the triangle shown is

A. 7.7 units **B.** 10.3 units

C. 12.9 units **D.** 20.6 units

CHALLENGER QUESTION

26. To the nearest hundredth, the shortest distance from the point (4, 1) to the line $y = 2x - 12$ is

A. 2.24 units **B.** 6.47 units

C. 9.20 units **D.** 10.05 units

Use the following information to answer the next multipart question.

27. A diameter of a circle has endpoints $A(-2, 3)$ and $B(4, 11)$.

Part A

Open Response

Determine the coordinates of the centre of the circle.

Show your work.

Part B

Open Response

Verify that the radius of the circle is 5 units in length.

Show your work.

Part C

Open Response

Verify that the point $P(-3, 10)$ is on the circle.

Show your work.

AG3.1 *determine, through investigation some characteristics and properties of geometric figures*

CHARACTERISTICS AND PROPERTIES OF TRIANGLES AND QUADRILATERALS

Through investigation, recall the following triangle characteristics and properties:

- A **right triangle** is a triangle that contains an angle of 90°.
- When each side of a triangle is equal in length, the triangle is defined as an **equilateral triangle**.
- When exactly two sides of a triangle are equal in length, the triangle is defined as an **isosceles triangle**.
- When each side of a triangle is different in length, the triangle is defined as a **scalene triangle**.

Example

Line segments AB and BC intersect at B. Line segments AC and AB intersect at A. Line segments AC and BC intersect at C. If AB = 4 cm, BC = 7 cm, and AC = 4 cm, then what type of geometric figure is formed?

Since there are three line segments, the figure is a triangle.

Since $AB = AC = 4$, the geometric figure is an isosceles triangle (two sides of the triangle are equal in length).

Through investigation, recall the following quadrilateral characteristics and properties:

- A **rectangle** is a quadrilateral in which opposite sides are parallel to one another and equal in length, and adjacent sides are perpendicular to one another.
- When opposite sides of a quadrilateral are equal in length and have equal slopes, the quadrilateral is called a **parallelogram**.
- It can be shown that the diagonals of a parallelogram bisect each other.
- When all the sides of a quadrilateral are equal in length and opposite sides have equal slopes, the quadrilateral is called a **rhombus**.
- A quadrilateral in which all four sides are equal in length, opposite sides are parallel, and adjacent sides are perpendicular is called a **square**.
- A quadrilateral in which the slope of exactly one pair of opposite sides is equal is called a **trapezoid**.

Example

Rectangle $ABCD$ has vertices $A(0, 0)$, $B(3, -2)$, $C(6, 3)$, and $D(x, y)$. What are the numerical coordinates for point D?

Begin with a sketch for clarity.

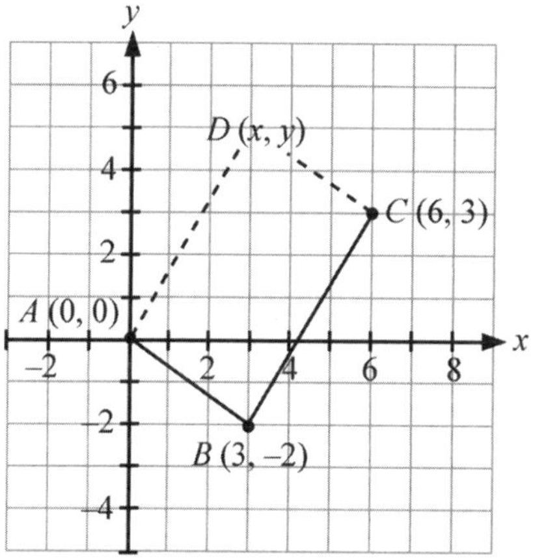

In a rectangle, opposite sides are parallel. Parallel line segments have equal slopes; therefore, it follows that $m_{AB} = m_{CD}$ and $m_{BC} = m_{AD}$.

$m = \dfrac{y_2 - y_1}{x_2 - x_1}$

$m_{AB} = \dfrac{-2-0}{3-0} = \dfrac{-2}{3}$

$m_{CD} = \dfrac{3-y}{6-x}$

Thus,

$\dfrac{-2}{3} = \dfrac{3-y}{6-x}$

$3(3-y) = -2(6-x)$

$9 - 3y = -12 + 2x$

$21 - 3y = 2x$ or $2x + 3y = 21$

Also, $m_{BC} = \dfrac{3-(-2)}{6-3} = \dfrac{5}{3} = m_{AD}\dfrac{y-0}{x-0} = \dfrac{y}{x}$

Thus,

$\dfrac{5}{3} = \dfrac{y}{x}$

$3y = 5x$

or $5x - 3y = 0$

Determine the coordinates of point D by solving the following system of equations using the elimination method:

Add the two equations to eliminate y

$2x + 3y = 21$

$\underline{5x - 3y = 0}$

$7x = 21$

$x = 3$

Substitute 3 for x into $5x - 3y = 0$

$5(3) - 3y = 0$

$15 - 3y = 0$

$3y = 15$

$y = 5$

Therefore, the coordinates of point D are $(3, 5)$.

Practice

28. In triangle PQR, line segment PT intersects the midpoint of line segment QR, forming a right angle at point T. Line segment PT is classified as the perpendicular

A. radius **B.** bisector

C. diagonal **D.** connector

Use the following information to answer the next question.

> Martha draws a quadrilateral with the following properties:
> - opposite sides are equal
> - opposite angles are equal
> - diagonals bisect each other at 90°

29. The quadrilateral that Martha draws is a

A. parallelogram **B.** rectangle

C. trapezoid **D.** square

AG3.2 *verify, using algebraic techniques and analytic geometry, some characteristics of geometric figures*

VERIFYING CHARACTERISTICS OF GEOMETRIC FIGURES

Characteristics of geometric figures can be verified using both algebraic and geometric techniques. Verifying a **conjecture** requires showing that a conjecture is true for a particular situation. An algebraic verification may require the use of previously developed definitions, formulas, or theorems.

Example

Verify that triangle ABC with vertices $A(2, 3)$, $B(6, 1)$, and $C(5, 4)$, and C $(5, 4)$ is an isosceles triangle.

To verify that triangle ABC is isosceles, determine the lengths of each of the three sides of the triangle, and show that exactly two sides have the same length. Recall the distance formula $d = \sqrt{(x_2 - x_1)^2 + (y_2 - y_1)^2}$.

Length of side AB

$= \sqrt{(6 - 2)^2 + (1 - 3)^2}$

$= \sqrt{16 + 4}$

$= \sqrt{20}$ units

Length of side BC

$= \sqrt{(5 - 6)^2 + (4 - 1)^2}$

$= \sqrt{1 + 9}$

$= \sqrt{10}$ units

Length of side AC

$= \sqrt{(5 - 2)^2 + (4 - 3)^2}$

$= \sqrt{9 + 1}$

$= \sqrt{10}$ units

Since the length of side BC is equal to the length of side AC, triangle ABC is isosceles. It is important to note that if all three sides of triangle ABC were the same length, triangle ABC would be an equilateral triangle.

Example

Verify that triangle DEF with vertices $D(3, 5)$, $E(5, 2)$, and $F(8, 4)$ is a right triangle.

To verify that triangle DEF is a right triangle, you need to show that either $\angle D$, $\angle E$, or $\angle F$ is a right angle. One approach is to determine the slope of each side of triangle DEF and then show that one side of the triangle is perpendicular to another side of the triangle. Remember that if two sides of a triangle are perpendicular to one another, then their respective slopes are negative reciprocals of each other $(m_1 \times m_2 = -1)$.

Find the slope of each side of triangle DEF by applying the slope formula, $m = \dfrac{y_2 - y_1}{x_2 - x_1}$.

Slope of DE:

$$m = \frac{2-5}{5-3}$$

$$m = \frac{-3}{2}$$

Slope of DF:

$$m = \frac{4-5}{8-3}$$

$$m = \frac{-1}{5}$$

Slope of EF:

$$m = \frac{4-2}{8-5}$$

$$m = \frac{2}{3}$$

Observe that the slope of side DE is the negative reciprocal of the slope of side EF.

$$\left(\frac{3}{-2} \times \frac{2}{3} = \frac{6}{-6} = -1\right)$$

Therefore, side DE is perpendicular to side EF.

It follows that $\angle E = 90°$.

Thus, triangle DEF is a right triangle.

Practice

30. If points $P(2, 4)$, $Q(6, 1)$, and $R(-1, 0)$ are the vertices of a triangle, then the triangle is

A. a scalene triangle

B. a right angle triangle

C. an equilateral triangle

D. a right angle isosceles triangle

Use the following information to answer the next question.

Points $J(-1, 3)$, $K(3, -2)$, and L $(5, 1)$ are plotted on the grid shown. Point N lies on the y-axis such that line LN is perpendicular to line JK.

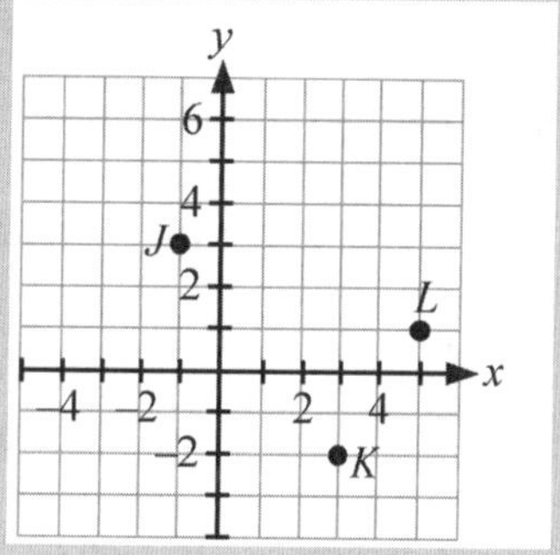

31. What are the coordinates of point N?

A. $(0, 3)$ **B.** $(0, -3)$

C. $\left(0, \frac{15}{4}\right)$ **D.** $\left(0, \frac{29}{4}\right)$

CHALLENGER QUESTION

Numerical Response

32. The graph of a particular line passes through the ordered pairs (3, 7) and (5, 15). The graph of a line that is perpendicular to this line could pass through the ordered pairs $(a, -6)$ and $(-2, -5)$. The value of a is ____.

AG3.3 *plan and implement a multi-step strategy that uses analytic geometry and algebraic techniques to verify a geometric property*

Problem Solving Using Analytical Geometry

Using analytical geometry to solve problems often requires a multi-step approach. These steps include sketching the given information, using appropriate formulas, and clearly stating the solution to the given problem.

Example

Given ΔABC with vertices $A(2, 5)$, $B(-4, -1)$, and $C(1, -1)$, verify that segment DE, formed by connecting the midpoint D of side AB and the midpoint E of side AC, is parallel to and half the length of side BC.

Step 1: Draw a sketch to represent the given information.

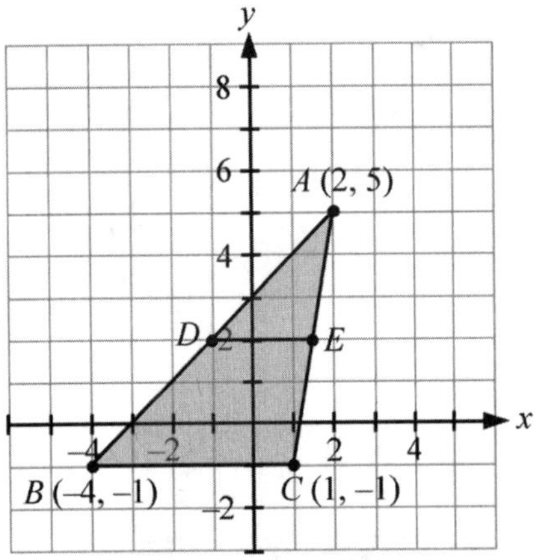

Step 2: Determine the coordinates of each of the midpoints D and E. Recall the midpoint formula:

$$M = \left(\frac{x_1 + x_2}{2}, \frac{y_1 + y_2}{2}\right)$$

$$D = M_{AB} = \left(\frac{2 + (-4)}{2}, \frac{5 + (-1)}{2}\right)$$

$$D = \left(\frac{-2}{2}, \frac{4}{2}\right) = (-1, 2)$$

$$E = M_{AC} = \left(\frac{2 + 1}{2}, \frac{5 + (-1)}{2}\right)$$

$$B = \left(\frac{3}{2}, \frac{4}{2}\right)$$

$$= \left(\frac{3}{2}, 2\right)$$

Step 3: Determine the slope of each of segments DE and BC. Remember:

$$m = \frac{y_2 - y_1}{x_2 - x_1}$$

$$m_{DE} = \frac{2 - 2}{-1 - \frac{3}{2}}$$

$$= \frac{0}{-\frac{5}{2}}$$

$$= 0$$

$$m_{BC} = \frac{-1 - (-1)}{1 - (-4)}$$

$$= \frac{0}{5}$$

$$= 0$$

$$m_{DE} = m_{BC}$$

$$= 0$$

Step 4: Determine the length of each of segments DE and BC.

Recall $d = \sqrt{(x_2 - x_1)^2 + (y_2 - y_1)^2}$.

$$d_{DE} = \sqrt{\left(\frac{3}{2} - (-1)\right)^2 + (2 - 2)^2}$$

$$d_{DE} = \sqrt{\left(\frac{5}{2}\right)^2 + 0^2} = \sqrt{\frac{25}{4}} = \frac{5}{2}$$

$$d_{BC} = \sqrt{(1 - (-4))^2 + (-1 - (-1))^2}$$

$$d_{BC} = \sqrt{25} = 5$$

Notice $d_{DE} = \frac{1}{2} d_{BC}$

Since the slope of DE is equal to the slope of BC and the length of DE is one-half the length of BC, it is verified that the segment DE is parallel to and half the length of BC.

Example

The vertices of a parallelogram are $A(-2, 4)$, $B(2, -1)$, $C(-2, -4)$, and $D(-6, 1)$. Verify that the diagonals bisect each other.

Step 1: Draw a sketch to represent the given information.

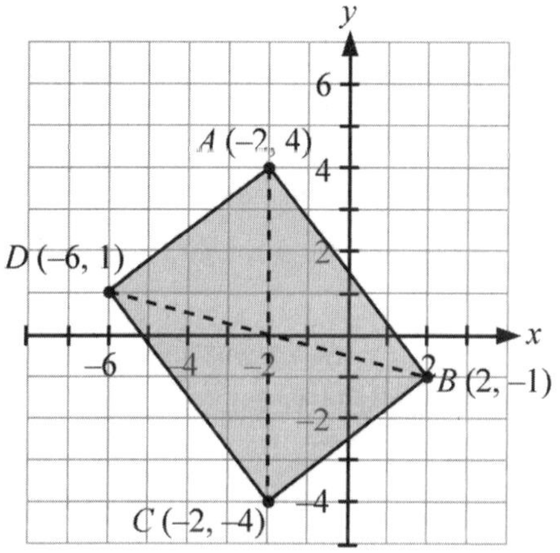

The diagonals of the parallelogram are line segments AC and BD.

If the diagonals bisect each other, then line segments AC and BD will have the same midpoint.

Step 2: Determine the coordinates of the midpoint of AC and the coordinates of the midpoint of BD.

Substitute appropriate values into the midpoint formula.

$$M = \left(\frac{x_1 + x_2}{2}, \frac{y_1 + y_2}{2}\right)$$

$$M_{AC} = \left(\frac{-2 + (-2)}{2}, \frac{4 + (-4)}{2}\right)$$

$$M_{AC} = \left(\frac{-4}{2}, \frac{0}{2}\right)$$

$$= (-2, 0)$$

$$M_{BD} = \left(\frac{2 + (-6)}{2}, \frac{-1 + (-1)}{2}\right)$$

$$M_{BD} = \left(\frac{-4}{2}, \frac{0}{2}\right)$$

$$= (-2, 0)$$

Since line segments AC and BD have the same midpoint, $(-2, 0)$, the diagonals of quadrilateral $ABCD$ bisect each other.

Practice

Use the following information to answer the next question.

Alex is asked to verify that the diagonals of the quadrilateral with vertices $(5, 4)$, $(7, 1)$, $(-4, -2)$, and $(-2, -5)$ are equal in length. He labelled the vertices $A(5, 4)$, $B(7, 1)$, $C(-4, -2)$, and $D(-2, -5)$ and made use of the distance formula $d = \sqrt{(x_2 - x_1)^2 + (y_2 - y_1)^2}$. He followed these steps:

Alex's Solution
Step 1 $d_{AC} = d_{BD}$
Step 2 $\sqrt{(5-(-4))^2 + (4-(-2))^2}$ $= \sqrt{(-2-7)^2 + (-5-1)^2}$
Step 3 $\sqrt{(9)^2 + (2)^2} = \sqrt{(-9)^2 + (-2)^2}$
Step 4 $\sqrt{85} = \sqrt{93}$

33. In which step was Alex's first error?

A. Step 1 **B.** Step 2

C. Step 3 **D.** Step 4

34. A line segment has endpoints $A(-8, 6)$ and $B(4, 6)$. Krystal is asked to verify that a particular point is on the perpendicular bisector of AB. Which of the following points is a possible point that Krystal could be asked to verify?

A. $(-4, 6)$ **B.** $(14, -4)$

C. $(-2, 14)$ **D.** $(6, -2)$

35. Three points are collinear if they are on the same line. Which of the following methods could **not** be used in order to determine if the points $A(-9,\ -2)$, $B(-6,\ 5)$, and $C(0,\ 19)$ are collinear?

A. Verify that the slope of segment AB is equal to the slope of segment BC.

B. Verify that the slope of segment AC is equal to the slope of segment AB.

C. Verify that the midpoint of line segment AB is equal to the midpoint of line segment BC.

D. Verify that the distance from point A to C is equal to the distance from point A to B plus the distance from point B to C.

Use the following information to answer the next multipart question.

36. In the diagram shown, AD is parallel to BC, and AB is parallel to CD.

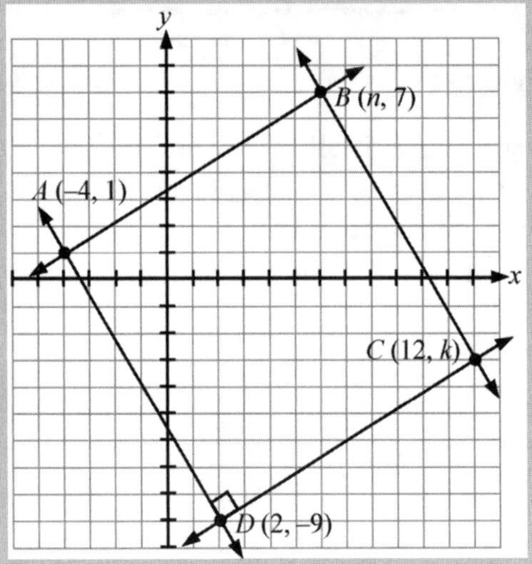

Part A

Open Response

Algebraically, determine the value of k in the diagram.

Show your work.

Part B

Open Response

Determine algebraically the value of n in the diagram.

Show your work.

Part C

Open Response

Verify that quadrilateral *ABCD* is a square.

Show your work.

SOLUTIONS–ANALYTIC GEOMETRY

1. B	**10. D**	**18. 20.6**	**27.** Part A- **OR**	**34. C**
2. D	**11.** Part A- **OR**	**19. A**	Part B- **OR**	**35. C**
3. B	Part B- **OR**	**20. C**	Part C- **OR**	**36.** Part A- **OR**
4. B	**12. A**	**21. B**	**28. B**	Part B- **OR**
5. A	**13. D**	**22. C**	**29. D**	Part C- **OR**
6. 15	**14. C**	**23. 4.2**	**30. D**	
7. B	**15. D**	**24. C**	**31. B**	
8. C	**16. C**	**25. B**	**32. 2**	
9. D	**17. A**	**26. A**	**33. A**	

1. B

In $Ax + By = 29$, substitute 2 for x and -5 for y.
This gives $2A - 5B = 29$.
Then substitute -5 for x and -2 for y.
This gives $-5A - 2B = 29$.
Now, solve as a system.

(1) $2A - 5B = 29$

(2) $-5A - 2B = 29$

Subtract the equations.

$$\begin{aligned} (1)\times 2 \quad 4A - 10B &= 58 \\ \underline{(2)\times 5 \quad -25A - 10B} &\underline{= 145} \\ 29A &= -87 \\ A &= -3 \end{aligned}$$

2. D

A vertical line can intersect other lines, thus, producing a solution to a system of equation.

3. B

If the lines are parallel, they must have the same slope.
For $-9x + 6y = 10$:
Add $9x$ to both sides.
$6y = 9x + 10$
Divide both sides by 6.
$y = \frac{9x}{6} + \frac{10}{6}$
Reduce fractions.
$y = \frac{3}{2}x + \frac{5}{3}$
For $Ax - 8y = 15$:
Subtract Ax from both sides.
$-8y = -Ax + 15$
Divide both sides by -8.
$y = \frac{Ax}{8} + \left(-\frac{15}{8}\right)$
Thus, the coefficients of x (the slope) must be equal.
$\frac{3}{2} = \frac{A}{8}$
Cross multiply.
$2A = 24$
Solve for A.
$A = 12$

4. B

Solve the system.
(1) $x + y = 365$
(2) $3x + 2y = 925$
Subtract the equations.
(1) $2x + 2y = 730$(2 × equation(1))
(2) $\underline{3x + 2y = 925}$
$-x = -195$
Solve for x.
$x = 195$
To find y, substitute 195 for x in one of the equations.
$195 + y = 365$
Subtract 195 from both sides.
$y = 170$
Rebecca must replace x with 195 and y with 170 in both equations.

5. A

Solve the system.
(1) $8x + 3y = -41$
(2) $6x - 5y = -9$
Add the equations, and solve for x.
$[(1) \times 5]\ 40x + 15y = -205$
$\underline{[(2) \times 3]\ 18x - 15y = -27}$
$58x = -232$
$x = -4$

6. 15

To have an infinite number of solutions, the equations must be equal.
First, $-16x - 20y = 12$ becomes $4x + 5y = -3$ by dividing both sides by -4.
For $12x + Ky = -9$, divide both sides by 3 to give $4x + \frac{K}{3}y = -3$.
Now, you have the same coefficients for x, and the constant terms are equal. You must also have the coefficients of y equal.
Thus, $\frac{K}{3} = 5$
Multiply both sides by 3.
$K = 15$

7. B

It is given that a represents the number of adult tickets sold and b represents the number of student tickets sold. It follows that $7a + 5b = 880$ is the equation showing income from sales and $b = 3a$ is the equation showing the number of student tickets as three times the number of adult tickets.

8. C

Steve has a better deal for the first 12 visits.
Both cost the same at 13 visits. The fitness gym that Noel uses is most cost-effective after 13 visits; therefore, it is false that Steve's gym would be the most cost-effective.

9. D

Let x = the number of pens purchased
Let y = the number of pencils purchased.
Create a system showing the two cases.
(1) $2x + 8y = 5.20$
(2) $3x + 4y = 5.80$
Multiply equation (2) by 2, then subtract the equations solving for x.
$2x + 8y = 5.20$
$\underline{6x + 8y = 11.60}$
$-4x = -6.40$
$x = 1.60$
Thus, one pen costs \$1.60.

10. D

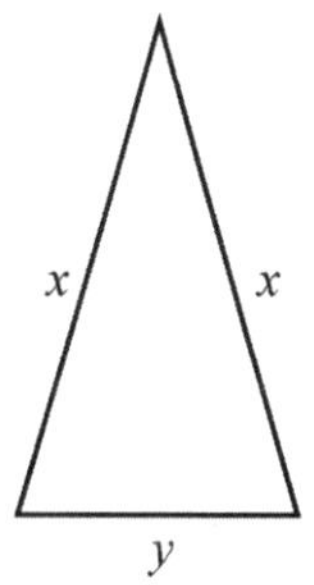

x is the length of each of the two equal sides.
y is the length of the base.
Create a system showing the two cases.
(1) $2x + y = 71$
(2) $y = 2x - 1$
Add 1 and subtract y from both sides.
$1 = 2x - y$
Thus, the system is as shown:
$2x + y = 71$
$2x - y = 1$

11. Part A – Open Response

Substitute \$2 500 for P, 0.042 for r, and 1 for t.
$I = Prt$
$I = \$2\,500 \times 0.042 \times 1$
$I = \$105$
Ken will earn \$105 in interest at the end of the first year of his investment.

Part B – Open Response

Let x = the amount of money Ken invested at 4%.

Let y = the amount of money Ken invested at 3.5%.

Change percentages to decimals.

4% = 0.04 and 3.5% = 0.035

(1) $x + y = 6\ 000$

(2) $0.04x = 30 + 0.035y$

Equation (2) can be rewritten as $40x = 30\ 000 + 35y$ when each term is multiplied by 1 000. Next, subtract 35 from both sides to get equation (2) as $40x - 35y = 30\ 000$.

Equation (1) and (2) can be solved by using the method of elimination as shown:

$$\begin{array}{lr} 35 \times (1) & 35x + 35y = 210\ 000 \\ (2) & \underline{40x - 35y = 30\ 000} \\ 35 \times (1) + (2) & 75x = 240\ 000 \\ & x = 3\ 200 \end{array}$$

The value of y can be determined by substituting 3 200 for x in equation (1) as follows:

$$x + y = 6\ 000$$
$$3\ 200 + y = 6\ 000$$
$$y = 2\ 800$$

Ken invested \$3 200 at 4% and \$2 800 at 3.5%.

12. A

A is the point $(-4, -1)$.

B is the point $(6, 5)$.

Use the midpoint formula.

$$M_{AB} = \left(\frac{x_1 + x_2}{2}, \frac{y_1 + y_2}{2}\right)$$

$$M_{AB} = \left(\frac{-4 + 6}{2}, \frac{-1 + 5}{2}\right)$$

$$M_{AB} = (1, 2)$$

The midpoint of line segment AB is $(1, 2)$.

13. D

Let (x, y) be the other endpoint.

Using the midpoint formula:

$$\frac{6 + x}{2} = 2 \qquad \frac{5 + y}{2} = -3$$

Multiply both sides of each equation by 2.

$$6 + x = 4 \qquad 5 + y = -6$$

Solve for x. Solve for y.

$$x = -2 \qquad y = -11$$

The other endpoint is $(-2, -11)$.

14. C

The point $(-1, 2)$ is the midpoint of the line segment with endpoints that are $(a, -4)$ and $(-7, b)$.

The values of a and b are

$$(-1, 2) = \left(\frac{a + (-7)}{2}, \frac{-4 + b}{2}\right)$$

$$\therefore -1 = a + \frac{-7}{2}, \qquad 2 = \frac{-4 + b}{2}$$

$$a + (-7) = -2, \qquad 4 = -4 + b$$

$$a - 7 = -2, \qquad b = 4 + 4$$

$$a = 7 - 2 = 5, \qquad b = 8$$

Hence, the values of a and b are 5 and 8, respectively.

15. D

The length of line segment AB can be calculated using the distance formula.

$$d = \sqrt{(x_2 - x_1)^2 + (y_2 - y_1)^2}$$

Use $A(0, 5)$ as point 1 and $B(-3, 1)$ as point 2.

$$d(\overline{AB}) = \sqrt{(-3 - 0)^2 + (1 - 5)^2}$$

$$AB = \sqrt{9 + 16} = \sqrt{25}$$

$$AB = 5$$

The length of line segment AB is 5 units.

16. C

Using the distance formula:

$$d = \sqrt{(1 - a)^2 + (1 - (-3))^2}$$

$$5 = \sqrt{(1 - a)^2 + 4^2}$$

$$5 = \sqrt{(1 - a)^2 + 16}$$

Square both sides.

$$25 = (1 - a)^2 + 16$$

Subtract 16 from both sides.

$$9 = (1 - a)^2$$

Take the square root of both sides.

$$\pm 3 = 1 - a$$

$$3 = 1 - a \quad \text{or} \quad -3 = 1 - a$$

$$2 = -a \qquad -4 = -a$$

Solve for a in both cases.

$-2 = a$, or $4 = a$

Since distance must be a positive value, one possible solution for a is 4.

17. A

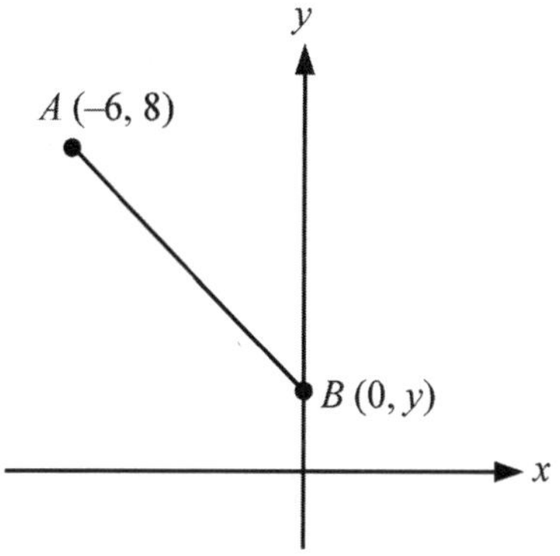

Using the distance formula:

$d_{AB} = \sqrt{(-6-0)^2 + (8-y)^2}$

$10 = \sqrt{(-6)^2 + (8-y)^2}$ (Note: d_{AB} is 10 as given)

$10 = \sqrt{36 + (8-y)^2}$

Square both sides.

$100 = 36 + (8-y)^2$

Subtract 36 from both sides.

$64 = (8-y)^2$

Take the square root of both sides.

$\pm 8 = 8 - y$

Solve for y in both cases.

$8 = 8 - y \qquad -8 = 8 - y$

$0 = -y \quad \text{or} \quad -16 = -y$

$0 = y \qquad 16 = y$

Point B could be (0, 0) or (0, 16) using the two possible solutions for y.

18. 20.6

Perimeter of triangle $ABC = \overline{AB} + \overline{AC} + \overline{BC}$

Use the distance formula.

$d = \sqrt{(x_2 - x_1)^2 + (y_2 - y_1)^2}$

$d(\overline{AB}) = \sqrt{(5-3)^2 + (-2-1)^2}$

$= \sqrt{4+9}$

$= \sqrt{13}$

$d(\overline{AC}) = \sqrt{(-3-3)^2 + (-5-1)^2}$

$= \sqrt{36+36} = \sqrt{72}$

$d(\overline{BC}) = \sqrt{(-3-5)^2 + (-5+2)^2}$

$= \sqrt{64+9} = \sqrt{73}$

The perimeter of triangle ABC

$= d(\overline{AB}) + d(\overline{AC}) + d(\overline{BC})$

$= \sqrt{13} + \sqrt{72} + \sqrt{73}$

$= 20.6$ units

19. A

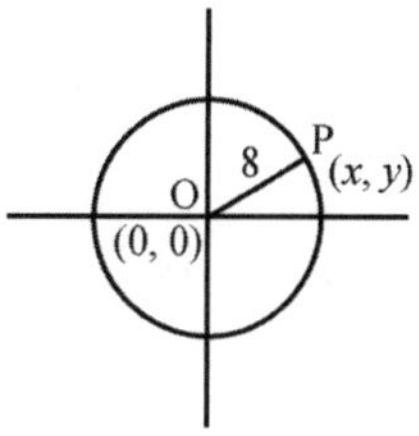

Let any point on the circumference of the circle be $P(x, y)$.

The radius of the circle is OP.

$\Rightarrow (OP) = 8$ units

$\Rightarrow \sqrt{(x-0)^2 + (y-0)^2} = 8$

$\Rightarrow x^2 + y^2 = 64$

The circle that has a radius of 8 units with its centre located at the origin has an equation of $x^2 + y^2 = 64$.

20. C

Recall that the radius of a circle is $\frac{1}{2}$ the diameter. Use the distance formula to determine the diameter of this circle.

$d = \sqrt{(x_2 - x_1)^2 + (y_2 - y_1)^2} = \sqrt{(a-c)^2 + (b-d)^2}$

Therefore, the radius will be $= \dfrac{\sqrt{(a-c)^2 + (b-d)^2}}{2}$

Recall that $x^2 + y^2 = r^2$ is the equation of a circle with its centre at (0, 0). Substitute the expression for the radius into this equation.

Thus, $x^2 + y^2 = \left(\dfrac{\sqrt{(a-c)^2 + (b-d)^2}}{2}\right)^2$

$x^2 + y^2 = \dfrac{(a-c)^2 + (b-d)^2}{4}$

Therefore, the equation of this circle could be

$x^2 + y^2 = \dfrac{(a-c)^2 + (b-d)^2}{4}$.

21. B

In the diagram, the radius of the circle is 6 units, and the centre of the circle is at (0, 0). In order to write the equation of the circle, substitute 6 for r in the equation $x^2 + y^2 = r^2$.

$x^2 + y^2 = (6)^2$

$x^2 + y^2 = 36$

Thus, the equation that defines the circle with centre (0, 0) and a radius of 6 units is $x^2 + y^2 = 36$.

22. C

The minimum length of the required border can be found by determining the circumference of the circle. Recall that circumference (C) is equal to $2\pi r$. To solve, you need to know the value of the radius of the flower bed. Since the equation $x^2 + y^2 = r^2$ represents a circle with centre (0, 0) and radius r, it follows that for the equation $x^2 + y^2 = 2.89$:

$r^2 = 2.89$

$r = \sqrt{2.89} = 1.7$ m

Now, substitute 1.7 for r in the circumference equation.

$C = 2\pi r$

$C = 2\pi(1.7)$

$C = 10.7$ m

Therefore, the minimum length of the required border material, to the nearest tenth, is 10.7 m.

23. 4.2

Since the equation $x^2 + y^2 = r^2$ represents a circle with centre (0,0) and radius r, it follows that:

$r^2 = 18$

$r = \sqrt{18} = 4.2$

Thus, the radius of the circle $x^2 + y^2 = 18$ is 4.2 units.

24. C

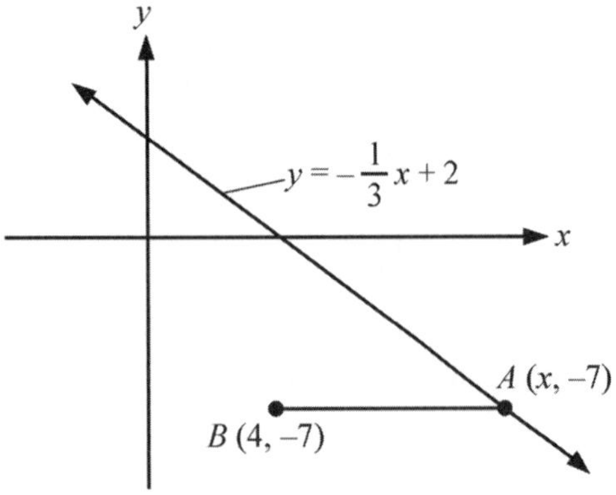

To be horizontal, A must be $(x, -7)$. It has the same y-coordinate as the given point $B(4, -7)$. Thus, for the line $y = -\frac{1}{3}x + 2$, $y = -7$.

This gives $-7 = -\frac{1}{3} + 2$.

Subtract 2 from both sides.

$-9 = -\frac{1}{3}x$

Multiply both sides by -3.

$27 = x$

Since AB is a horizontal line segment, the distance can be found by taking the absolute value of the difference of the x-coordinates.

$d = |27 - 4|$

$d = 23$

Thus, the horizontal distance is 23 units.

Note: You could also find the distance using the distance formula.

25. B

First, find all the midpoints.

$M_{AB} = \left(\frac{-3+1}{2}, \frac{-4+4}{2}\right) = (-1, 0)$

$M_{AC} = \left(\frac{-3+3}{2}, \frac{-4+0}{2}\right) = (0, -2)$

$M_{BC} = \left(\frac{1+3}{2}, \frac{4+0}{2}\right) = (2, 2)$

Let these midpoints be $P(-1, 0)$, $Q(0, -2)$, and $R(2, 2)$. Now, find the distances of PQ, PR, and QR.

$d_{PQ} = \sqrt{(-1-0)^2 + (0-(-2))^2}$

$d_{PQ} = \sqrt{(-1)^2 + 2^2}$

$d_{PQ} = \sqrt{5}$

$d_{PQ} = 2.24$

$d_{PR} = \sqrt{(-1-2)^2 + (0-2)^2}$

$d_{PR} = \sqrt{(-3)^2 + (-2)^2}$

$d_{PR} = \sqrt{13}$

$d_{PR} = 3.61$

$d_{QR} = \sqrt{(0-2)^2 + (-2-2)^2}$

$d_{QR} = \sqrt{(-2)^2 + (-4)^2}$

$d_{QR} = \sqrt{20}$

$d_{QR} = 4.47$

Thus, the perimeter is $2.24 + 3.61 + 4.47 = 10.32$ or 10.3 units.

26. A

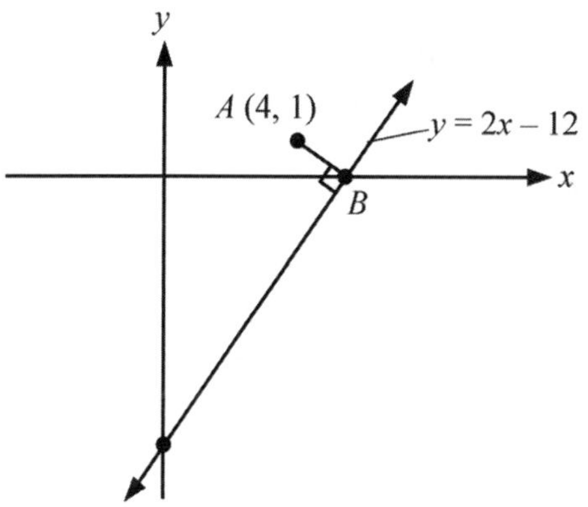

For $y = 2x - 12$, the slope m is 2 (coefficient of x).

Thus, the slope of AB (as shown in the diagram) is $-\frac{1}{2}$.

It is the negative reciprocal of 2.

The equation for AB can be determined using the point slope formula.

$y = m(x - x_1) + y_1$

$y = -\frac{1}{2}(x - 4) + 1$

$y = -\frac{1}{2}x + 2 + 1$

$y = -\frac{1}{2}x + 3$

The intersection point B can be found by solving the system involving the two equations.

$y = 2x - 12$

$y = -\frac{1}{2}x + 3$

Substitute.

$-\frac{1}{2}x + 3 = 2x - 12$

Multiply both sides by 2.

$-x + 6 = 4x - 24$

$6 = 5x - 24$

$30 = 5x$

$6 = x$

Substitute $x = 6$ into $y = 2x - 12$ to solve for y.

$y = 2(6) - 12$

$y = 0$

Thus, point B (from the diagram) is (6, 0).

Use the distance formula to find the distance form A to B.

$d_{AB} = \sqrt{(4-6)^2 + (1-0)^2}$

$d_{AB} = \sqrt{(-2)^2 + 1^2}$

$d_{AB} = \sqrt{5}$

$d_{AB} = 2.24$

27. Part A – Open Response

The centre of the circle can be found by determining the midpoint of the diameter as shown:

$m = \left(\frac{x_1 + x_2}{2}, \frac{y_1 + y_2}{2}\right)$

$m_{AB} = \left(\frac{-2+4}{2}, \frac{3+11}{2}\right)$

$m_{AB} = (1, 7)$

The coordinates of the centre of the circle are $(1, 7)$.

Part B – Open Response

The radius is half the length of the diameter. The length of the diameter can be determined by applying the distance formula as shown:

$d = \sqrt{(x_2 - x_1)^2 + (y_2 - y_1)^2}$

$d_{AB} = \sqrt{(4-(-2))^2 + (11-3)^2}$

$d_{AB} = \sqrt{(6)^2 + (8)^2}$

$d_{AB} = \sqrt{36 + 64}$

$d_{AB} = \sqrt{100}$

$d_{AB} = 10$

Since the diameter is 10 units in length, the radius is 5 units in length.

Part C – Open Response

If the point $P(-3, 10)$ is on the circle, then the distance from the centre, C, of the circle to this point must be 5 units in length. Verify this by applying the distance formula as shown:

$d = \sqrt{(x_2 - x_1)^2 + (y_2 - y_1)^2}$

Recall the centre of the circle is at (1,7).

$d_{CP} = \sqrt{(-3-1)^2 + (10-7)^2}$

$d_{CP} = \sqrt{(-4)^2 + (3)^2}$

$d_{CP} = \sqrt{16 + 9}$

$d_{CP} = \sqrt{25}$

$d_{CP} = 5$

Since CP is 5 units in length, point P must be on the circle.

28. B

A line segment that bisects any side of a triangle and makes a right angle at the midpoint is known as the perpendicular bisector of that side of the triangle. Thus, line segment PT is the perpendicular bisector of side QR.

29. D

A quadrilateral in which all four sides (both sets of opposite sides) are equal in length and opposite sides are parallel and adjacent sides are perpendicular is called a square, as shown in the figure. Only in a square will the diagonals bisect each other at 90°

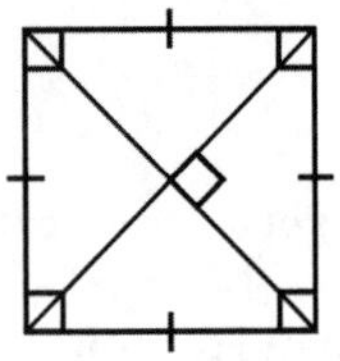

30. D

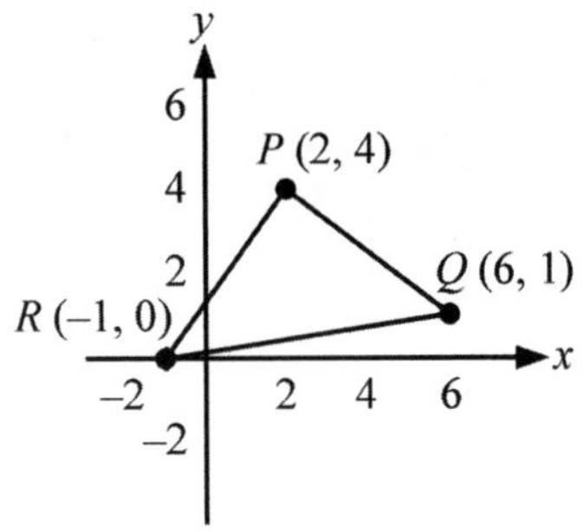

First, check the slopes of all three sides.

m of $PQ = \dfrac{4-1}{2-6} = \dfrac{3}{-4}$

m of $PR = \dfrac{4-0}{2-(-1)} = \dfrac{4}{3}$

m of $RQ = \dfrac{0-1}{-1-6} = \dfrac{-1}{-7} = \dfrac{1}{7}$

The slopes of PQ and PR are negative reciprocals.
Thus, there is a right angle at P since PQ and PR are perpendicular.
Also, check the length (distance) of each side.

$d_{PQ} = \sqrt{(2-6)^2 + (4-1)^2}$

$d_{PQ} = \sqrt{(-4)^2 + 3^2}$

$d_{PQ} = \sqrt{25}$

$d_{PQ} = 5$

$d_{PR} = \sqrt{(2-(-1))^2 + (4-0)^2}$

$d_{PR} = \sqrt{3^2 + 4^2}$

$d_{PR} = \sqrt{25}$

$d_{PR} = 5$

$d_{RQ} = \sqrt{(6-(-1))^2 + (1-0)^2}$

$d_{RQ} = \sqrt{7^2 + 1^2}$

$d_{RQ} = \sqrt{50}$

The triangle is also isosceles since $PQ = PR$.
The triangle is a right angle isosceles triangle.

31. B

First, find the slope of JK.

$m = \dfrac{-2-3}{3-(-1)} = -\dfrac{5}{4}$

Thus, the slope of LN must be $\dfrac{4}{5}$, which is the negative reciprocal of $-\dfrac{5}{4}$.

Let N be the point $(0, y)$ since N is on the y-axis.
The slope of LN is

$m = \dfrac{y-1}{0-5} = \dfrac{y-1}{-5}$

This must equal the actual slope of $\dfrac{4}{5}$.

Thus,

$\dfrac{y-1}{-5} = \dfrac{4}{5}$

$5y - 5 = -20$

$5y = -15$

$y = -3$

The coordinates of point N are $(0, -3)$.

32. 2

Begin by finding the slope of the given line segment.

$$m = \frac{y_2 - y_1}{x_2 - x_1}$$

$$m = \frac{15 - 7}{5 - 3}$$

$$m = \frac{8}{2} = 4$$

Since the lines are perpendicular to one another, their respective slopes are negative reciprocals of each other $(m_1 \times m_2 = -1)$.

Therefore, the slope of the line perpendicular to the line that passes through the given points is $-\frac{1}{4}$.

Use the slope formula again for the perpendicular line.

$$m = \frac{y_2 - y_1}{x_2 - x_1}$$

$$m = \frac{-5 - (-6)}{-2 - a}$$

$$m = \frac{-5 + 6}{-2 - a} = \frac{1}{-2 - a}$$

Since the slope is $-\frac{1}{4}$,

$$\frac{1}{-2 - a} = -\frac{1}{4}$$

$$4 = -(-2 - a)$$

$$4 = 2 + a$$

$$2 = a$$

The value of a is 2.

33. A

The first error occurs in step 1 because the student is asked to verify that the *diagonals* of the quadrilateral are equal in length. Alex's solution is attempting to verify that the opposite sides of the quadrilateral are equal in length. As shown in the sketch, the diagonals are line segments AD and BC and not AC and BD.

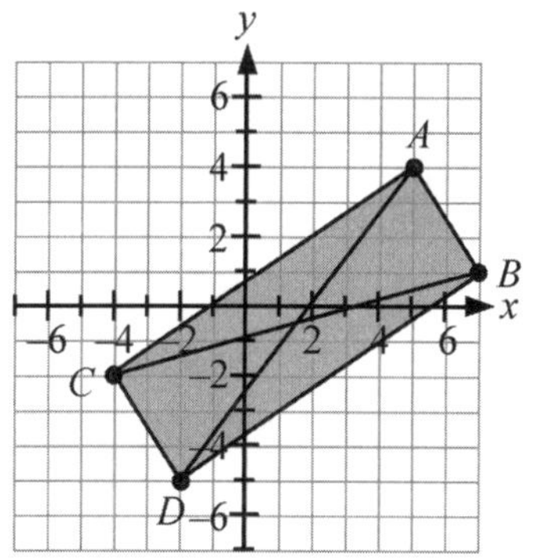

34. C

Begin by determining the midpoint of line segment AB since the perpendicular bisector will pass through this point.

$$M_{AB} = \left(\frac{x_1 + x_2}{2}, \frac{y_1 + y_2}{2}\right) = \left(\frac{-8 + 4}{2}, \frac{6 + 6}{2}\right)$$

$$= \left(\frac{-4}{2}, \frac{12}{2}\right) = (-2, 6)$$

The perpendicular bisector must be a vertical line passing through the point $(-2, 6)$. All points on the vertical line will be equidistant from either endpoint. Therefore, the x-coordinate of any ordered pair on the perpendicular bisector must have a value of -2.

The sketch shown below illustrates the preceding statements.

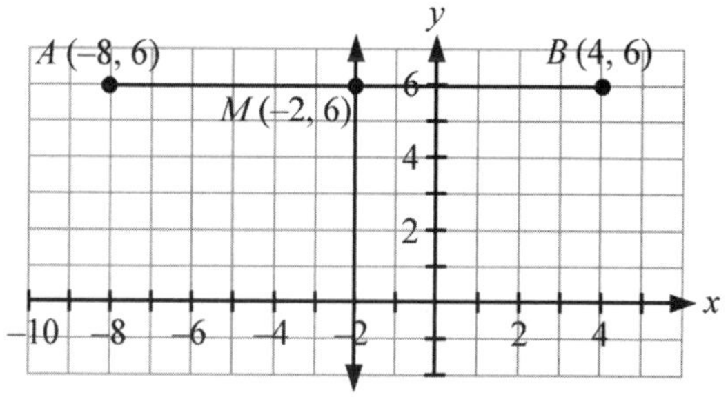

On the graph, the only possible point that can be verified algebraically will be the point $(-2, 14)$, since it will also be on the line $x = -2$, which is the perpendicular bisector of segment AB.

An alternate method is to verify algebraically by applying the distance formula.

The ordered pair $P(x, y)$ must be equidistant from either endpoint of line segment AB.

Thus,

$$d_{PA} = d_{PB}$$

$$\sqrt{(x - (-8))^2 + (y - 6)^2} = \sqrt{(x - 4)^2 + (y - 6)^2}$$

From the given ordered pairs, the only point that satisfies this equation is the point $(-2, 14)$.

35. C

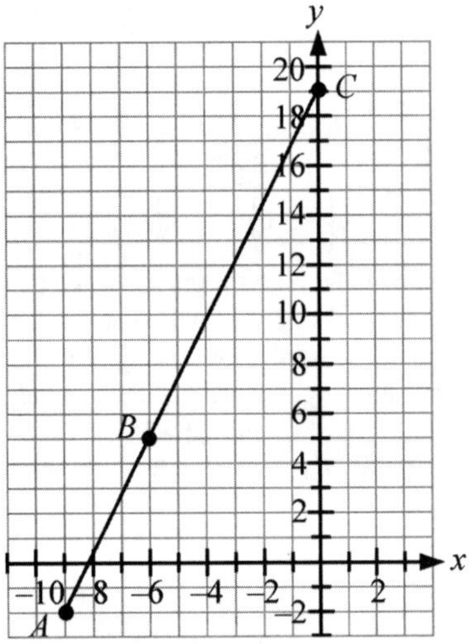

If points A, B, and C on a line are collinear, then:

- the slope of segment AB is equal to the slope of segment BC
- the distance from point A to C is equal to the distance from point A to B plus the distance from point B to C
- the slope of segment AC is equal to the slope of segment AB

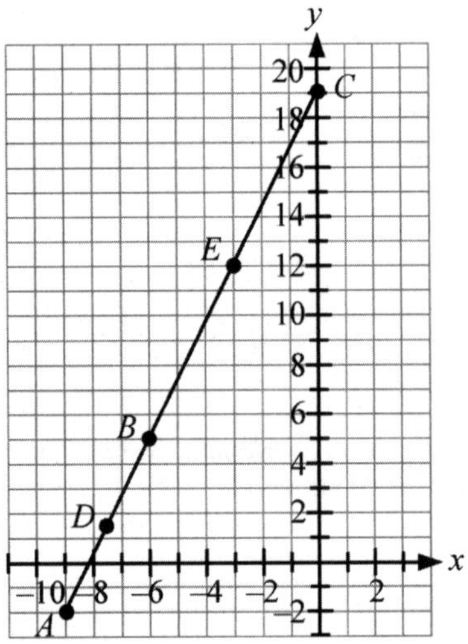

From the diagram, you can see that the midpoint of line segment AB (D) is not equal to the midpoint of line segment BC (E).

36. Part A – Open Response

AD is perpendicular to DC given that $\angle ADC = 90°$. The value of k can be determining by making use of the slope formula, $m = \frac{y_2 - y_1}{x_2 - x_1}$.

Slope of $AD = \frac{-9-1}{2-(-4)}$

$= \frac{-10}{6}$

$= \frac{-5}{3}$

Slope of $DC = \frac{k-(-9)}{12-2}$

$= \frac{k+9}{10}$

Since $AD \perp DC$,

$\frac{3}{5} = \frac{k+9}{10}$ (The negative reciprocal of $\frac{-5}{3}$ is $\frac{3}{5}$.)

Cross multiply.

$5k + 45 = 30$

$5k = -15$

$k = -3$

The value of k is -3.

Part B – Open Response

The value of n can be found given that AD is parallel to BC and by making use of the slope formula.

Slope of $AD = -\frac{5}{3}$ as determined above.

Slope of $BC = \frac{7-(-3)}{n-12}$, since $k = -3$.

$= \frac{7+3}{n-12}$

$= \frac{10}{n-12}$

Since AD is parallel to BC, it follows that

$\frac{-5}{3} = \frac{10}{n-12}$

Cross multiply.

$-5n + 60 = 30$

$-5n = -30$

$n = 6$

The value of $n = 6$.

Part C – Open Response

Verify that quadrilateral $ABCD$ is a square by showing that each side of quadrilateral $ABCD$ is equal in length. The length of each side can be determined by using the distance formula.

$d = \sqrt{(x_2 - x_1)^2 + (y_2 - y_1)^2}$

$d_{AB} = \sqrt{(6 - (-4))^2 + (7 - 1)^2}$ Recall $n = 6$.

$d_{AB} = \sqrt{(10)^2 + (6)^2}$

$d_{AB} = \sqrt{100 + 36}$

$d_{AB} = \sqrt{136}$

$d_{BC} = \sqrt{(12 - 6)^2 + (-3 - 7)^2}$ Recall $k = -3$.

$d_{BC} = \sqrt{(6)^2 + (-10)^2}$

$d_{BC} = \sqrt{36 + 100}$

$d_{BC} = \sqrt{136}$

$d_{CD} = \sqrt{(2 - 12)^2 + (-9 - (-3))^2}$

$d_{CD} = \sqrt{(-10)^2 + (-6)^2}$

$d_{CD} = \sqrt{100 + 36}$

$d_{CD} = \sqrt{136}$

$d_{AD} = \sqrt{(2 - (-4))^2 + (-9 - 1)^2}$

$d_{AD} = \sqrt{(6)^2 + (-10)^2}$

$d_{AD} = \sqrt{36 + 100}$

$d_{AD} = \sqrt{136}$

Since $d_{AB} = d_{BC} = d_{CD} = d_{AD}$, quadrilateral $ABCD$ is a square.

NOTES

Unit Test

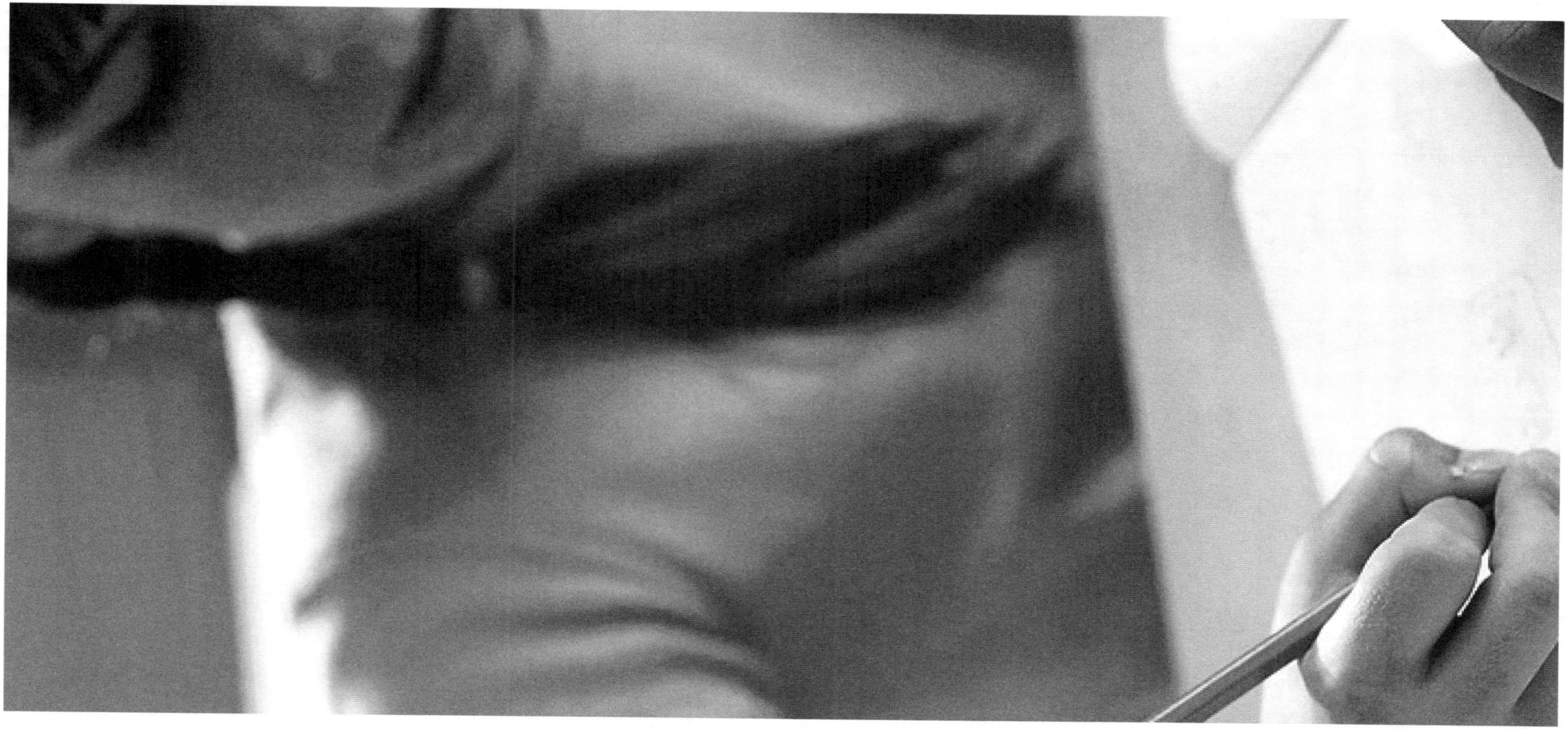

Use the following information to answer the next question.

A System of Linear Equations

$4x + 2y = 20$

$x - 3y = 12$

1. The value of x in the solution to the system is

A. -6 **B.** -2

C. 6 **D.** 18

Use the following information to answer the next question.

A System of Linear Equations

$-3x - 4y = -2$

$5x + 6y = 4$

2. The system of linear equations shown can be solved using the elimination method. To eliminate y by addition, the first equation is multiplied by 3. By what value must the second equation be multiplied?

A. -4 **B.** -2

C. 2 **D.** 4

3. The value of y in the solution to the system of linear equations $x + y = 1$ and $5x - 2y = -16$ is

A. 3 **B.** -2

C. -3 **D.** -7

4. The solution to the system of linear equations $x - \frac{1}{3}y = 2$ and $3x + 2y - 24 = 0$ is obtained by using the method of substitution. A possible substitution that could be made to solve this system is to replace

A. x with $\frac{y+2}{2}$

B. y with $1 + 2x$

C. y with $1 - 2x$

D. y with $\frac{24 - 3x}{2}$

CHALLENGER QUESTION

Numerical Response

Use the following information to answer the next question.

A System of Linear Equations

$11y = -ax + 4$

$3y = -45x + 13$

5. To the nearest whole number, what is the value of a if the system has no solutions?__

CHALLENGER QUESTION

6. Two numbers have a sum of 80. If the larger number is 10 more than the smaller, then the smaller number is

A. 30 **B.** 35 **C.** 50 **D.** 55

Use the following information to answer the next multipart question.

7. Crates of oranges have a different mass depending on the number of oranges in the crate. A crate contains 18larger oranges, each with a mass of 0.15 kg.

Part A

Open Response

If the crate has a mass of 0.50 kg, what is the total mass of the crate of oranges?

Part B

Open Response

Set up a system of two linear equations involving two variables, and then use this system to solve the following problem.

A crate of 48 smaller oranges has a total mass of 6.75 kg. When 12 oranges are removed, the total mass becomes 5.25 kg. If each orange has the same mass, determine the mass of the crate and the mass of a smaller orange.

Show your work.

8. The sum of the present ages of Samantha and Jocelyn is 22 years. In four years, Samantha will be twice as old as Jocelyn. If x represents the present age of Samantha and y represents the present age of Jocelyn, then the system of linear equations that could be solved in order to determine the present age of each girl is

A. $x + y = 22$ and $x - 2y = 4$

B. $x + y = 22$ and $x = 2(y - 4)$

C. $x + y = 22$ and $x = 2(y + 4)$

D. $x + y = 22$ and $2x - y = -4$

Use the following information to answer the next question.

To make a blend of two teas, a store owner mixed Orange Blossom tea selling at \$6.40 per kilogram with Red Dragon tea selling at \$7.20 per kilogram. The owner sold 10 kg of the blended tea at \$6.72 per kilogram.

9. If x represents the number of kilograms of Orange Blossom tea used and y represents the number of kilograms of Red Dragon tea used, then a system of linear equations that could be solved in order to determine the amount of each type of tea used to make the blended tea is

A. $x + y = 10$
$6.40x + 7.20y = 6.72$

B. $6.40x + 7.20y = 10$
$x + y = 6.72$

C. $x + y = 10$
$6.40x + 7.20y = 67.20$

D. $6.40x + 7.20y = 10$
$6.40x + 7.20y = 67.20$

Use the following information to answer the next question.

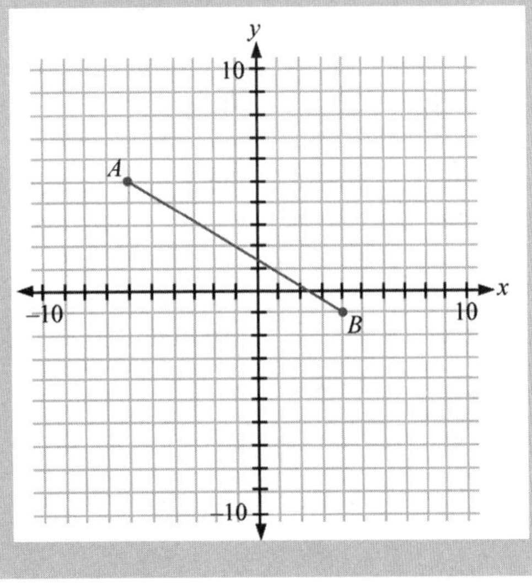

10. The midpoint of line segment AB is

A. $(-1, 2)$ **B.** $(-2, 1)$

C. $(2, 1)$ **D.** $(-1, 1)$

11. The point $M(2, 4)$ is at the midpoint of the line segment, where $A(8, 4)$ and $B(x, y)$. The coordinates of point B are

A. $(-4, 4)$ **B.** $(4, -4)$

C. $(4, 5)$ **D.** $(5, 4)$

Use the following information to answer the next question.

Points $C(4.2, -1.9)$ and $D(-3.6, -6.7)$ are the endpoints of line segment CD.

12. Which of the following expressions represents the length of line segment CD?

A. $\sqrt{(4.2 + 3.6)^2 + ((-1.9) - 6.7)^2}$

B. $\sqrt{(4.2 - (-1.9))^2 + ((-3.6) - (6.7))^2}$

C. $\sqrt{(4.2 - (-6.7))^2 + ((-1.9) - (-3.6))^2}$

D. $\sqrt{(4.2 - (-3.6))^2 + ((-1.9) - (-6.7))^2}$

13. The distance formula can **best** be derived by

A. applying the concept of $\frac{\text{rise}}{\text{run}}$

B. applying the Pythagorean theorem

C. determining how far each of two given points is from the origin

D. placing two given points on a coordinate system and then measuring the distance between the two points with a ruler

CHALLENGER QUESTION

Numerical Response

14. Point A is 10 km west of point B, point C is 30 km north of point B, and point D is 20 km east of point C. What is the distance from A to D?

____

(To the nearest tenth)

15. A circle with a centre of $(0, 0)$ and passing through the point $(3, 4)$ is shown.

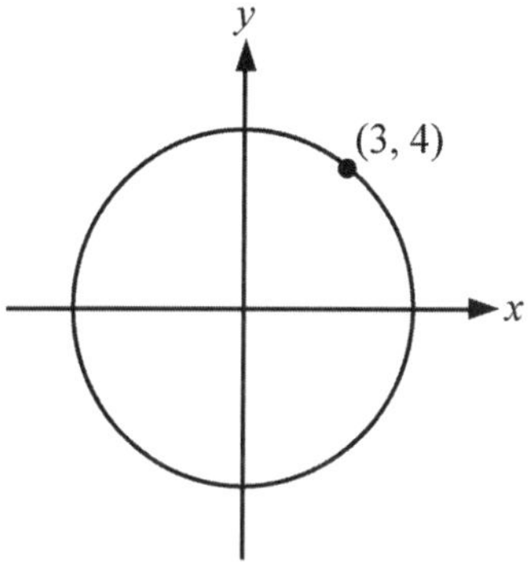

Another point that this circle will pass through is

A. $(-5, 5)$ **B.** $(0, 25)$

C. $(4, -5)$ **D.** $(-4, -3)$

16. Two concentric circles are shown in the diagram.

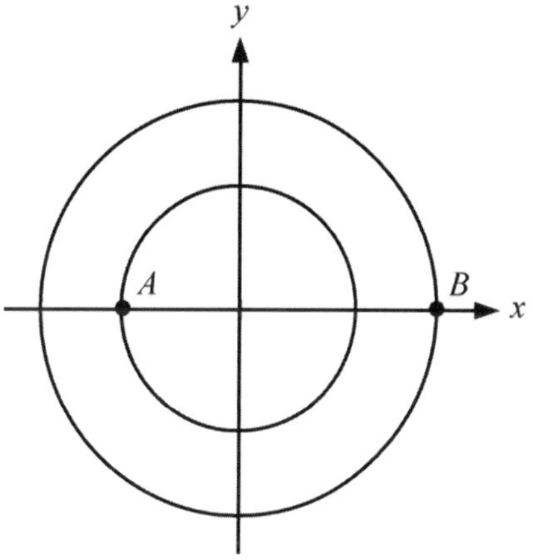

If the smaller circle is defined by the equation $x^2 + y^2 = 9$ and the larger circle is defined by the equation $x^2 + y^2 = 25$, then the distance from point A to point B is

A. 8 units **B.** 11 units

C. 16 units **D.** 34 units

17. A circle has its centre at (0, 0) and a diameter that is 16 units in length. The equation that defines this circle is

A. $x^2 + y^2 = 8$

B. $x^2 + y^2 = 16$

C. $x^2 + y^2 = 64$

D. $x^2 + y^2 = 256$

CHALLENGER QUESTION

Numerical Response

Use the following information to answer the next question.

The diagram illustrates Mrs. Ruby's circular flower bed, sketched on a Cartesian plane.

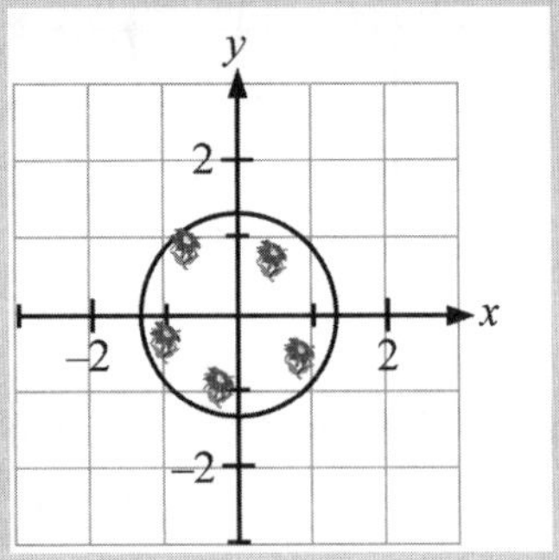

18. The equation that defines the outside edge of Mrs. Ruby's flower bed is $x^2 + y^2 = 1.44$, where the radius is expressed in metres. So the flowers do not become root-bound, the minimum area allocated to each flower is 0.09 m^2. The maximum number of flowers Mrs. Ruby can plant in her flower bed is ____.

19. To the nearest tenth, the vertical distance between the point $(-5, -4)$ and the line $2x + 3y + 15 = 0$ is

A. 1.0 units **B.** 2.3 units

C. 3.3 units **D.** 5.7 units

CHALLENGER QUESTION

20. If a line segment has endpoints at points $C(-5, -4)$ and $D(1, 1)$, then the equation of the perpendicular bisector of the line segment CD will be

A. $y = \frac{-6}{5}x - \frac{39}{10}$

B. $y = \frac{5}{6}x - 4$

C. $y = \frac{-6}{5}x + 4$

D. $y = -\frac{5}{6}x + \frac{1}{6}$

21. Part A

Open Response

To the nearest tenth, determine the shortest distance between point $P(-4, 8)$ and point $Q(-9, -7)$.

Show your work.

Part B

Open Response

To the nearest tenth, determine the shortest distance between point $P(-4, 8)$ and the line defined by the equation $y = 2x + 1$.

Show your work.

Use the following information to answer the next question.

Jody and Brittany are asked to verify that ΔABC with vertices $A(-3, 1)$, $B(-1, 5)$, and $C(5, 2)$ is a right triangle with $\angle ABC = 90°$. Each student's partial solution is shown below.

Jody's Partial Solution

It is given that $\angle ABC = 90°$. In order to verify that ΔABC is a right triangle, it is necessary to verify that segments AB and BC are perpendicular.

Step 1: Slope of

$$AB = \frac{5-1}{-1-(-3)} = \frac{4}{2} = 2$$

Step 2: Slope of $BC = \dfrac{2-5}{5-(-1)} = \dfrac{-3}{6}$

Brittany's Partial Solution

It is given that $\angle ABC = 90°$. In order to verify that ΔABC is a right triangle, it is necessary to show that $(AB)^2 + (BC)^2 = (AC)^2$.

Step 1: $AB = \sqrt{(-1-(-3))^2 + (5-1)^2}$

$AB = \sqrt{(2)^2 + (4)^2}$

$AB = \sqrt{20}$

Step 2: $BC = \sqrt{(5-(-1))^2 + (2-5)^2}$

$BC = \sqrt{(6)^2 + (-3)^2}$

$BC = \sqrt{45}$

Step 3: $AC = \sqrt{(5-(-3))^2 + (2-1)^2}$

22. Which of the following statements is **true** with respect to the partial solution obtained by each of the two students?

A. Both girls have a correct partial solution.

B. Both girls have an incorrect partial solution.

C. Jody has a correct partial solution, and Brittany has an incorrect partial solution.

D. Jody has an incorrect partial solution, and Brittany has a correct partial solution.

CHALLENGER QUESTION

Numerical Response

23. Two of the vertices of ΔABC are $A(6, 5)$ and $B(8, 4)$. If $\angle ABC = 90°$, then vertex C could be the ordered pair $(d, -2)$. The value of d is ____.

24. In which of the following types of quadrilaterals do the diagonals **not** bisect each other?

A. Square

B. Rectangle

C. Trapezoid

D. Parallelogram

25. The points $P(-4, 0)$, $Q(0, \sqrt{48})$, and $R(4, 0)$ are the vertices of triangle PQR. If the length of side PQ is 8 units, then ΔPQR is

A. a scalene triangle

B. an isosceles triangle

C. a right angle triangle

D. an equilateral triangle

26. Which of the following pairs of equations represents a pair of perpendicular lines?

A. $y = x - 4$ and $y = x + \frac{1}{4}$

B. $y = 75x$ and $y = -75x$

C. $y = -3x + 7$ and $y = -\frac{1}{3}x + 4$

D. $y = 4x - 5$ and $y = -\frac{1}{4}x + 5$

27. The vertices of a parallelogram are $A(-4, -2)$, $B(-1, 2)$, $C(8, 6)$, and $D(6, 2)$. Which of the following methods could be used to determine that the diagonals AC and BD bisect each other?

A. Verify that segment AC is perpendicular to segment BD.

B. Verify that segment AC and segment BD have the same midpoint.

C. Verify that the slope of segment AC is equal to the slope of segment BD.

D. Verify that the length of segment AC is equal to the length of segment BD.

Use the following information to answer the next multipart question.

28. The vertices of a quadrilateral are $A(7, 6)$, $B(11, 2)$, $C(3, -6)$, and $D(1, 4)$.

Part A

Open Response

Sketch the quadrilateral on the grid below.

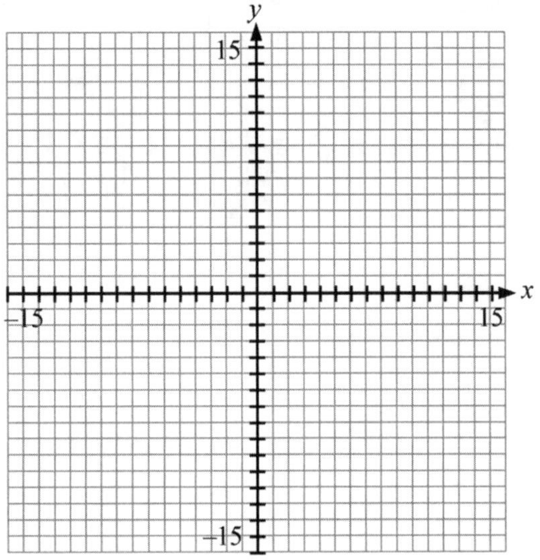

Part B

Open Response

Determine the midpoint of each side of the quadrilateral.

Show your work.

Part C

Open Response

Verify that the quadrilateral formed by joining the four midpoints is a parallelogram.

Show your work.

SOLUTIONS

1. C	Part B- **OR**	14. 42.4	21. Part A- **OR**	27. B
2. C	8. A	15. D	Part B- **OR**	28. Part A- **OR**
3. A	9. C	16. A	22. A	Part B- **OR**
4. D	10. A	17. C	23. 5	Part C- **OR**
5. 165	11. A	18. 50	24. C	
6. B	12. D	19. B	25. D	
7. Part A- **OR**	13. B	20. A	26. D	

1. C

Solve as a system.

(1) $4x + 2y = 20$

(2) $x - 3y = 12$

(1) × 3 $12x + 6y = 60$

(2) × 2 $\underline{2x - 6y = 24}$

$14x = 84$

$x = 6$

2. C

(1) $-3x - 4y = -2$

(2) $5x + 6y = 4$

$[(1) \times 3] - 9x - 12y = -6$

To use addition to eliminate y, the coefficient of y in equation (2) must be 12.

This can be obtained by multiplying equation (2) by 2.

3. A

(1) $x + y = 1$

(2) $3x - 2y = -16$

(1) × 5 $5x + 5y = 5$

(2) $\underline{5x - 2y = -16}$

$7y = 21$

$y = 3$

4. D

$3x + 2y - 24 = 0$

Add 24 and subtract $3x$ from both sides.

$2y = 24 - 3x$

Divide both sides by 2.

$y = \dfrac{24 - 3x}{2}$

Thus, y could be replaced by $\dfrac{24 - 3x}{2}$.

5. 165

In order to have no solution, the lines must be parallel; that is, have the same slope.

For $3y = -45x + 13$:

$y = -15x + \dfrac{13}{3}$ [Divide both sides by 3.]

Here, the slope is -15.

For $11y = -ax + 4$:

$y = \dfrac{-a}{11}x + \dfrac{4}{11}$ [Divide both sides by 11.]

Here, the slope is $\dfrac{-a}{11}$.

Thus, $\dfrac{-a}{11} = -15$

$-a = -165$ [Multiply both sides by 11.]

$a = 165$ [Solve for a.]

6. B

Let x be the larger number.

Let y be the smaller number.

The numbers have a sum of 80.

(1) $x + y = 80$

The larger number is 10 more than the smaller.

(2) $x = y + 10$

Substitute $y + 10$ for x in (1).

$y + 10 + y = 80$

Simplify.

$2y + 10 = 80$

Subtract 10 from both sides.

$2y = 70$

Solve for y.

$y = 35$

Thus, the smaller number is 35.

7. Part A – Open Response

The total mass of the larger oranges is $18 \times 0.15 = 2.7$ kg. Therefore, the total mass of the crate of oranges is $2.7 + 0.50 + 3.2$ kg.

Part B – Open Response

Let x = the mass of the crate.

Let y = the mass of a smaller orange.

Thus, (1) $x + 48y = 6.75$

When 12 oranges are removed, 36 oranges remain.

(2) $x + 36y = 5.25$

Equations (1) and (2) can be solved by using the method of elimination as shown:

$$\begin{array}{ll} (1) & x + 48y = 6.75 \\ (2) & \underline{x + 36y = 5.25} \\ (1)-(2) & 12y = 1.50 \\ & y = 0.125 \end{array}$$

The value of x can be determined by substituting 0.125 for y in either equation (1) or (2). Using equation (1) has the following result:

$$\begin{aligned} x + 48y &= 6.75 \\ x + 48(0.125) &= 6.75 \\ x + 6 &= 6.75 \\ x &= 0.75 \end{aligned}$$

The mass of the crate is 0.75 kg, and the mass of a smaller orange is 0.125 kg.

8. A

1. $x + y = 22$ (the sum of their ages)
   Since $x + 4$ = Samantha's age in 4 years, and $y + 4$ = Jocelyn's age in 4 years:
2. $x + 4 = 2(y + 4)$(Samantha is twice as old as Jocelyn in 4 years)
   $x + 4 = 2y + 8$ [Expand.]
   $x - 2y = 4$ [Subtract 4 and $2y$ from both sides.]

Thus, the system is as shown:

(1) $x + y = 22$

(2) $x - 2y = 4$

9. C

Create the system.

(1) $x + y = 10$ (the total weight of the two blends)

(2) $6.40x + 7.20y = 67.20$ (the total amount of all sales)

10. A

Point A is at $(-6, 5)$.

Point B is at $(4, -1)$.

Use the midpoint formula.

$$M_{AB} = \left(\frac{x_1 + x_2}{2}, \frac{y_1 + y_2}{2}\right)$$

$$M_{AB} = \left(\frac{-6 + 4}{2}, \frac{5 + (-1)}{2}\right)$$

$$M_{AB} = (-1, 2)$$

11. A

Using the midpoint formula:

$\frac{8 + x}{2} = 2$ and $\frac{4 + y}{2} = 4$

Multiply both equations by 2.

$8 + x = 4$ and $4 + y = 8$

Solve for x and y.

$x = -4$ and $y = 4$

Thus, coordinates of point B are $(-4, 4)$.

12. D

Use the distance formula $d = \sqrt{(x_2 - x_1)^2 + (y_2 - y_1)^2}$.

Substitute the values from points C and D into the formula.

$d = \sqrt{(4.2 - (-3.6))^2 + ((-1.9) - (-6.7))^2}$.

13. B

The distance formula is an application of the Pythagorean theorem.

14. 42.4

Set up a coordinate system where point B is represented by the origin.

Then, A is at $(-10, 0)$, C is at $(0, 30)$, and D is at $(20, 30)$.

Find the distance between $(-10, 0)$ and $(20, 30)$.

Recall that the distance between two points (x_1, y_1) and (x_2, y_2) is given by the formula

$d(\overline{AD}) = \sqrt{(x_2 - x_1)^2 + (y_2 - y_1)^2}$.

Use $A(-10, 0)$ as point 1 and $D(20, 30)$ as point 2.

$$\begin{aligned} d(\overline{AD}) &= \sqrt{(20 + 10)^2 + (30 - 0)^2} \\ &= \sqrt{(30)^2 + (30)^2} = \sqrt{900 + 900} \\ &= \sqrt{1\ 800} = 30\sqrt{2} \\ &= 30 \times 1.414 \\ &= 42.4 \end{aligned}$$

The distance between A and D is 42.4 km.

15. D

The distance between the centre $(0, 0)$ and the point $(3, 4)$ is the radius of the circle. Find the length of the radius using the distance formula.

$d = \sqrt{(x_2 - x_1)^2 + (y_2 - y_1)^2}$

$= \sqrt{(3 - 0)^2 + (4 - 0)^2}$

$= \sqrt{9 + 16} = \sqrt{25} = 5$

Since the radius of the circle is 5 units, the distance from the centre to any other point on the circle must also be 5 units.

Determine the distance from the centre to each of the other points provided in each choice.

Choice A: For the point $(-5, 5)$: $= \sqrt{(-5 - 0)^2 + (5 - 0)^2}$
$= \sqrt{25 + 25} = \sqrt{50} = 7.1$

Choice B: For the point $(0, 25)$: $= \sqrt{(0 - 0)^2 + (25 - 0)^2}$
$= \sqrt{0 + 625} = \sqrt{625} = 25$

Choice C: For the point $(4, -5)$: $= \sqrt{(4 - 0)^2 + (-5 - 0)^2}$
$= \sqrt{16 + 25} = \sqrt{41} = 6.4$

Choice D: For the point $(-4, -3)$: $= \sqrt{(-4 - 0)^2 + (-3 - 0)^2}$
$= \sqrt{16 + 9} = \sqrt{25} = 5$

Since the point $(-4, -3)$ is 5 units from the centre, it is another point that this circle will pass through.

16. A

Since the equation $x^2 + y^2 = r^2$ represents a circle with centre of (0,0) and radius r, it follows that:

Smaller circle:

$r^2 = 9$

$r = \sqrt{9} = 3$

Larger circle:

$r^2 = 25$

$r = \sqrt{25} = 5$

Thus, the radius of the circles $x^2 + y^2 = 9$ and $x^2 + y^2 = 25$ are 3 and 5 units, respectively.

Label the diagram as follows:

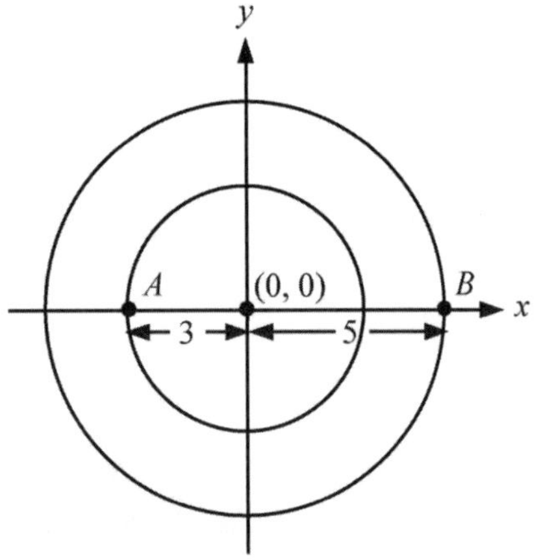

As the diagram shows, the distance from point A to point B can be found by adding the two radii together. Therefore, the distance from point A to point B is 8 units $(3 + 5 = 8)$.

17. C

Since the diameter is twice the length of the radius, the radius of the circle is 8 units. In order to write the equation of the circle, substitute 8 for r in the equation $x^2 + y^2 = r^2$.

$x^2 + y^2 = (8)^2$

$x^2 + y^2 = 64$

Thus, the equation that defines a circle with its centre at (0, 0) and a diameter of 16 units is $x^2 + y^2 = 64$.

18. 50

To determine the maximum number of flowers Mrs. Ruby can plant, first determine the total area of the flower bed. Recall that the area of a circle is $A = \pi r^2$. To solve, find the value of the radius of the flower bed. Since the equation $x^2 + y^2 = r^2$ represents a circle with a centre of $(0, 0)$ and a radius r, it follows that for the equation $x^2 + y^2 = 1.44$:

$r^2 = 1.44$

$r = \sqrt{1.44} = 1.2$ m

Now, substitute 1.2 for r in the area of a circle equation.

$A = \pi r^2$

$A = \pi(1.2)^2$

$A = 1.44\pi$

$A = 4.5 \text{ m}^2$

Since the minimum area allocated to each flower is 0.09 m^2, divide the total area of the flower bed by the minimum area of each flower.

$\frac{4.5 \text{ m}^2}{0.09 \text{ m}^2} = 50$

Therefore, the maximum number of flowers Mrs. Ruby can plant in her flower bed is 50.

19. B

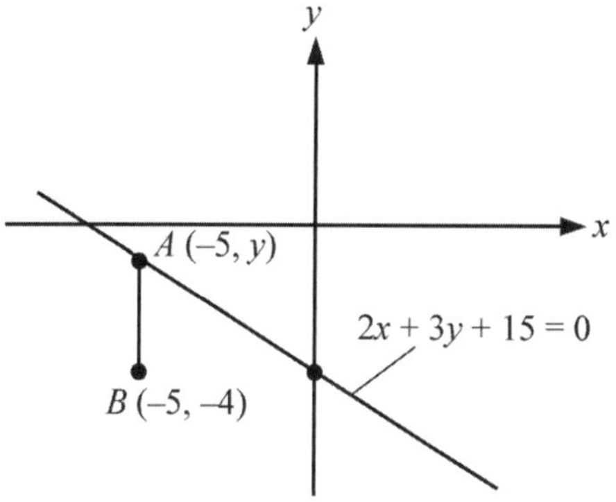

To be vertical, point A must be $(-5, y)$. It has the same x-coordinate as the given point $(-5, -4)$.
Thus, for the line $2x + 3y + 15 = 0$, $x = -5$

$$2(-5) + 3y + 15 = 0$$
$$-10 + 3y + 15 = 0$$
$$3y + 5 = 0$$
$$3y = -5$$
$$y = -\frac{5}{3}$$

Since AB is a vertical line segment, find the distance using the distance formula.

$$d = \sqrt{(x_2 - x_1)^2 + (y_2 - y_1)^2}$$
$$d = \sqrt{(-5-(-5))^2 + \left(-4 - \left(-\frac{5}{3}\right)\right)^2}$$
$$d = \sqrt{(-5+5)^2 + \left(-4 + \frac{5}{3}\right)^2}$$
$$d = \sqrt{(0)^2 + \left(-\frac{7}{3}\right)^2}$$
$$d = \frac{7}{3}$$

The distance is $\frac{7}{3}$ or 2.3 units.

20. A

Using the slope formula, find the slope of CD.

$$m = \frac{-4-1}{-5-1}$$
$$m = \frac{-5}{-6}$$
$$m = \frac{5}{6}$$

The slope of the perpendicular bisector will be $\frac{-6}{5}$, which is the negative reciprocal of $\frac{5}{6}$.

Find the midpoint of CD.

$$M_{CD} = \left(\frac{-5+1}{2}, \frac{-4+1}{2}\right)$$
$$M_{CD} = \left(-2, \frac{-3}{2}\right)$$

The perpendicular bisector of CD has a slope of $\frac{-6}{5}$ and passes through the point $\left(-2, \frac{-3}{2}\right)$.

Using the point-slope form, find the equation of this line.

$$y = m(x - x_1) + y_1$$
$$y = \frac{-6}{5}(x - (-2)) - \frac{3}{2}$$
$$y = -\frac{6}{5}(x + 2) - \frac{3}{2}$$
$$y = -\frac{6}{5}x - \frac{12}{5} - \frac{3}{2}$$

Use a common denominator.

$$y = -\frac{6}{5}x - \frac{24}{10} - \frac{15}{10}$$
$$y = -\frac{6}{5}x - \frac{39}{10}$$

21. Part A – Open Response

The shortest distance from point P to point Q is a line segment and can be determined by applying the distance formula as shown:

$$d = \sqrt{(x_2 - x_1)^2 + (y_2 - y_1)^2}$$
$$d_{PQ} = \sqrt{(-9-(-4))^2 + (-7-8)^2}$$
$$d_{PQ} = \sqrt{(-5)^2 + (-15)^2}$$
$$d_{PQ} = \sqrt{25 + 225}$$
$$d_{PQ} = \sqrt{250}$$
$$d_{PQ} \approx 15.81$$

To the nearest tenth, the distance between point P and point Q is 15.8 units.

Part B – Open Response

The shortest distance from point P to the line $y = 2x + 1$ is the length of the line segment PQ, where point Q is on the line $y = 2x + 1$ and PQ is perpendicular to the line $y = 2x + 1$.

The first step is to determine the equation of PQ. The slope of the line $y = 2x + 1$ is 2 (the coefficient of x).

Therefore, the slope of PQ is $-\frac{1}{2}$ (since PQ is perpendicular to the line $y = 2x + 1$). The equation of line segment PQ can be found by applying the point-slope formula as shown below.

$y = m(x - x_1) + y_1$

Substitute $-\frac{1}{2}$ for m, -4 for x_1, and 8 for y_1.

$y = -\frac{1}{2}(x - (-4)) + 8$

$y = -\frac{1}{2}(x + 4) + 8$

$y = -\frac{1}{2}x - 2 + 8$

$y = -\frac{1}{2}x + 6$

Multiply each term by 2.

$2y = -x + 12$

$2y = -x + 12$

$x + 2y = 12$

The next step is to determine the coordinates of point Q by solving the system of linear equations $y = 2x + 1$ and $x + 2y = 12$. Solve this system of equations by using the method of substitution as follows:

(1) $y = 2x + 1$

(2) $x + 2y = 12$

Substitute $2x + 1$ for y in equation (2).

$x + 2(2x + 1) = 12$

$x + 4x + 2 = 12$

$5x + 2 = 12$

$5x = 10$

$x = 2$

The value of y can be determined by substituting 2 for x in equation (1).

(1) $y = 2x + 1$

$y = 2(2) + 1$

$y = 4 + 1$

$y = 5$

Thus, the coordinates of point Q are $(2, 5)$.

Finally, determine the distance from point P to point Q by using the distance formula as shown:

$d = \sqrt{(x_2 - x_1)^2 + (y_2 - y_1)^2}$

$d_{PQ} = \sqrt{(2 - (-4))^2 + (5 - 8)^2}$

$d_{PQ} = \sqrt{(6)^2 + (-3)^2}$

$d_{PQ} = \sqrt{36 + 9}$

$d_{PQ} = \sqrt{45}$

$d_{PQ} \approx 6.71$

To the nearest tenth, the shortest distance from point P to the line $y = 2x + 1$ is 6.7 units.

22. A

In order to verify that ΔABC is a right triangle using the fact that $\angle ABC = 90°$, there are two main methods.
Method 1:
Verify that segments AB and BC are perpendicular by using the slope formula $m = \frac{y_2 - y_1}{x_2 - x_1}$ to determine the slopes of line segments AB and BC.
Step 1: Determine the slope of
$AB = \frac{5-1}{-1-(-3)} = \frac{4}{2} = 2$
Step 2: Determine the slope of
$BC = \frac{2-5}{5-(-1)} = \frac{-3}{6} = -\frac{1}{2}$
Note that $2 \times -\frac{1}{2} = -1$. Since $m_1 \times m_2 = -1$, line segments AB and BC are perpendicular.
Method 2:
Verify the Pythagorean theorem for this triangle, such that $(AB)^2 + (BC)^2 = (AC)^2$.
Use the distance formula $d = \sqrt{(x_2 - x_1)^2 + (y_2 - y_1)^2}$ to determine the distance of each of the line segments.
Step 1: $AB = \sqrt{(-1-(-3))^2 + (5-1)^2}$
$AB = \sqrt{(2)^2 + (4)^2}$
$AB = \sqrt{20}$
Step 2: $BC = \sqrt{(5-(-1))^2 + (2-5)^2}$
$BC = \sqrt{(6)^2 + (-3)^2}$
$BC = \sqrt{45}$
Step 3: $AC = \sqrt{(5-(-3))^2 + (2-1)^2}$
$AC = \sqrt{(8)^2 + (1)^2}$
$AC = \sqrt{65}$
Step 4: Substitute the distance values into $(AB)^2 + (BC)^2 = (AC)^2$.
$(\sqrt{20})^2 + (\sqrt{45})^2 = (\sqrt{65})^2$
$20 + 45 = 65$
$65 = 65$
Since the Pythagorean theorem has been verified for this triangle, it is a right triangle.
Compare the full solutions with the partial student solutions to see that both girls have a correct partial solution.

23. 5

Begin by finding the slope of the given line segment AB.
$m = \frac{y_2 - y_1}{x_2 - x_1}$
$m = \frac{4-5}{8-6} = \frac{-1}{2}$
Since the line segments AB and BC form a 90° or are perpendicular to one another, their respective slopes are negative reciprocals of each other $(m_1 \times m_2 = -1)$.
Therefore, the slope of the line segment perpendicular to the line segment AB is 2.
Use the slope formula again for the perpendicular line segment BC.
$m = \frac{y_2 - y_1}{x_2 - x_1}$
$m = \frac{-2-4}{d-8} = \frac{-6}{d-8}$
Since the slope is 2,
$\frac{-6}{d-8} = 2$
$-6 = 2(d-8)$
$-6 = 2d - 16$
$10 = 2d$
$\frac{10}{2} = d$
$5 = d$
The value of d is 5.

24. C

The diagonals of parallelograms, rectangles, and squares bisect each other. In a trapezoid, they do not bisect each other.

25. D

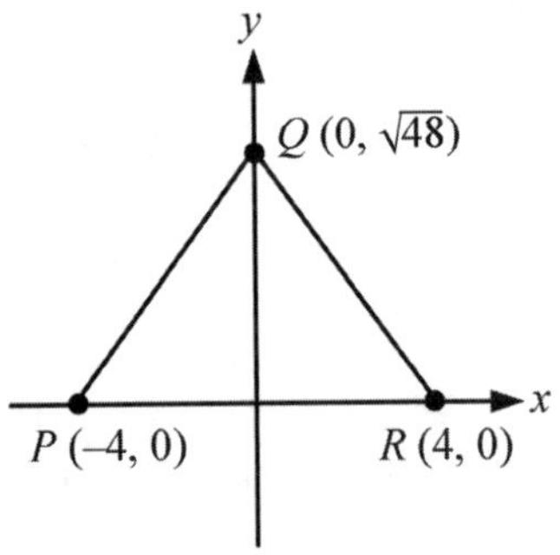

Find the length of each side of the triangle using the distance formula.

$d_{PQ} = 8$ (given)

$d_{RQ} = \sqrt{(0-4)^2 + (\sqrt{48}-0)^2}$

$d_{RQ} = \sqrt{(-4)^2 + (\sqrt{48})^2}$

$d_{RQ} = \sqrt{16+48}$

$d_{RQ} = \sqrt{64}$

$d_{RQ} = 8$

$d_{PR} = \sqrt{(4-(-4))^2 + (0-0)^2} = \sqrt{64} = 8$

$d_{PR} = 8$ (the horizontal distance from P to R)

Thus, all three sides are 8 units long. The triangle is equilateral.

26. D

For two lines to be perpendicular, their slopes must be negative reciprocals of each other.

The slopes are negative reciprocals only in choice **D** $y = 4x - 5$ and $y = -\frac{1}{4}x + 5$. The two slopes are 4 and $-\frac{1}{4}$.

27. B

A sketch of the parallelogram is shown.

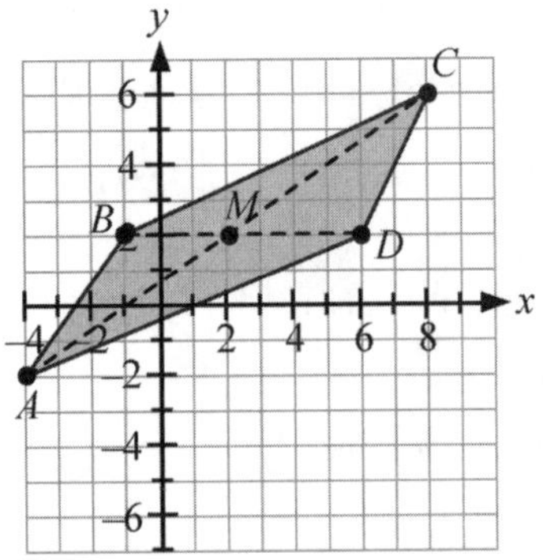

The diagram shows that the diagonals of the parallelogram are line segments AC and BD.

If the diagonals bisect each other, then line segments AC and BD will have the same midpoint M.

Therefore, the procedure in which you must verify that segment AC and segment BD have the same midpoint could be used to determine if the diagonals bisect each other.

28. Part A – Open Response

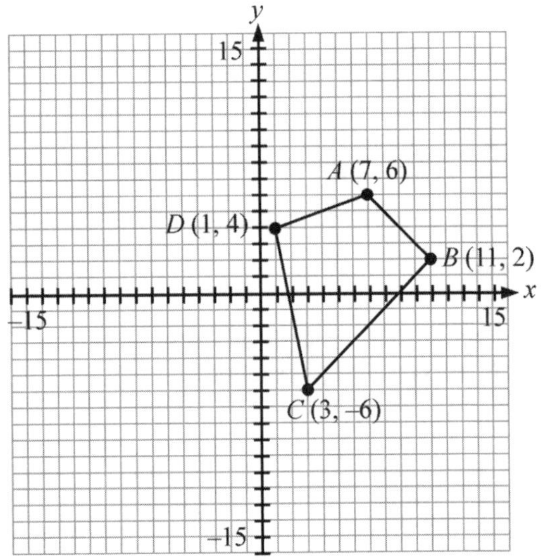

Part B – Open Response

The midpoint of each side of the quadrilateral can be determined by applying the midpoint formula $M = \left(\frac{x_1 + x_2}{2}, \frac{y_1 + y_2}{2}\right)$.

$$M_{AB} = \left(\frac{7 + 11}{2}, \frac{6 + 2}{2}\right) \quad M_{BC} = \left(\frac{11 + 3}{2}, \frac{2 + (-6)}{2}\right)$$

$$M_{AB} = \left(\frac{18}{2}, \frac{8}{2}\right) \quad M_{BC} = \left(\frac{14}{2}, \frac{-4}{2}\right)$$

$$M_{AB} = (9, 4) \quad M_{BC} = (7, -2)$$

$$M_{CD} = \left(\frac{3 + 1}{2}, \frac{-6 + 4}{2}\right) \quad M_{DA} = \left(\frac{1 + 7}{2}, \frac{4 + 6}{2}\right)$$

$$M_{CD} = \left(\frac{4}{2}, \frac{-2}{2}\right) \quad M_{DA} = \left(\frac{8}{2}, \frac{10}{2}\right)$$

$$M_{CD} = (2, -1) \quad M_{DA} = (4, 5)$$

Part C – Open Response

Denote the midpoint of AB as P, the midpoint of BC as Q, the midpoint of CD as R, and the midpoint of DA as T. In order to verify that $PQRT$ is a parallelogram, use the slope formula $m = \frac{y_2 - y_1}{x_2 - x_1}$ to show that side PT is parallel to side QR and side RT is parallel to side PQ.

$$m_{PT} = \frac{5 - 4}{4 - 9}$$

$$m_{PT} = \frac{1}{-5} = -\frac{1}{5}$$

$$m_{QR} = \frac{-1 - (-2)}{2 - 7}$$

$$m_{QR} = \frac{-1 + 2}{2 - 7}$$

$$m_{QR} = \frac{1}{-5} = -\frac{1}{5}$$

Since $m_{PT} = m_{QR}$, side PT is parallel to side QR.

$$m_{RT} = \frac{5 - (-1)}{4 - 2}$$

$$m_{RT} = \frac{5 + 1}{2}$$

$$m_{RT} = \frac{6}{2} = 3$$

$$m_{PQ} = \frac{-2 - 4}{7 - 9}$$

$$m_{PQ} = \frac{-6}{-2} = 3$$

Since $m_{RT} = m_{PQ}$, side RT is parallel to side PQ.

The opposite sides of quadrilateral $PQRT$ are parallel; therefore, quadrilateral $PQRT$ is a parallelogram.

NOTES

Trigonometry

Trigonometry

Table of Correlations

Specific Expectation	Practice Questions	Unit Test Questions
TR1 Investigating Similarity and Solving Problems Involving Similar Triangles		
TR1.1 *verify, through investigation the properties of similar triangles*	1, 2	1
TR1.2 *describe and compare the concepts of similarity and congruence*	3, 4	2
TR1.3 *solve problems involving similar triangles in realistic situations*	5, 6, 7	3, 4
TR2 Solving Problems Involving the Trigonometry of Right Triangles		
TR2.1 *determine, through investigation the relationship between the ratio of two sides in a right triangle and the ratio of the two corresponding sides in a similar right triangle, and define the sine, cosine, and tangent ratios*	8, 9	5
TR2.2 *determine the measures of the sides and angles in right triangles, using the primary trigonometric ratios and the Pythagorean theorem*	10, 11, 12, 13	6, 7, 8, 9
TR2.3 *solve problems involving the measures of sides and angles in right triangles in real life applications using the primary trigonometric ratios and the Pythagorean theorem.*	14, 15, 16, 17, 18a, 18b	10, 11, 12, 13, 14a, 14b
TR3 Solving Problems Involving the Trigonometry of Acute Triangles		
TR3.1 *explore the development of the sine law within acute triangles*	19, 20	15
TR3.2 *explore the development of the cosine law within acute triangles*	21, 22	16
TR3.3 *determine the measures of sides and angles in acute triangles, using the sine law and the cosine law*	23, 24, 25, 26, 27	17, 18, 19, 20
TR3.4 *solve problems involving the measures of sides and angles in acute triangles*	28a, 28b, 29, 30, 31, 32	21, 22, 23, 24a, 24b

TR1.1 *verify, through investigation the properties of similar triangles*

Verifying the Properties of Similar Triangles

Through investigation, the following properties of similar triangles can be verified:

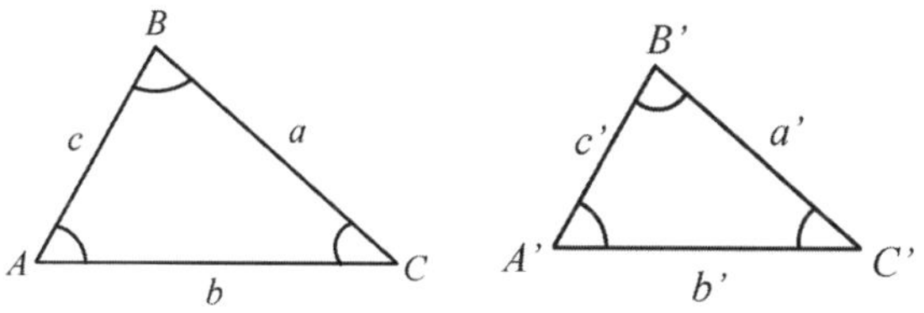

1. **Corresponding angles** are equal.
   $A = A'$ and $B = B'$ and $C = C'$
2. **Corresponding sides** have proportional lengths.
   $\frac{a}{a'} = \frac{b}{b'} = \frac{c}{c'}$

Example

Triangle ABC is similar to triangle DEF, as shown. What is the value of $\angle A - \angle C + \angle E$?

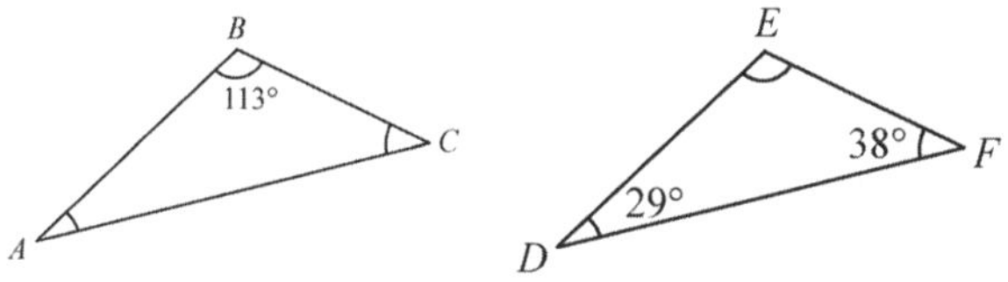

Since corresponding angles are equal, it follows that $\angle A = \angle D$, $\angle B = \angle E$, and $\angle C = \angle F$. From the diagram, $\angle D = 29° = \angle A$, $\angle F = 38° = \angle C$, and $\angle B = 113° = \angle F$. Therefore, substitute these values into $\angle A - \angle C + \angle E$ to get $29° - 38° + 113° = 104°$.

Practice

1. To guarantee that ΔABC is similar to ΔDEF, a student can verify that $\angle A = \angle D$ and verify that

A. $\angle C = \angle F$

B. $\angle B + \angle C = \angle E + \angle F$

C. AB is proportional to DE

D. BC is proportional to EF

2. Which of the following statements is **true** for similar triangles?

A. The measure of corresponding sides are equal in length.

B. The ratio of corresponding sides are equal and the measure of corresponding angles are equal.

C. Similar triangles always have the same shape and the same size.

D. The ratio of corresponding sides is equal to the ratio of corresponding angles.

TR1.2 *describe and compare the concepts of similarity and congruence*

Comparing Similarity and Congruence

Two triangles are **congruent** if all pairs of corresponding sides and angles are equal. That means the triangles are exactly the same size, but may have a different orientation.

The sign for congruent is ≅ .

There are three methods to verifying congruency:

1. SSS: If all three sides of one triangle are equal to the corresponding sides of the other triangle.

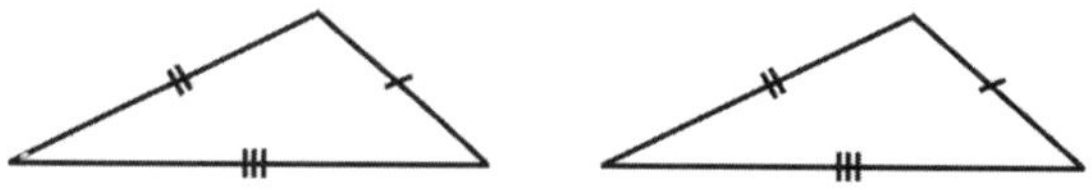

2. SAS: If any two sides and the angle contained within them is equal to the corresponding sides and contained angle of the other triangle.

3. ASA: If any two angles and the side contained within them is equal to the corresponding angles and contained side of the other triangle.

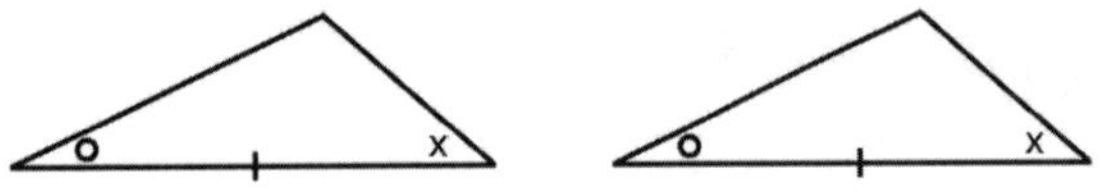

Example

Prove triangle $ABC \cong \Delta DEF$.
Side AB is equal in length to corresponding side EF.
Side AC is equal in length to corresponding side ED.
Side BC is equal in length to corresponding side DF.
All three sides of triangle ABC are equal to the corresponding sides of triangle DEF.
Therefore, by SSS, $\Delta ABC \cong \Delta DEF$.

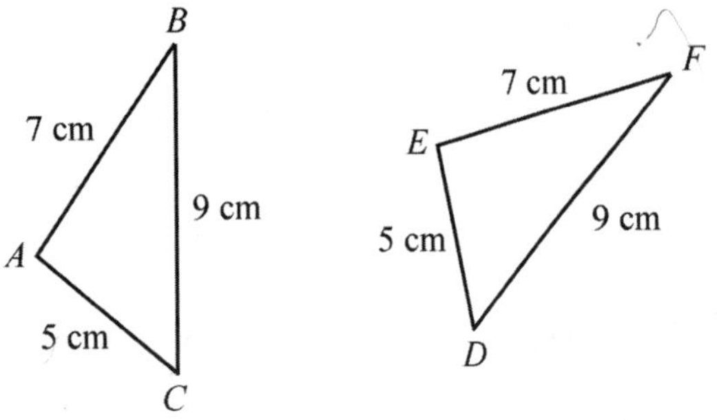

Similar triangles have the same shape, but not necessarily the same size. Two triangles are similar if the measures of the corresponding angles are equal or if the ratios of the corresponding sides are equal.
The symbol for similar is ~.

Example

The diagram below shows how two triangles can be used to find the width of a river.

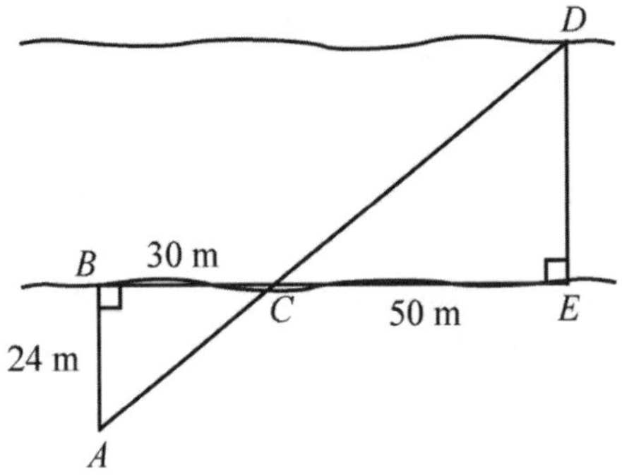

Determine the length of the river at DE.

$\angle ABC = \angle CED = 90°$
$\angle ACB = \angle DCE$ (Opposite angles are equal.)
If two sets of angles in two triangles are equal, then the third set must also be equal .
Therefore, all corresponding angles are equal, so $\Delta ABC \sim \Delta DEC$.

Since the triangles are similar, it follows that the ratio of the corresponding sides must also be equal.

$$\frac{DE}{AB} = \frac{CE}{CB}$$

$$\frac{DE}{24 \text{ m}} = \frac{50 \text{ m}}{30 \text{ m}}$$

$$DE = \frac{(24 \text{ m})(50 \text{ m})}{30 \text{ m}}$$

$$DE = \frac{1\ 200 \text{ m}}{30 \text{ m}}$$

$DE = 40$ m
The width of the river at DE is 40 m.

Practice

3. What is the length of side y?

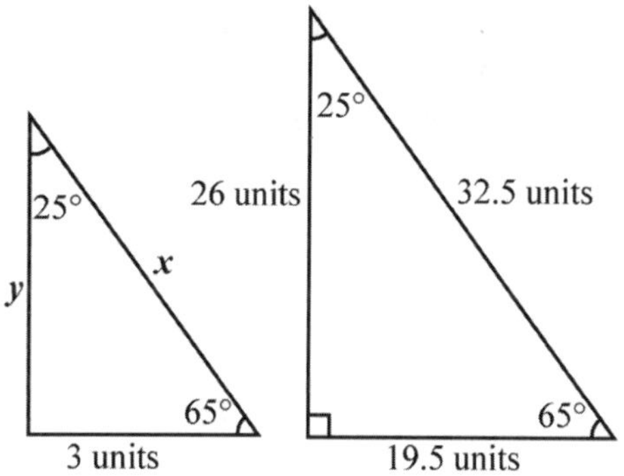

A. 4.0 units **B.** 4.5 units

C. 5.0 units **D.** 6.0 units

4. The two given triangles can be described as congruent because

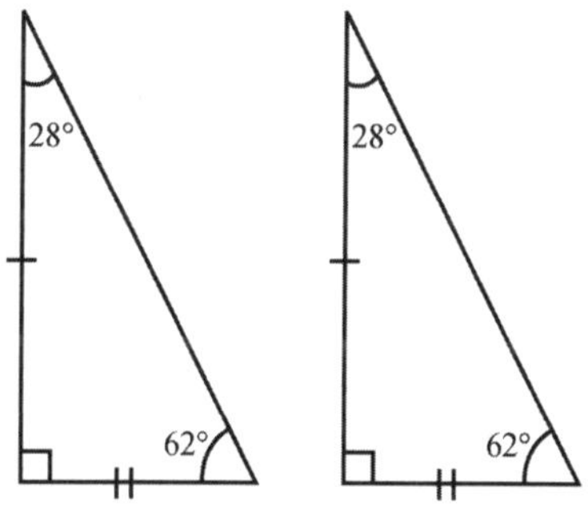

A. all of their corresponding angles are equal

B. they each contain a 90° angle

C. the sum of the angles in each triangle is 180° angle

D. all of their corresponding angles and sides are equal

TR1.3 *solve problems involving similar triangles in realistic situations*

Solving Similar Triangle Problems

Similar triangles are often used to solve problems in realistic situations.

Example

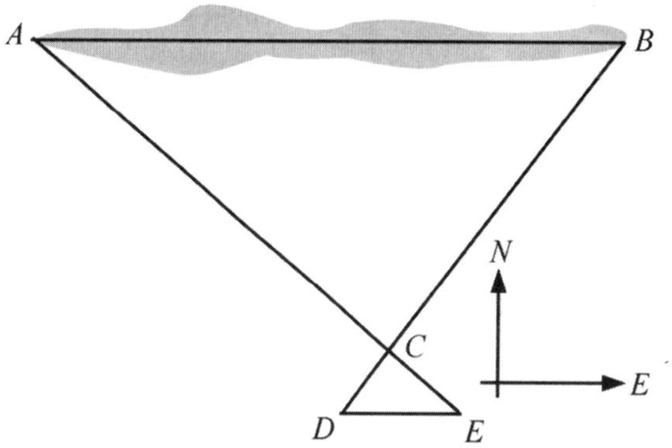

To determine the distance from A to B across a lake, two triangles are drawn as shown. The following distances were measured: DE = 412 m, DC = 260 m, BC = 1 264 m, and CE = 308 m. Also, AB is parallel to DE. What is the distance across the lake to the nearest metre?

Using properties of geometry, it is given that $AB \parallel DE$.
Therefore, lines AE and DB act as transversals across these parallel lines. This means that $\angle A = \angle E$ and $\angle B = \angle D$ (which form opposite interior angles in both cases).
Thus,

$\angle C = \angle C$

$\angle A = \angle E$

$\angle B = \angle D$

It follows that $\Delta ABC \sim \Delta EDC$.
Draw the two triangles with the same orientation, and label with the given distances, as shown.

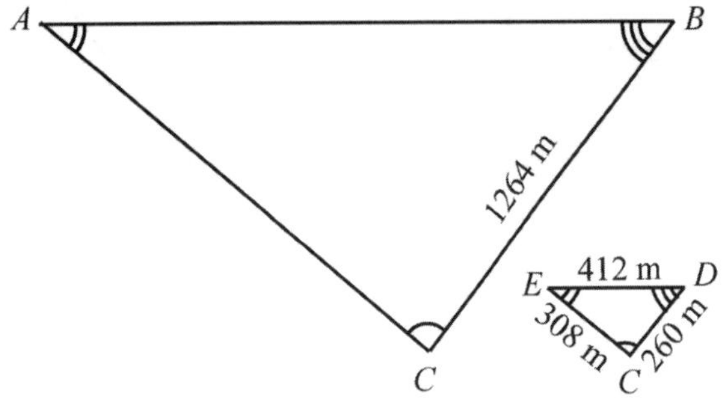

Since $\Delta ABC \sim \Delta EDC$,

$$\frac{BC}{DC} = \frac{AC}{EC} = \frac{AB}{ED}$$

Substitute the given distances into this equation.

$$\frac{1\,264 \text{ m}}{260 \text{ m}} = \frac{AC}{308 \text{ m}} = \frac{AB}{412 \text{ m}}$$

Since all three of these ratios are equal, equate the first and last to get $\frac{1\,264 \text{ m}}{260 \text{ m}} = \frac{AB}{412 \text{ m}}$.

$$AB = \frac{1\,264 \text{ m}}{260 \text{ m}} \times 412 \text{ m} = 2\,002.95 \text{ m}$$

Therefore, the distance from point A to point B across the lake is 2 003 m.

Practice

5. In the school storage room, a tennis racket and a ski pole are both leaning against a wall at the same angle. The length of the tennis racket is 60.0 cm, and it touches the floor 30.0 cm away from the wall. The ski pole touches the floor 67.5 cm away from the wall. What is the length of the ski pole?

A. 135.0 cm **B.** 124.0 cm

C. 37.5 cm **D.** 33.8 cm

Use the following information to answer the next question.

The diagram shows shadows cast by a tree and a statue at the same point in time.

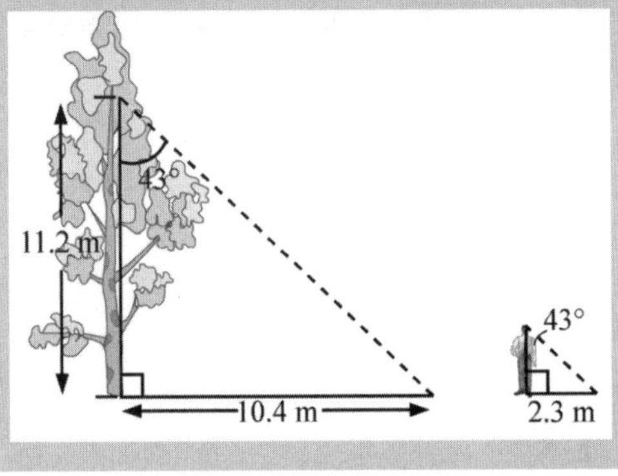

6. To the nearest tenth of a metre, how tall is the statue?

A. 2.2 m **B.** 2.5 m

C. 4.5 m **D.** 11.7 m

Numerical Response

7. Two lookout bridges AB and CD are built across a pond as shown in the diagram.

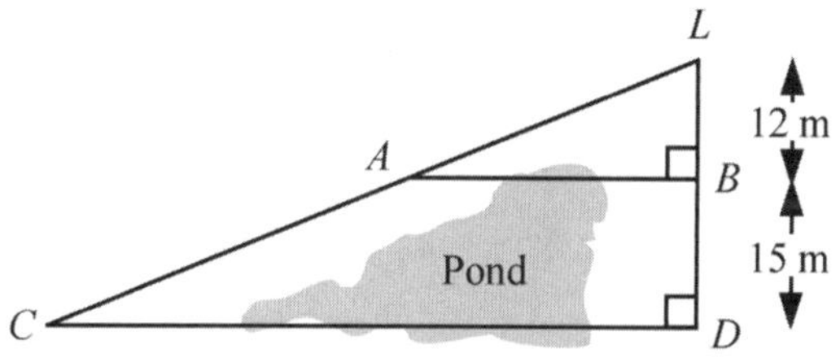

If bridge AB is 30 m in length, then the length in metres of bridge CD, correct to one decimal place, is ___.

TR2.1 *determine, through investigation the relationship between the ratio of two sides in a right triangle and the ratio of the two corresponding sides in a similar right triangle, and define the sine, cosine, and tangent ratios*

Primary Trigonometric Ratios

Through investigation, you can determine the relationship between the ratios of the lengths of two sides in a right triangle relative to an angle other than the right angle. Recall that a right triangle is a triangle containing a 90° angle. A triangle can be labelled as follows:

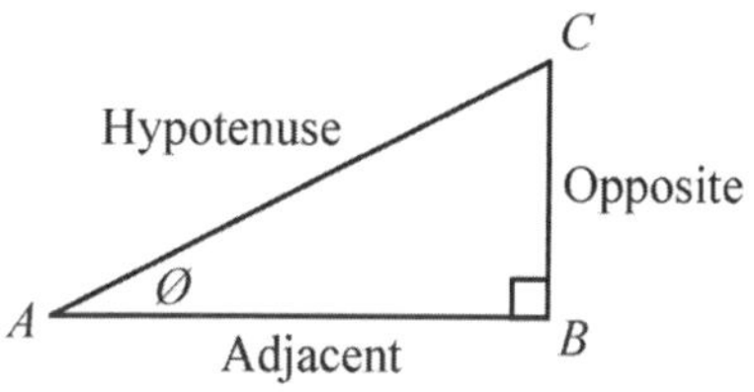

- OPPOSITE is always the side across from the angle.
- ADJACENT is always the side right next to the angle.
- HYPOTENUSE is the longest side and is always across from the 90° angle.

When you compare the lengths of the different sides of similar right triangles that hold the same acute angle, investigation will show that the ratios of the lengths of the three sides will remain the same, regardless of the right triangles that are chosen. This is summarized in the following illustration:

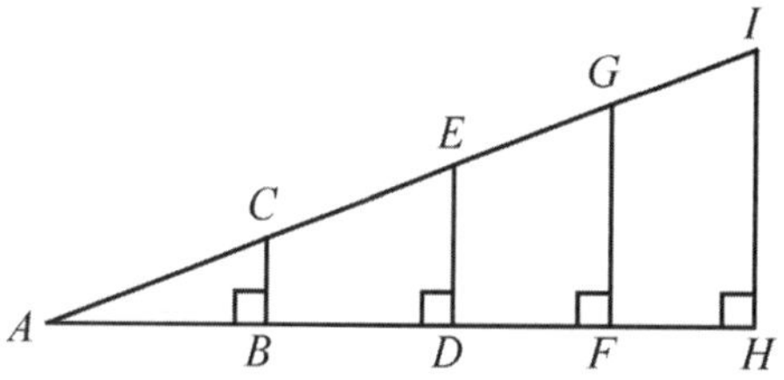

Given the acute angle A, it follows that:

- $\frac{BC}{AC} = \frac{DE}{AE} = \frac{FG}{AG} = \frac{HI}{AI} = \frac{\text{opposite}}{\text{hypotenuse}}$
- $\frac{AB}{AC} = \frac{AD}{AE} = \frac{AF}{AG} = \frac{AH}{AI} = \frac{\text{adjacent}}{\text{hypotenuse}}$
- $\frac{BC}{AB} = \frac{DE}{AD} = \frac{FG}{AF} = \frac{HI}{AH} = \frac{\text{opposite}}{\text{adjacent}}$

These ratios are known as the primary trigonometric ratios:

Sine ratio: $\sin A = \frac{\text{opposite}}{\text{hypotenuse}}$

Cosine ratio: $\cos A = \frac{\text{adjacent}}{\text{hypotenuse}}$

Tangent ratio: $\tan A = \frac{\text{opposite}}{\text{adjacent}}$

To remember these ratios, think of this mnemonic: SOH CAH TOA.

Example

Write the three primary trigonometric ratios for θ.

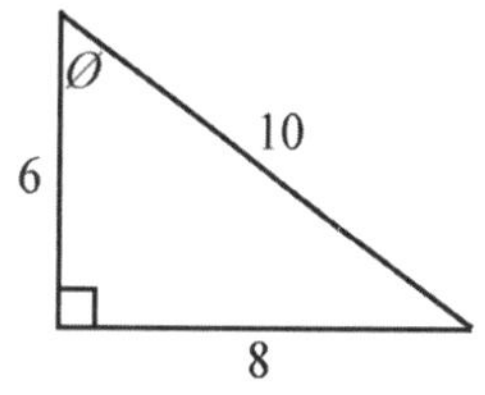

Begin by labelling the triangle as follows:

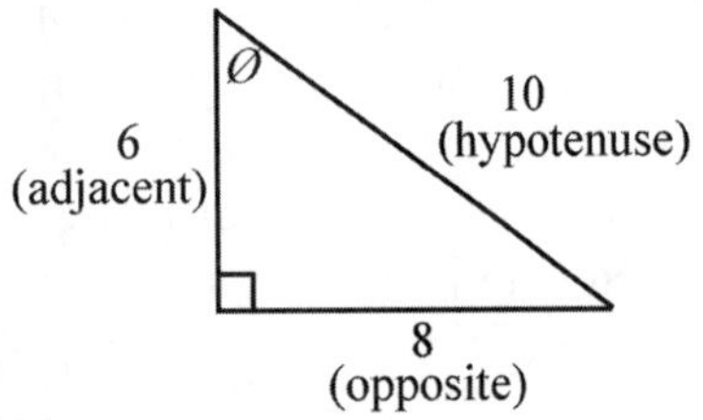

$$\sin\theta = \frac{\text{opposite}}{\text{hypotenuse}} = \frac{8}{10} = \frac{4}{5}$$

$$\cos\theta = \frac{\text{adjacent}}{\text{hypotenuse}} = \frac{6}{10} = \frac{3}{5}$$

$$\tan\theta = \frac{\text{opposite}}{\text{adjacent}} = \frac{8}{6} = \frac{4}{3}$$

Practice

8. In a right triangle, if $\cos\theta = \frac{12}{13}$ and $\tan\theta = \frac{5}{12}$, what is the value of $\sin\theta$?

A. $\frac{5}{13}$ **B.** $\frac{5}{12}$

C. 1 **D.** $\frac{12}{5}$

Use the following information to answer the next question.

In the given triangle, tan 72° = 3.1.

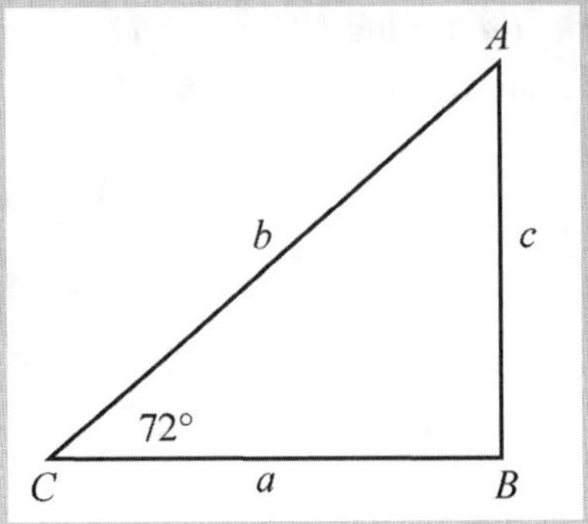

9. Which of the following ratios is equal to 3.1?

A. $\frac{a}{c}$ **B.** $\frac{c}{a}$

C. $\frac{b}{a}$ **D.** $\frac{a}{b}$

TR2.2 *determine the measures of the sides and angles in right triangles, using the primary trigonometric ratios and the Pythagorean theorem*

Determining the Measures of Sides and Angles in Right Triangles

The primary trigonometric ratios and the Pythagorean theorem are mathematical tools that can be used to determine the value of an unknown side or angle in a right triangle.

Example

Determine the measure of the indicated angle to the nearest tenth of a metre.

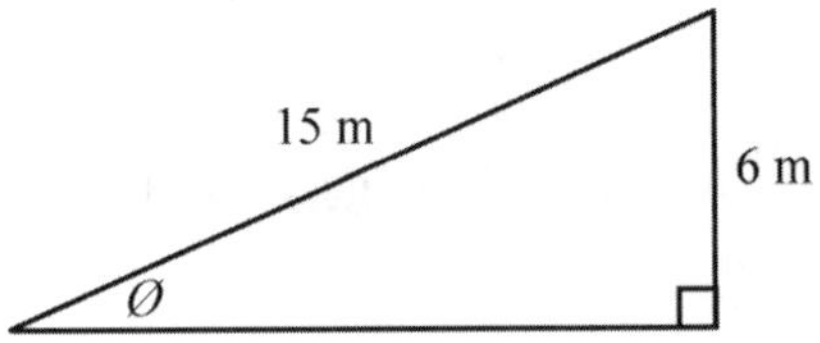

Begin by labelling the triangle as follows:

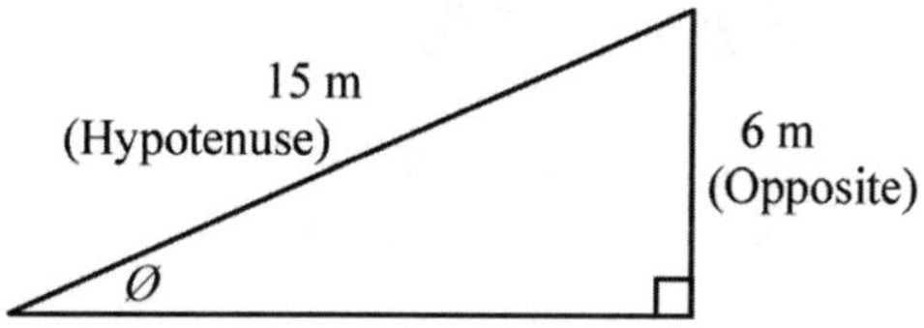

$$\sin\theta = \frac{\text{opposite}}{\text{hypotenuse}}$$

$$\sin\theta = \frac{6}{15}$$

$$\theta = \sin^{-1}\left(\frac{6}{15}\right)$$

$$\theta \approx 23.6°$$

Solving a Triangle

Solving a triangle involves determining all the unknown sides and angles of a triangle. In order to solve a triangle, it is common to use the Pythagorean theorem, the rule that the sum of the angles in a triangle equals 180°, and the trigonometric ratios.

Example

Solve the following triangle.

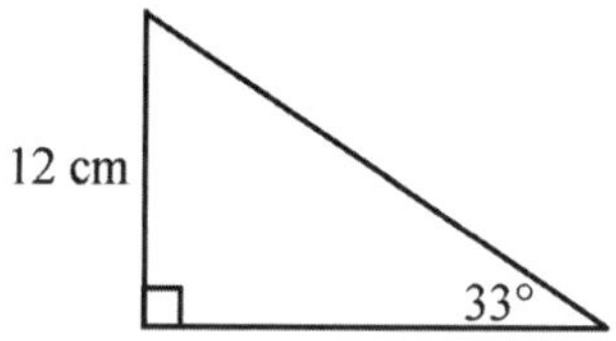

Begin by labelling the unknown sides and angles as follows:

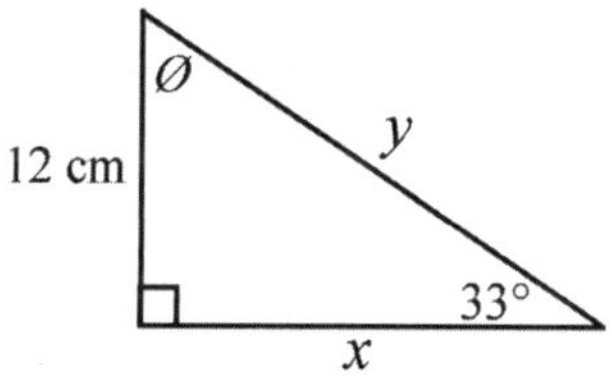

$$90° + 33° + \theta = 180°$$

$$\theta = 57°$$

Next, the length of x can be calculated using the tangent ratio.

$$\tan\theta = \frac{\text{opposite}}{\text{adjacent}}$$

$$\tan 33° = \frac{12}{x}$$

$$x\tan 33° = 12$$

$$x = \frac{12}{\tan 33°}$$

$$x \approx 18.5 \text{ cm}$$

The final side, y, can be determined either by using the Pythagorean theorem or by using a trigonometric ratio.

Using the Pythagorean theorem:

$$c^2 = a^2 + b^2$$

$$y^2 = 12^2 + x^2$$

$$y^2 = 12^2 + \left(\frac{12}{\tan 33°}\right)^2$$

$$y = \sqrt{12^2 + \left(\frac{12}{\tan 33°}\right)^2}$$

$$y \approx 22.0 \text{ cm}$$

Using the sine ratio:

$$\sin\theta = \frac{\text{opposite}}{\text{hypotenuse}}$$

$$\sin 33° = \frac{12}{y}$$

$$y\sin 33° = 12$$

$$y = \frac{12}{\sin 33°}$$

$$y \approx 22.0 \text{ cm}$$

Practice

Use the following information to answer the next question.

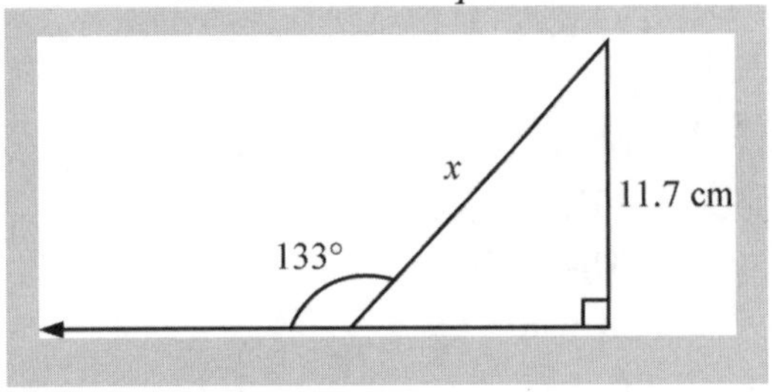

10. What is the length of side x to the nearest tenth?

A. 8.0 cm **B.** 8.6 cm

C. 16.0 cm **D.** 17.2 cm

11. If the hypotenuse of a right triangle is 90 cm and a second side is 45 cm, then what is the length of the third side to the nearest whole number?

A. 78 cm **B.** 80 cm

C. 82 cm **D.** 85 cm

Use the following information to answer the next question.

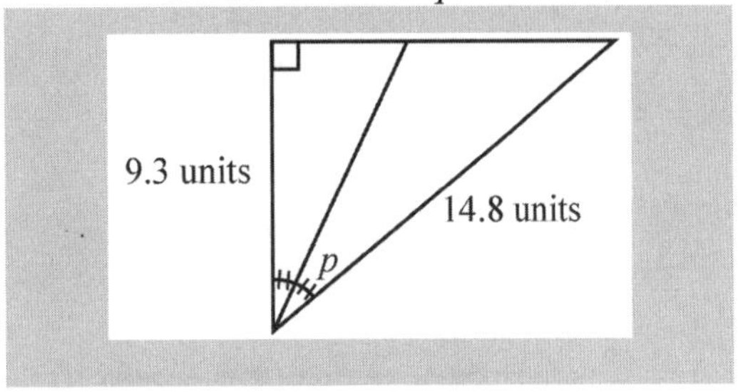

12. What is the measure of angle p to the nearest tenth?

A. 16.5° **B.** 25.5°

C. 33.0° **D.** 51.0°

CHALLENGER QUESTION

Numerical Response

Use the following information to answer the next question.

A diagram of two right angle triangles is shown.

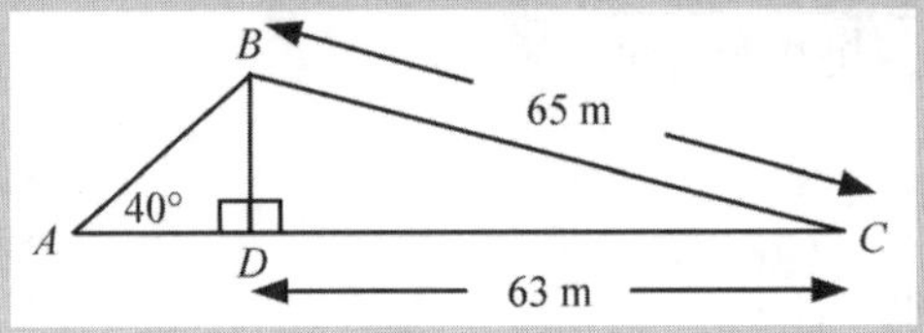

13. Correct to the nearest tenth, the length in metres of side AB is ____.

TR2.3 *solve problems involving the measures of sides and angles in right triangles in real life applications using the primary trigonometric ratios and the Pythagorean theorem.*

Solving Right Triangle Problems

The primary trigonometric ratios and the Pythagorean theorem can be used to solve problems involving the measures of sides and angles in real-life applications. When solving these types of problems, recall these key definitions:

- The **angle of elevation** is up from the horizontal.
- The **angle of depression** is down from the horizontal.

Example

A cat watches a bird in a tree. The bird is at an angle of elevation of 40° from the cat. If the cat is 7.1 m from the base of the tree, how high up in the tree is the bird?

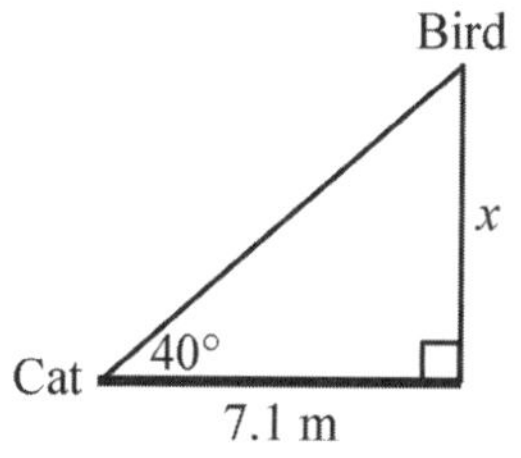

$$\tan 40° = \frac{x}{7.1}$$

$$x = 7.1\tan 40°$$

$$x \approx 6.0 \text{ m}$$

The bird is 6.0 m from the ground.

Example

Lexi is standing in her yard. She sees a cat sitting directly west of her. Directly east of her is a dog. Lexi's eye level is 1.48 m high. To look directly at where the cat is sitting, she looks down at an angle of depression of 30°. To the dog, the angle of depression is 25°. How far apart are the cat and dog?

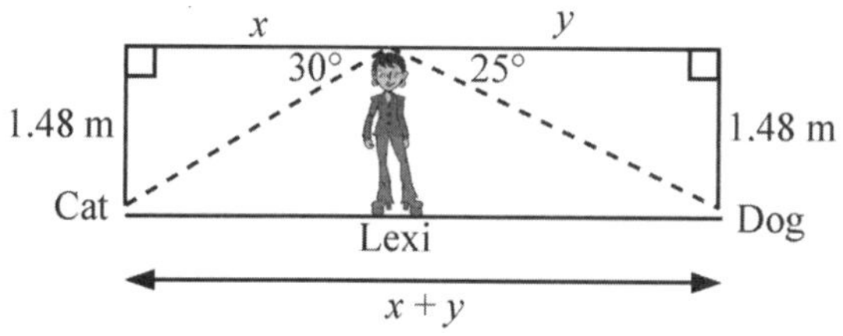

Notice that $x + y$ at eye level will be the same as $x + y$ on the ground.

The distance between the cat and dog = $x + y$.

$$\tan 30° = \frac{1.48}{x}$$

$$x = \frac{1.48}{\tan 30°}$$

$$\tan 25° = \frac{1.48}{y}$$

$$y = \frac{1.48}{\tan 25°}$$

$$\text{distance} = x + y$$

$$= \frac{1.48}{\tan 30°} + \frac{1.48}{\tan 25°}$$

$$\approx 5.74 \text{ m}$$

The cat and the dog are 5.74 m apart.

Practice

Use the following information to answer the next question.

A telephone pole is kept vertical by two wires that run from the top of the pole to the ground as illustrated in the given diagram. The wire closest to the pole measures 13.2 m in length and makes an angle of 36° with the ground. The other wire measures 15.8 m in length.

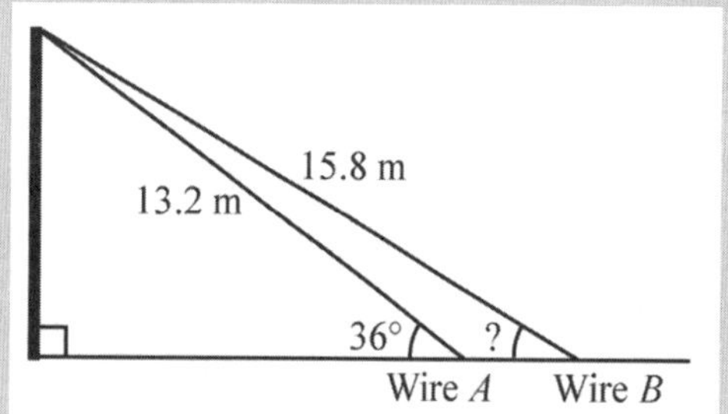

14. Correct to the nearest degree, what is the angle between Wire B and the ground?

A. 29° **B.** 31° **C.** 45° **D.** 57°

Use the following information to answer the next question.

Simon is pitching a tent. Each wall of the tent is 3.5 m long when the centre pole is erected.

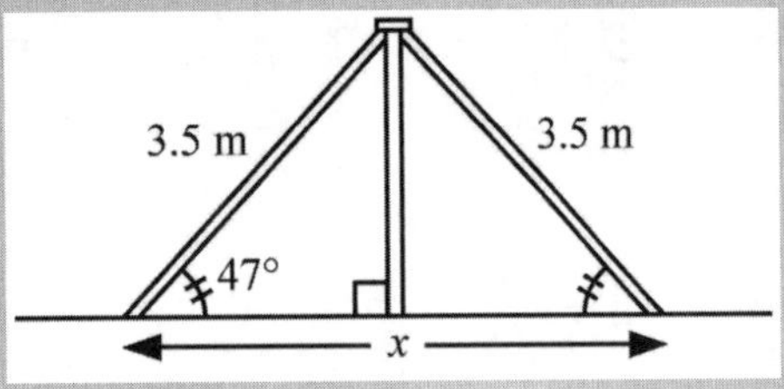

15. What is the width, x, of the tent at its base, to the nearest tenth?

A. 2.4 m **B.** 2.6 m

C. 4.8 m **D.** 5.2 m

CHALLENGER QUESTION

Use the following information to answer the next question.

Two buildings are 40 m apart, as illustrated in the given diagram. From a point at the top of the shorter building, the angle of elevation to the top of the taller building is 37°. From the same point, the angle of depression to the foot of the taller building is 26°.

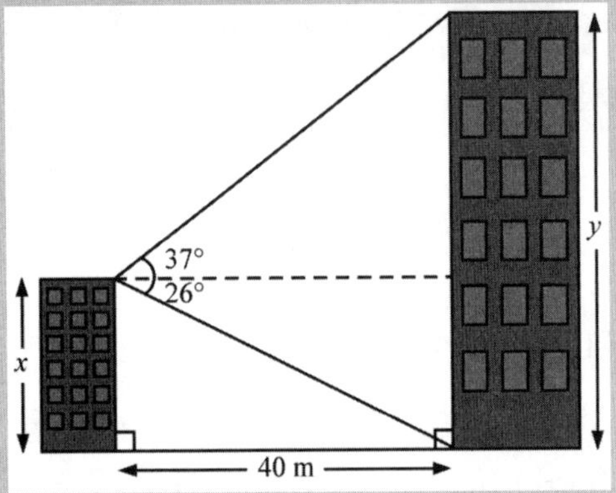

16. The height of the taller building, y, correct to the nearest tenth of a metre, is

A. 52.8 m **B.** 51.4 m

C. 49.7 m **D.** 27.1 m

Use the following information to answer the next question.

This map shows routes that Marrah often takes. Every Friday, Marrah goes from school to the café before going home.

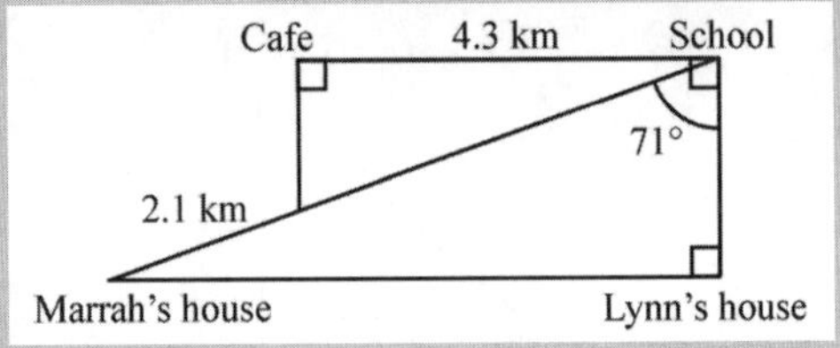

17. What is the total distance from school to the café to Marrah's house?

A. 1.5 km **B.** 4.3 km

C. 5.8 km **D.** 7.9 km

Use the following information to answer the next multipart question.

18. A ladder sits between two trees at a point 3.5 m from the base of the first tree. The ladder makes an angle of 70° with the ground when its top is placed against that tree. If the ladder is turned and its top is placed against the second tree with the foot of the ladder remaining in the same location, the ladder makes an angle of 66°, as shown in the diagram.

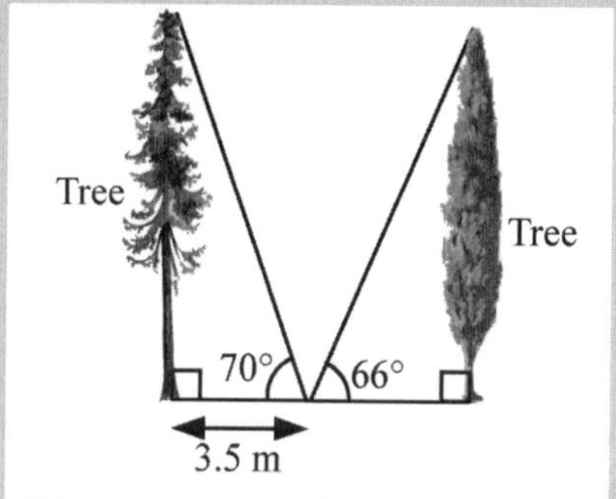

Diagram not to scale

Part A

Open Response

What is the length of the ladder to the nearest tenth of a metre?

Part B

Open Response

To the nearest tenth of a metre, what is the distance between the bases of the two trees?

TR3.1 *explore the development of the sine law within acute triangles*

The Sine Law

Any triangle that is not a right angle triangle is called an **oblique triangle**. If all angles in a triangle are acute, this is called an **acute triangle**. An acute triangle is a particular type of oblique triangle. The primary trigonometric ratios can only be directly applied when given a right angle triangle, so a new procedure needs to be developed when presented with an acute triangle.

Consider ΔABC.

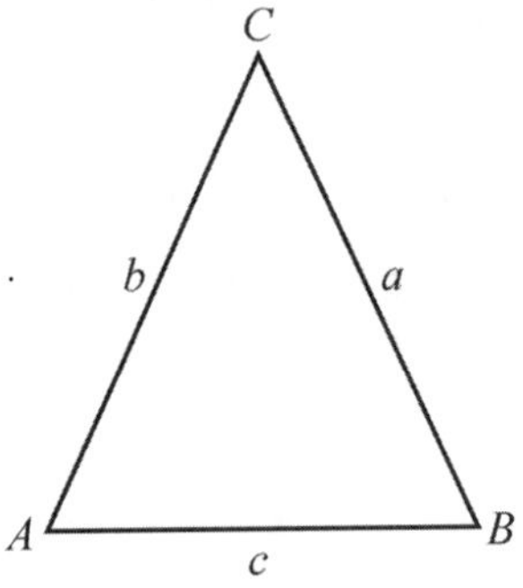

Side BC is opposite angle A and can be denoted by a. Similarly, side AC can be denoted by b, and side AB can be denoted by C.

In ΔABC, draw DC perpendicular to AB in order to form two right triangles as follows. DC is the height, h, of ΔABC.

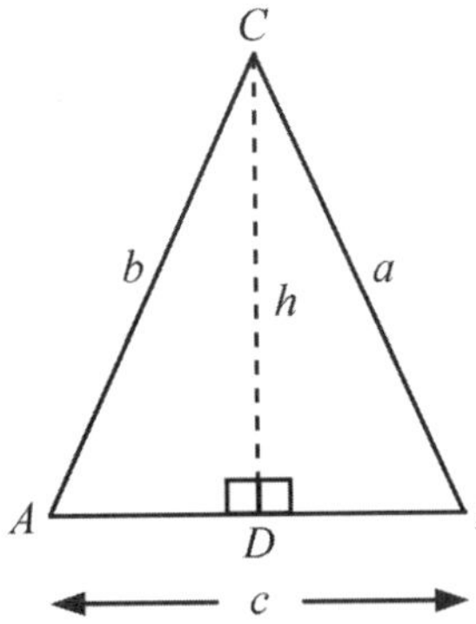

In ΔADC: In ΔBDC:

$\sin A = \frac{h}{b}$ $\sin B = \frac{h}{a}$

$b\sin A = h$ $a\sin B = h$

Since the value of h is identical for ΔADC and ΔBDC, $b\sin A = a\sin B$. The equation $b\sin A = a\sin B$ can be rewritten as

$$\frac{a}{\sin A} = \frac{b}{\sin B}.$$

If you draw a line perpendicular to AC and follow the preceding steps, the equation $\frac{a}{\sin A} = \frac{c}{\sin C}$ can be generated.

Combining the derived results gives the equation $\frac{a}{\sin A} = \frac{b}{\sin B} = \frac{c}{\sin C}$. This equation is called the sine law.

The law of sines can be illustrated by examining each of the following triangles.

Example

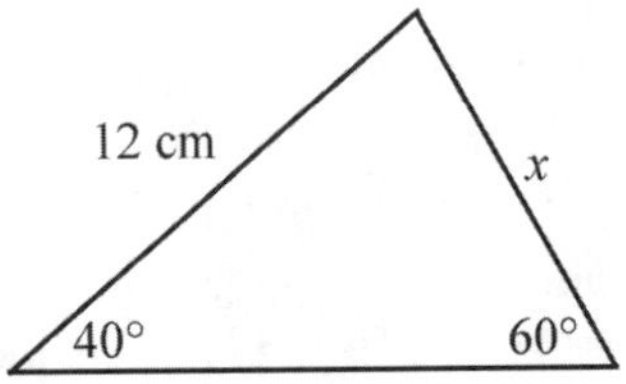

Since the side measuring x cm is opposite the 40° angle and the side measuring 12 cm is opposite the 60° angle, $\frac{12}{\sin 60°} = \frac{x}{\sin 40°}$.

Example

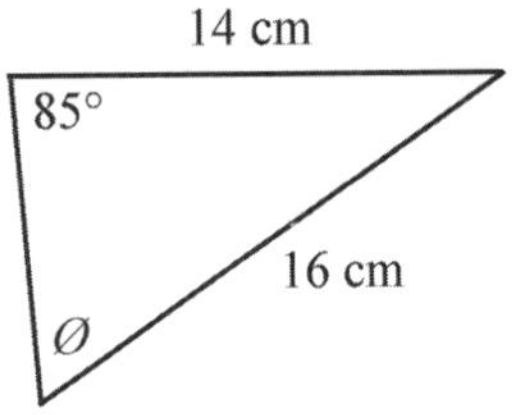

Since the side measuring 14 cm is opposite angle θ and the side measuring 16 cm is opposite the 85° angle, $\frac{14}{\sin \theta} = \frac{16}{\sin 85°}$.

Example

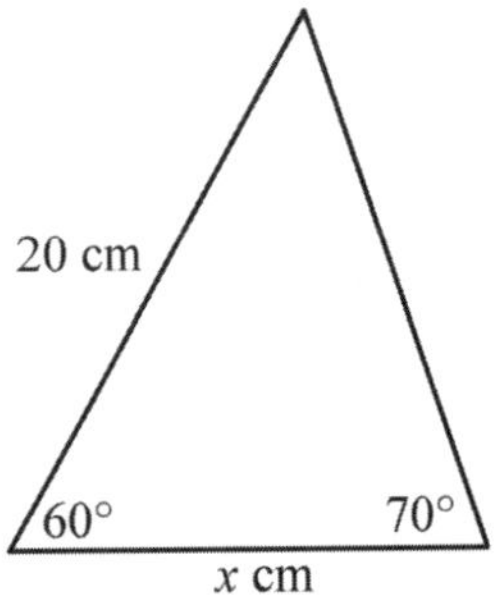

Recall that the sum of the interior angles of a triangle is equal to 180°. Therefore, the angle opposite the side measuring x cm is equal to 50°(180° – 60° – 70°). Since the side measuring 20 cm is opposite the 70° angle, $\frac{x}{\sin 50°} = \frac{20}{\sin 70°}$.

Practice

Use the following information to answer the next question.

A student drew the diagram shown in order to derive the law of sines.

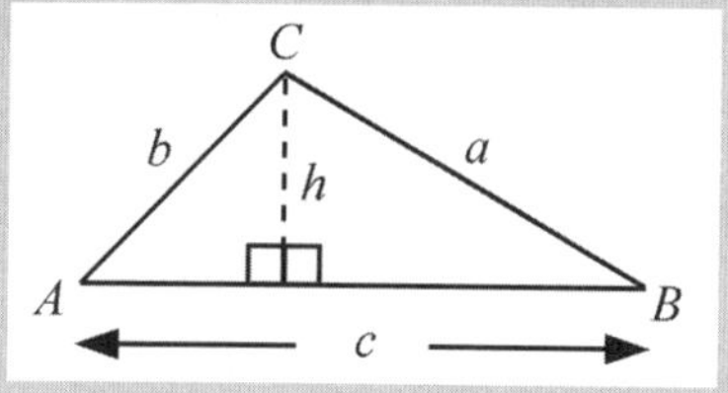

19. If the student correctly determined that $\sin A = \dfrac{h}{b}$ and $\sin B = \dfrac{h}{a}$, then which of the following equations is correct?

A. $h = \dfrac{b\sin A}{a\sin B}$

B. $h = \dfrac{a\sin A}{b\sin B}$

C. $b\sin B = a\sin A$

D. $b\sin A = a\sin B$

20. For which of the following triangles can the equation $\dfrac{80}{\sin 50^\circ} = \dfrac{65}{\sin x^\circ}$ be used to determine the measure of angle x?

A.

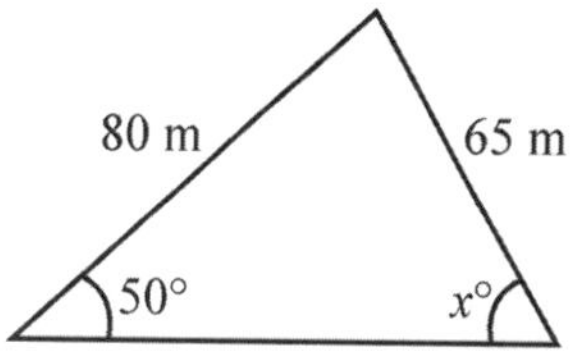

B.

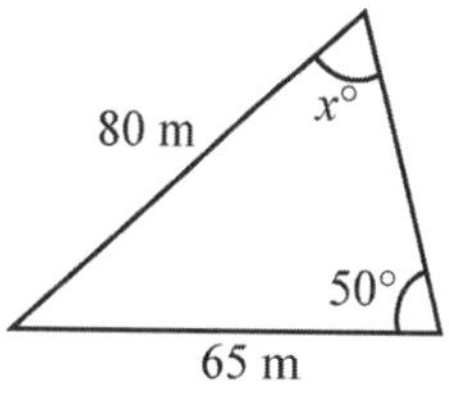

C.

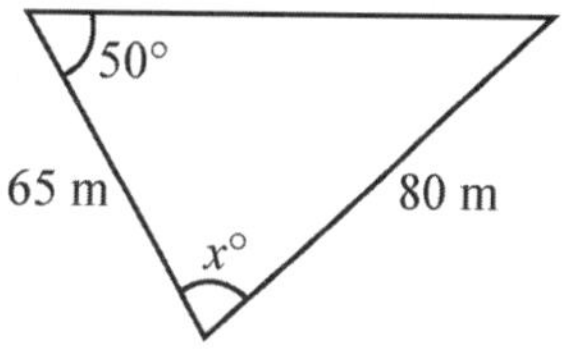

D.

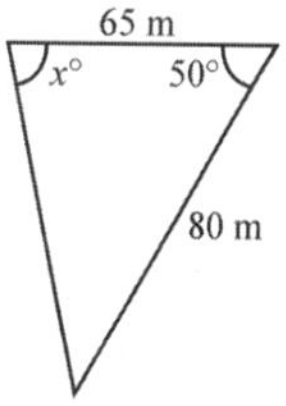

TR3.2 *explore the development of the cosine law within acute triangles*

The Cosine Law

There are acute triangles that can not be solved directly by using the law of sines. Once again, a new procedure needs to be developed.

Consider ΔABC.

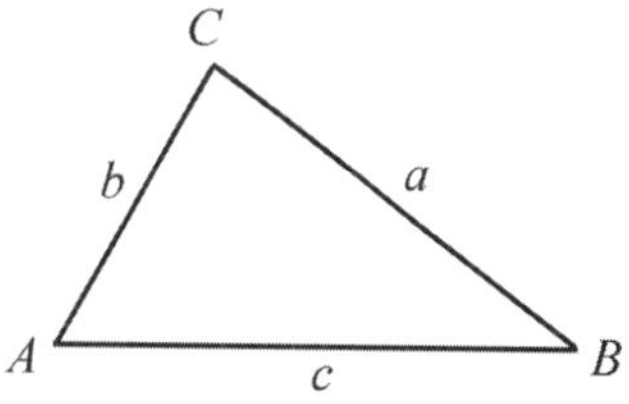

In ΔABC, draw DC perpendicular to AB in order to form two right triangles. Recall that DC is the height, h, of ΔABC. Denote side AD by x. It follows that side $DB = c - x$.

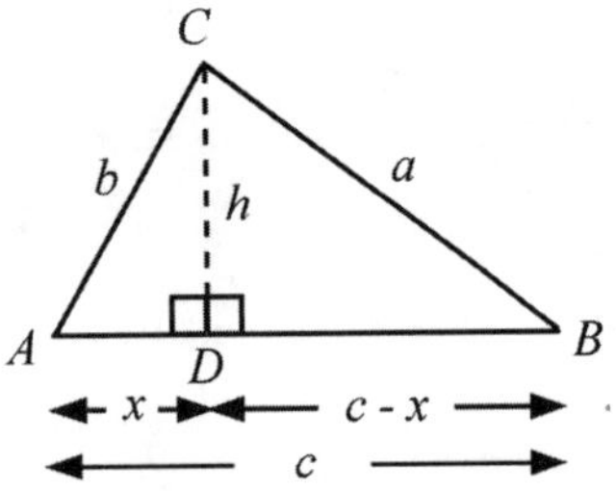

Apply the Pythagorean theorem to both ΔADC and ΔBDC.

In ΔADC, $b^2 = x^2 + h^2$ or $b^2 - x^2 = h^2$.

In ΔBDC, $a^2 = h^2 + (c - x)^2$.

Substitute $b^2 - x^2$ for h^2 in the equation

$a^2 = h^2 + (c - x)^2$.

$a^2 = b^2 - x^2 + (c - x)^2$

Expand $(c - x)^2$.

$a^2 = b^2 - x^2 + c^2 - 2cx + x^2$

Collect like terms.

$a^2 = b^2 + c^2 - 2cx$

Also, in ΔADC, $\cos A = \frac{x}{b}$ or $b\cos A = x$.

By substituting $b\cos A$ for x in the equation $a^2 = b^2 + c^2 - 2cx$, the equation $a^2 = b^2 + c^2 - 2bc\cos A$ can be generated. This equation is called the law of cosines.

Similar equations can be derived that involve $\cos B$ and $\cos C$:

$b^2 = a^2 + c^2 - 2ac\cos B$

$c^2 = a^2 + b^2 - 2ab\cos C$

The law of cosines can be used to find the measure of an angle in a triangle when the lengths of all three sides of the triangle are known. In this case, one of the following forms of the law of cosines is useful.

$$\cos A = \frac{b^2 + c^2 - a^2}{2bc}$$

$$\cos B = \frac{a^2 + c^2 - b^2}{2ac}$$

$$\cos C = \frac{a^2 + b^2 - c^2}{2ab}$$

The law of cosines can be illustrated by examining each of the following triangles.

Example

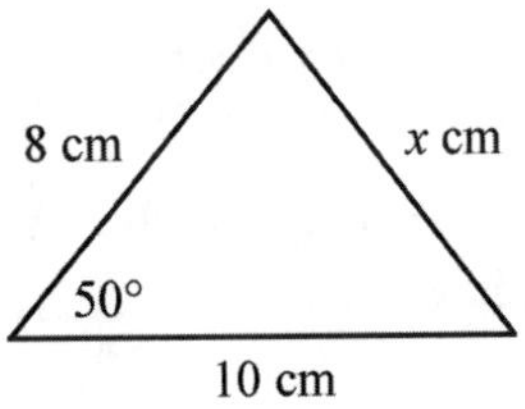

Since the side measuring x cm is opposite the 50° angle, $x^2 = 8^2 + 10^2 - 2(8)(10)\cos 50°$.

Example

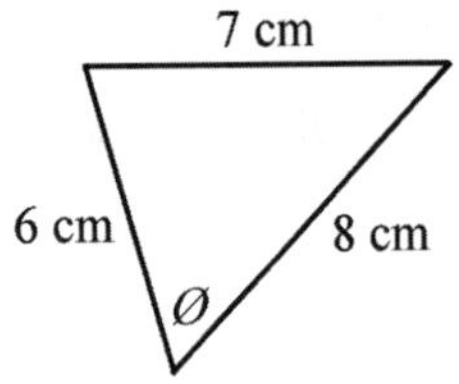

Since the angle measuring θ is opposite the side measuring 7 cm, $\cos\theta = \frac{6^2 + 8^2 - 7^2}{2(6)(8)}$.

Practice

21. The equation $\cos x° = \dfrac{15^2 + 20^2 - 17^2}{2(15)(20)}$ applies to which of the following acute triangles?

A.

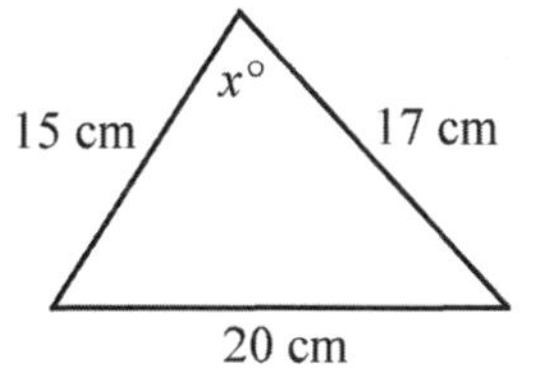

B.

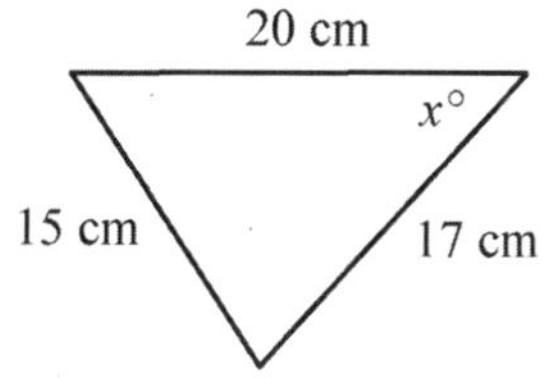

C.

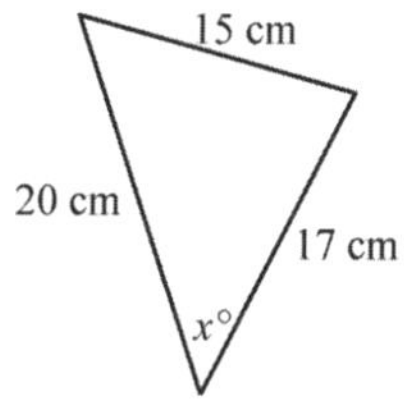

D.

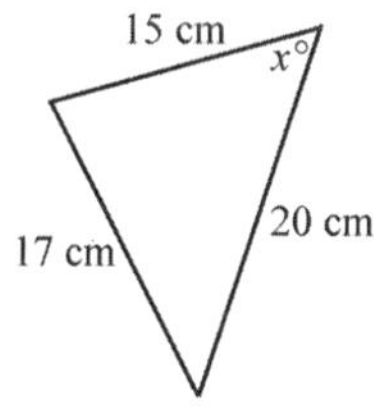

Use the following information to answer the next question.

Acute ΔPQR is shown.

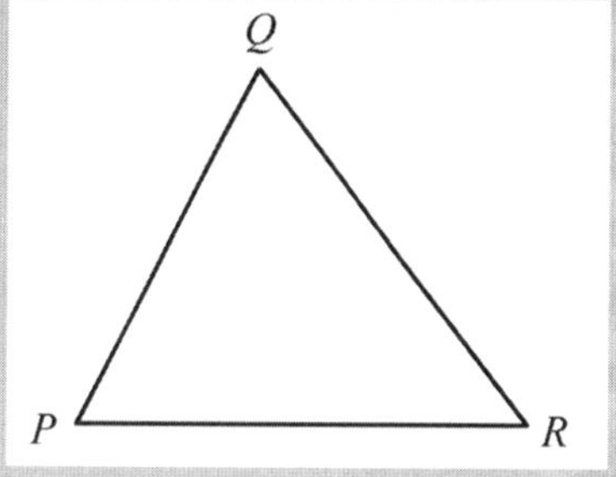

22. Which of the following equations correctly illustrates the law of cosines with respect to ΔPQR?

A. $\dfrac{QR}{\cos P} = \dfrac{PQ}{\cos R}$

B. $\dfrac{PR}{\cos P} = \dfrac{QR}{\cos Q}$

C. $(PQ)^2 = (PR)^2 + (QR)^2 - 2(PR)(QR)\cos Q$

D. $(QR)^2 = (QP)^2 + (PR)^2 - 2(QP)(PR)\cos P$

TR3.3 *determine the measures of sides and angles in acute triangles, using the sine law and the cosine law*

Using the Sine and Cosine Laws

The law of sines or the law of cosines can be used to determine either a missing side length or a missing angle measure in an acute triangle.
For example, consider the following problems.

Example

Determine the value of x to the nearest tenth.

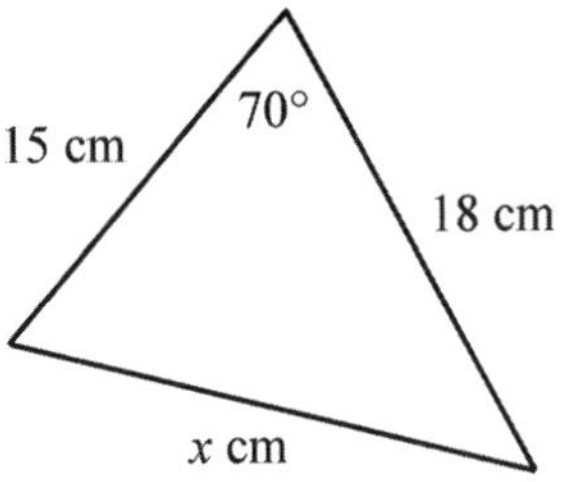

In the triangle, two sides and an included angle (SAS) are given; therefore, directly apply the law of cosines $a^2 = b^2 + c^2 - 2bc\cos A$ as follows:
Since the side measuring x cm is opposite the 70° angle, write the following:

$$x^2 = 15^2 + 18^2 - 2(15)(18)\cos 70°$$

$$x^2 \approx 225 + 324 - 184.69$$

$$x^2 \approx 364.31$$

$$x \approx \sqrt{364.31}$$

$$x \approx 19.1$$

Example

In ΔABC, $\angle A = 40°$, $\angle B = 60°$, and $AC = 18$ cm. Determine the length of side BC to the nearest tenth.
To begin, draw a sketch of the given triangle, and place the indicated measurements in the appropriate location.

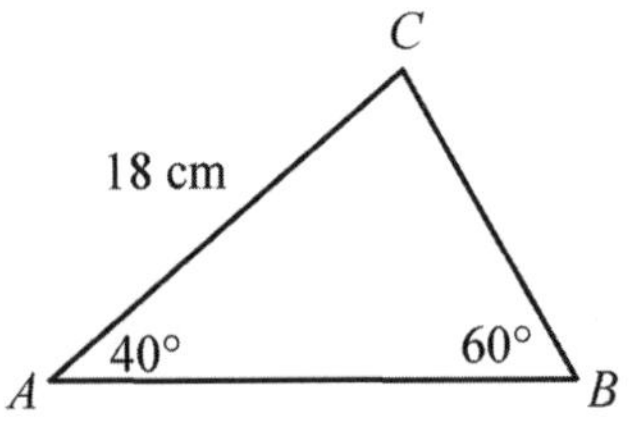

Since this is not an SAS situation, apply the law of sines $\frac{a}{\sin A} = \frac{b}{\sin B} = \frac{c}{\sin C}$.
The side measuring 18 cm is opposite the 60° angle, and side BC is opposite the 40° angle. Thus, write the following:

$$\frac{BC}{\sin 40°} = \frac{18}{\sin 60°}$$

$$BC\sin 60° = 18\sin 40°$$

$$\frac{BC\sin 60°}{\sin 60°} = \frac{18\sin 40°}{\sin 60°}$$

$$BC = \frac{18\sin 40°}{\sin 60°}$$

$$BC = 13.4 \text{ cm (to the nearest tenth)}$$

Example

Determine the measure of angle θ, to the nearest tenth, in the triangle shown below.

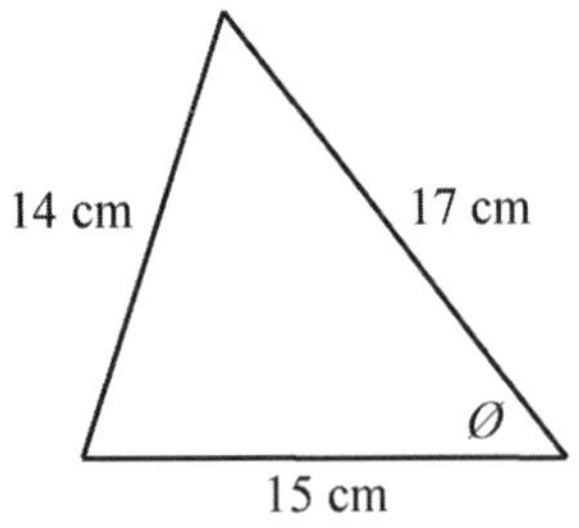

The lengths of all three sides (SSS) of the triangle are given; therefore, apply the law of cosines $\cos A = \frac{b^2 + c^2 - a^2}{2bc}$ as follows:
Since the side measuring 14 cm is opposite angle θ, write the following:

$$\cos\theta = \frac{17^2 + 15^2 - 14^2}{2(17)(15)}$$

$$\cos\theta = \frac{289 + 225 - 196}{510}$$

$$\cos\theta = \frac{318}{510}$$

$$\theta = 51.4° \text{ (to the nearest tenth)}$$

Example

In ΔDEF, $\angle D = 48°$, $EF = 27$ cm, and $DF = 32$ cm. Determine the measure of $\angle E$ to the nearest tenth.

To begin, draw a sketch of the given triangle, and place the indicated measurements in the appropriate location.

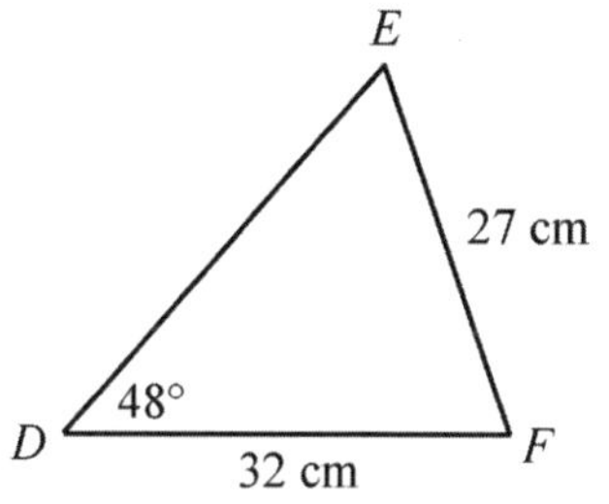

Since this is not an *SSS* situation, apply the law of sines as follows:
Since the side measuring 27 cm is opposite the 48° angle and the side measuring 32 cm is opposite $\angle E$, write the following:

$$\frac{27}{\sin 48°} = \frac{32}{\sin E}$$

$$27\sin E = 32\sin 48°$$

$$\frac{27\sin E}{27} = \frac{32\sin 48°}{27}$$

$$\sin E = \frac{32\sin 48°}{27}$$

$$E = 61.7° \text{ (to the nearest tenth)}$$

Practice

23. Triangle *ABC* has sides measuring 17 m, 23 m, and 24 m. Correct to the nearest degree, what is the measure of the angle opposite the side measuring 23 m?

A. 35° **B.** 42° **C.** 66° **D.** 72°

Use the following information to answer the next question.

A student is asked to determine the length of side x in the given diagram.

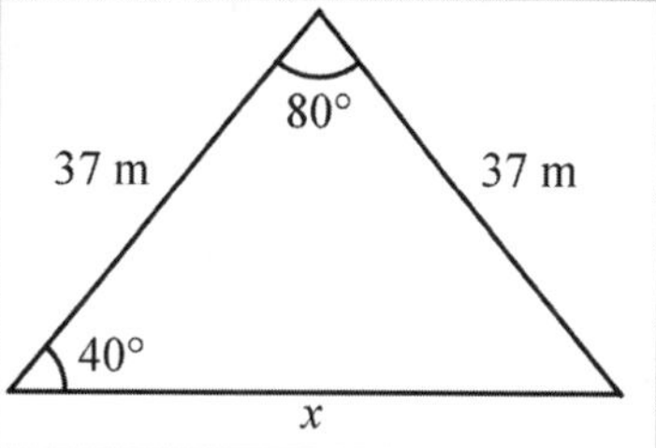

24. Which of the following equations can the student use in order to solve for the length of side x?

A. $\frac{x}{\sin 40} = \frac{37}{\sin 80}$

B. $\sin 40 = \frac{37}{x}$

C. $x^2 = 37^2 + 37^2 - 2(37)(37)\cos(80°)$

D. $x^2 = 37^2 + 37^2 - 2(37)(37)\cos(40°)$

Use the following information to answer the next question.

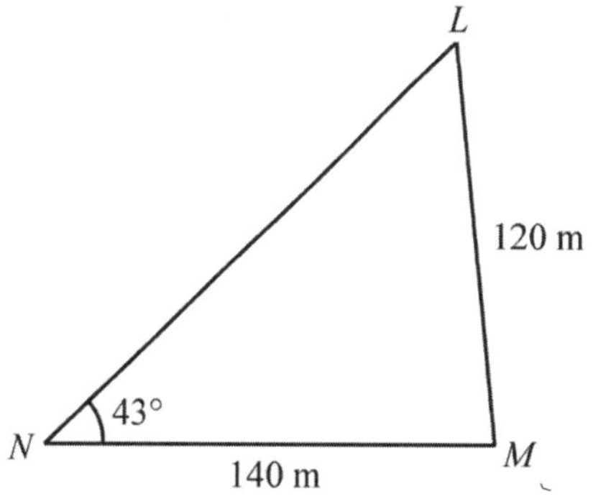

25. To the nearest degree, what is the measure of angle M?

A. 84° **B.** 72° **C.** 53° **D.** 36°

Use the following information to answer the next question.

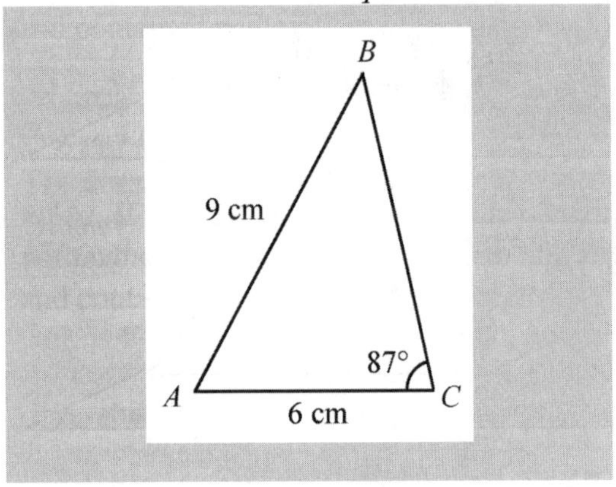

26. Correct to the nearest degree, what is the measure of $\angle B$?

A. 87° **B.** 34°

C. 40° **D.** 42°

CHALLENGER QUESTION

Numerical Response

27.

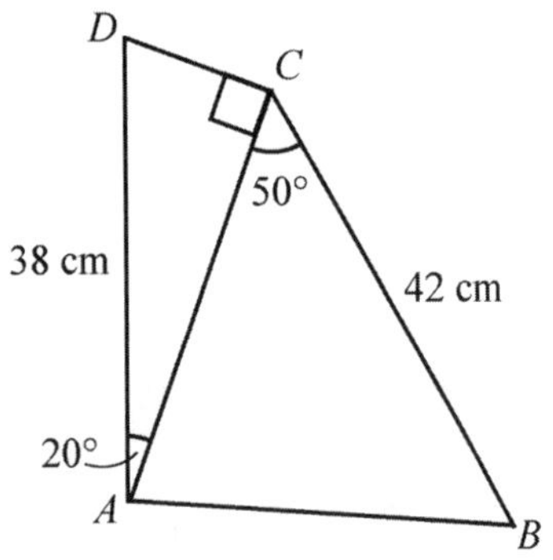

Correct to the nearest centimetre, what is the perimeter of ΔABC?

TR3.4 *solve problems involving the measures of sides and angles in acute triangles*

Solving Problems Using the Sine and Cosine Laws

The law of sines and the law of cosines can be used to solve problems involving acute triangles.
Here are some problem solving suggestions:

1. Read the problem carefully. Determine what it is you are asked to solve for and what information you are given.
2. If a diagram is not given, draw a sketch to represent the situation presented in the problem.
3. Examine the diagram in order to decide whether to make use of the law of sines or the law of cosines.
4. If you are asked to find a "missing" side length, then apply the law of cosines in a side-angle-side situation; otherwise, apply the law of sines.
5. If you are asked to find a "missing" angle measure, apply the law of cosines in a side-side-side situation; otherwise, apply the law of sines.
6. Make substitutions into the appropriate formula, and then use correct algebraic steps to solve for the unknown value.
7. Check your calculations.
8. Write a concluding statement.

Some of these problem solving suggestions are used in the following four problems.

Example

A radar tracking station locates a fishing boat at a distance of 3.4 km from the tracking station and a passenger ferry at a distance of 5.6 km from the tracking station. From the tracking station, the angle between the line of sight to the two ships is 86°. To the nearest tenth, determine the distance between the two ships.

Let x represent the distance between the two ships.

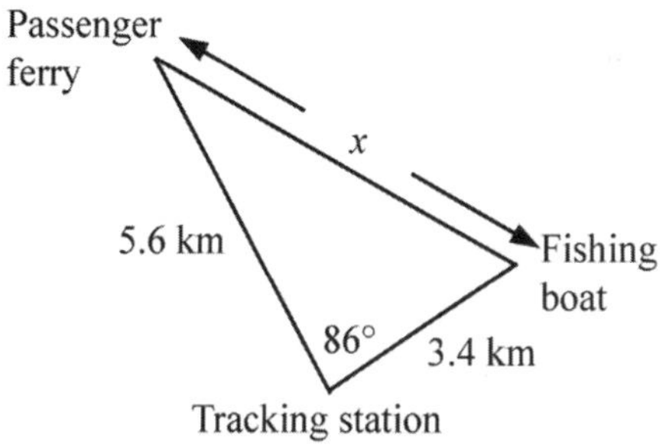

Since it is a side-angle-side situation, use the law of cosines. Side x is opposite the 86° angle; therefore, solve for x as follows:

$$x^2 = 5.6^2 + 3.4^2 - 2(5.6)(3.4)\cos 86°$$

$$x^2 \approx 31.36 + 11.56 - 2.66$$

$$x^2 \approx 40.26$$

$$x \approx \sqrt{40.26}$$

$$x \approx 6.3$$

The distance between the fishing boat and the passenger ferry, to the nearest tenth, is 6.3 km.

Example

Two points, A and B, are separated by a body of water. In order to find the distance between the two points, line AC is measured and found to be 600 m in length. A measuring device is then used to determine that $\angle BAC = 49°$ and $\angle ACB = 68°$. What is the distance between points A and B to the nearest tenth?

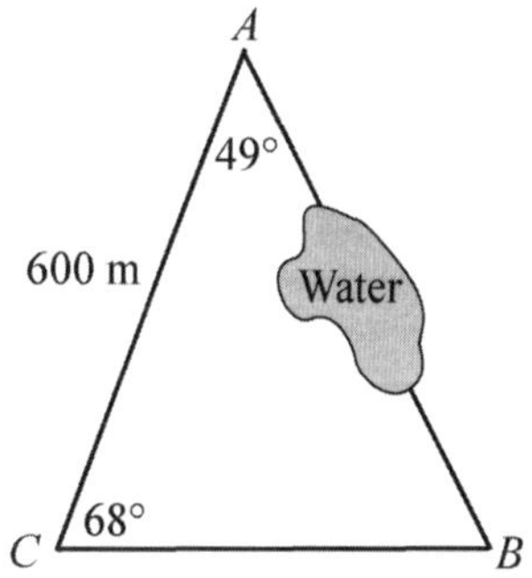

Since it is not a side-angle-side situation, make use of the law of sines. Side AB is opposite the 68° angle, and side AC (600 m) is opposite angle B. The measure of $\angle B$ is $63°(180° - 49° - 68°)$. Now, solve for AB as follows:

$$\frac{AB}{\sin 68°} = \frac{600}{\sin 63°}$$

$$AB\sin 63° = 600\sin 68°$$

$$\frac{AB\sin 63°}{\sin 63°} = \frac{600\sin 68°}{\sin 63°}$$

$$AB = \frac{600\sin 68°}{\sin 63°}$$

$$AB = 624.4 \text{ (to the nearest tenth)}$$

The distance between points A and B, to the nearest tenth, is 624.4 km.

Example

To display the Stanley Cup, staff at a hockey arena roped off a triangular area and installed a security camera, as shown below.

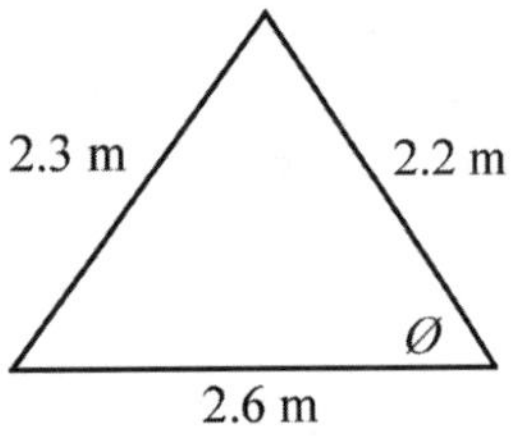

The security camera was installed so that it rotated continuously between the two indicated ropes. To the nearest tenth, determine the measure of angle θ.

Since it is a side-side-side situation, make use of the law of cosines. Angle θ is opposite the side measuring 2.3 m, so solve for θ as follows:

$$\cos\theta = \frac{2.6^2 + 2.2^2 - 2.3^2}{2(2.6)(2.2)}$$

$$\cos\theta = \frac{6.76 + 4.84 - 5.29}{11.44}$$

$$\cos\theta = \frac{6.31}{11.44}$$

$$\theta = 56.5° \text{ (to the nearest tenth)}$$

To the nearest tenth, the measure of angle θ is 56.5°.

Example

During hockey practice, the players performed the following drill as shown in the given diagram. Player A passed the puck to player B, who is 12 m away. Player B redirected the puck at an angle of 40° to player C. Player C then passed the puck back to player A who was standing 9 m away.

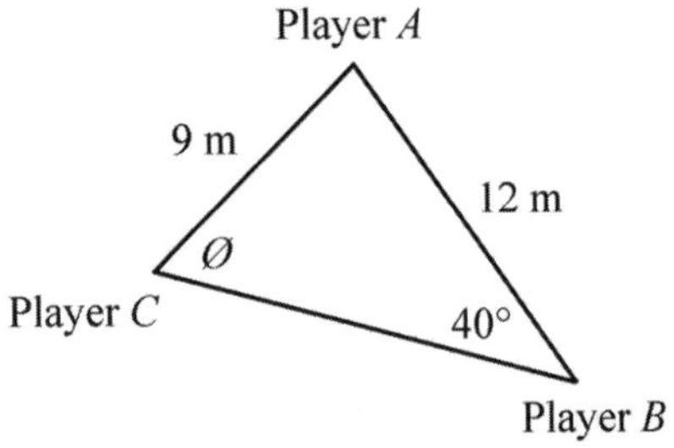

To the nearest degree, determine the measure of angle θ.

Since it is not a side-side-side situation, make use of the law of sines. The side measuring 9 m is opposite the 40° angle and the side measuring 12 m is opposite angle θ. Solve for θ as follows:

$$\frac{9}{\sin 40°} = \frac{12}{\sin\theta}$$

$$9\sin\theta = 12\sin 40°$$

$$\frac{9\sin\theta}{9} = \frac{12\sin 40°}{9}$$

$$\sin\theta = \frac{12\sin 40°}{9}$$

$$\theta = 59° \text{ (to the nearest tenth)}$$

The measure of angle θ, to the nearest degree, is 59°.

Practice

Use the following information to answer the next multipart question.

28. Danny is in a 90 m high watchtower. Lily and Bryan are out searching for clues in regards to the route taken by an escaped prisoner. Lily radios to Danny that she has found some evidence and estimates that she is 350 m from the base of the watchtower. Danny radios this information to Bryan, who estimates that from this location, the angle of elevation to the top of the watchtower is 20°. Danny estimates that the angle from Bryan to the base of the watchtower to Lily is 85°, as shown in the diagram.

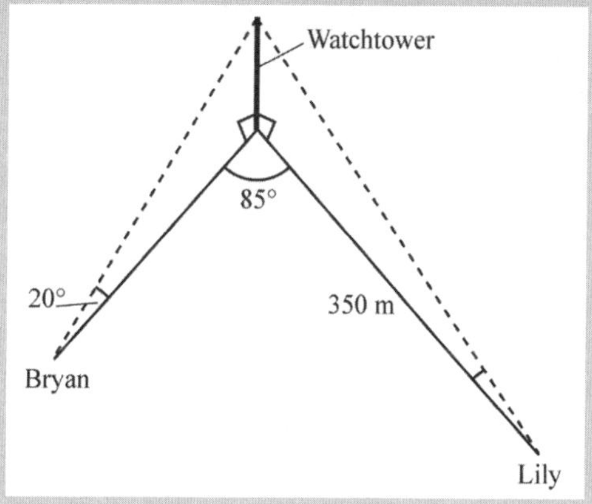

Part A

Open Response

To the nearest metre, how far is Bryan from the base of the watchtower?

Part B

Open Response

To the nearest metre, how far apart are Bryan and Lily?

Use the following information to answer the next question.

A power station is situated on a cliff h metres above a river. A surveyor maps out a triangle across the river with measurements as indicated in the diagram shown. From the surveyor's position at S, the angle of elevation to the base of the power station is 65°.

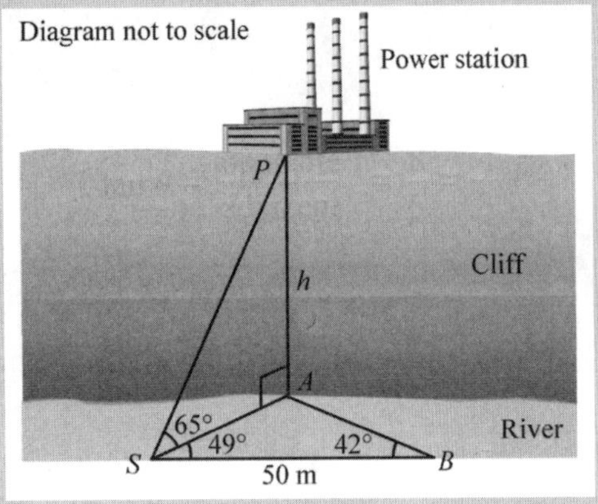

29. To the nearest metre, what is the height of the cliff, h?

A. 72 m **B.** 81 m

C. 95 m **D.** 121 m

Use the following information to answer the next question.

A golf course designer wishes to design a risk-reward golf hole around a small pond as shown in the diagram.

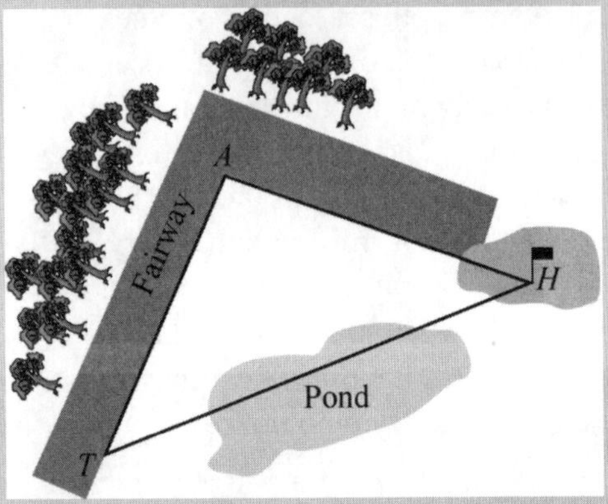

A golfer has two options. He can play "save-and-shoot" from point T to point A and then from point A to point H, or he can play a high-risk shot and attempt to shoot directly from point T to point H.

30. A golfer estimates that the distance from point T to point A is 175 m, the measure of angle ATH = 45°, and the measure of angle TAH = 95°. If the golfer's estimates are accurate, then the distance from point T to point H, correct to the nearest metre, is

A. 193 m **B.** 247 m

C. 265 m **D.** 271 m

Use the following information to answer the next question.

The Royal Caribbean, the Norwegian, and the Princess cruise ships are moored in the harbour off George Town, Grand Cayman. The distance between the Norwegian and the Princess is 250 m. The angle formed by the Royal Caribbean, the Princess, and the Norwegian is 85°, and the angle formed by the Royal Caribbean, the Norwegian, and the Princess is 24° as shown in the diagram.

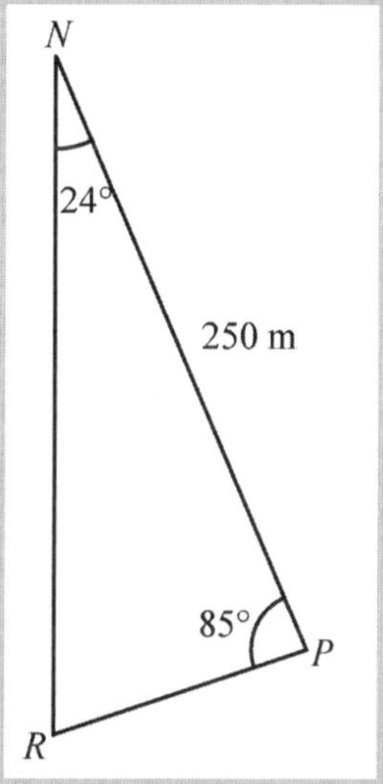

R = Royal Caribbean

P = Princess

N = Norwegian

31. Correct to the nearest metre, what is the distance between the Royal Caribbean and the Norwegian cruise ships?

A. 237 m **B.** 263 m

C. 581 m **D.** 612 m

CHALLENGER QUESTION

Use the following information to answer the next question.

A golf course engineer designs a golf hole that curves to the right. In golf terms, this is called a "dog-leg right." The designer places four reference points on his sketch of the hole. One reference point (T) is at the starting location, one is at each side of the dog leg (A and B), and the last point is where the hole is (G), as shown in the diagram.

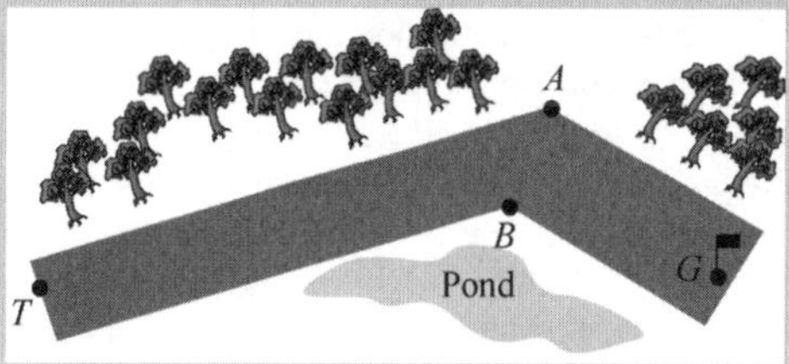

32. In the designer's sketch, distance TA = 240 m, distance TB = 210 m, $\angle ATB$ = 10°, $\angle GAB$ = 68°, and $\angle GBA$ = 84°. Correct to the nearest metre, distance BG is

A. 46 m **B.** 53 m

C. 97 m **D.** 104 m

SOLUTIONS–TRIGONOMETRY

1. A	**8. A**	**15. C**	**21. D**	**28.** Part A- **OR**
2. B	**9. B**	**16. C**	**22. D**	Part B- **OR**
3. A	**10. C**	**17. D**	**23. C**	**29. A**
4. D	**11. A**	**18.** Part A- **OR**	**24. C**	**30. D**
5. A	**12. B**	Part B- **OR**	**25. A**	**31. B**
6. B	**13. 24.9**	**19. D**	**26. D**	**32. C**
7. 67.5	**14. A**	**20. B**	**27. 111**	

1. A

In similar triangles, corresponding angles are equal, and the length of corresponding sides are proportional.
If ΔABC is similar to ΔDEF, then $\angle A = \angle D$ and $\angle C = \angle F$, which means the remaining angles are also equal ($\angle B = \angle E$).
Therefore, by verifying $\angle C = \angle F$, the two triangles are guaranteed to be similar since all corresponding angles are equal.

2. B

Similar triangles have the same shape, but not necessarily the same size and have the following properties:

1. Corresponding angles are equal.
   $\angle A = \angle A'$ and $\angle B = \angle B'$ and $\angle C = \angle C'$
2. Corresponding sides have proportional lengths.
   $\frac{a}{a'} = \frac{b}{b'} = \frac{c}{c'}$

Therefore, the ratio of corresponding sides are equal and the measure of corresponding angles are equal.

3. A

The two triangles are similar since the corresponding angles are equal.

$$\frac{3}{y} = \frac{19.5}{26}$$
$$3 \times 26 = 19.5 \times y$$
$$78 = 19.5y$$
$$78 \div 19.5 = y$$
$$4 = y$$

The length of side y is 4.0 units.

4. D

By definition, two triangles are congruent if all pairs of corresponding sides and angles are equal. In this case, all angles are the same, and two corresponding sides are marked as equal, so by SAS, the triangles are congruent.

5. A

Draw a diagram for clarity.

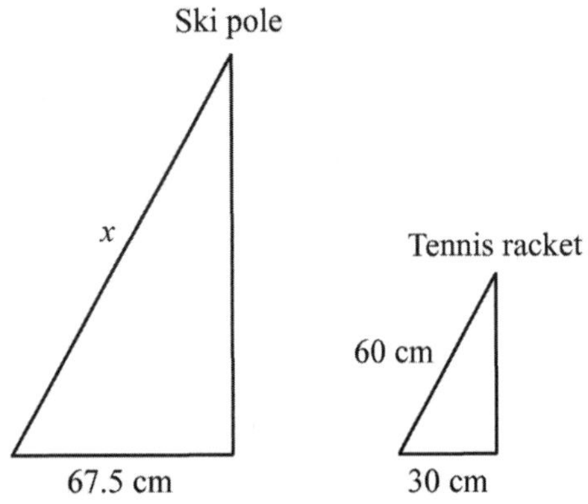

Since both triangles are right triangles (perpendicular with the floor) and have equal angles at the top, the remaining corresponding angles will also be equal. Thus, the triangles are similar.
Therefore, the ratios of the corresponding sides are equal.

$$\frac{x}{67.5 \text{ cm}} = \frac{60.0}{30.0}$$
$$x = \frac{60.0 \times 67.5}{30.0}$$
$$x = 135$$

The length of the ski pole is 135.0 cm.

6. B

The triangles are similar since they are formed using the shadows created by the same angle of the sun at the same point in time, and the remaining corresponding angles are equal. Therefore, corresponding sides will have equal ratios.

$$\frac{10.4}{11.2} = \frac{2.3}{x}$$
$$x = \frac{2.3 \times 11.2}{10.4}$$
$$x \approx 2.4769$$

The height of the statue, to the nearest tenth of a metre, is 2.5 m tall.

7. 67.5

$\angle ABL = \angle CDL$, $\angle BAL = \angle DCL$, and $\angle ALB = \angle CLD$.
Therefore, ΔLAB is similar to ΔLCD.
In similar triangles, the length of corresponding sides are proportional; thus, $\frac{LB}{LD} = \frac{AB}{CD}$.

Solve for CD as follows:

Substitute 12 for LB, $27(12 + 15)$ for LD, and 30 for AB.

$\frac{12}{27} = \frac{30}{CD}$

$12 \times CD = 30 \times 27$

$CD = \frac{30 \times 27}{12}$

$CD = 67.5$

The length of bridge CD is 67.5 m.

8. A

Recall the primary trigonometry ratio.

$\cos\theta = \frac{\text{adjacent}}{\text{hypotenuse}}$ $\quad \cos\theta = \frac{12}{13}$

$\tan\theta = \frac{\text{opposite}}{\text{adjacent}}$ $\quad \tan\theta = \frac{5}{12}$

From the given ratios the following triangle can be drawn

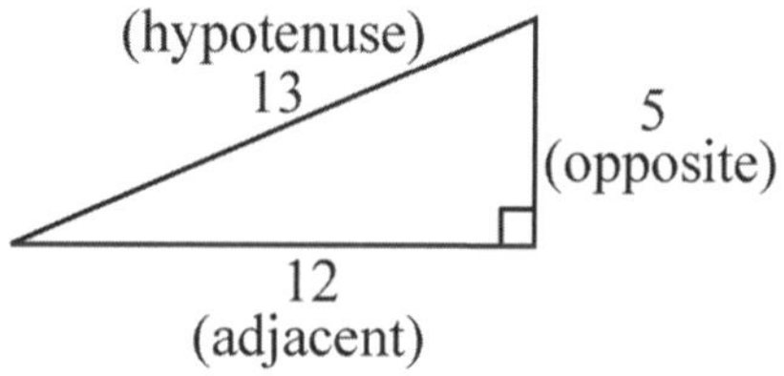

$\sin\theta = \frac{\text{opposite}}{\text{hypotenuse}}$

$\sin\theta = \frac{5}{13}$

9. B

$\tan\theta = \frac{\text{opposite}}{\text{adjacent}}$

$\tan 72° = \frac{c}{a}$

Since $\tan 72° = 3.1$, it follows that $3.1 = \frac{c}{a}$.

10. C

The angle inside the triangle adjacent to 133° is 47° because they are supplementary angles $(180° - 133° = 47°)$.
Therefore,

$\sin 47° = \frac{\text{opposite}}{\text{hypotenuse}} = \frac{11.7}{x}$

$x = \frac{11.7}{\sin 47°}$

$x \approx 15.998$ cm

The length of side x, to the nearest tenth, is 16.0 cm.

11. A

Begin by sketching a diagram to represent the given problem.

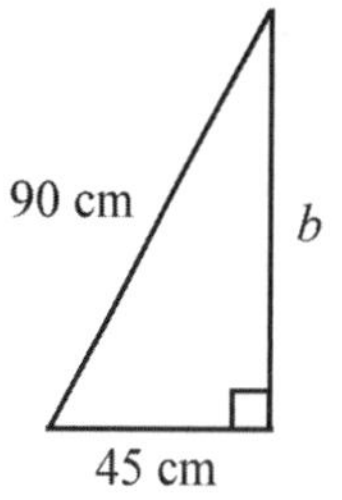

To solve, use the Pythagorean theorem $c^2 = a^2 + b^2$.
Substitute 90 for c and 45 for a.

$(90)^2 = (45)^2 + b^2$

Now, solve for b.

$8\,100 = 2\,025 + b^2$

$6\,075 = b^2$

$b = \sqrt{6\,075}$

$b = \approx 77.942$ cm

To the nearest centimetre, the length of the third side is 78 cm.

12. B

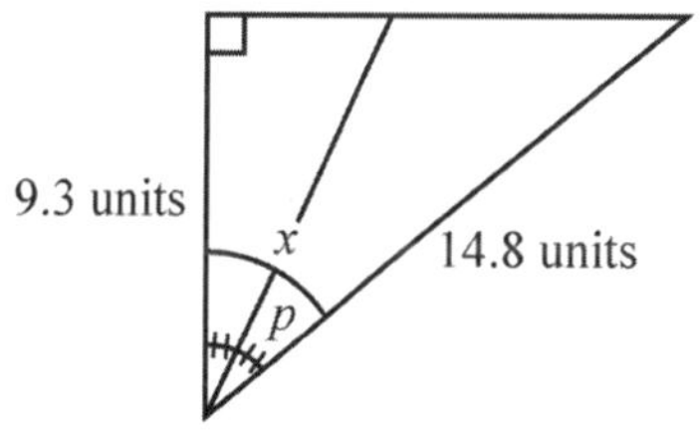

Using the cosine ratio, determine the angle that represents $2p$. The angle is labelled x in the diagram shown.

$\cos x = \frac{\text{adjacent}}{\text{hypotenuse}}$

$\cos x = \frac{9.3}{14.8}$

$\cos x = 0.628378$

$\cos^{-1}(0.628378) = x$

$x \approx 51.069°$

Since $x = 2p$, the measure of angle $p = \frac{x}{2} \approx \frac{51.069°}{2} = 25.5°$.

13. 24.9

Begin by applying the Pythagorean theorem in ΔBDC as follows:

$(BD)^2 + (CD)^2 = (BC)^2$

Substitute 63 for CD and 65 for BC

$(BD)^2 + (63)^2 = (65)^2$

$(BD)^2 + 3\,969 = 4\,225$

$(BD)^2 = 256$

$BD = \sqrt{256}$

$BD = 16$

In ΔABD, $\sin 40° = \frac{BD}{AB}$

Substitute 16 for BD.

$\sin 40° = \frac{16}{AB}$

$AB \sin 40° = 16$

$AB = \frac{16}{\sin 40°}$

$AB \approx 24.89$

Correct to the nearest tenth, the length of side AB is 24.9 m.

14. A

Let x represent the unknown angle between Wire B and the ground. Since there are two right triangles in the diagram, use the smaller right triangle to solve for the vertical distance of the telephone pole. This is needed to solve for the unknown angle. Let y represent the vertical distance of the telephone pole.

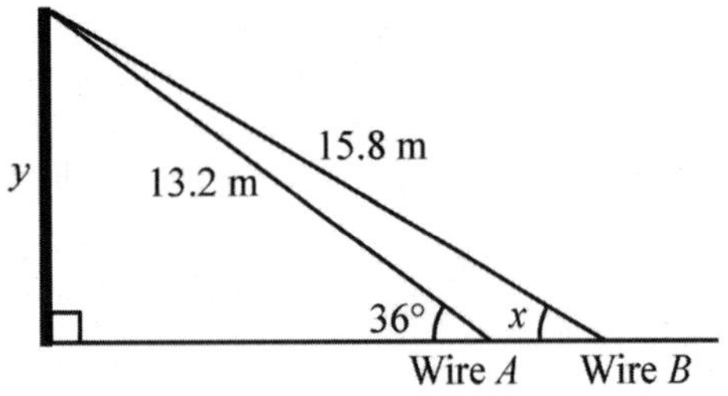

Use the sine ratio to solve for y.

$\sin\theta = \frac{\text{opposite}}{\text{hypotenuse}}$

$\sin 36° = \frac{y}{13.2}$

$y = 13.2 \times \sin 36°$

$y \approx 7.759$ m

Use the sine ratio again to solve for x.

$\sin\theta = \frac{\text{opposite}}{\text{hypotenuse}}$

$\sin x \approx \frac{7.759}{15.8}$

$\sin^{-1}\left(\frac{7.759}{15.8}\right) \approx x$

$x \approx 29.411$

The angle between Wire B and the ground to the nearest degree is 29°.

15. C

The tent is made up of two congruent right triangles. Use the cosine ratio to determine the length of $\frac{1}{2}x$, labelled y, as shown below.

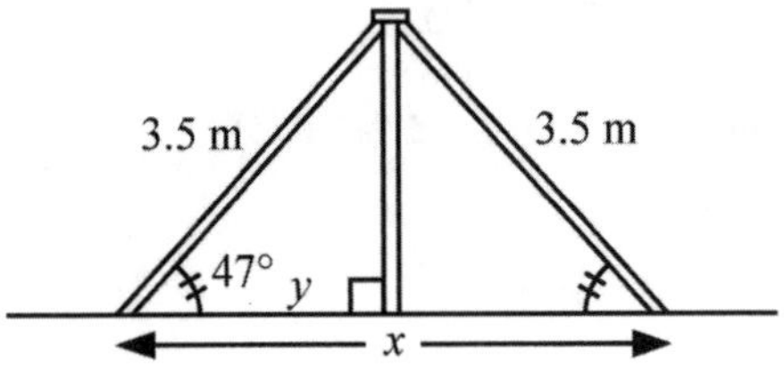

$\cos\theta = \frac{\text{adjacent}}{\text{hypotenuse}}$

$\cos 47° = \frac{y}{3.5}$

$y = (3.5)(\cos 47°)$

$y \approx 2.387$

Since $x = 2y$, $x \approx 2(2.387) \approx 4.774$

The width of the tent at its base, to the nearest tenth, is 4.8 m.

16. C

Represent the distance from the top of the shorter building to the top of the second building as w.

Thus, $y = w + x$. To determine x, use the tangent ratio.

$\tan\theta = \frac{\text{opposite}}{\text{adjacent}}$

$\tan 26° = \frac{x}{40}$

$40 \times \tan 26° = x$

$x \approx 19.509$

Similarly for w,

$\tan\theta = \frac{\text{opposite}}{\text{adjacent}}$

$\tan 37° = \frac{w}{40}$

$40 \times \tan 37° = w$

$w \approx 30.142$

Substitute the values of x and y into the equation $y = w + x$.

$y \approx 19.509 + 30.142$

$y \approx 49.651$

The height of the taller building, to the nearest tenth, is 49.7 m.

17. D

Since there is a right angle from Lynn's house to school to the café, determine the acute angle 19°(90° – 71°) inside the right triangle formed from the café to the school. To determine the total distance from school to the café and then to Marrah's house, determine the unknown side x, as shown below, using the tangent ratio.

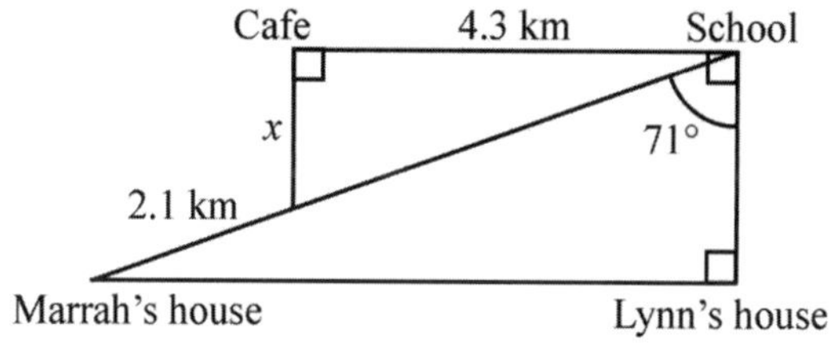

$\tan \theta = \dfrac{\text{opposite}}{\text{adjacent}}$

$\tan 19° = \dfrac{x}{4.3}$

$4.3 \times \tan 19° = x$

$x = 1.5$ km to the nearest tenth

The total distance is calculated by adding the three distances that make up the route from the school to the café to Marrah's house.

4.3 km + 1.5 km + 2.1 km = 7.9 km

18. Part A – Open Response

The given diagram can be labelled as shown below.

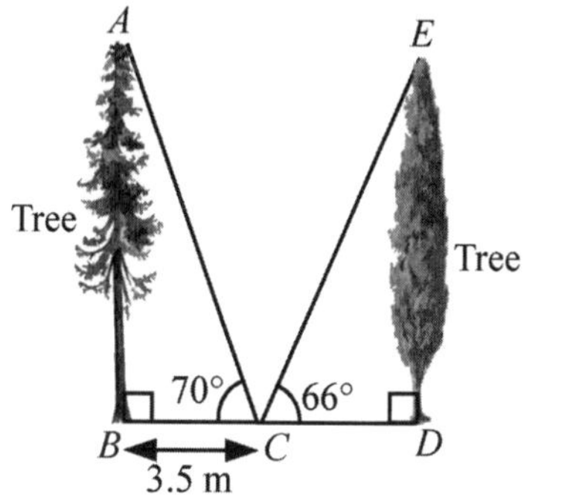

Diagram not to scale

In ΔABC, the length of the ladder, AC, can be determined as follows:

$\cos 70° = \dfrac{BC}{AC}$

Substitute 3.5 for BC.

$\cos 70° = \dfrac{3.5}{AC}$

$AC \times \cos 70° = 3.5$

$AC = \dfrac{3.5}{\cos 70°}$

$AC \approx 10.23$

The length of the ladder correct to the nearest tenth is 10.2 m.

Part B – Open Response

The distance between the bases of the two trees is equal to the distance from B to D. Since $BD = BC + CD$, it is necessary to determine the length of BC and CD.

Since $BC = 3.5$ m, solve for CD using the following procedure:

In ΔCDE, $\cos 66° = \dfrac{CD}{CE}$

Substitute 10.23 for CE, since $CE = AC$.

$\cos 66° = \dfrac{CD}{10.23}$

$CD = 10.23 \times \cos 66°$

$CD = 4.2$ (to the nearest tenth)

Recall that $BD = BC + CD$.

Thus, $BD = 3.5 + 4.2 = 7.7$

To the nearest tenth, the distance between the bases of the two trees is 7.7 m.

19. D

$\sin A = \dfrac{h}{b}$ implies that $b \times \sin A = h$.

$\sin B = \dfrac{h}{a}$ implies that $a \times \sin B = h$.

Since the value of h is identical in each equation, it follows that $b \times \sin A = a \times \sin B$ or $b\sin A = a\sin B$.

20. B

In general, the law of sines states that $\dfrac{a}{\sin A} = \dfrac{b}{\sin B}$.

Thus, in the ratio $\dfrac{80}{\sin 50°} = \dfrac{65}{\sin x°}$, the 50° angle must be opposite the side measuring 80 m and the $x°$ angle must be opposite the side measuring 65 m.

21. D

One form of the law of cosines is $\cos A = \dfrac{b^2 + c^2 - a^2}{2bc}$.

The equation $\cos x° = \dfrac{15^2 + 20^2 - 17^2}{2(15)(20)}$ implies that the side measuring 17 cm is opposite to the angle measuring $x°$.

22. D

The law of cosines can be represented by the general equation $a^2 = b^2 + c^2 - 2bc\cos A$.

This equation implies that angle A is opposite side a.

In the given triangle, angle R is opposite PQ, angle P is opposite QR, and angle Q is opposite PR. Thus, the equation

$(QR)^2 = (QP)^2 + (PR)^2 - 2(QP)(PR)\cos P$ correctly represents the law of cosines.

23. C

Begin by sketching triangle ABC and placing the given measurements in the appropriate location. One possible sketch is shown below.

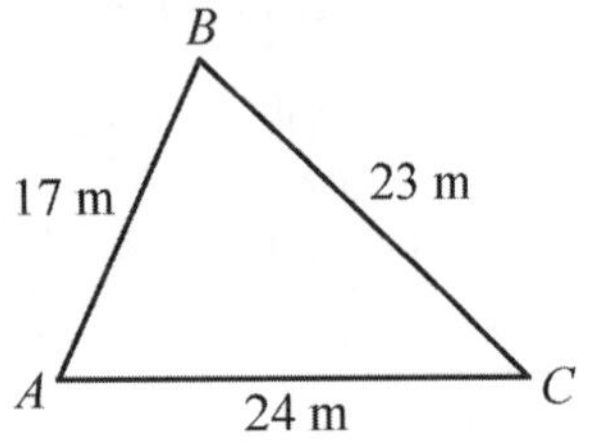

In the given sketch, $\angle A$ is opposite the side measuring 23 m. Since this is a side-side-side situation, determine the measure of $\angle A$ by applying the law of cosines as follows:

$\cos A = \dfrac{(AB)^2 + (AC)^2 - (BC)^2}{2(AB)(AC)}$

Substitute 17 for AB, 24 for AC, and 23 for BC.

$\cos A = \dfrac{17^2 + 24^2 - 23^2}{2(17)(24)}$

$\cos A = \dfrac{336}{816}$

$\cos A \approx 0.4118$

$A \approx 65.68°$

The measure of the angle opposite the side measuring 23 m, to the nearest degree, is 66°.

24. C

In the given triangle, it is a side-angle-side situation, so use the law of cosines in order to solve for x.

The general form of the law of cosines is $a^2 = b^2 + c^2 - 2bc \cos A$. By making the appropriate substitutions, the equation becomes $x^2 = 37^2 + 37^2 - 2(37)(37)\cos(80°)$.

25. A

In ΔLMN, it is not a side-side-side situation; therefore, use the law of sines in order to determine the measure of angle M as follows:

To begin, determine the measure of angle L since angle L is opposite side MN.

$\dfrac{MN}{\sin L} = \dfrac{LM}{\sin N}$

Substitute 140 for MN, 120 for LM, and 43° for N.

$\dfrac{140}{\sin L} = \dfrac{120}{\sin 43°}$

$120 \times \sin L = 140 \times \sin 43°$

$\sin L = \dfrac{140 \times \sin 43}{120}$

$\sin L = 0.795$

$L = 52.7°$

To the nearest degree, the measure of angle M is 84° (180° – 43° – 53°).

26. D

In ΔABC, it is not a side-angle-side situation; therefore, use the law of sines to determine the measure of $\angle B$ as follows:

$\dfrac{AC}{\sin B} = \dfrac{AB}{\sin C}$

Substitute 6 for AC, 9 for AB, and 87° for C.

$\dfrac{6}{\sin B} = \dfrac{9}{\sin 87°}$

$9 \times \sin B = 6 \times \sin 87°$

$\sin B = \dfrac{6 \times \sin 87°}{9}$

$\sin B \approx 0.6658$

$B \approx 41.7°$

The measure of $\angle B$, to the nearest degree, is 42°.

27. 111

In order to determine the perimeter of ΔABC, find the length of each of the three sides of the triangle. The length of side BC is given, but the lengths of side AC and AB must be determined.

In ΔDAC, $\cos \angle DAC = \dfrac{AC}{AD}$

Substitute 20° for $\angle DAC$ and 38 for AD.

$\cos 20° = \dfrac{AC}{38}$

$AC = 38 \times \cos 20°$

$AC \approx 35.71$

In ΔABC, use the law of cosines to determine AB as follows:

$(AB)^2 = (AC)^2 + (BC)^2 - 2(AC)(BC)\cos \angle ACB$

Substitute 35.71 for AC, 42 for BC, and 50° for $\angle ACB$.

$(AB)^2 = (35.71)^2 + (42)^2 - 2(35.71)(42)\cos 50°$

$(AB)^2 \approx 1\,111.07$

$AB \approx 33.33$

The perimeter of ΔABC, to the nearest centimetre, is 111 cm (42 + 35.71 + 33.33).

28. Part A – Open Response

ΔABC

$\tan B = \dfrac{AC}{BC}$

Substitute 20° for $\angle B$ and 90 for AC.

$\tan 20° = \dfrac{90}{BC}$

$BC \times \tan 20° = 90$

$BC = \dfrac{90}{\tan 20°}$

$BC \approx 247.27$

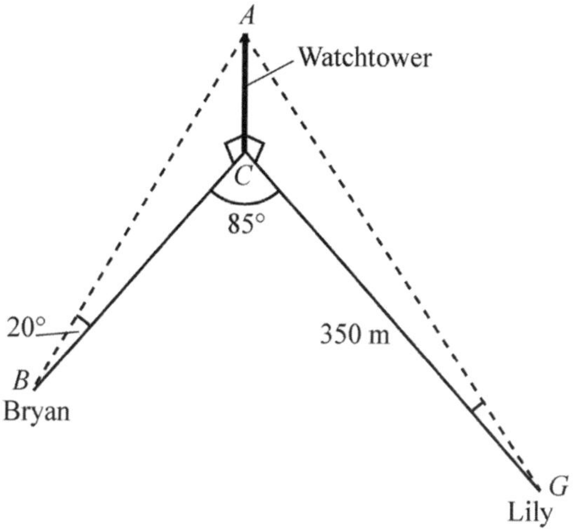

To the nearest metre, Bryan is 247 m from the base of the watchtower.

Part B – Open Response

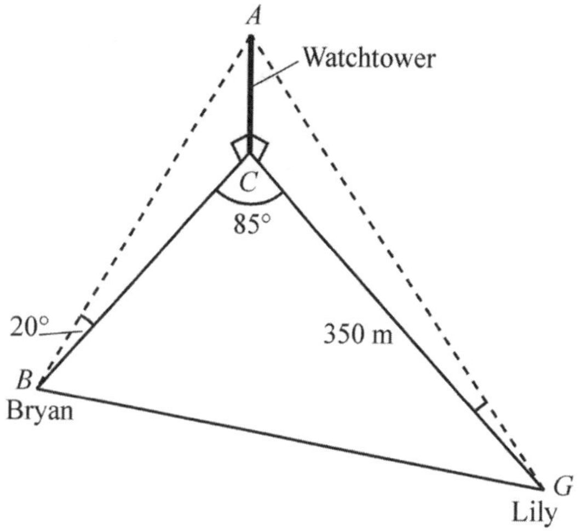

Connect B to G. In ΔBCG, make use of the law of cosines as follows:

$(BG)^2 = (BC)^2 + (CG)^2 - 2(BC)(CG)\cos \angle BCG$

Substitute 247.27 for BC, 350 for CG, and 85° for $\angle BCG$.

$(BG)^2 = 247.27^2 + 350^2 - 2(247.27)(350)\cos 85°$

$(BG)^2 \approx 61\,142.45 + 122\,500 - 15\,085.70$

$(BG)^2 \approx 168\,556.75$

$BG \approx \sqrt{168\,556.75}$

$BG \approx 410.56$

To the nearest metre, Bryan and Lily are 411 m apart.

29. A

Begin by determining the distance from point S to point A in ΔSAB by applying the law of sines as shown:

$\dfrac{SA}{\sin \angle SBA} = \dfrac{SB}{\sin \angle SAB}$

Substitute 42° for $\angle SBA$, 50 for SB, and 89° (180° – 49° – 42°) for $\angle SAB$.

$\dfrac{SA}{\sin 42°} = \dfrac{50}{\sin 89°}$

$SA \times \sin 89° = 50 \times \sin 42°$

$SA = \dfrac{50 \times \sin 42°}{\sin 89°}$

$SA \approx 33.46$

Next, solve for h in right triangle SAP as follows:

$\tan \angle PSA = \dfrac{PA}{SA}$

Substitute 65° for $\angle PSA$, h for PA, and 33.46 for SA.

$\tan 65° = \dfrac{h}{33.46}$

$h = 33.46 \times \tan 65°$

$h \approx 71.76$

To the nearest metre, the height of the cliff is 72 m.

30. D

In ΔTAH, it is not a side-angle-side situation; therefore, determine the distance from point T to point H by applying the law of sines as show:

$$\frac{\text{TH}}{\sin \angle TAH} = \frac{\text{AT}}{\sin \angle AHT}$$

Substitute 95° for $\angle TAH$, 175 for AT, and 40° $(180° - 95° - 45°)$ for $\angle AHT$.

$$\frac{\text{TH}}{\sin 95°} = \frac{175}{\sin 40°}$$

$TH \times \sin 40° = 175 \times \sin 95°$

$$TH = \frac{175 \times \sin 95°}{\sin 40°}$$

$TH \approx 271.22$

The distance from point T to point H, to the nearest metre, is 271 m.

31. B

In ΔNPR, it is not a side-angle-side situation, so determine the distance between the Royal Caribbean and the Norwegian cruise ships by applying the law of sines as shown:

$$\frac{\text{RN}}{\sin \angle RPN} = \frac{\text{NP}}{\sin \angle NRP}$$

Substitute 85°for $\angle RPN$, 250 for NP, and 71°$(180° - 24° - 85°)$ for $\angle NRP$.

$$\frac{\text{RN}}{\sin 85°} = \frac{250}{\sin 71°}$$

$RN \times \sin 71° = 250 \times \sin 85°$

$$RN = \frac{250 \times \sin 85°}{\sin 71°}$$

$RN \approx 263.40$

To the nearest metre, the distance between the Royal Caribbean and the Norwegian cruise ships is 263 m.

32. C

The given diagram can be labelled as follows:

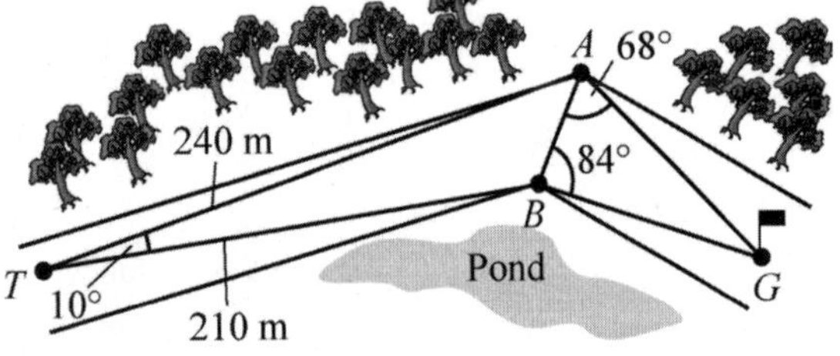

To begin, determine the distance from point A to point B. In ΔATB, it is a side-angle-side situation; therefore, solve for AB by applying the law of cosines as shown:

$(AB)^2 = (TA)^2 + (TB)^2 - 2(TA)(TB)\cos \angle ATB$

Substitute 240 for TA, 210 for TB, and 10° for $\angle ATB$.

$(AB)^2 = 240^2 + 210^2 - 2(240)(210)\cos 10°$

$(AB)^2 \approx 57\,600 + 44\,100 - 99\,268.62$

$(AB)^2 \approx 2\,431.38$

$AB \approx \sqrt{2\,431.38}$

$AB \approx 49.31$

Now, use ΔGAB and apply the law of sines in order to determine the distance BG as follows:

$$\frac{BG}{\sin \angle GAB} = \frac{AB}{\sin \angle AGB}$$

Substitute 68° for $\angle GAB$, 49.31 for AB, and 28°$(180° - 68° - 84°)$ for$\angle AGB$.

$$\frac{BG}{\sin 68°} = \frac{49.31}{\sin 28°}$$

$BG \times \sin 28° = 49.31 \times \sin 68°$

$$BG = \frac{49.31 \times \sin 68°}{\sin 28°}$$

$BG \approx 97.38$

Distance BG, to the nearest metre, is 97 m.

Unit Test

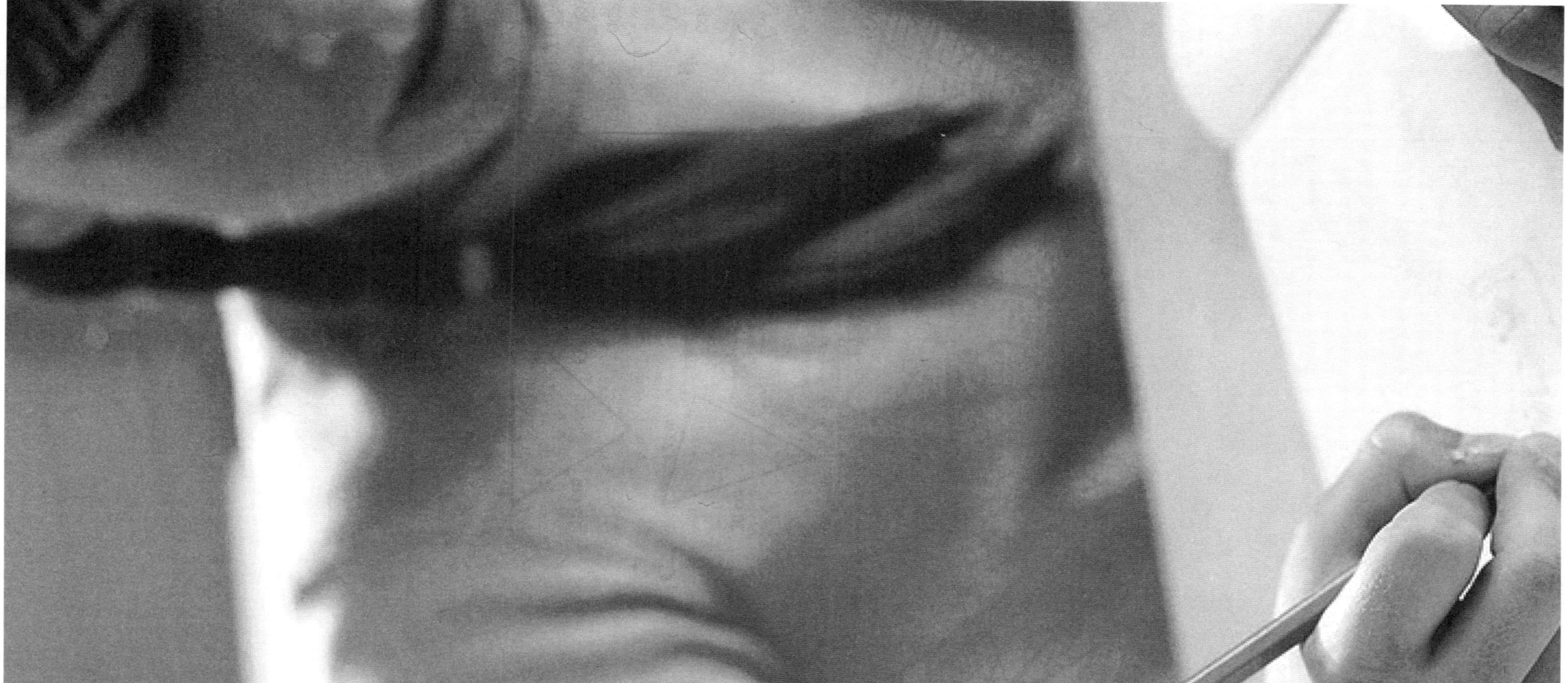

1. Two different triangles are shown.

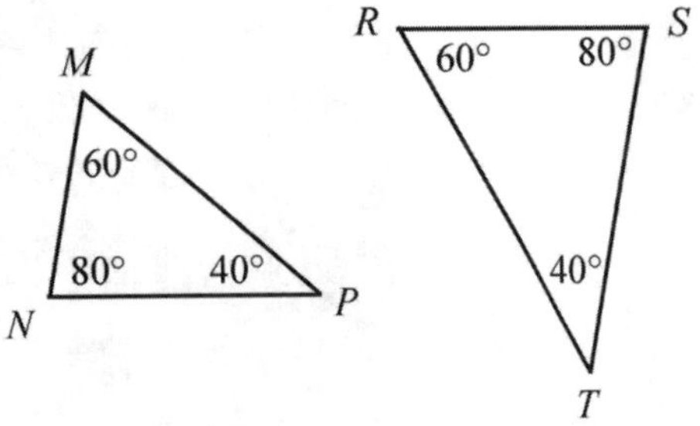

Which of the following equations is **incorrect** with respect to ΔMNP and ΔRST?

A. $\frac{MN}{NP} = \frac{RS}{ST}$

B. $\frac{NP}{ST} = \frac{MP}{RT}$

C. $\frac{MN}{RS} = \frac{MP}{RT}$

D. $\frac{NP}{ST} = \frac{MN}{RT}$

2. Which of the following conditions does **not** guarantee that two triangles are congruent?

A. The measures of the three side lengths of the two triangles are the same.

B. The measures of the three interior angles of the two triangles are the same.

C. The measures of two of the interior angles and the side included by them are the same.

D. The measures of two of the side lengths and the interior angle included by them are the same.

Use the following information to answer the next question.

Mitchell made a drawing of a poster in the shape of a right triangle as shown.

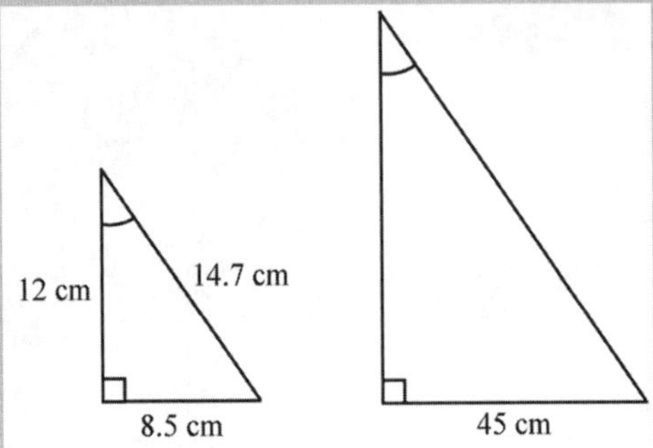

(Diagram not to scale)

3. If one of the sides of the actual poster is 45 cm, what are the actual lengths of the other two sides of the poster, correct to the nearest tenth of a centimetre?

A. 26.7 cm and 45 cm

B. 48.5 cm and 51.2 cm

C. 60.5 cm and 75.8 cm

D. 63.5 cm and 77.8 cm

Numerical Response

4. A 6 m high vertical pole casts a shadow 4 m long. The pole is right beside a building that casts a shadow with a length of 64 m. The approximate height in metres of the building is ___.

Use the following information to answer the next question.

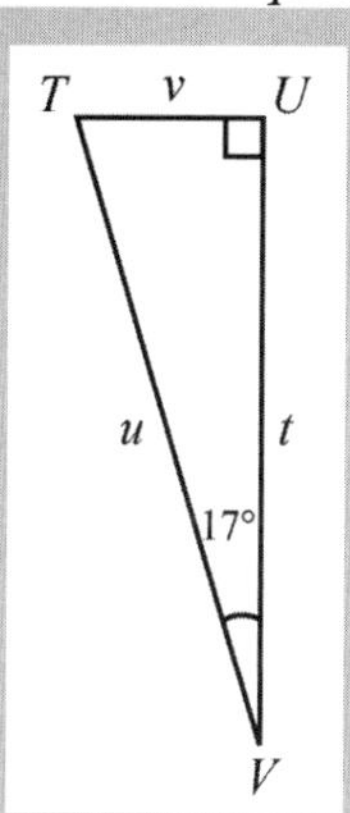

5. What trigonometric ratio is represented by $\frac{t}{v}$ in the diagram?

   A. sin 17° **B.** tan 17°

   C. sin 73° **D.** tan 73°

6.

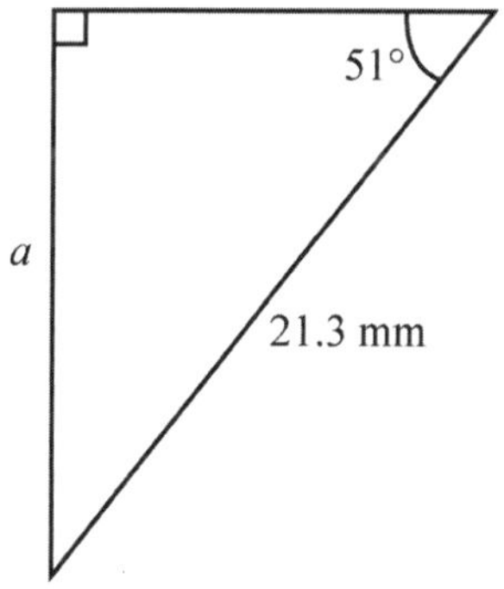

What is the length of side a?

A. 13.4 mm **B.** 16.6 mm

C. 26.3 mm **D.** 27.4 mm

7. The length of the hypotenuse of a right triangle is 30.5 cm. If the length of another side is 5.5 cm, what is the length of the third side of this triangle?

   A. 25 cm **B.** 30 cm

   C. 31 cm **D.** 36 cm

Use the following information to answer the next question.

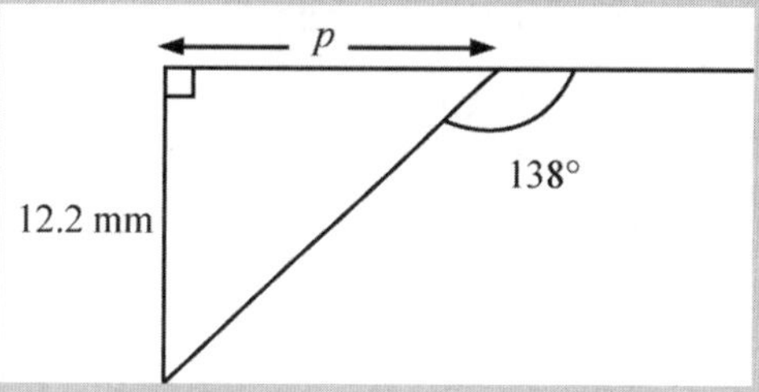

8. What is the length of p?

   A. 8.2 mm **B.** 9.1 mm

   C. 11.0 mm **D.** 13.5 mm

Numerical Response

Use the following information to answer the next question.

A design involving two right triangles is shown.

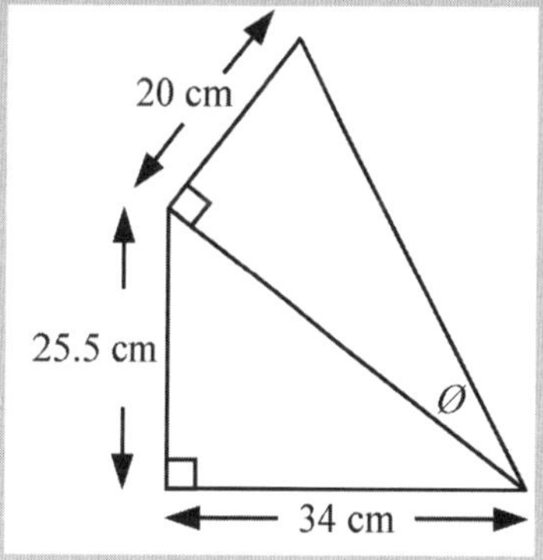

9. To the nearest tenth, the measure of $\angle\theta$ in the design is ____ degrees.

CHALLENGER QUESTION

Use the following information to answer the next question.

To support a score clock in an arena, two cables are attached from the ceiling to the score clock, as shown.

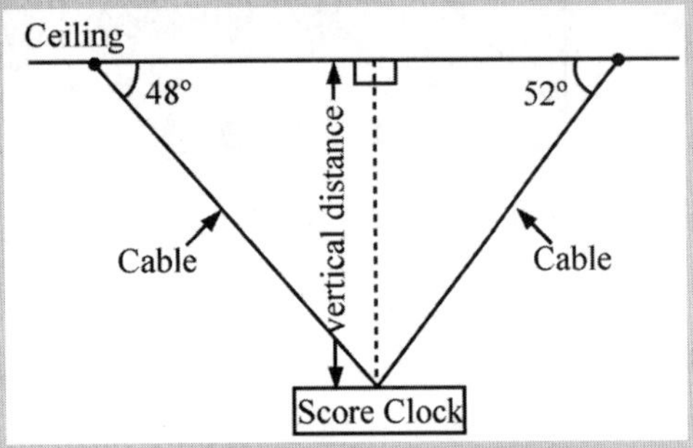

10. If the vertical distance between the top of the score clock and the ceiling is 16 m, then the distance, correct to the nearest tenth of a metre, between the two cables at the point where they are attached to the ceiling is

A. 26.9 m **B.** 29.4 m

C. 30.2 m **D.** 34.9 m

Use the following information to answer the next question.

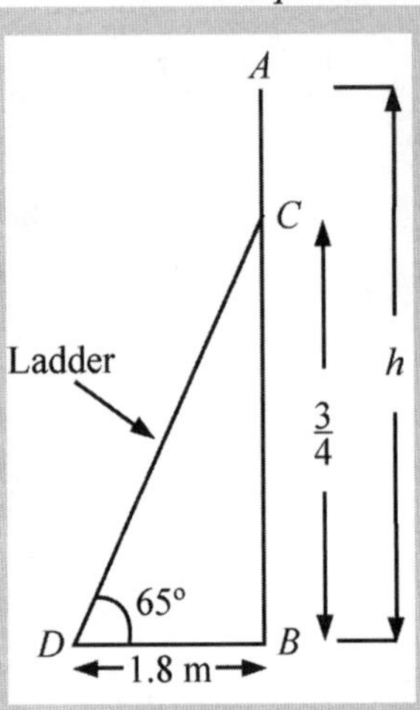

11. In order to paint a pole, George places a ladder against it. The foot of the ladder is 1.8 m away from the pole, and the top of the ladder rests against the pole at a position that is three-quarters up the pole. If the ladder is at an angle of 65° to the ground, what is the actual height of the pole, to the nearest thousandth?

A. 5.193 m **B.** 5.147 m

C. 4.931 m **D.** 4.903 m

Use the following information to answer the next question.

When light is reflected off a smooth surface, such as polished glass, the path it follows can easily be determined.
Almost 2 000 years ago, Hero of Alexandria concluded that the angle at which light strikes a mirror (the angle of incidence) is exactly equal to the angle at which it reflects (the angle of reflection).

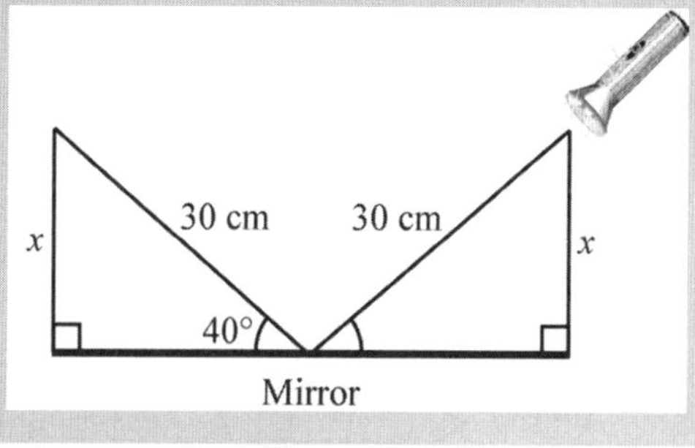

12. If the light from a flashlight reflects off a mirror at a 40° angle and the distance the light travels to the mirror is 30 cm, then, rounded to the nearest tenth of a centimetre, how far is the flashlight from the mirror?

A. 19.3 cm **B.** 23.0 cm

C. 25.2 cm **D.** 46.7 cm

CHALLENGER QUESTION

Numerical Response

Use the following information to answer the next question.

A cellphone transmitter is placed at the top of a vertical tower. Cables are used to help support the tower. One end of a cable is anchored to the ground, and the other end is attached to an anchor at the top of the tower. As shown, two supporting cables are anchored to the ground at points A and B, which are 12 m apart. The angle between the ground and the cable anchored to points A and B is 62° and 72°, respectively.

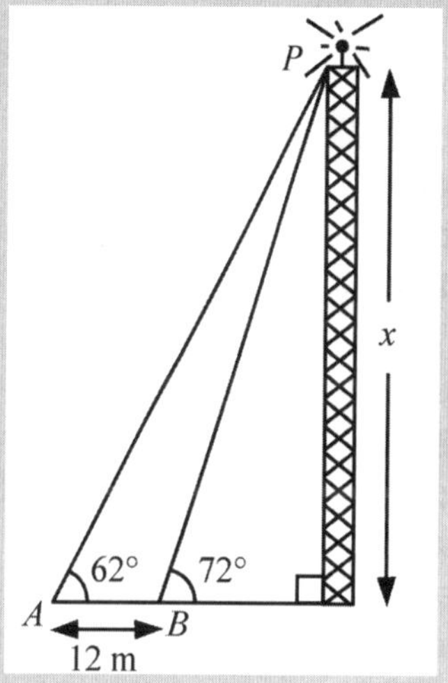

13. To the nearest metre, the height of the tower, x, is ___.

Use the following information to answer the next multipart question.

14. George built a shelf 50 cm in length. In order to keep it secure, he built two supports *BE* and *CD*, as shown in the diagram.

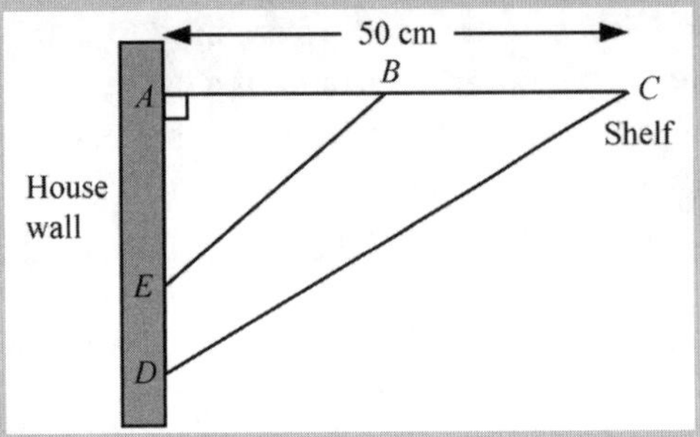

Part A

Open Response

If $\angle ADC = 60°$, what is the length of *CD* to the nearest tenth of a centimetre?

Part B

Open Response

If the distance between anchor point *A* and anchor point *E* is 20 cm, what is the distance between anchor point *D* and *E* to the nearest tenth of a centimetre?

15. The equation $\dfrac{60}{\sin 48°} = \dfrac{x}{\sin 62°}$ applies to which of the following acute triangles?

A.

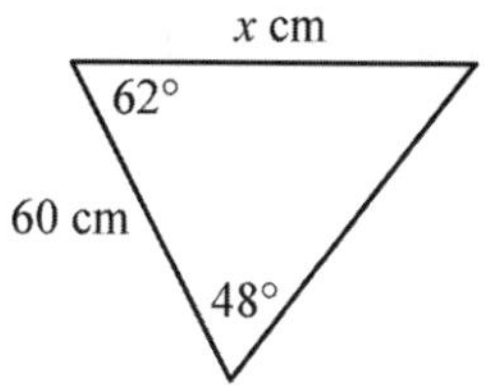

B.

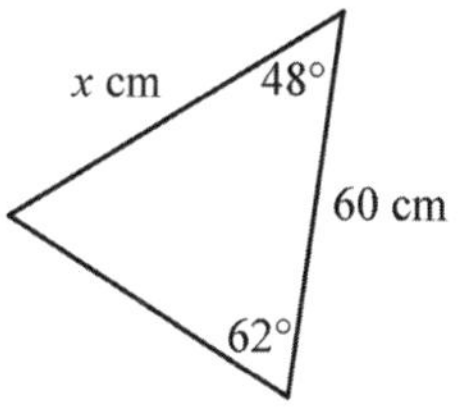

C.

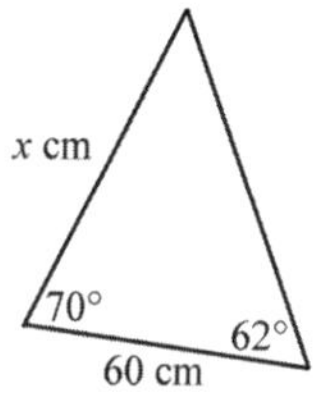

D.

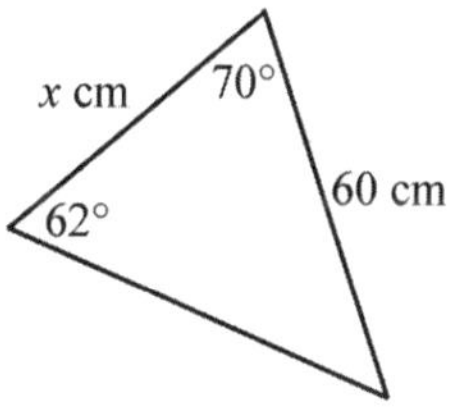

16. For which of the following triangles could the equation
$x^2 = 45^2 + 50^2 - 2(45)(50)\cos 78°$be used to determine the length of side x?

A.

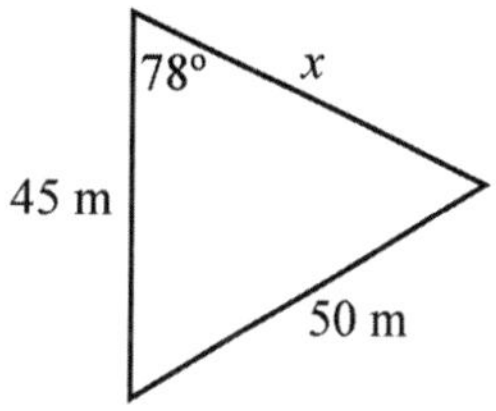

B.

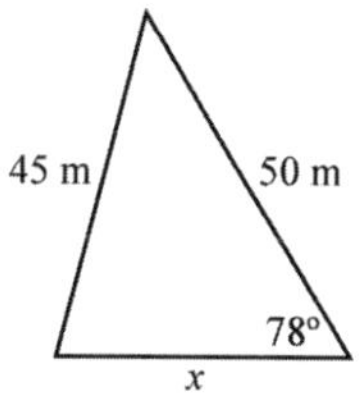

C.

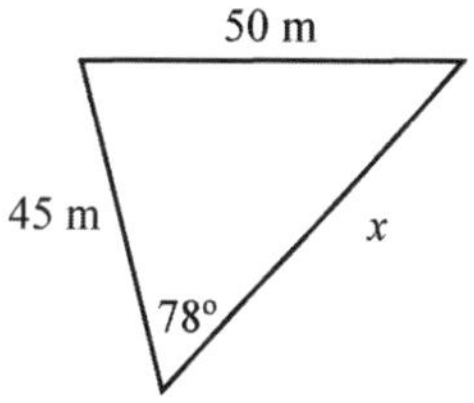

D.

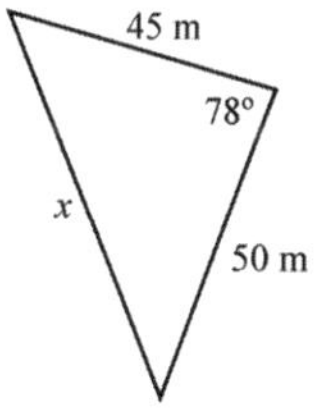

Use the following information to answer the next question.

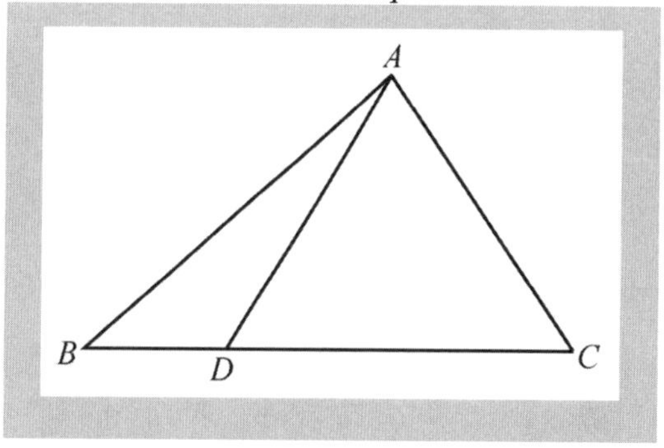

17. If $\angle BAC = 84°$, $AD = 3.4$ m, $CD = 3.8$ m, and $AC = 3.5$ m, then the measure of $\angle BAD$, correct to the nearest tenth, is

A. 26.1° **B.** 24.7°

C. 19.4° **D.** 17.2°

Use the following information to answer the next question.

The diagram illustrates triangle MNP, where MN = 46 cm, NP = 54 cm, and $\angle MPN$ = 48°.

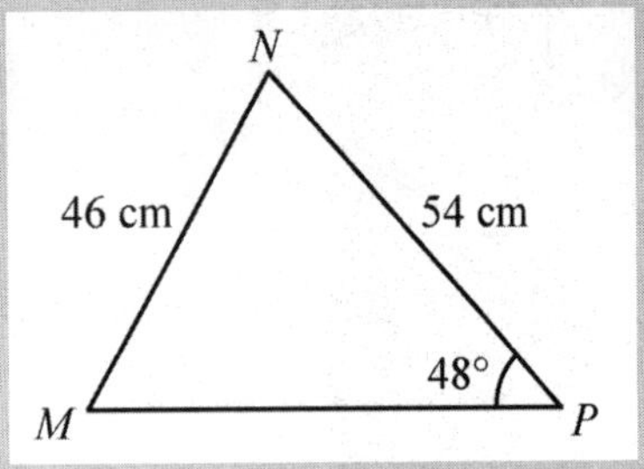

18. Correct to the nearest tenth of a degree, what is the measure of $\angle NMP$?

A. 71.8° **B.** 60.7°

C. 52.4° **D.** 39.3°

19. In triangle PQR, PR = 12.2 cm, $\angle R$ = 38°, and $\angle P$ = 74°. The length of side PQ, correct to the nearest tenth of a centimetre, is

A. 7.8 cm **B.** 8.1 cm

C. 14.3 cm **D.** 18.4 cm

Numerical Response

20.

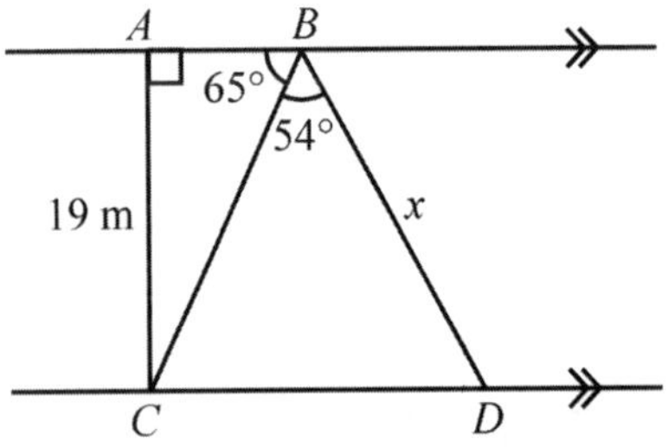

If AB is parallel to CD, then what is the value of x, correct to the nearest metre?

CHALLENGER QUESTION

Use the following information to answer the next question.

An engineer needs to calculate the distance across a deep canyon. She takes a sighting from a point A and then from a point C, which are both on the same side of the canyon, to a point B on the opposite side of the canyon, as shown in the diagram.

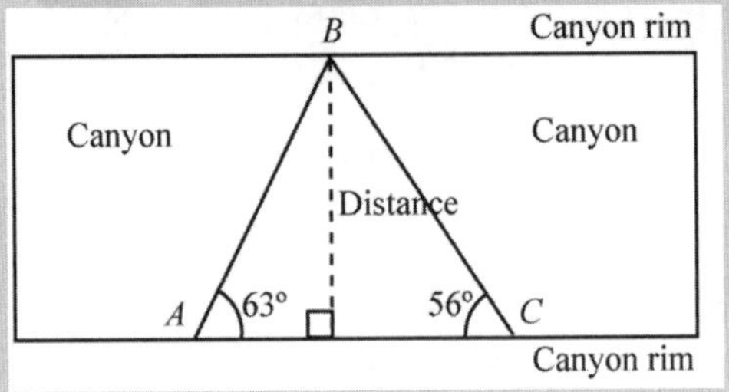

21. If points A and C are 70 m apart, then the distance across the canyon, correct to the nearest tenth of a metre, is

A. 51.9 m **B.** 59.1 m

C. 60.3 m **D.** 68.7 m

Use the following information to answer the next question.

The game of curling involves throwing rocks down a sheet of ice toward a bull's-eye painted on the ice.

The diagram illustrates a curling rock released from point A and striking a stationary rock at point B before ending up at location C.

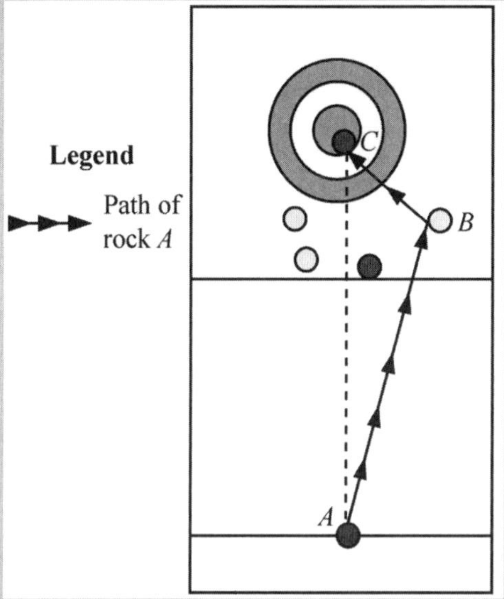

22. If $AB = 24$ m, $BC = 8.5$ m, and $\angle ABC = 115°$, then what is the distance from point A to point C, correct to the nearest tenth?

A. 31.2 m **B.** 28.6 m

C. 25.4 m **D.** 21.8 m

CHALLENGER QUESTION

Use the following information to answer the next question.

From a prison watchtower, there are two floodlights lighting the prison yard. The triangular shaded region in the given diagram represents the section of the prison yard lit by the two floodlights and has an area of 2 670 m^2.

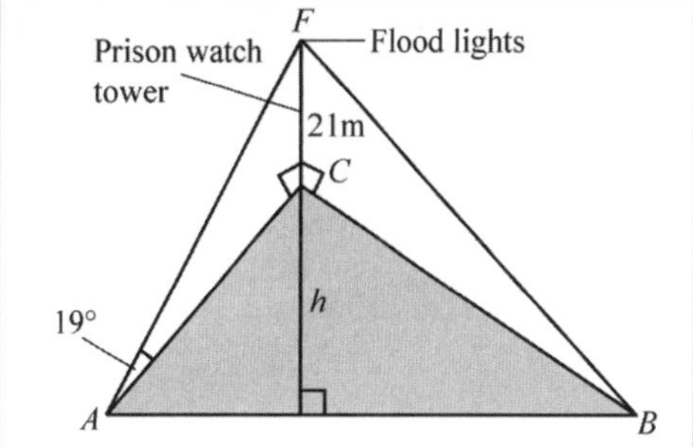

Diagram not to scale

23. If $\angle ACB = 98°$ and the length of side BC is 84.51m, then the height, h, of the shaded triangle that represents the section of the prison yard lit by the floodlights, to the nearest metre, is

A. 84 m **B.** 80 m

C. 48 m **D.** 44 m

Use the following information to answer the next multipart question.

24. An engineer is asked to calculate the width, w, of a river. He takes a sighting from point X and another sighting from point Y, both on the shore of the same side of the river to a point A on the opposite shore of the river. The engineer's measurements are shown in the diagram.

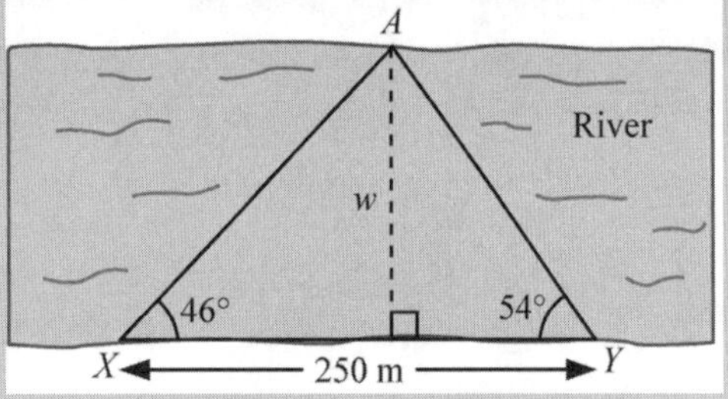

Part A

Open Response

What is the measure of $\angle XAY$?

Justify your answer.

Part B

Open Response

What is the width, w, of the river to the nearest tenth of a metre?

Solutions

1. D	**7. B**	**13. 58**	**18. B**	**24.** Part A- **OR**
2. B	**8. D**	**14.** Part A- **OR**	**19. B**	Part B- **OR**
3. D	**9. 25.2**	Part B- **OR**	**20. 22**	
4. 96	**10. A**	**15. C**	**21. B**	
5. D	**11. B**	**16. D**	**22. B**	
6. B	**12. A**	**17. D**	**23. C**	

1. D

In ΔMNP and ΔRST, ΔMNP is similar to ΔRST since the angles in ΔMNP are equal to the angles in ΔRST.
Thus, the ratios of corresponding sides are equal. The correct ratios are $\frac{MN}{NP} = \frac{RS}{ST}$, $\frac{NP}{ST} = \frac{MP}{RT}$, and $\frac{MN}{RS} = \frac{MP}{RT}$.

The incorrect ratio $\frac{NP}{ST} = \frac{MN}{RT}$ could be replaced with the correct ratios $\frac{NP}{ST} = \frac{MP}{RT}$ or $\frac{NP}{ST} = \frac{MN}{RS}$.

2. B

There are three approaches to verifying congruency:

1. **SSS:** The measures of the three side lengths of two triangles are the same.
2. **SAS:** The measures of two of the side lengths and the interior angle included by them are the same.
3. **ASA:** The measures of two of the interior angles and the side included by them are the same.

Therefore, if the measures of the three interior angles of the two triangles are the same, it does not guarantee congruency.

3. D

Since both triangles are right triangles and they have an equal angle at the top, the remaining angle will also be equal. The triangles are similar.
Therefore, the ratios of the corresponding sides are equal.
Label the larger triangle as follows:

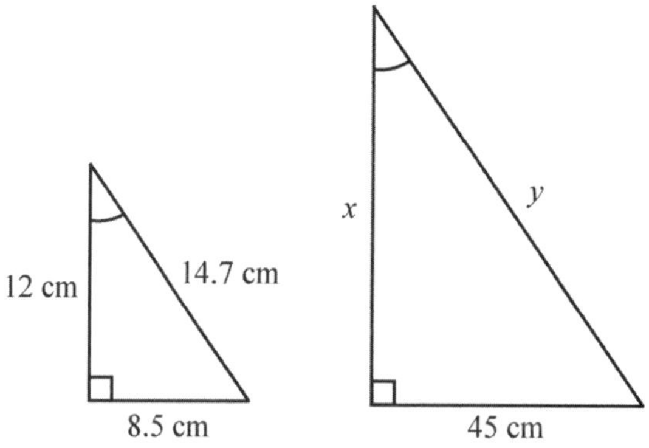

(Diagram not to scale)

$$\frac{x}{45 \text{ cm}} = \frac{12 \text{ cm}}{8.5 \text{ cm}}$$

$$x = \frac{12 \text{ cm} \times 45 \text{ cm}}{8.5 \text{ cm}} = 63.5 \text{ cm}$$

$$\frac{y}{45 \text{ cm}} = \frac{14.7 \text{ cm}}{8.5 \text{ cm}}$$

$$y = \frac{14.7 \text{ cm} \times 45 \text{ cm}}{8.5 \text{ cm}} = 77.8 \text{ cm}$$

The actual lengths of the other two sides of the poster are 63.5 cm and 77.8 cm.

4. 96

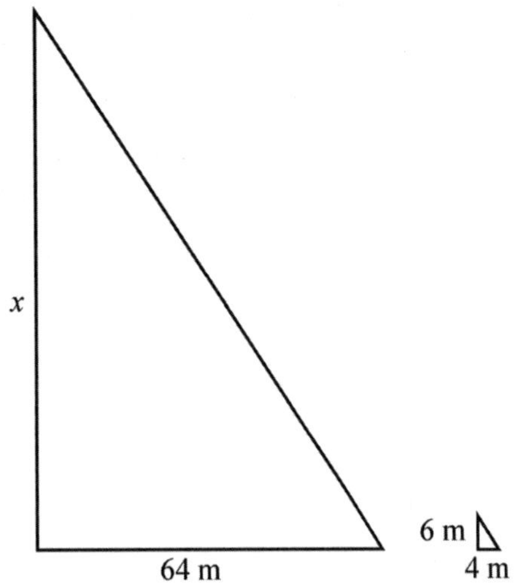

The triangles are similar since they are formed using the shadows created by the same angle of the sun at the same point in time, and the remaining corresponding angles are equal. Therefore, corresponding sides will have equal ratios.

$$\frac{x}{64} = \frac{6}{4}$$

$$x = \frac{6 \times 64}{4}$$

$$x = 96 \text{ m}$$

5. D

When using 17° as the point of reference, the sides are labelled t = adjacent, v = opposite, and u = hypotenuse. Therefore, the primary trigonometric ratios are:

$$\sin\theta = \frac{\text{opposite}}{\text{hypotenuse}}$$

$$\sin 17^\circ = \frac{v}{u}$$

$$\cos\theta = \frac{\text{adjacent}}{\text{hypotenuse}}$$

$$\cos 17^\circ = \frac{t}{u}$$

$$\tan\theta = \frac{\text{opposite}}{\text{adjacent}}$$

$$\tan 17^\circ = \frac{v}{t}$$

The third angle in the triangle is 73°, (180° – 90° – 17° = 73°).

When using 73° as a point of reference, the sides are labelled t = opposite, v = adjacent, and u = hypotenuse.

$$\sin\theta = \frac{\text{opposite}}{\text{hypotenuse}}$$

$$\sin 73^\circ = \frac{t}{u}$$

$$\cos\theta = \frac{\text{adjacent}}{\text{hypotenuse}}$$

$$\cos 17^\circ = \frac{v}{u}$$

$$\tan\theta = \frac{\text{opposite}}{\text{adjacent}}$$

$$\tan 17^\circ = \frac{t}{v}$$

Thus, the trigonometric ratio represented by $\frac{t}{v}$ is tan 73°.

6. B

$$\sin\theta = \frac{\text{opposite}}{\text{hypotenuse}} = \sin 51^\circ = \frac{a}{21.3}$$

$$a = (21.3)(\sin 51^\circ)$$

$$a = 16.6 \text{ mm}$$

The length of side a is 16.6 mm.

7. B

Begin with a sketch for clarity.

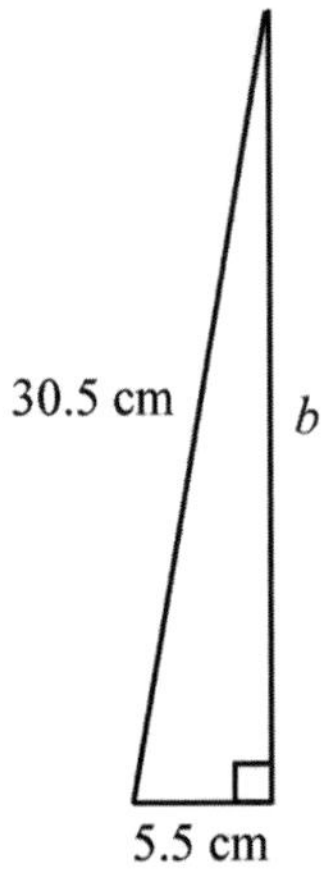

To solve, use the Pythagorean theorem $c^2 = a^2 + b^2$. Substitute the value of the hypotenuse, (c = 30.5 cm), and the value of a, (a = 5.5 cm) into the equation.

$$(30.5)^2 = (5.5)^2 + b^2$$

Now, solve for b.

$$930.25 = 30.25 + b^2$$

$$900 = b^2$$

$$b = \sqrt{900}$$

$$b = 30 \text{ cm}$$

The length of the third side is 30 cm.

8. D

The angle inside the triangle is 42° because of supplementary angles (180° – 138° = 42°). Therefore,

$$\tan 42^\circ = \frac{\text{opposite}}{\text{adjacent}} = \frac{12}{p}$$

$$p = \frac{12}{\tan 42^\circ}$$

$$p = 13.5 \text{ mm}$$

The length of p is 13.5 mm.

9. 25.2

The given diagram can be labelled as shown below

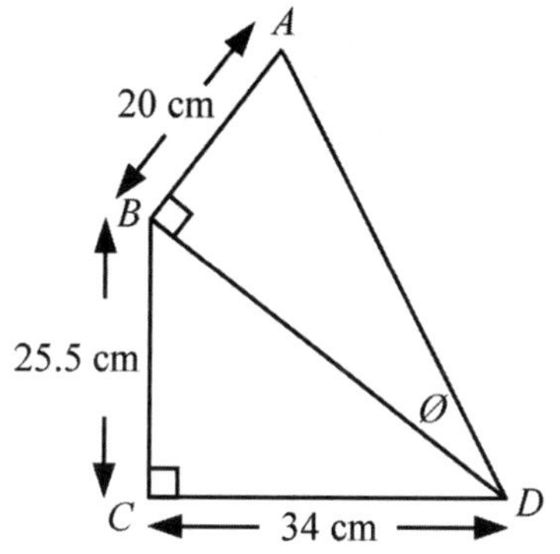

Apply the Pythagorean theorem to ΔBCD as follows:

$(BC)^2 + (CD)^2 = (BD)^2$

Substitute 25.5 for BC and 34 for CD.

$25.5^2 + 34^2 = (BD)^2$

$650.25 + 1\ 156 = (BD)^2$

$1\ 806.25 = (BD)^2$

$\sqrt{1\ 806.25} = BD$

$42.5 = BD$

In ΔABD, $\tan\theta = \dfrac{AB}{BD}$

Substitute 20 for AB and 42.5 for BD.

$\tan\theta = \dfrac{20}{42.5}$

$\theta = \tan^{-1}\left(\dfrac{20}{42.5}\right)$

$\theta \approx 25.20$

To the nearest tenth, the measure of $\angle\theta$ is 25.2°.

10. A

Label the diagram as follows:

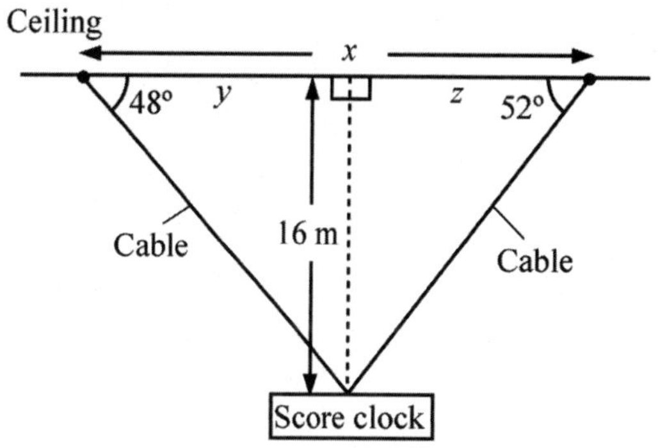

From the diagram, $x = y + z$. Therefore, determine the values of y and z to determine x. To determine y, use the tangent ratio.

$\tan\theta = \dfrac{\text{opposite}}{\text{adjacent}}$

$\tan 48° = \dfrac{16}{y}$

$y = \dfrac{16}{\tan 48°}$

$y = 14.4$ m

Similarly, determine z.

$\tan\theta = \dfrac{\text{opposite}}{\text{adjacent}}$

$\tan 52° = \dfrac{16}{z}$

$z = \dfrac{16}{\tan 52°}$

$z = 12.5$ m

Substitute these values into $x = y + z$.

$x = 14.4 \text{ m} + 12.5 \text{ m}$

$x = 26.9$ m

The distance between the two cables is 26.9 m.

11. B

To determine the height of the pole (BA), first determine the distance BC. Use the tangent ratio.

$\tan\theta = \dfrac{\text{opposite}}{\text{adjacent}}$

$\tan 65° = \dfrac{BC}{1.8}$

$1.8 \times \tan 65° = BC$

$BC = 3.860$ m

Since $BC = \dfrac{3}{4}BA$,

$BA = \dfrac{4}{3}BC$

$BA = \dfrac{4}{3}(3.860)$

$BA = 5.147$ m

12. A

In the diagram, the distance between the flashlight and the mirror is the side of a right triangle opposite the 40° angle.

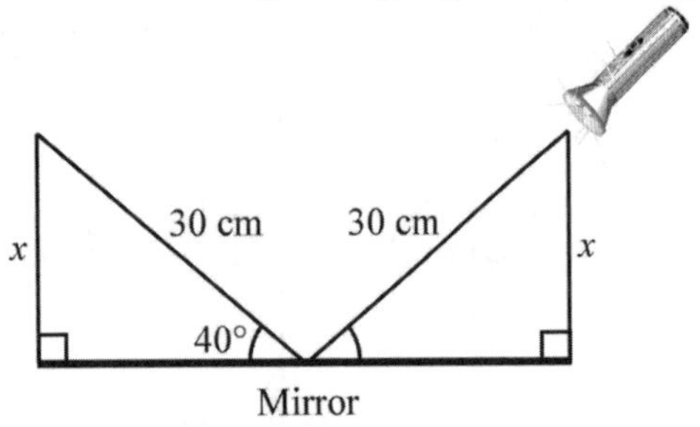

Since the hypotenuse of the triangle is 30 cm, use the sine ratio to determine the distance between the flashlight and the mirror. Let x equal the distance between the flashlight and the mirror.

$\frac{x}{30} = \sin 40°$

$x = \sin 40 \times 30$

$x = 19.3$ cm

Therefore, $\frac{x}{30} \doteq 0.643$

Multiply both sides of the equation by 30 cm.

$\frac{x}{30} \times 30 \doteq 30 \times 0.643$

$x \doteq 19.28 \text{ cm} \doteq 19.3 \text{ cm}$

13. 58

By looking at the larger triangle, you can determine that $\angle APC$ at the top is 28° and $\angle BPC$ is 18°. Let y represent the distance from the bottom of the transmitter to the anchor at point B.

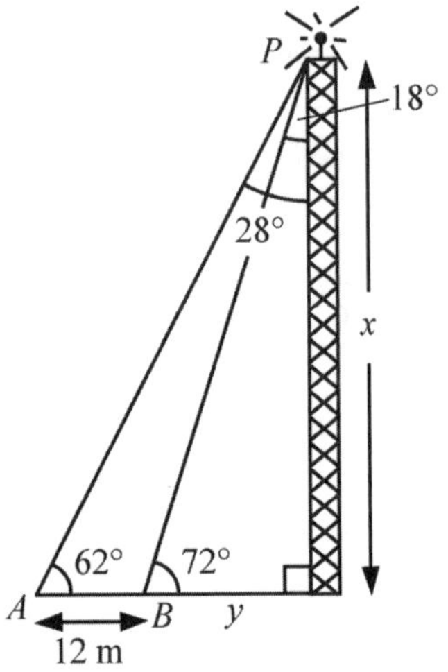

Now, examine the two tangent ratios that can be formed.

$\tan \theta = \frac{\text{opposite}}{\text{adjacent}}$

$\tan 28° = \frac{12 + y}{x}$

$\tan 18° = \frac{y}{x}$

Rearrange the two equations as follows:

$x\tan 28° = 12 + y$

$x\tan 18° = y$

Substitute $x\tan 18°$ for y in the equation $x\tan 28° = 12 + y$, and solve for x.

$x\tan 28° = 12 + (x\tan 18°)$

$x\tan 28° - x\tan 18° = 12$

$x(\tan 28° - \tan 18°) = 12$

$x = \frac{12}{\tan 28° - \tan 18°}$

$x = \frac{12}{0.5317 - 0.3249}$

$x = \frac{12}{0.269}$

$x = 58$ m

14. Part A – Open Response

In ΔACD, the length of CD can be determined by the following procedure:

$\sin 60° = \frac{AC}{CD}$

$\sin 60° = \frac{50}{CD}$

$CD \times \sin 60° = 50$

$CD = \frac{50}{\sin 60°}$

$CD = 57.7$

To the nearest tenth of a centimetre, the length of CD is 57.7.

Part B – Open Response

In order to determine the distance between anchor points D and E, it is necessary to determine the distance between anchor points A and D as well as the distance between anchor points A and E since $AD = AE + DE$.
Since $AE = 20$ cm, solve for AD as shown:
In ΔACD, apply the Pythagorean theorem.

$(AD)^2 + (AC)^2 = (CD)^2$

Substitute 57.74 for CD.

$(AD)^2 + 50^2 = 57.74^2$

$(AD)^2 + 2\ 500 \approx 3\ 333.91$

$(AD)^2 \approx 3\ 333.91 - 2\ 500$

$(AD)^2 \approx 833.91$

$AD \approx \sqrt{833.91}$

$AD = 28.9$ (to the nearest tenth)

Note: AD can also be determined as follows:

$\tan 60° = \dfrac{AC}{AD}$

Substitute 50 for AC.

$\tan 60° = \dfrac{50}{AD}$

$AD \times \tan 60° = 50$

$AD = \dfrac{50}{\tan 60°}$

$AD = 28.9$ (to the nearest tenth)

Recall that $AD = AE + DE$.
Substitute 20 for AE and 28.9 for AD.

$28.9 = 20 + DE$

$28.9 - 20 = DE$

$8.9 = DE$

To the nearest tenth, the distance between anchor points D and E is 8.9 cm.

15. C

The ratio $\dfrac{60}{\sin 48°} = \dfrac{x}{\sin 62°}$ implies that the side measuring 60 cm is opposite to the 48° angle. (The missing angle measurement is 48°).

16. D

In general, the law of cosines states that $a^2 = b^2 + c^2 - 2bc\cos A$. Therefore, the equation $x^2 = 45^2 + 50^2 - 2(45)(50)\cos 78°$ applies to a triangle where the side-angle-side situation is given and the 78° angle is opposite the side measuring x.

17. D

The measure of $\angle BAD$ is equal to the measure of $\angle BAC$ minus the measure of $\angle CAD$. The measure of $\angle BAC$ is given, but it is necessary to determine the measure of $\angle CAD$. In ΔCAD, determine the measure of $\angle CAD$ by applying the law of cosines as follows:

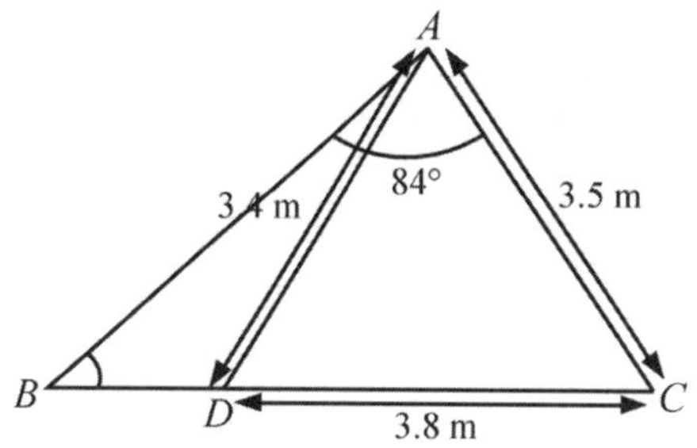

$\cos \angle CAD = \dfrac{(AD)^2 + (AC)^2 - (CD)^2}{2(AD)(AC)}$

Substitute 3.4 for AD,3.5 for AC, and 3.8 for CD.

$\cos \angle CAD = \dfrac{3.4^2 + 3.5^2 - 3.8^2}{2(3.4)(3.5)}$

$\cos \angle CAD = \dfrac{9.37}{23.8}$

$\cos \angle CAD = 0.3937$

$\cos \angle CAD = \cos^{-1}(0.3937)$

$\cos \angle CAD = 66.82$

To the nearest tenth, the measure of $\angle CAD$ is 66.8°.
Thus, $\angle BAD = 84° - 66.8°$

$\angle BAD = 17.2°$

18. B

In ΔMNP, it is not a side-side-side situation; therefore, use the law of sines to determine the measure of $\angle NMP$ as follows:

$\dfrac{NP}{\sin \angle NMP} = \dfrac{MN}{\sin \angle MPN}$

Substitute 54 for NP, 46 for MN, and 48° for $\angle MPN$.

$\dfrac{54}{\sin \angle NMP} = \dfrac{46}{\sin 48°}$

$46 \times \sin \angle NMP = 54 \times \sin 48°$

$\sin \angle NMP = \dfrac{54 \times \sin 48°}{46}$

$\sin \angle NMP = 0.8724$

$\angle NMP = \sin^{-1}(0.8724)$

$\angle NMP = 60.74$

To the nearest tenth, the measure of $\angle NMP$ is 60.7°.

19. B

Begin by sketching triangle PQR and placing the given measurements in the appropriate location.

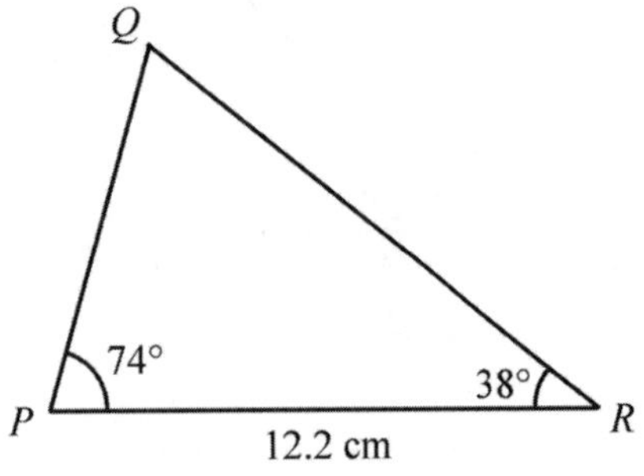

In ΔPQR, it is not a side-angle-side situation; therefore, solve for PQ by using the law of sines as follows:

Observe that PR is opposite $\angle PQR$ and the measure of $\angle PQR = 68° = (180° - 74° - 38)$.

$$\frac{PQ}{\sin \angle PRQ} = \frac{PR}{\sin \angle PQR}$$

Substitute 38° for $\angle PRQ$, 12.2 for PR, and 68° for $\angle PQR$.

$$\frac{PQ}{\sin 38°} = \frac{12.2}{\sin 68°}$$

$$PQ \times \sin 68° = 12.2 \times \sin 38°$$

$$PQ = \frac{12.2 \times \sin 38°}{\sin 68°}$$

$PQ = 8.10$

To the nearest tenth, the length of side PQ is 8.1 cm.

20. 22

Begin by determining the length of side BC.

In $\triangle ABC$, $\sin \angle ABC = \frac{AC}{BC}$

Substitute 65° for $\angle ABC$ and 19 for AC.

$$\sin 65° = \frac{19}{BC}$$

$$BC \times \sin 65° = 19$$

$$BC = \frac{19}{\sin 65°}$$

$BC \approx 20.96$

Since $\angle ABC$ and $\angle DCB$ are alternate angles, the measure of $\angle ABC$ is equal to the measure of $\angle DCB$. Thus, the measure of $\angle DCB$ is 65°.

In $\triangle BCD$, it is not a side-angle-side situation, so use the law of sines to determine the value of x as follows:

$$\frac{x}{\sin \angle DCB} = \frac{BC}{\sin \angle CDB}$$

Substitute 20.96 for BC, 65° for $\angle DCB$, and 61° $(180° - 65° - 54°)$ for $\angle CDB$.

$$\frac{x}{\sin 65°} = \frac{20.96}{\sin 61°}$$

$$x \times \sin 61° = 20.96 \times \sin 65°$$

$$x = \frac{20.96 \times \sin 65°}{\sin 61°}$$

$x \approx 21.72$

The value of x, to the nearest metre, is 22 m.

21. B

The given diagram can be labelled as shown below.

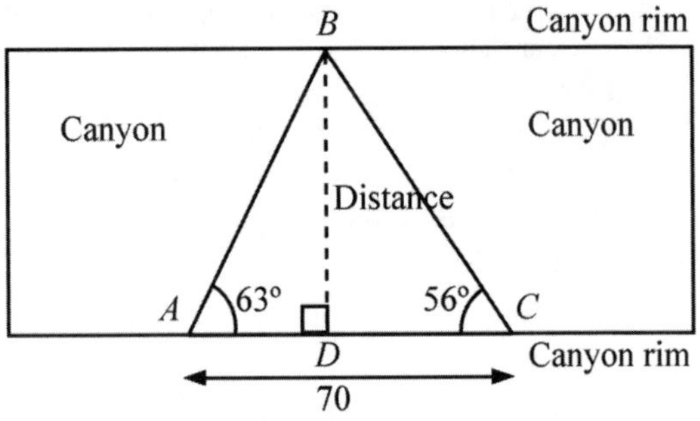

To begin, determine the length of either side AB or CB by applying the law of sines with respect to ΔABC. The length of AB can be determined as follows:

$$\frac{AB}{\sin \angle BCA} = \frac{AC}{\sin \angle ABC}$$

Substitute 56° for $\angle BCA$, 70 for AC, and 61°$(180° - 63° - 56°)$ for $\angle ABC$.

$$\frac{AB}{\sin 56°} = \frac{70}{\sin 61°}$$

$$AB \times \sin 61° = 70 \times \sin 56°$$

$$AB = \frac{70 \times \sin 56°}{\sin 61°}$$

$AB \approx 66.35$

Now, solve for BD by examining ΔADB.

In ΔADB, $\sin \angle BAD = \frac{BD}{AB}$

Substitute 63° for $\angle BAD$ and 66.35 for AB.

$$\sin 63° = \frac{BD}{66.35}$$

$BD = 66.35 \times \sin 63°$

$BD \approx 59.12$

The distance across the canyon, BD, to the nearest tenth, is 59.1m.

Note: A similar procedure can be used to determine the length of side BC, and then the sine ratio can be used with respect to ΔBCD.

22. B

In ΔABC, it is a side-angle-side situation, so determine the distance from point A to point C by applying the law of cosines as shown:

$$(AC)^2 = (AB)^2 + (BC)^2 - 2(AB)(BC)\cos \angle ABC$$

Substitute 24 for AB, 8.5 for BC, and 115° for $\angle ABC$.

$$(AC)^2 = 24^2 + 8.5^2 - 2(24)(8.5)\cos(115°)$$

$$(AC)^2 \approx 576 + 72.25 + 172.43$$

$$(AC)^2 \approx 820.68$$

$$AC \approx \sqrt{820.68}$$

$AC \approx 28.648$

The distance from point A to point C, to the nearest tenth, is 28.6 m.

23. C

Begin by determining the distance from point A to point C in the right triangle FAC as follows:

$$\tan \angle FAC = \frac{FC}{AC}$$

Substitute 19° for $\angle FAC$ and 21 for FC.

$$AC \times \tan 19° = 21$$

$$\tan 19° = \frac{21}{AC}$$

$$AC = \frac{21}{\tan 19°}$$

$$AC \approx 60.99$$

Next, determine the distance from point A to point B in ΔACB by applying the law of cosines as shown:

$$(AB)^2 = (AC)^2 + (BC)^2 - 2(AC)(BC)\cos\angle ACB$$

Substitute 60.99 for AC, 84.51 for BC, and 98° for $\angle ACB$.

$$(AB)^2 = (60.99)^2 + (84.51)^2 - 2(60.99)(84.51)\cos 98°$$

$$(AB)^2 \approx 3\ 19.78 + 7\ 141.94 + 1\ 434.67$$

$$(AB)^2 \approx 12\ 296.39$$

$$AB \approx 110.89$$

Recall that the area of a triangle is given by the formula $A = \frac{bh}{2}$.

Thus, for ΔABC,

$$\Delta ABC = \frac{AB \times h}{2}$$

Substitute 2 670 for the area of ΔABC and 110.89 for AB.

$$2\ 670 = \frac{110.89 \times h}{2}$$

$$110.89 \times h = 2\ 670 \times 2$$

$$h = \frac{2\ 670 \times 2}{110.89}$$

$$h \approx 48.16$$

The height, h, of the shaded triangle, to the nearest metre, is 48 m.

24. Part A – Open Response

The sum of the measures of the three interior angles of a triangle is equal to 180°.

Thus, $\angle X + \angle Y + \angle XAY = 180°$

Substitute 46° for $\angle X$ and 54° for $\angle Y$.

$$46° + 54° + \angle XAY = 180°$$

$$100° + \angle XAY = 180°$$

$$\angle XAY = 180° - 100°$$

The measure of $\angle XAY$ is 80°.

Part B – Open Response

The given diagram can be labelled as shown:

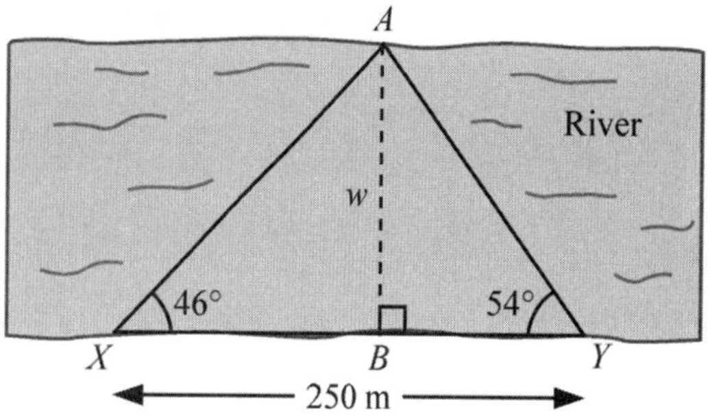

For ΔXAY, apply the law of sines as follows:

$$\frac{XY}{\sin \angle XAY} = \frac{AX}{\sin \angle XAY}$$

Substitute 250 for XY, 80° for $\angle XAY$, and 54° for $\angle XYA$.

$$\frac{250}{\sin 80°} = \frac{AX}{\sin 54°}$$

$$AX \times \sin 80° = 250 \times \sin 54°$$

$$AX = \frac{250 \times \sin 54°}{\sin 80°}$$

$$AX \approx 205.37$$

ΔABX is a right angle triangle; therefore, $\sin \angle X = \frac{AB}{AX}$.

Substitute 46° for $\angle X$, w for AB, and 205.37 for AX.

$$\sin 46° = \frac{w}{205.37}$$

$$w = 205.37 \times \sin 46°$$

$$w \approx 147.73$$

The width of the river to the nearest tenth is 147.7 m.

Note: an alternate solution is shown:

In ΔXAY, $\frac{XY}{\sin \angle XAY} = \frac{AY}{\angle AXY}$

$$\frac{250}{\sin 80°} = \frac{AY}{\sin 46°}$$

$$AY \times \sin 80° = 250 \times \sin 46°$$

$$AY = \frac{250 \times \sin 46°}{\sin 80°}$$

$$AY \approx 182.61$$

In ΔABY, $\sin \angle Y = \frac{AB}{AY}$

$$\sin 54° = \frac{w}{182.61}$$

$$w = 182.61 \times \sin 54°$$

$$w \approx 147.73$$

$$w = 147.7 \text{ m}$$

NOTES

KEY Strategies for Success on Tests

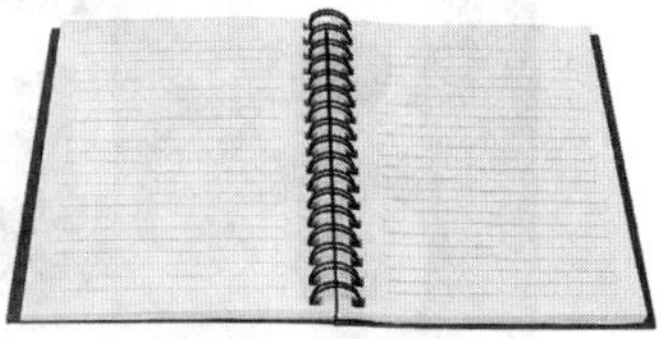

TEST PREPARATION AND TEST-TAKING SKILLS

Things to Consider When Taking a Test

- It is normal to feel anxious before you write a test. You can manage this anxiety by:
    - thinking positive thoughts. Visual imagery is a helpful technique to try.
    - making a conscious effort to relax by taking several slow, controlled, deep breaths. Concentrate on the air going in and out of your body.
- Before you begin the test, ask questions if you are unsure of anything.
- Jot down key words or phrases from any oral directions.
- Look over the entire test to assess the number and kinds of questions on the test.
- Read each question closely and reread if necessary.
- Pay close attention to key vocabulary words. Sometimes these are bolded or italicized, and they are usually important words in the question.
- Mark your answers on your answer sheet carefully. If you wish to change an answer, erase the mark completely and then ensure your final answer is darker than the one you have erased.
- On the test booklet, use highlighting to note directions, key words, and vocabulary that you find confusing or that are important to answering the question.
- Double-check to make sure you have answered everything before handing in your test.

When taking tests, the easy words are often overlooked. Failure to pay close attention to these words can result in an incorrect answer. One way to avoid this is to be aware of these words and to underline, circle, or highlight these words while you are taking the test.

Even though some words are easy to understand, they can change the meaning of the entire question, so it is important that you pay attention to them. Here are some examples.

all	**always**	**most likely**	**probably**	**best**	**not**
difference	**usually**	**except**	**most**	**unlikely**	**likely**

Example

1. Which of the following equations is **not** correct?

A. $3 + 2 = 5$

B. $4 - 3 = 1$

C. $5 \times 4 = 15$

D. $6 \times 3 = 18$

Helpful Strategies for Answering Multiple-Choice Questions

A multiple-choice question provides some information for you to consider and then asks you to select a response from four choices. Each question has one correct answer. The other answers are distractors, which are incorrect.

Below are some strategies to help you when answering multiple-choice questions.

- Quickly skim through the entire test. Find out how many questions there are and plan your time accordingly.
- Read and reread questions carefully. Underline key words and try to think of an answer before looking at the choices.
- If there is a graphic, look at the graphic, read the question, and go back to the graphic. Then, you may want to underline the important information from the question.
- Carefully read the choices. Read the question first and then each answer that goes with it.
- When choosing an answer, try to eliminate those choices that are clearly wrong or do not make sense.
- Some questions may ask you to select the best answer. These questions will always include words like **best**, **most appropriate**, or **most likely**. All of the answers will be correct to some degree, but one of the choices will be better than the others in some way. Carefully read all four choices before choosing the answer you think is the best.
- If you do not know the answer or if the question does not make sense to you, it is better to guess than to leave it blank.
- Do not spend too much time on any one question. Make a mark (*) beside a difficult question and come back to it. If you are leaving a question to come back to later, make sure you also leave the space on the answer sheet.
- Remember to go back to the difficult questions at the end of the test; sometimes clues are given throughout the test that will provide you with answers.
- Note any negative words like **no** or **not** and be sure your choice fits the question.
- Before changing an answer, *be sure* you have a very good reason to do so.
- Do not look for patterns on your answer sheet.

Helpful Strategies for Answering Open-Response Questions

A written response requires you to respond to a question or directive such as **explain**, **predict**, **list**, **describe**, **show your work**, **solve**, or **calculate.** In preparing for open-response tasks you may wish to:

- Read and reread the question carefully.
- Recognize and pay close attention to **directing words** such as **explain**, **show your work, and describe**.
- Underline key words and phrases that indicate what is required in your answer, such as explain, estimate, answer, calculate, or show your work.
- Write down rough, point-form notes regarding the information you want to include in your answer.
- Think about what you want to say and organize information and ideas in a coherent and concise manner within the time limit you have for the question.
- Be sure to answer every part of the question that is asked.
- Include as much information as you can when you are asked to explain your thinking.
- Include a picture or diagram if it will help to explain your thinking.
- Try to put your final answer to a problem in a complete sentence to be sure it is reasonable.
- Reread your response to ensure you have answered the question.
- **Think**: does your answer make sense
- **Listen**: does it sound right?
- Use appropriate subject vocabulary and terms in your response.

About Mathematics Tests

What You Need to Know about Mathematics Tests

To do well on a mathematics test, you need to understand and apply your knowledge of mathematical concepts. Reading skills can also make a difference in how well you perform. Reading skills can help you follow instructions and find key words, as well as read graphs, diagrams, and tables. They can also help you solve mathematics problems.

Mathematics tests usually have two types of questions: questions that ask for understanding of mathematics ideas and questions that test how well you can solve mathematics problems.

How You Can Prepare for the Mathematics Test

Below are some strategies that are particular to preparing for and writing mathematics tests.

- Know how to use your calculator and, if it is allowed, use your own for the test.
- Note-taking is a good way to review and study important information from your class notes and textbook.
- Sketch a picture of the problem, procedure, or term. Drawing is helpful for learning and remembering concepts.
- Check your answer to practice questions by working backward to the beginning. You can find the beginning by going step-by-step in reverse order.
- When answering questions with graphics (pictures, diagrams, tables, or graphs), read the test question carefully.
    - Read the title of the graphic and any key words.
    - Read the test question carefully to figure out what information you need to find in the graphic.
    - Go back to the graphic to find the information you need.
- Decide which operation is needed.
- Always pay close attention when pressing the keys on your calculator. Repeat the procedure a second time to be sure you pressed the correct keys.

TEST PREPARATION COUNTDOWN

There is little doubt that if you develop a plan for studying and test preparation, you *will* perform well on tests.

Below is a general plan to follow seven days before you write a test.

Countdown: 7 Days before the Test

1. Use "Finding Out About the Test" to help you make your own personal test preparation plan.
2. Review the following information:
   - areas to be included on the test
   - types of test items
   - general and specific test tips
3. Start preparing for the test at least 7 days before the test. Develop your test preparation plan and set time aside to prepare and study.

Countdown: 6, 5, 4, 3, 2 Days before the Test

1. Review old homework assignments, quizzes, and tests.
2. Rework problems on quizzes and tests to make sure you still know how to solve them.
3. Correct any errors made on quizzes and tests.
4. Review key concepts, processes, formulas, and vocabulary.
5. Create practice test questions for yourself and then answer them. Work out many sample problems.

Countdown: The Night before the Test

1. The night before the test is for final preparation, which includes reviewing and gathering material needed for the test before going to bed.
2. Most important is getting a good night's rest and knowing you have done everything possible to do well on the test.

Test Day

1. Eat a healthy and nutritious breakfast.
2. Ensure you have all the necessary materials.
3. Think positive thoughts: "I can do this." "I am ready." "I know I can do well."
4. Arrive at your school early so you are not rushing, which can cause you anxiety and stress.

SUMMARY OF HOW TO BE SUCCESSFUL DURING THE TEST

The following are some strategies you may find useful for writing your test.

- Take two or three deep breaths to help you relax.
- Read the directions carefully and underline, circle, or highlight any important words.
- Survey the entire test to understand what you will need to do.
- Budget your time.
- Begin with an easy question or a question you know you can answer correctly rather than following the numerical question order of the test.
- If you cannot remember how to answer a question, try repeating the deep breathing and physical relaxation activities first. Then, move to visualization and positive self-talk to get you going.
- Write down anything you remember about the subject on the reverse side of your test paper. This activity sometimes helps you to remind yourself that you *do* know something and you *are* capable of writing the test.
- Look over your test when you have finished and double-check your answers to be sure you did not forget anything.

NOTES

Practice Tests

Practice Tests

Table of Correlations

Specific Expectation	Practice Test 1	Practice Test 2
QR1 Investigating the Basic Properties of Quadratic Relations		
QR1.1 *collect data that can be represented as a quadratic relation, from experiments using appropriate equipment and technology or from secondary sources ; graph the data and draw a curve of best fit, if appropriate, with or without the use of technology*	1	1
QR1.2 *determine, through investigation with and without the use of technology, that a quadratic relation of the form* $y = ax^2 + bx + c (a \neq 0)$ *can be graphically represented as a parabola, and that the table of values yields a constant second difference*	2	2
QR1.3 *identify the key features of a graph of a parabola, and use the appropriate terminology to describe them*	3	3
QR1.4 *compare, through investigation using technology, the features of the graph of* $y = x^2$ *and the graph of* $y = 2^x$*, and determine the meaning of a negative exponent and of zero as an exponent*	4	4
QR2 Relating the Graph of $y = x^2$ and Its Transformations		
QR2.1 *identify, through investigation using technology, the effect on the graph of* $y = x^2$ *of transformations by considering separately each parameter* a, h, *and* k	5	5
QR2.2 *explain the roles of* a, h, *and* k *in* $y = a(x - h)^2 + k$, *using the appropriate terminology to describe the transformations, and identify the vertex and the equation of the axis of symmetry*	6	6
QR2.3 *sketch, by hand, the graph of* $y = a(x - h)^2 + k$ *by applying transformations to the graph of* $y = x^2$	7	7
QR2.4 *determine the equation, in the form* $y = a(x - h)^2 + k$, *of a given graph of a parabola*	8	8
QR3 Solving Quadratic Equations		
QR3.1 *expand and simplify second-degree polynomial expressions using a variety of tools and strategies*	9	9
QR3.2 *factor polynomial expressions involving common factors, trinomials, and differences of squares using a variety of tools and strategies*	10	10
QR3.3 *determine, through investigation, and describe the connection between the factors of a quadratic expression and the* x*-intercepts of the graph of the corresponding quadratic relation, expressed in the form* $y = a(x - r)(x - s)$	11	11
QR3.4 *interpret real and non-real roots of quadratic equations, through investigation using graphing technology, and relate the roots to the* x*-intercepts of the corresponding relations*	12	12
QR3.5 *express* $y = ax^2 + bx + c$ *in the form* $y = a(x - h)^2 + k$ *by completing the square in situations involving no fractions, using a variety of tools*	13	13
QR3.6 *sketch or graph a quadratic relation whose equation is given in the form* $y = ax^2 + bx + c$, *using a variety of methods*	14	14
QR3.8 *solve quadratic equations that have real roots, using a variety of methods*	15, 16, 17	15, 41a, 41b, 41c, 41d
QR4 Solving Problems Involving Quadratic Relations		
QR4.1 *determine the zeros and the maximum or minimum value of a quadratic relation from its graph or from its defining equation*	18	16

Specific Expectation	Practice Test 1	Practice Test 2
QR4.2 *solve problems arising from a realistic situation represented by a graph or an equation of a quadratic relation, with and without the use of technology.*	19, 41a, 41b, 41c, 41d	17, 18, 19
AG1 Using Linear Systems to Solve Problems		
AG1.1 *solve systems of two linear equations involving two variables, using the algebraic method of substitution or elimination*	20, 21	20, 21
AG1.2 *solve problems that arise from realistic situations described in words or represented by linear systems of two equations involving two variables, by choosing an appropriate algebraic or graphical method*	22, 42a, 42b	22, 23
AG2 Solving Problems Involving Properties of Line Segments		
AG2.1 *develop the formula for the midpoint of a line segment, and use this formula to solve problems*	23	24
AG2.2 *develop the formula for the length of a line segment, and use this formula to solve problems*	24	25
AG2.3 *develop the equation for a circle with centre (0, 0) and radius r, by applying the formula for the length of a line segment;*	25	26
AG2.4 *determine the radius of a circle with centre (0, 0), given its equation; write the equation of a circle with centre (0, 0), given the radius; and sketch the circle, given the equation in the form* $x^2 + y^2 = r^2$	26	27
AG2.5 *solve problems involving the slope, length, and midpoint of a line segment.*	27, 28	28, 29
AG3 Using Analytic Geometry to Verify Geometric Properties		
AG3.2 *verify, using algebraic techniques and analytic geometry, some characteristics of geometric figures*	29	30
AG3.3 *plan and implement a multi-step strategy that uses analytic geometry and algebraic techniques to verify a geometric property*	30	42a, 42b, 42c, 42d
TR1 Investigating Similarity and Solving Problems Involving Similar Triangles		
TR1.3 *solve problems involving similar triangles in realistic situations*	31, 32	31, 32
TR2 Solving Problems Involving the Trigonometry of Right Triangles		
TR2.2 *determine the measures of the sides and angles in right triangles, using the primary trigonometric ratios and the Pythagorean theorem*	33, 34	33
TR2.3 *solve problems involving the measures of sides and angles in right triangles in real life applications using the primary trigonometric ratios and the Pythagorean theorem.*	35, 36, 37	43a, 43b
TR3 Solving Problems Involving the Trigonometry of Acute Triangles		
TR3.1 *explore the development of the sine law within acute triangles*	38	34
TR3.2 *explore the development of the cosine law within acute triangles*	39	35
TR3.3 *determine the measures of sides and angles in acute triangles, using the sine law and the cosine law*	40	36, 37
TR3.4 *solve problems involving the measures of sides and angles in acute triangles*	43a, 43b	38, 39, 40

NOTES

Practice Test 1

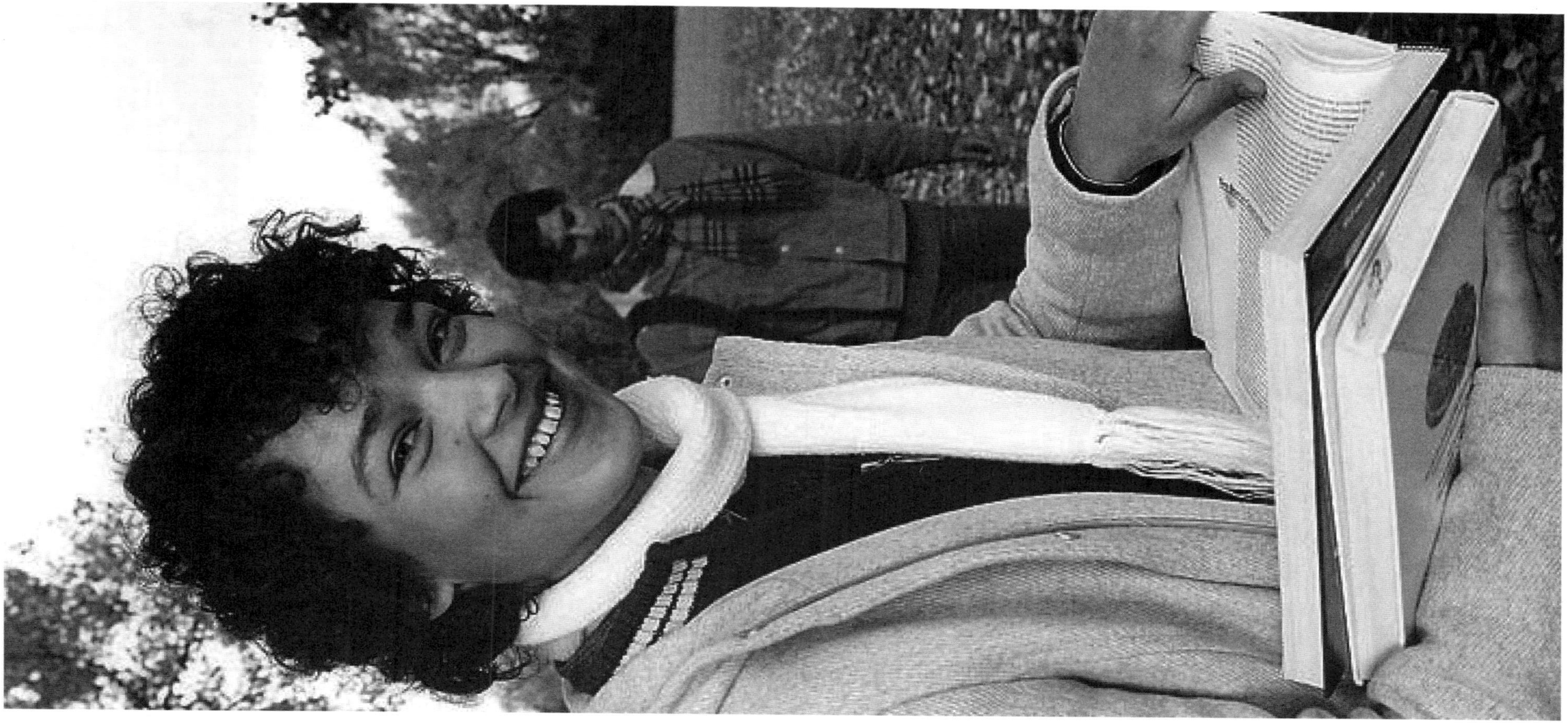

Ontario Math 10 Academic

Practice Test 1

1. A model rocket was launched from a platform, and its height, h, in metres, above the ground with respect to time, t, in seconds was recorded. The data obtained is shown in the table.

Time (s)	0	1	3	8	14	20	25
Height (m)	3	148	410	890	1 140	1 025	700

Which of the following graphs could represent the data shown in the table?

A.
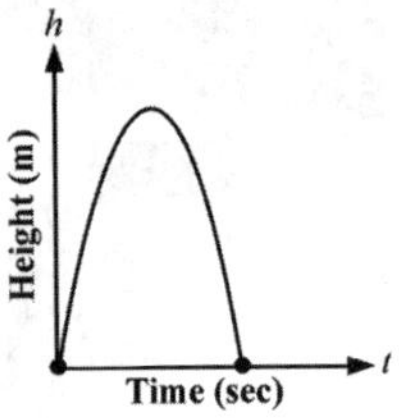

B.
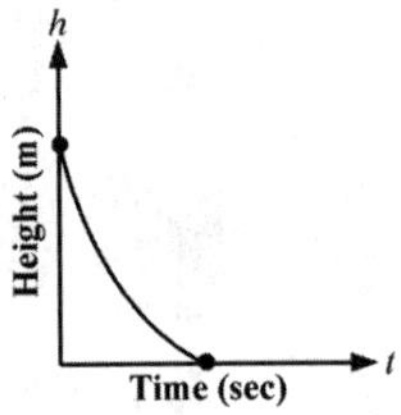

C.
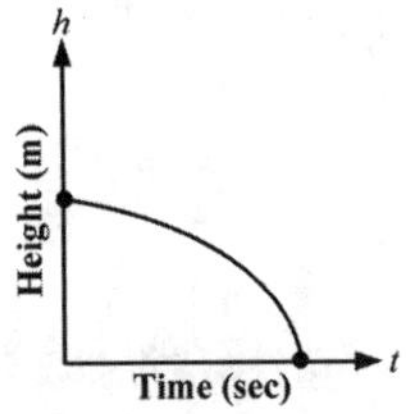

D.
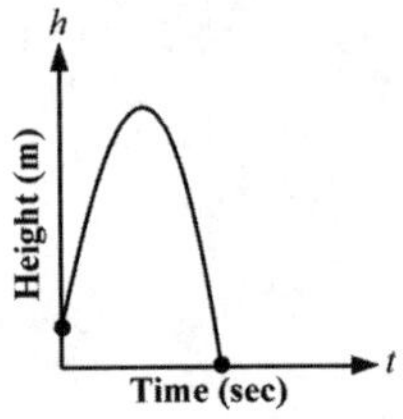

2. Which of the following quadratic function has a corresponding graph that opens downward and has a second difference of −8.4?

F. $y = 8.4x^2 - 8.4$

G. $y = -8.4x^2 + 5$

H. $y = 4.2x^2 - 8.4$

J. $y = -4.2x^2 + 5$

3. The partial graph of a parabola is shown.

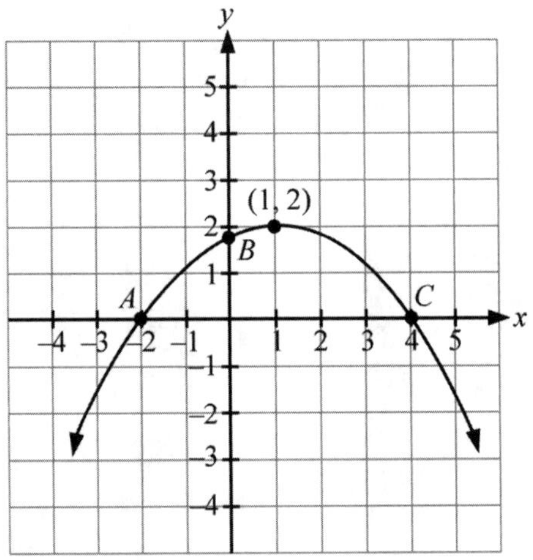

Which of the following statements about the graph of the parabola shown is correct?

A. The y-intercept is A, and the zeros occur at B and C.

B. The y-intercept is B, and the zeros occur at A and C.

C. The coordinates of the vertex are (1, 2), and the zeros occur at A and B.

D. The coordinates of the vertex are (−1, 2), and the zeros occur at A and B.

4. A partial table of values for the graph of $y = 2^x$ is shown.

x	−3	0	3
y	a	b	c

What are the respective values of a, b, and c?

F. −6, 0, and 6

G. −8, 0, and 6

H. $\frac{1}{6}$, 1, and 6

J. $\frac{1}{8}$, 1, and 8

5. Two different quadratic functions are defined by the equations
$h(x) = 3(x - h)^2 - 7$ and
$g(x) = -3(x - h)^2 + 7$, respectively.

If the value of h is the same for each equation, then the graph of each function will have the same

A. range
B. vertex
C. y-intercepts
D. axis of symmetry

6. The vertex of the parabola defined by the equation $y = -3(x - 2)^2 + 5$ is located at the ordered pair

F. (5, −2)
G. (2, −5)
H. (2, 5)
J. (−2, 5)

7. The following four transformations are applied, in the given order, to the graph of $y = x^2$:

- a reflection about the x-axis
- a vertical stretch about the x-axis by a factor of 3
- a horizontal translation 2 units to the right
- a vertical translation 4 units downward

Point (3, 9) on the graph of $y = x^2$ becomes point (a, b) on the transformed graph. What are the values of a and b?

A. $a = 5$ and $b = -23$

B. $a = 5$ and $b = -31$

C. $a = 1$ and $b = -23$

D. $a = 1$ and $b = -31$

8. The graph of a parabola is shown.

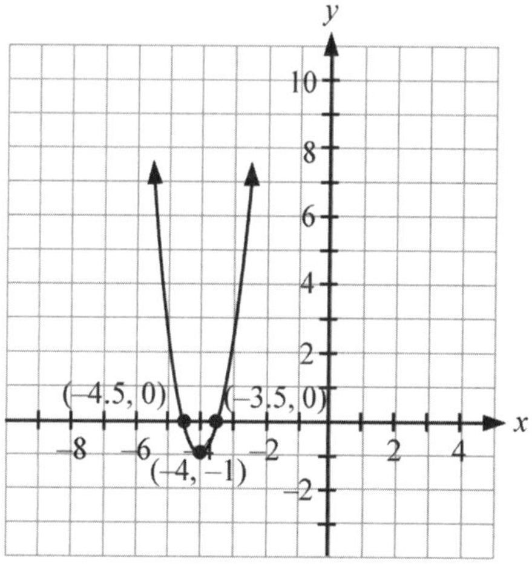

What is the equation of the given parabola?

F. $y = 4(x + 4)^2 + 1$

G. $y = 4(x + 4)^2 - 1$

H. $y = -4(x - 4)^2 + 1$

J. $y = -4(x + 4)^2 - 1$

9. The expanded form of the expression $\left(m-\frac{n}{5}\right)^2$ is

A. $m^2+\frac{2}{5}mn-\frac{n^2}{5}$

B. $m^2+\frac{2}{5}mn+\frac{n^2}{25}$

C. $m^2-\frac{2}{5}mn+\frac{n^2}{25}$

D. $m^2-\frac{2}{5}mn-\frac{n^2}{25}$

10. The expression $x+3$ is **not** a factor of

F. x^2+3x

G. x^2-9

H. x^2+6x+9

J. $x^2+13x-30$

11. A factored form of a polynomial function that has zeros of $\frac{3}{5}$ and −6 is

A. $y=(5x-3)(x+6)$

B. $y=(5x+3)(x+6)$

C. $y=(5x-5)(x-6)$

D. $y=\left(\frac{3}{5}x+3\right)(x-6)$

12. Two equations are given.

$x^2+4=0$ (i)

$x^2-2x+3=0$ (ii)

Which of the following statements about the given equations is **true**?

F. Both equations have real roots.

G. Both equations have non-real roots.

H. Equation (i) has real roots, and equation (ii) has non-real roots.

J. Equation (i) has non-real roots, and equation (ii) has real roots.

13. To convert the quadratic function $y=4x^2-4x-3$ into the completed square form $y=a(x-h)^2+k$, a student performed the following steps:

Step 1: $y=4(x^2-x)-3$

Step 2: $y=4\left(x^2-x+\frac{1}{4}\right)-3-1$

Step 3: $y=4\left(x-\frac{1}{2}\right)^2-4$

Which of the following statements about the student's solution is correct?

A. The student made an error in step 1.

B. The student made an error in step 2.

C. The student made an error instep 3.

D. The student did not make an error.

14. Which of the following graphs could be a sketch of the quadratic function $y = -24x^2 + 1\,000x - 3\,250$?

F.

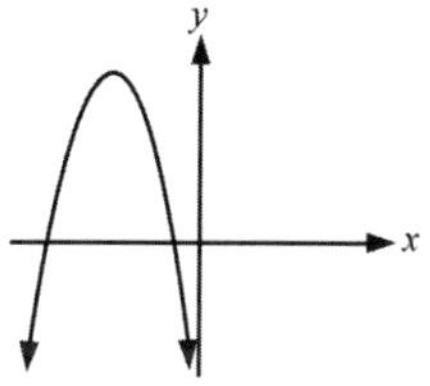

G.

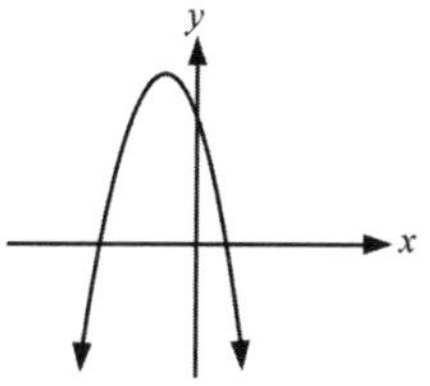

H.

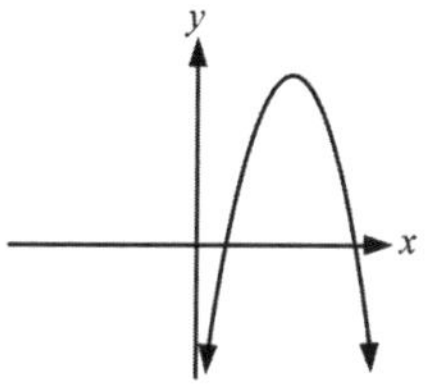

J.

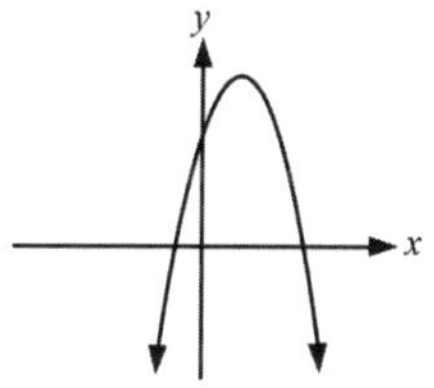

15. The graphs of $y = -2x - 2$ and $y = x^2 + x - 6$ are shown.

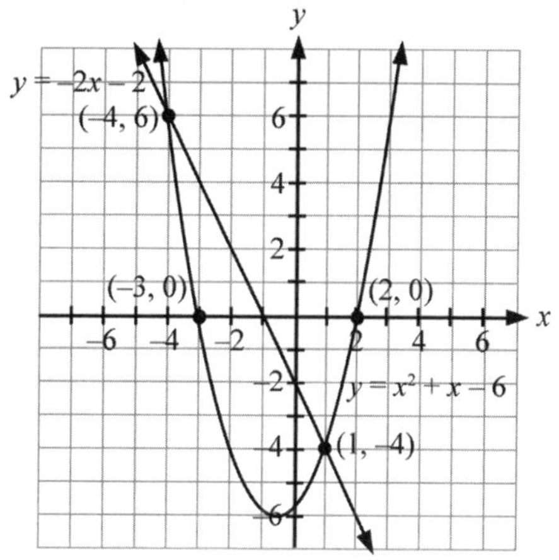

The largest root of the quadratic equation $x^2 + x - 6 = -2(x + 1)$ is ____.

16. The solution to the quadratic equation $2x^2 + 5x + 1 = 0$ is

F. $x = \dfrac{-5 \pm \sqrt{13}}{4}$ **G.** $x = \dfrac{-5 \pm \sqrt{17}}{4}$

H. $x = \dfrac{-5 \pm \sqrt{15}}{2}$ **J.** $x = \dfrac{-5 \pm \sqrt{19}}{4}$

17. The procedures used by four different students in order to solve the equation $3x^2 - 5x = 1$ by using a graphical approach are given:

Sergei

Graph $y_1 = 3x^2 - 5x$ and $y_2 = 1$. Determine the x-coordinate of each point of intersection of the two graphs.

Jeremy

Graph $y_1 = 3x^2$ and $y_2 = 1 + 5x$. Determine the x-coordinate of each point of intersection of the two graphs.

Alexi

Graph $y_1 = 3x^2 - 5x - 1$. Determine the zeros of the resulting graph.

Beyonce

Rewrite the equation as $x(3x - 5) - 1 = 0$. Graph $y_1 = x(3x - 5)$. Subtract 1 from each of the zeros of the graph of $y_1 = x(3x - 5)$.

The student who has an **incorrect** procedure is

A. Sergei **B.** Jeremy

C. Alexi **D.** Beyonce

18. The roots of the equation $ax^2 + bx - 16 = 0$ where a and b are real numbers, are 2 and 4. What is the maximum value of the quadratic function $y = ax^2 + bx - 16$?

F. 1 **G.** 2 **H.** 3 **J.** 4

19. A stone is thrown upward from the top of a building. The height of the stone, y in metres, above the ground is given by the function $y = -2x^2 + 8x + 27$, where x is the time in seconds. What is the maximum height attained by the stone?

A. 30 m **B.** 35 m **C.** 40 m **D.** 45 m

20. If the ordered pair $(K, -3)$ is the solution to the system of equations $8x + 3y = -41$ and $6x - 5y = -9$, then what is the value of K?

F. 4 **G.** 1

H. –4 **J.** $\frac{-25}{4}$

21. Sally has this system of equations in her notebook.

$2x - 3y = 3$

$-x + 4y = 1$

In verifying that (3, 1) is a solution to this system of equations, Sally must replace x with 3

A. and replace y with 1 in both equations

B. and replace y with 1 in the first equation only

C. and replace y with 1 in the second equation only

D. in the first equation and replace y with 1 in the second equation

22. A rock concert drew 55 300 fans to a venue in London. The price of each ticket in sections A to M was $55 and the price of each ticket in sections N to Z was $85. The concert brought in a total of $3 740 500 in ticket sales revenue.

How many tickets in sections N to Z were sold?

F. 9 000 **G.** 23 300

H. 32 000 **J.** 55 300

23. What is the midpoint of one of the diagonals of a parallelogram with vertices (–5, 5), (5, 10), (3, –1), and (–7, –6)?

A. (–2, 4) **B.** (–6, –0.5)

C. (4, 4.5) **D.** (–1, 2)

24. Points $A(-2, 2)$, $B(1, -4)$, and $C(2, 6)$ are shown on the given coordinate axis.

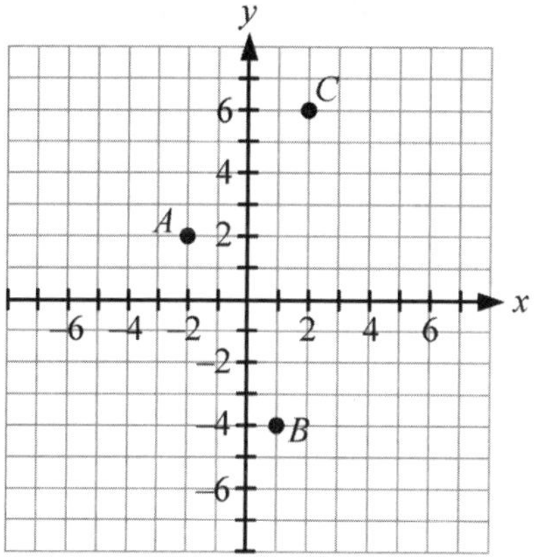

The perimeter of triangle ABC is equal to

F. $\sqrt{178}$

G. $3\sqrt{5} + 4\sqrt{2} + \sqrt{101}$

H. $\sqrt{5} + \sqrt{13} + 8$

J. 28

25. The equation of the circle with centre (0, 0) that passes through the point (5, −2) is

A. $x^2 + y^2 = \sqrt{29}$ **B.** $x^2 + y^2 = 29$

C. $x^2 + y^2 = \sqrt{21}$ **D.** $x^2 + y^2 = 21$

26. Rami sketched the circle defined by the equation $x^2 + y^2 = 16$. Jacqueline decided to sketch a circle with a diameter that was twice as long as the diameter of Rami's circle. Which of the following diagrams represents a sketch of Jacqueline's circle?

F.

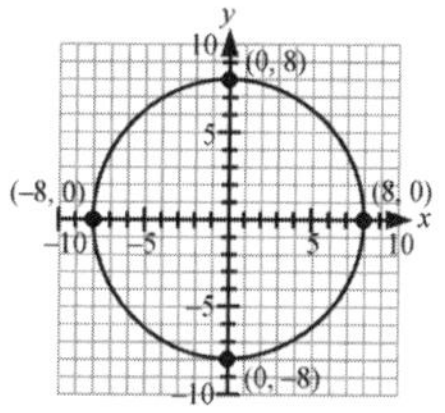

G.

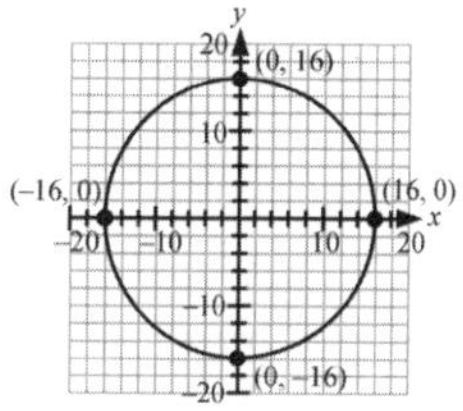

H.

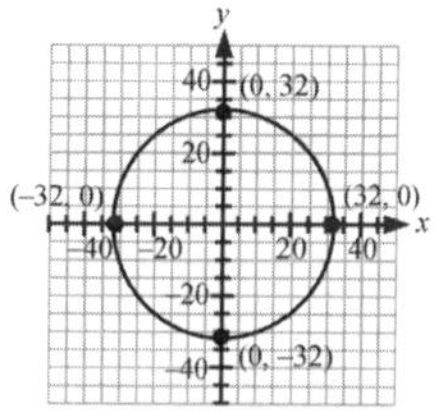

J.

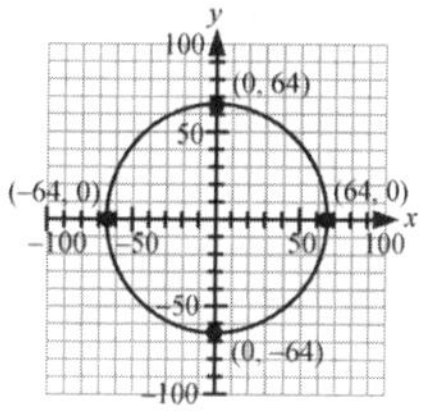

Go On

27. The median of a triangle is a line segment from one vertex to the midpoint of the opposite side. The vertices of triangle *ABC* are *A*(−5, 0), *B*(−1, 4), and *C*(1, −1), as shown in the diagram.

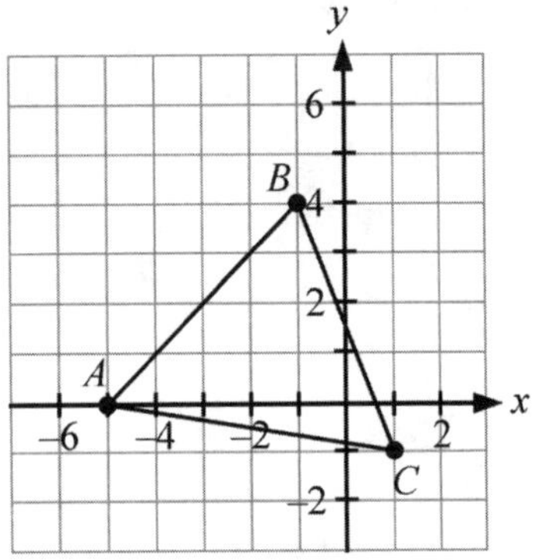

What is the length of the median from point *C* to line segment *AB*?

A. 4 units **B.** 5 units

C. 6 units **D.** 7 units

Numerical Response

28. The ordered pair (1, *K*) is located on the right bisector of a line segment with endpoints (2, −6) and (−8, −4). The value of *K* is ____.

29. The chart shows the slopes of six different pairs of lines.

	Slope of First Line	Slope of Second Line
Pair I	$\frac{3}{4}$	$\frac{3}{4}$
Pair II	−1	1
Pair III	$\frac{1}{2}$	−2
Pair IV	0	0
Pair V	$-\frac{8}{7}$	$\frac{7}{8}$
Pair VI	$\frac{5}{6}$	$\frac{6}{5}$

Perpendicular lines are given by pairs

A. I and IV only

B. III and V only

C. II, III, and V only

D. II, III, V, and VI only

30. Cody is asked to use the diagram shown to verify that the perpendicular bisector of a chord of a circle passes through the centre of the circle.

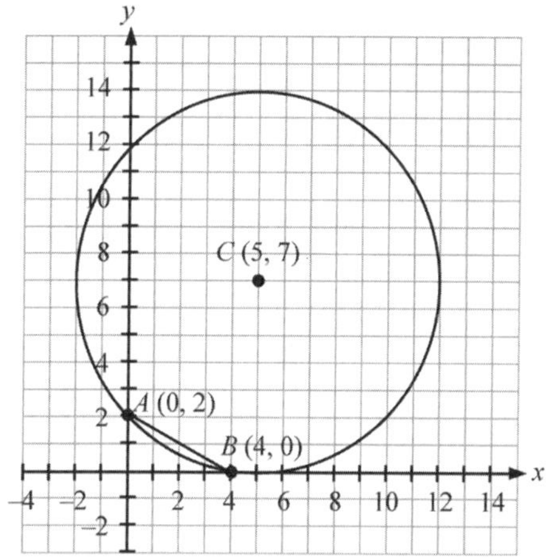

Cody's Plan

Determine the equation of the perpendicular bisector of chord *AB*, and then determine if the point (5, 7) is on this perpendicular bisector.

Cody's Partial Solution

Step 1: Determine the slope, *m*, of chord *AB*.

$$m = \frac{2-0}{0-4} = -\frac{1}{2}$$

Step 2: Determine the midpoint, *M*, of chord *AB*.

$$M = \left(\frac{0+4}{2}, \frac{2+0}{2}\right) = (2, 1)$$

Step 3: Determine the equation of the perpendicular bisector of chord *AB* by applying the formula $y = m(x - x_1) + y_1$.

$$y = -\frac{1}{2}(x-2) + 1$$

$$y = -\frac{1}{2}x + 1 + 1$$

$$y = -\frac{1}{2}x + 2$$

Step 4: Verify that the point (5, 7) is on the line $y = -\frac{1}{2}x + 2$.

Which of the following statements with respect to Cody's plan and partial solution is **true**?

F. Cody's plan is incorrect.

G. Cody's plan and partial solution are both correct.

H. Cody's partial solution is incorrect because he made his first error in step 1.

J. Cody's partial solution is incorrect because he made his first error in step 3.

31. The sails of two sailboards are similar triangles, as shown below.

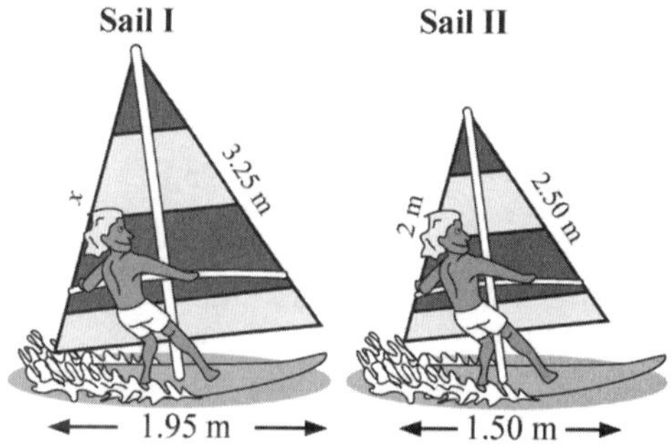

What is the length of side *x* of sail I?

A. 2.45 m **B.** 2.60 m

C. 2.75 m **D.** 3.80 m

32. During an afternoon soccer game, Samira casts a 62 cm shadow, and Leah casts a 77 cm shadow.

If Leah is 158 cm tall, what is Samira's height, to the nearest cm?

F. 124 cm **G.** 127 cm

H. 143 cm **J.** 173 cm

33. The hypotenuse of a right triangle is 3*x*, and the other two sides are 8 cm and 12 cm. What is the value of *x*, to the nearest hundredth?

A. 4.81 cm **B.** 7.23 cm

C. 11.16 cm **D.** 14.42 cm

Go On

34. A sketch of an ice cream cone is shown.

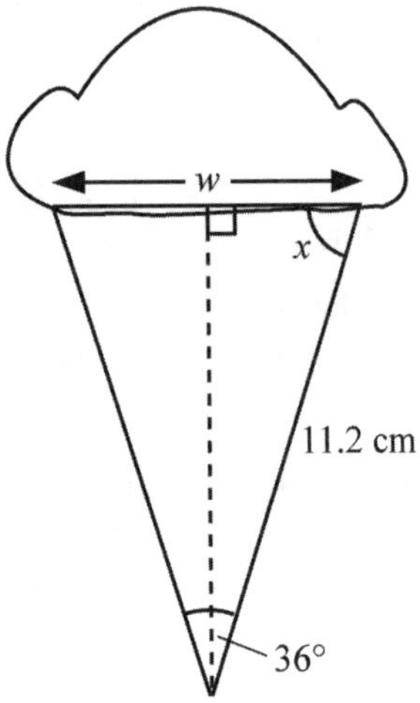

What is the width, w, to the nearest tenth of the ice-cream cone's opening?

F. 3.5 cm **G.** 5.4 cm

H. 7.0 cm **J.** 10.7 cm

35. A rectangular garden that has a length of 50 m will have a sidewalk built diagonally across it, as shown in the diagram. This sidewalk will be at a 32° angle to the longer side.

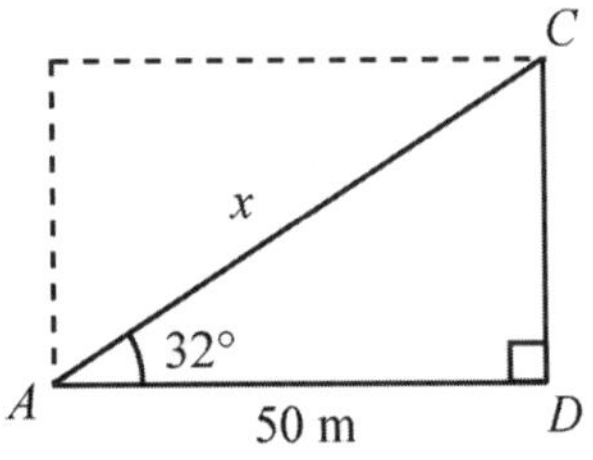

To the nearest metre, what is the length of the sidewalk?

A. 42 m **B.** 57 m **C.** 59 m **D.** 94 m

36.

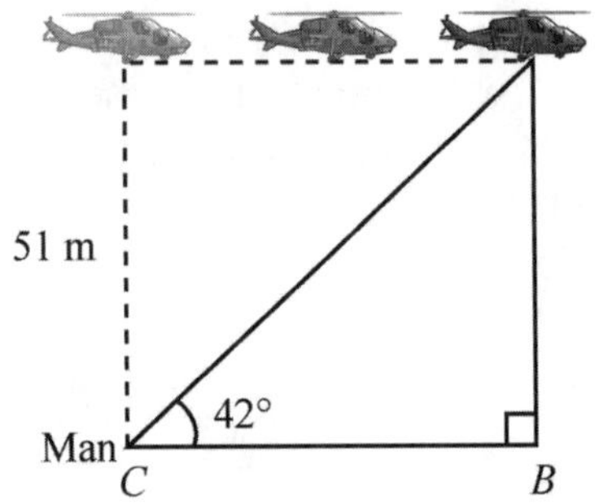

A rescue helicopter is at a height of 51 m above sea level. To save a drowning man at point C, the helicopter needs to lift him to point B on the shore with the help of a rope.

What is the distance that the man travels from point C to point B?

F. 54.64 m **G.** 55.66 m

H. 56.64 m **J.** 65.55 m

37. Standing beneath an apple tree, Ted spotted an apple at a height of 10 m. By throwing a rock at an angle of 45° from the ground, Ted managed to hit the apple and knock it down from the tree. Standing in the same place, he saw another apple directly above where the first had been. This time, by throwing a rock at an angle of 50° from the ground, Ted knocked the second apple from the tree.

Before Ted knocked them down, the distance between the two apples was ____ m.

38. The equation $\dfrac{50}{\sin 40°} = \dfrac{x}{\sin 58°}$ applies to which of the following acute triangles?

F.

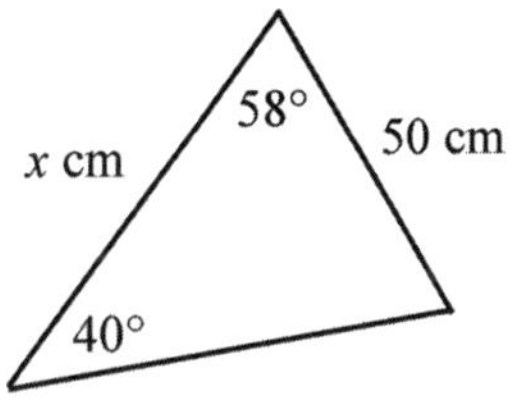

G.

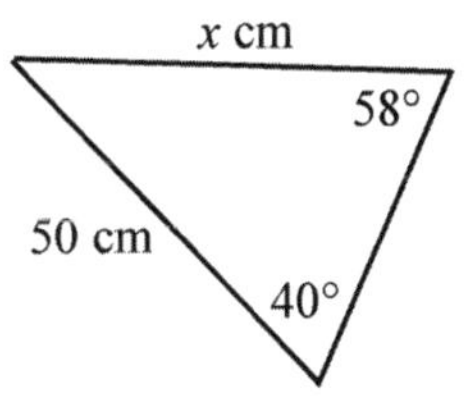

H.

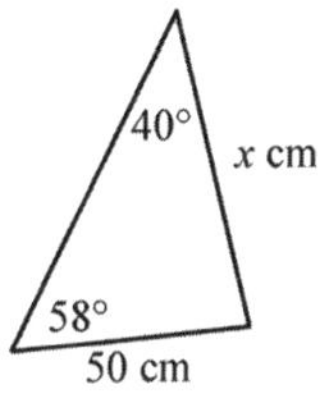

J.

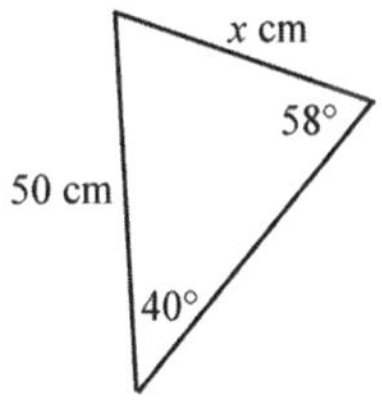

39. A student drew the diagram shown in order to derive the law of cosines.

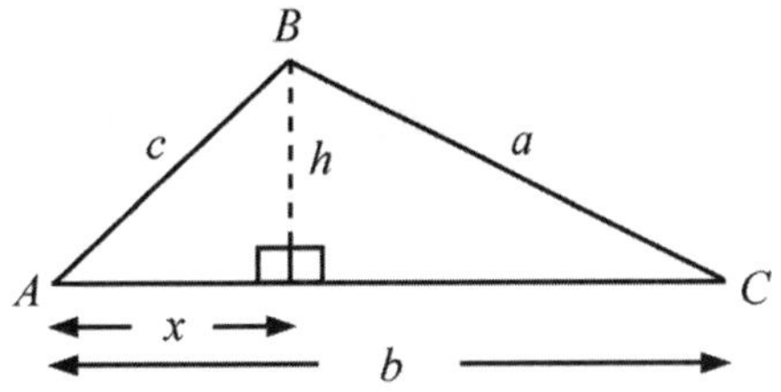

If the student correctly determined that $x^2 + h^2 = c^2$ and $(b - x)^2 + h^2 = a^2$, then which of the following equations is correct?

A. $x^2 + c^2 = (b - x)^2 + a^2$

B. $a^2 - (b - x)^2 = c^2 - x^2$

C. $h^2 = \dfrac{c^2 - x^2}{a^2 - (b - x)^2}$

D. $h^2 = \dfrac{a^2 + (b - x)^2}{x^2 + c^2}$

40. The given diagram illustrates triangle RST, where $RS = 37$ cm, $ST = 28$ cm, and $\angle SRT = 49°$.

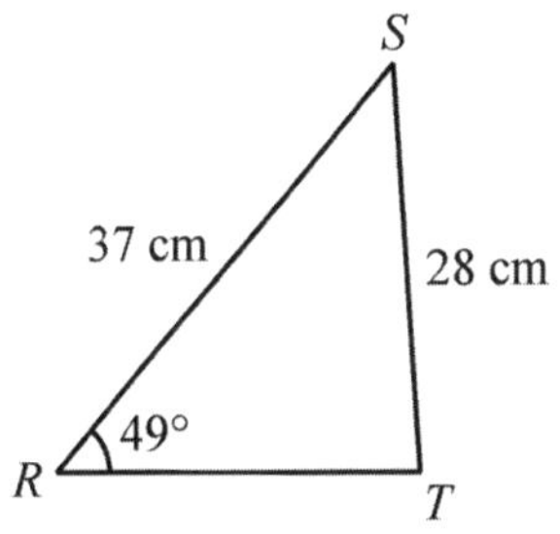

Correct to the nearest tenth of a degree, what is the measure of $\angle RTS$?

F. 85.8° **G.** 74.6°

H. 60.2° **J.** 34.8°

41. A ball is thrown in the air from a balcony of an apartment building and falls to the ground. The height, y metres, of the ball with respect to the ground x seconds after being thrown is given by the equation $y = -4.9x^2 + 24.5x + 6$.

Part A

Open Response

On the grid below, draw a graph that represents the path of the ball. Make use of your graphing calculator.

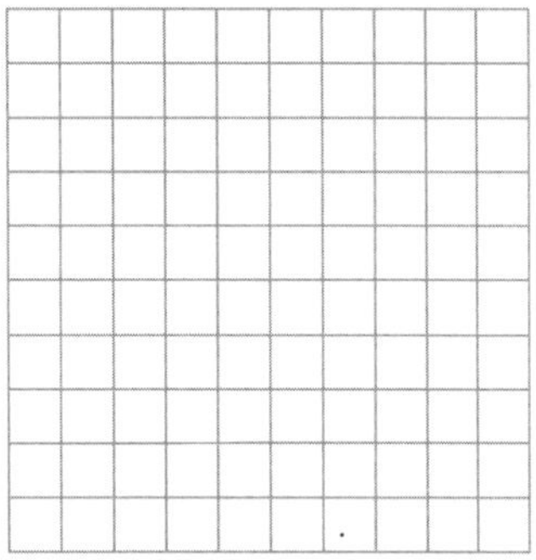

Part B

Open Response

What is the maximum height, to the nearest tenth, of the ball above the ground?

Part C

Open Response

To the nearest tenth, what are the domain and range for the path of the ball?

Part D

Open Response

To the nearest tenth of a second, how long is the ball more than 25 m above the ground.

Justify your answer.

42. Part A

Open Response

As part of an end of the year school function, a teacher and 23 students attend a special showing of a movie at a downtown theatre. All the students and the teacher each purchase a large bag of popcorn. If each large bag of popcorn sells for $4.75, what will be the total cost of the popcorn?

Part B

Open Response

Set up a system of two linear equations involving two variables, and then use this system to solve the following problem.

At a particular theatre, adult tickets cost $12.50 each, and student tickets cost $8 each. At a certain show, only adult and student tickets were sold. If twice as many student tickets as adult tickets were sold and the total sales were $2 280, then how many adult and how many student tickets were sold?

Show your work.

Go On

43. A weather balloon is flying in a field outside of London, Ontario. One end of a lightweight rope is attached to the base of the weather balloon, and the other end of the rope is anchored to the ground at point *P*. On a windy day, Rachel decides to determine the length of the rope, *x*, between *P* and the connection point located at the base of the weather balloon. She locates two points *A* and *B* that are 200 m apart and records the measurements shown in the diagram.

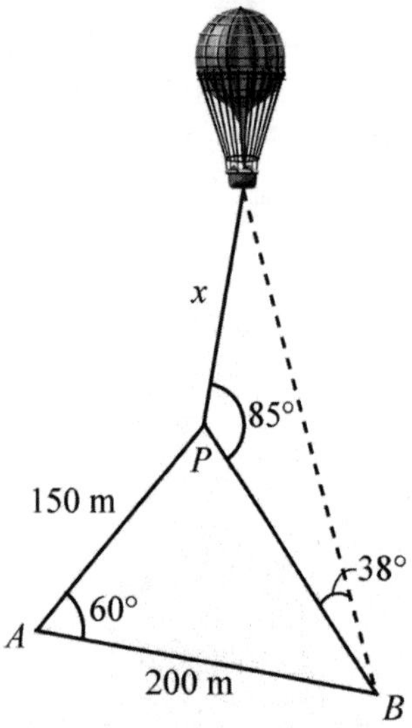

Diagram not to scale

Part A

Open Response

To the nearest metre, what is the distance from anchor point *P* to point *B*?.

Part B

Open Response

What is the value of *x* to the nearest metre?

Practice Test 2

Ontario Math 10 Academic

Practice Test 2

1. A model rocket was launched from a platform and its height, h, in metres, above the ground, with respect to time, t, in seconds was recorded. The data obtained is shown is the table.

Time (s)	0	1	3	8	14	20	25
Height (m)	3	148	410	890	1 140	1 025	700

If a quadratic regression was done on the data, the best estimate of the height of the model rocket after 6 s is

A. 680 m **B.** 725 m

C. 780 m **D.** 820 m

2. Which of the following graphs could be the graph of the quadratic function $y = ax^2 - 12x + 7$, $a < 0$?

F.

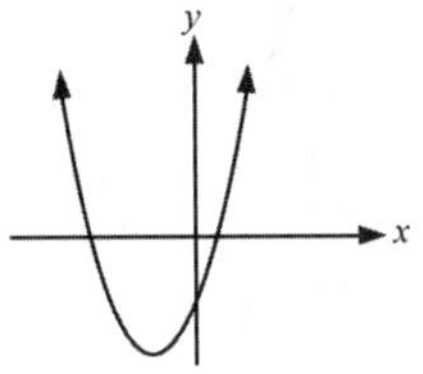

G.

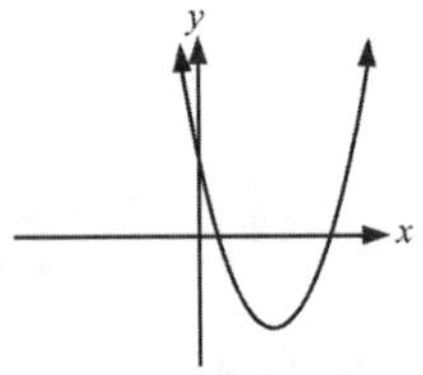

H.

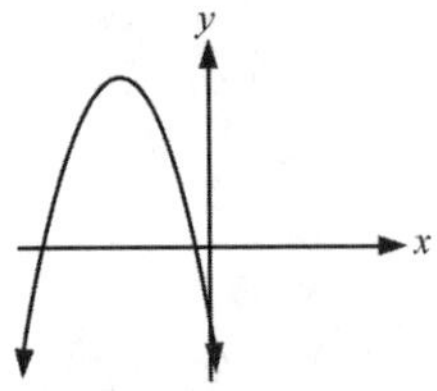

J.

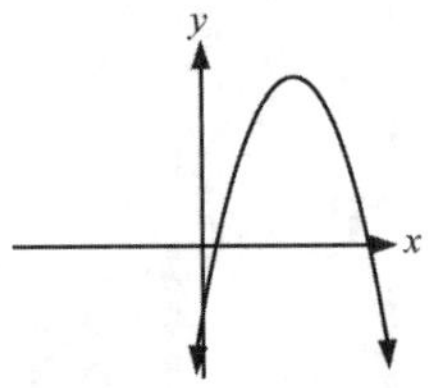

3. The graphs of two different parabolas with the same vertex are shown in the diagram.

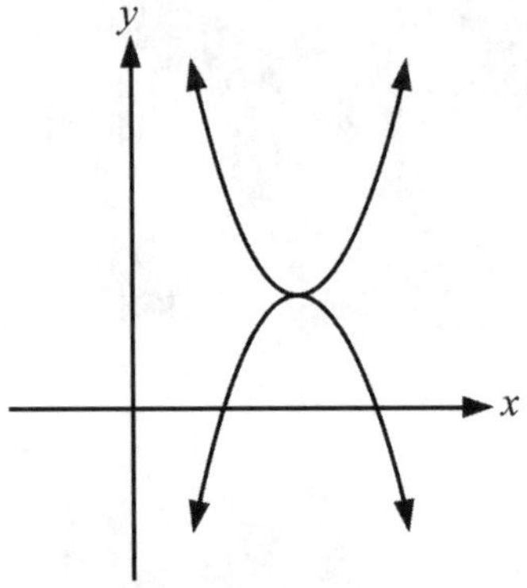

A student analyzed the two parabolas and made the following statements:

I. The parabolas will have the same domain.

II. The parabolas will have the same zeros.

III. The parabolas will have the same equation of the axis of symmetry.

IV. The parabolas will have the same maximum value.

V. The parabolas will have the same minimum value.

Which statements are correct?

A. Only I and II

B. Only I and III

C. Only II, III, and IV

D. Only I, III, and V

4. In order for the equation $2^x \times 2^a = 1$, $x \neq 0$, to be correct, the value of a must be

F. 0 **G.** 1 **H.** x **J.** $-x$

5. The graph of $y = x^2$ is translated left 4 units and down 3 units. Which of the following graphs depicts the new parabola?

A.

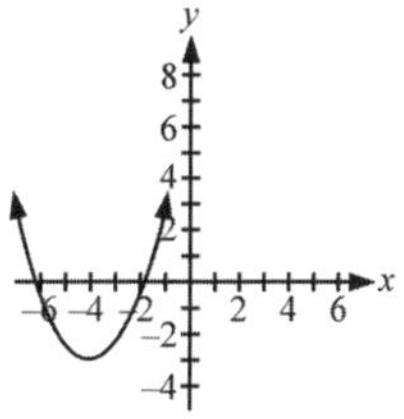

B.

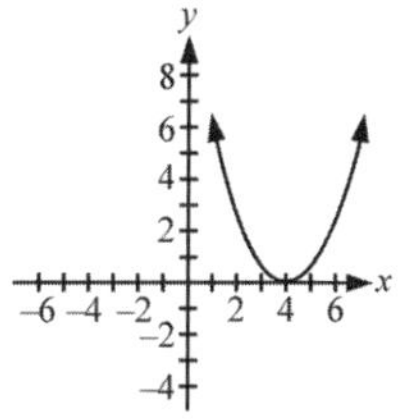

C.

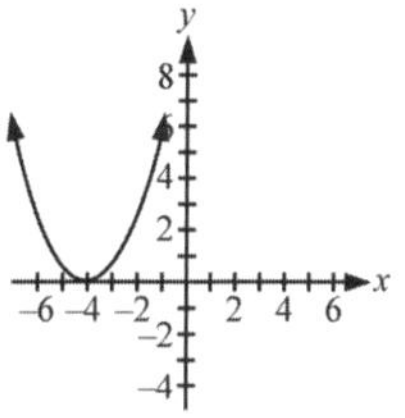

D.

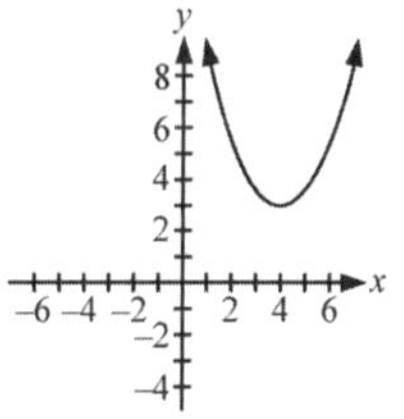

6. The graph of the function $y = x^2$ is transformed to become the function $y = -3(x - h)^2 + k$. Respectively, what are the equation of the axis of symmetry and the location of the vertex of the transformed function?

F. $x = k$ and (h, k)

G. $x = -h$ and $(-h, k)$

H. $x = h$ and (h, k)

J. $x = k$ and (k, h)

7. In the order shown, the following transformations were applied to the graph of $y = x^2$.

1. A vertical stretch by a factor of 2 about the x-axis.
2. A reflection in the x-axis.
3. A horizontal translation 2 units left.
4. A vertical translation 3 units up.

Which of the following graphs **best** represents the graph of the transformed function?

A.

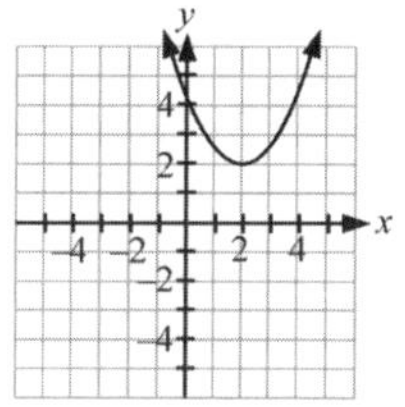

B.

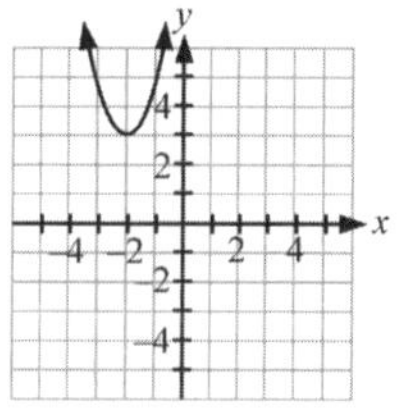

C.

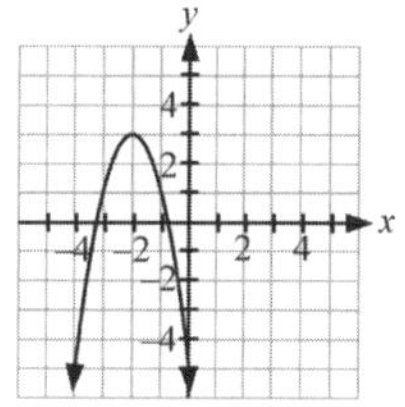

D.

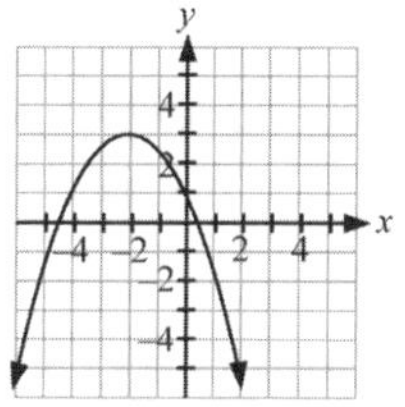

Go On

8. 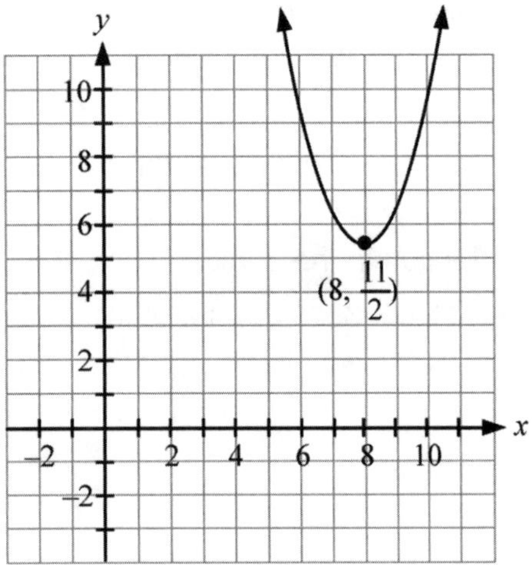

Which of the following quadratic relations is **best** illustrated by the given graph?

F. $y = (x - 8)^2 + \frac{11}{2}$

G. $y = (x - 8)^2 - \frac{11}{2}$

H. $y = 2(x - 8)^2 - \frac{11}{2}$

J. $y = -2(x - 8)^2 + \frac{11}{2}$

9. If $-2(3x + 5)^2 = ax^2 + bx + c$, then the value of $a + c$ is

A. −34 **B.** −68

C. −78 **D.** −110

10. Which of the following expressions is **not** a factor of $9mn^2 - 12mn - 12m$?

F. $3m$ **G.** $n - 4$

H. $3n + 2$ **J.** $n - 2$

11. The graph of a particular quadratic relation is shown.

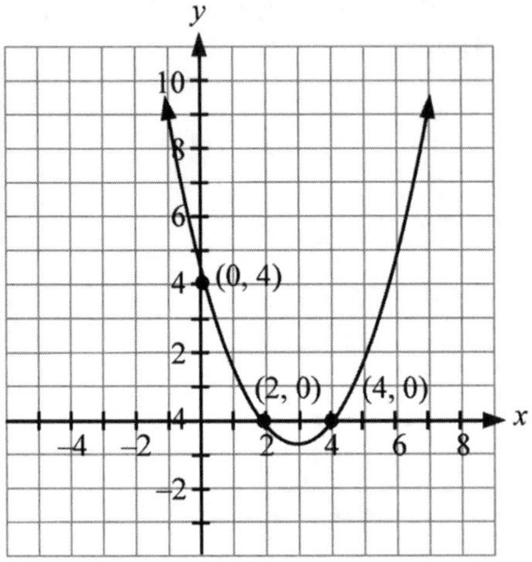

The equation of the quadratic relation is

A. $y = \frac{1}{2}(x + 2)(x + 4)$

B. $y = 2(x + 2)(x + 4)$

C. $y = \frac{1}{2}(x - 2)(x - 4)$

D. $y = 2(x - 2)(x - 4)$

12. Which of the following graphs could be used to illustrate a quadratic equation with no real roots?

F.

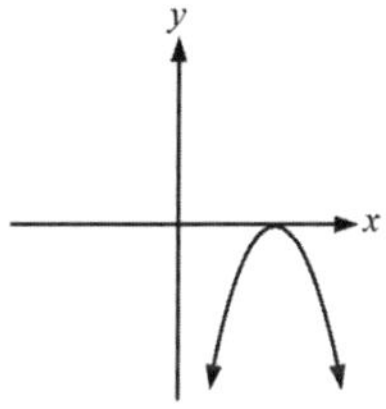

G.

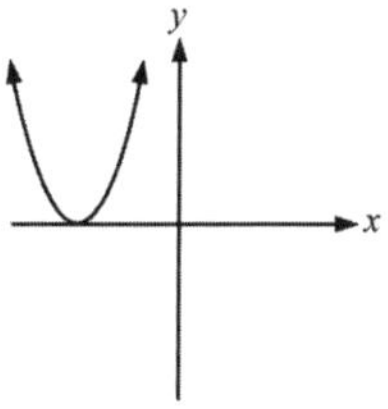

H.

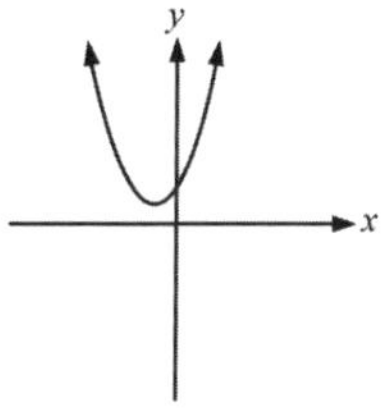

J.

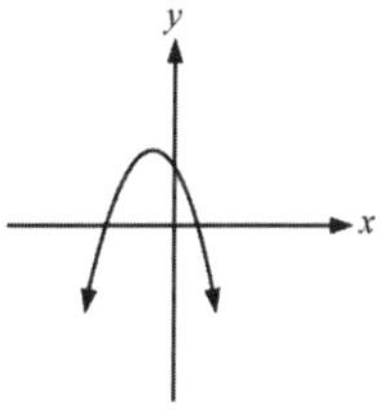

13. If the equation $y = 3x^2 + 42x + 142$ is written in the completed square form $y = a(x - h)^2 + k$, then the value of k is

A. –7 **B.** –5 **C.** 5 **D.** 7

14. Roman is attempting to sketch the graph of the quadratic function $y = -2(x^2 + 6x + 8)$. He makes the following four statements:

Statement I: The y-intercept of the graph is 8.

Statement II: The x-intercepts of the graph are –4 and –2.

Statement III: The vertex of the graph is (3, –2).

Statement IV: The equation of the axis of symmetry of the graph is $x = -3$.

Which of Roman's statements are correct?

F. Only II and IV **G.** Only II and III

H. I, II, and III **J.** I, II, and IV

15. A math teacher asks her class to solve the quadratic equation $6x^2 - 13x = 5$. The partial solution of each of two students is given.

Rhett
$6x^2 - 13x = 5$
$6x^2 - 13x - 5 = 0$
$6x^2 - 10x - 3x - 5 = 0$
$2x(3x - 5) - 1(3x - 5) = 0$
$(3x - 5)(2x - 1) = 0$

Vlad
$6x^2 - 13x = 5$
$6x^2 - 13x - 5 = 0$
$x = \dfrac{13 \pm \sqrt{(-13)^2 - 4(6)(-5)}}{2(6)}$
$x = \dfrac{13 \pm \sqrt{169 - 120}}{12}$
$x = \dfrac{13 \pm \sqrt{49}}{12}$

Which of the following statements is **true**?

A. Rhett's work and Vlad's work will each lead to a correct solution.

B. Rhett's work and Vlad's work will each lead to an incorrect solution.

C. Rhett's work will lead to a correct solution, and Vlad's work will lead to an incorrect solution.

D. Rhett's work will lead to an incorrect solution, and Vlad's work will lead to a correct solution.

16. The minimum value of the function $y = 4x^2 - 12x + 15$ is

F. −12 **G.** −4

H. 4 **J.** 6

Numerical Response

17. The path of a roller coaster car can be modelled by the function $h = -7t^2 + 61t + 98$ for the section of the ride where $1 \le t \le 10$. For this function, h is the height of the car above the ground in feet and t is the time in seconds elapsed since the beginning of the ride.

To the nearest tenth of a second, over what time period is the roller coaster car 200 feet or more above the ground?

____

18. If a bullet is fired vertically at an initial speed of 100 m/s, then the height, h, after t seconds is given by the equation $h = 100t - 5t^2$.

What is the maximum height attained by the bullet?

F. 10 m **G.** 20 m

H. 100 m **J.** 500 m

19. Maj held a soccer ball in front of her. She kicked the ball, which followed a path that can be modelled by the equation $y = -4.9x^2 + 13.7x + 0.7$, where y is the height above the ground in metres and x is the time in seconds.

At what height above the ground was Maj holding the soccer ball when she kicked it?

A. 0.0 m **B.** 0.7 m

C. 1.4 m **D.** 2.8 m

20. This system of equations was given to two students to solve.

$4x + y = -14$

$3x + 2y = -8$

Minesh's Partial Solution
1. Multiply the first equation by 3.
2. Multiply the second equation by 4.
3. Subtract the second equation from the first equation. $12x + 3y = -42$ $\underline{12x + 8y = -32}$ $-5y = -10$
4. Solve for y.
5. Now, solve for x.

Cameron's Partial Solution
1. Rearrange the first equation in the form $y = -4x - 14$
2. Rearrange the second equation in the form $y = -\frac{3}{2}x - 4$
3. Graph both equations using technology.
4. Find the point of intersection of the two lines.

Which of the following statements about these partial solutions is **true**?

F. Minesh's partial solution is wrong, and Cameron's partial solution is correct.

G. Cameron's partial solution is wrong, and Minesh's partial solution is correct.

H. Minesh and Cameron each made an error that will lead to a wrong answer.

J. Minesh's partial solution and Cameron's partial solution will both lead to the same correct answer.

Numerical Response

21. If $5x + y = 93$ and $2x + y = 48$, then what is the value of y in the solution to this system of equations?

____

22. At a particular fast food restaurant, the cost of 2 hamburgers and 1 small french fries is \$7.00. The cost of 1 hamburger and 2 small french fries is \$5.75. What is the cost of 1 hamburgers?

F. \$2.25 **G.** \$2.50

H. \$2.75 **J.** \$2.80

23. Harold invested his savings of \$5 000. He invested part of his savings at 4% per annum and part at 6% per annum. At the end of one year, the interest from the amount invested at 4% was \$50 more than the interest from the amount invested at 6%.

If x represents the amount of money invested at 4% and y represents the amount of money invested at 6%, then the system of equations that could be solved in order to determine the amount of money invested at each rate is

A. $x + y = 5\,000$ and $4x = 6y + 5\,000$

B. $x + y = 5\,000$ and $6y - 4x = 5\,000$

C. $4x + 6y = 5\,000$ and $x = y - 60$

D. $4x + 6y = 5\,000$ and $x - 60 = y$

24. If point $(-3, 4)$ is the midpoint of point $A(2, 1)$ and point $B(x, 7)$, then the value of x is

F. −8 **G.** −6 **H.** 6 **J.** 8

25. The given diagram represents a situation in which coast guard ship A is located 4 km west and 12 km north of a reference point denoted by (0, 0), and coast guard ship B is located 1 km west and 8 km north of the reference point. A third coast guard ship, C, is located such that coast guard ship B is the midpoint of the line segment connecting coast guard ship A to coast guard ship C. Cruise ship D, which is sailing in the area, issues a distress signal. It is determined that the distance from coast guard ship A to cruise ship D is the same as the distance from coast guard ship A to coast guard ship C.

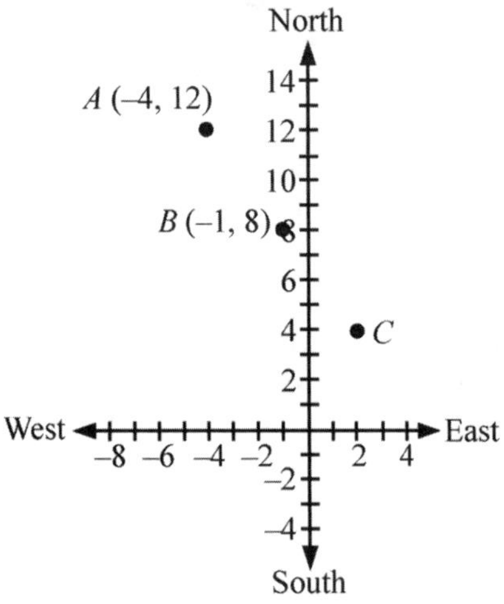

If the coordinates of cruise ship D are $(2, y)$, then the value of y is

A. 18 **B.** 20 **C.** 22 **D.** 24

26. The point (a, b) is located on a particular circle with centre (0, 0) as shown.

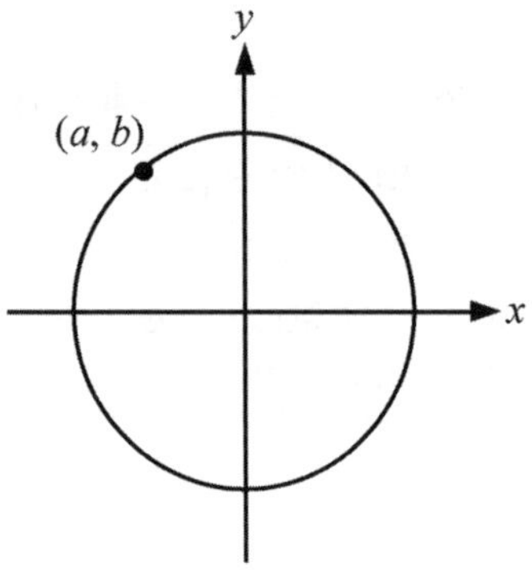

The radius of this circle is given by the expression

F. $a^2 + b^2$ **G.** $\sqrt{a^2 + b^2}$

H. $a^2 - b^2$ **J.** $\sqrt{a^2 - b^2}$

27. A circle is defined by the equation $4x^2 + 4y^2 = 36$. What is the length of the radius of this circle?

A. 2 units **B.** 3 units

C. 6 units **D.** 9 units

28. A perpendicular bisector is a line that intersects the midpoint of another line at a right angle. Triangle PQR has vertices $Q(6, 2)$, $R(-2, 8)$ and $P(2, -4)$.

The equation of the perpendicular bisector of side QR is given by

F. $y = \frac{3}{4}x + 2$

G. $y = \frac{4}{3}x - \frac{1}{3}$

H. $y = \frac{4}{3}x + \frac{7}{3}$

J. $y = -\frac{3}{4}x + \frac{13}{2}$

29. To the nearest tenth, the shortest distance between the point $(-1, 2)$ and the line $3x - 4y - 36 = 0$ is

A. 5.2 units **B.** 8.4 units

C. 9.4 units **D.** 11.0 units

30. The points $A(1, 5)$, $B(-3, 1)$, and $C(6, -4)$ are the vertices of triangle ABC. If the length of side AB is $\sqrt{32}$ units and the length of side AC is $\sqrt{106}$ units, then ΔABC is

F. a scalene triangle

G. an isosceles triangle

H. a right angle triangle

J. an equilateral triangle

31. At 11:30 A.M on a sunny day, a 6 foot tall man casts an 8 foot long shadow. What is the approximate length of the shadow cast by a 45 foot high building at the same time?

A. 33.75 ft **B.** 47.00 ft

C. 60.00 ft **D.** 85.00 ft

32. Jim wants to measure the width of a small river that is near his house. He draws the following diagram based on measurements that he knows, where A, B, and C represent points in a nearby park.

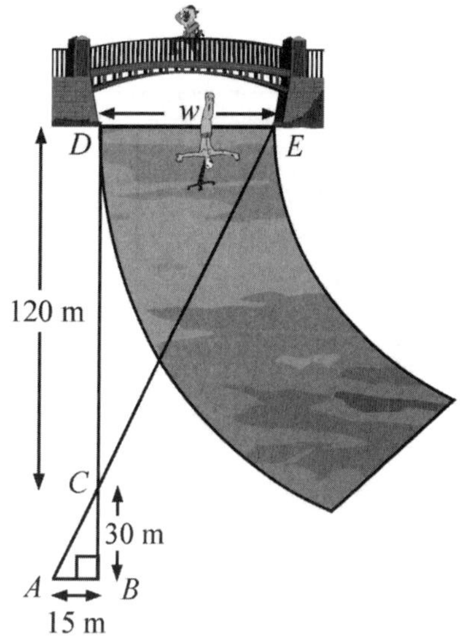

What is the width of the river?

F. 40 m **G.** 60 m

H. 80 m **J.** 240 m

33.

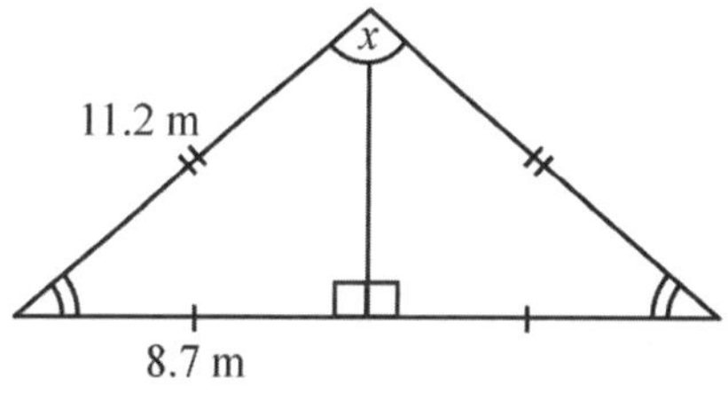

A triangle

What is the measure of angle x to the nearest degree?

A. 102° **B.** 78° **C.** 51° **D.** 39°

34. Acute ΔMNP is shown.

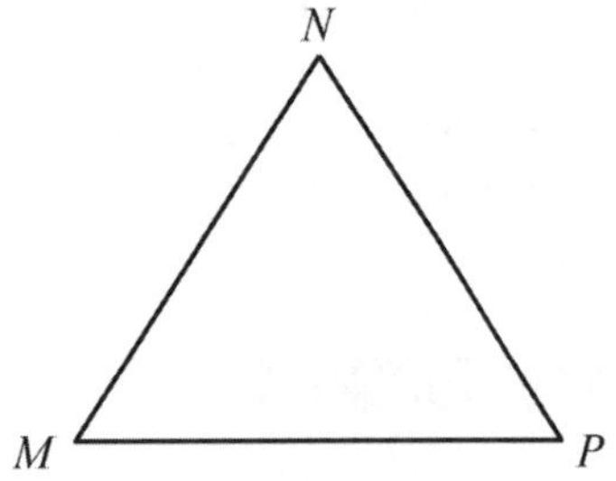

Which of the following equations correctly illustrates the law of sines with respect to ΔMNP?

F. $\dfrac{NP}{\sin M} = \dfrac{MP}{\sin P}$

G. $\dfrac{MN}{\sin P} = \dfrac{MP}{\sin N}$

H. $(MP)^2 = (MN)^2 + (NP)^2 - 2(MN)(NP)\sin M$

J. $(NP)^2 = (MN)^2 + (MP)^2 - 2(MN)(MP)\sin P$

35. The equation $x^2 = 80^2 + 95^2 - 2(80)(95)\cos 73°$ applies to which of the following triangles?

A.

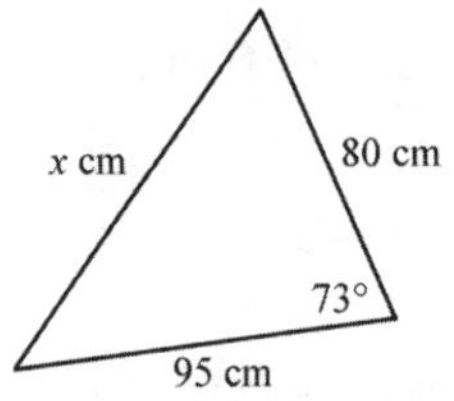

B.

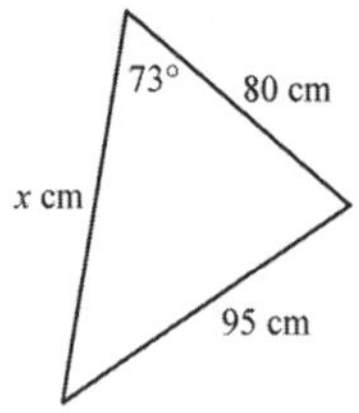

C.

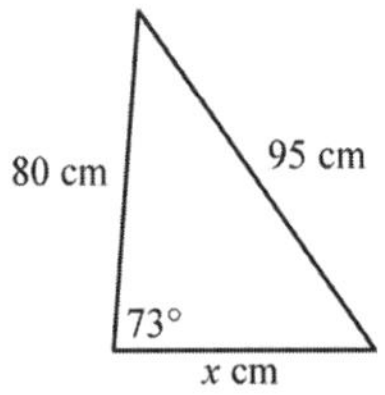

D.

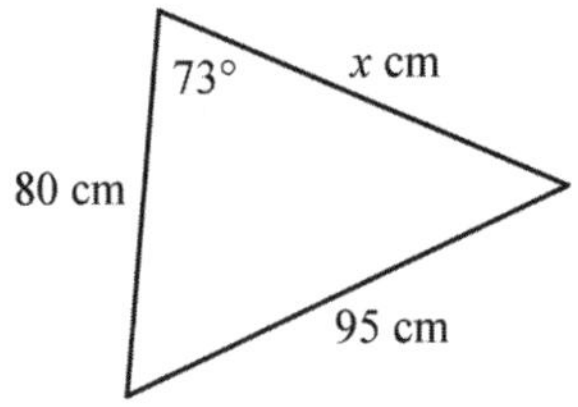

36.

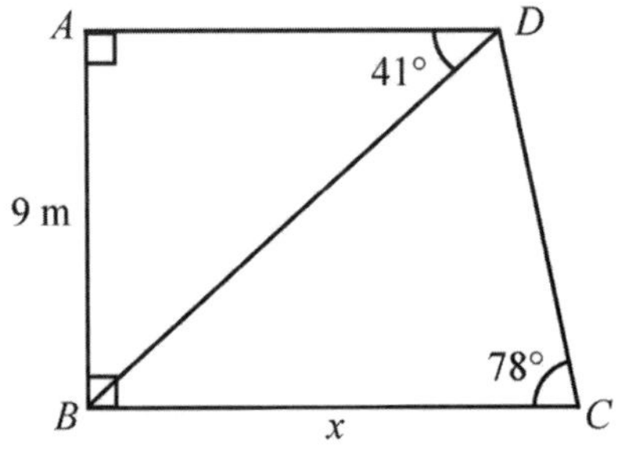

Correct to the nearest tenth, what is the length of side x in the given diagram?

F. 9.2 m　　**G.** 11.2 m

H. 12.3 m　　**J.** 13.7 m

37.

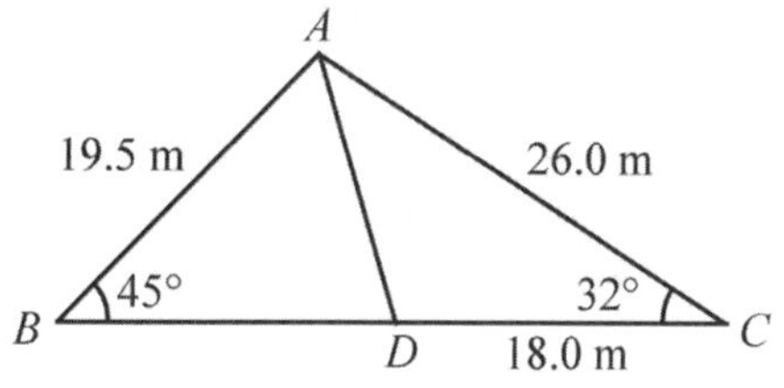

Correct to the nearest degree, what is the measure of ∠*ADB*?

A. 58° **B.** 64° **C.** 68° **D.** 74°

38. From a particular point, Jennifer determined that the angle of elevation to the top of her school was 18°. When she walked 12.5 m closer to the school, she determined that the angle of elevation to the top of the school was 29°, as illustrated in the diagram.

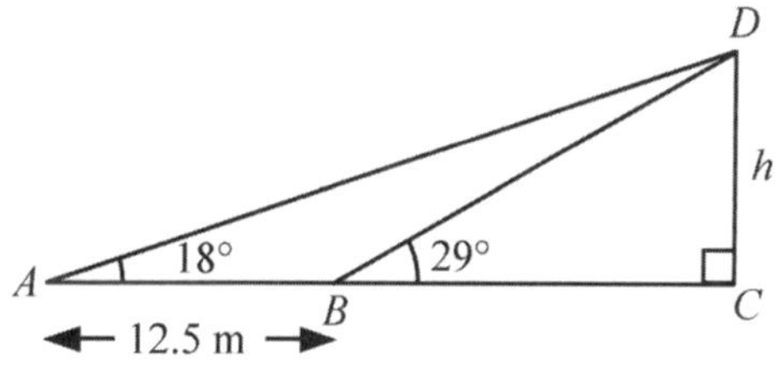

Correct to the nearest metre, the height of the school, h, is ____ m.

39. A boat is towing two wakeboarders. Wakeboarder 1 has a rope that is 65 feet long, and Wakeboarder 2 has a rope that is 70 feet long. At one point in time, the angle between the two ropes is 38°, as illustrated in the diagram.

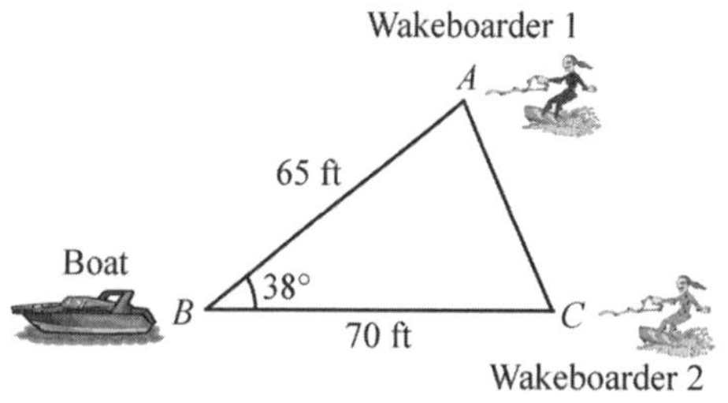

To the nearest tenth, how far apart are the wakeboarders at the given point in time?

A. 4.4 ft **B.** 43.1 ft

C. 44.2 ft **D.** 50.8 ft

40. A construction site at the University of Toronto is in the shape of a kite. Because of the size of the area and the busy traffic around the university, a road was built through the site for construction vehicles only, as shown in the diagram.

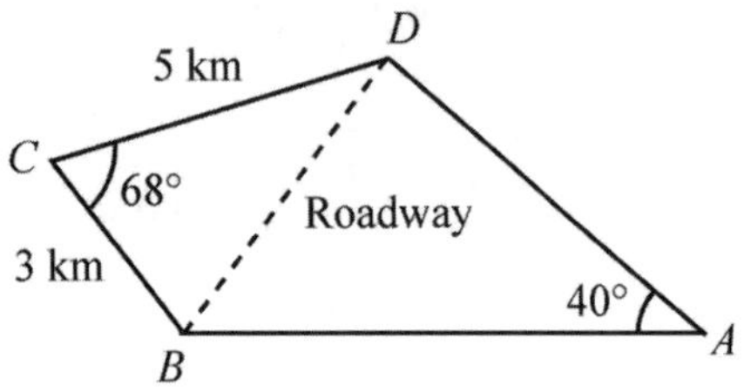

An equation that could be used to determine the length of the roadway, *BD*, in kilometres is

F. $BD = \dfrac{3\sin 68^\circ}{\sin 40^\circ}$

G. $BD = \dfrac{5\sin 68^\circ}{\sin 40^\circ}$

H. $BD = \sqrt{3^2 + 5^2 + 2(3)(5)\cos 68^\circ}$

J. $BD = \sqrt{3^2 + 5^2 - 2(3)(5)\cos 68^\circ}$

41. The cost, *C*, in dollars of manufacturing *x* Road Racer bicycles at Cycle World's production plant can be modelled by the function $C = 2x^2 - 700x + 92\,750$.

Part A

Open Response

What are two possible values for *x* if the cost, *C*, of manufacturing Road Racer bicycles is $62 750?

Part B

Open Response

Algebraically, determine the number of Road Racer bicycles that must be manufactured to minimize the cost.

Part C

Open Response

What is the minimum cost of manufacturing Road Racer bicycles?

Part D

Open Response

To the nearest whole number, what is the fewest number of bicycles that can be manufactured for a cost of $50 000? Use a graphing calculator.

42. A soccer field is part of a sports complex. The given diagram shows the soccer field placed on a coordinate grid where the coordinates are expressed in yards.

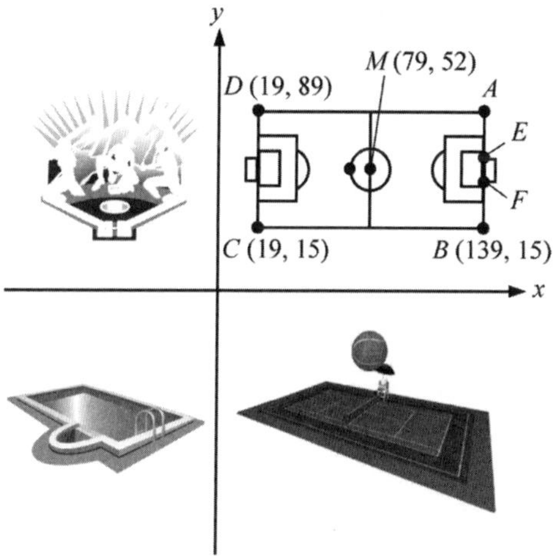

Part A

Open Response

Determine the coordinates of corner post *A*.

Part B

Open Response

The soccer nets are centered on the back lines of the playing field and are 8 yards in width. Determine the coordinates of points *E* and *F* in the diagram.

Justify your answer.

Part C

Open Response

If player *P* located at coordinates (54, 41) wants to pass the soccer ball to player *Q* located at coordinates (83, 62), what is the minimum distance, to the nearest tenth, that the ball must travel.

Show your work.

Part D

Open Response

Verify that the diagonals of the playing field bisect each other at the centre mark M.

Show your work.

43. To estimate the amount of new water pipe required for part of a golf course, the golf course designer used the diagram shown with the indicated measurements.

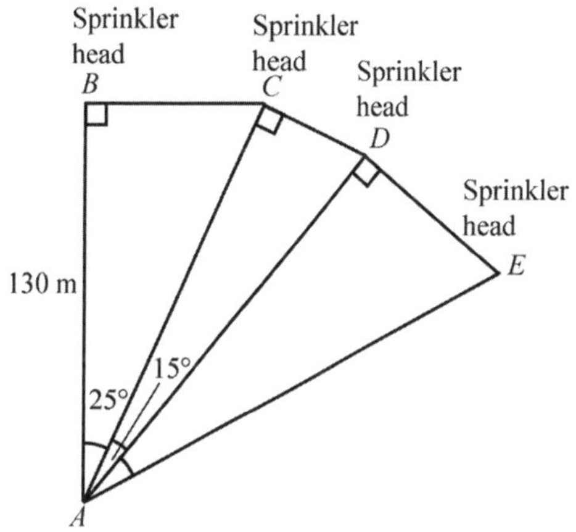

Part A

Open Response

What is the correct distance from the sprinkler head at point B to the sprinkler head at point C to the nearest tenth of a metre?

Part B

Open Response

What is the correct distance from the sprinkler head at point D to the sprinkler head at point E to the nearest metre?

SOLUTIONS–PRACTICE TEST 1

1. D	**11. A**	**21. A**	**31. B**	**41.** Part A- **OR**
2. J	**12. G**	**22. G**	**32. G**	Part B- **OR**
3. B	**13. D**	**23. D**	**33. A**	Part C- **OR**
4. J	**14. H**	**24. G**	**34. H**	Part D- **OR**
5. D	**15. 1**	**25. B**	**35. C**	**42.** Part A- **OR**
6. H	**16. G**	**26. F**	**36. H**	Part B- **OR**
7. B	**17. D**	**27. B**	**37. 1.9**	**43.** Part A- **OR**
8. G	**18. G**	**28. 15**	**38. H**	Part B- **OR**
9. C	**19. B**	**29. C**	**39. B**	
10. J	**20. H**	**30. J**	**40. F**	

1. D

The shape of the graph can be determined by sketching by hand or by using technology. Use a TI-83 Plus graphing calculator to get the following graph:

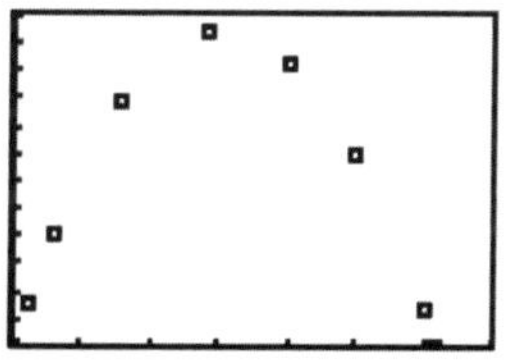

The shape of the graph models a parabola. Examine the first set of ordered pairs from the table to see that when time is 0, the height is 3. Therefore, the graph that best represents the data is graph D.

2. J

If $a < 0$ in the equation $y = ax^2 + bx + c$, the parabola opens downward; therefore, $y = -8.4x^2 + 5$ and $y = -4.2x^2 + 5$ are two possible equations.

From the table of values, calculate the second difference for each equation.

$y = -8.4x^2 + 5$:

x	y	1st diff	2nd diff
1	–3.4		
		} 25.2	
2	–28.6		} –16.8
		} 42	
3	–70.6		} –16.8
		} 58.8	
4	–129.4		} –16.8
		} 75.6	
5	–205		} –16.8
		} 92.4	
6	–297.4		

$y = -4.2x^2 + 5$:

x	y	1st diff	2nd diff
1	0.8		
		} 12.6	
2	–11.8		} –8.4
		} 21	
3	–32.8		} –8.4
		} 29.4	
4	–62.2		} –8.4
		} 37.8	
5	–100		} –8.4
		} 46.2	
6	–146.2		

Therefore, the quadratic function that opens downward and has a second difference of $-8.4 y = -4.2x^2 + 5$ is.

3. B

The graph of the function shown is a parabola that opens downward and has the following features:

- The vertex of the parabola is $(1, 2)$.
- The zeros are $x = -2$ and $x = 4$, which are points A and C, respectively.
- The parabola passes through the y-axis at point B.

Therefore, the y-intercept is B, and the zeros occur at A and C.

4. J

Substitute each x-value into the equation $y = 2^x$.

$y = 2^{(-3)} = \frac{1}{2^3} = \frac{1}{8}$

$y = 2^{(0)} = 1$ (Any number or variable with an exponent of zero is equal to 1; $x^0 = 1$.)

$y = 2^{(3)} = 8$

5. D

The h-value causes a horizontal translation (shifting the parabola left or right) and affects the axis of symmetry. Since the h value is the same for each equation, the axis of symmetry for the graph of each given function will be the same.

For a quadratic function of the form $y = a(x - h)^2 + k$, the range, vertex, and y-intercepts are affected by the parameter k.

6. H

For the equation $y = -3(x - 2)^2 + 5$, it follows that $a = -3$, $h = 2$, and $k = 5$. The vertex of a quadratic relation is (h, k); therefore, the vertex for $y = -3(x - 2)^2 + 5$ is located at the ordered pair $(2, 5)$.

7. B

All points on the transformed graph must satisfy the given transformations.
A reflection about the x-axis will change $(3, 9)$ to $(3, -9)$.
A vertical stretch about the x-axis by a factor of 3 will change $(3, -9)$ to $(3, -27)$.
A horizontal translation 2 units to the right changes $(3, -27)$ to $(5, -27)$.
A vertical translation 4 units downward changes $(5, -27)$ to $(5, -31)$.
The respective values of a and b are 5 and -31.

8. G

The parabola shown can have an equation of the form $y = a(x - h)^2 + k$, where (h, k) is the vertex.
Since the vertex is at $(-4, -1)$, $h = -4$ and $k = -1$.
Substitute -4 for h and -1 for k into $y = a(x - h)^2 + k$ to get $y = a(x + 4)^2 - 1$.
Since the equation passes through the point $(-3.5, 0)$, $x = -3.5$ and $y = 0$.

$y = a(x + 4)^2 - 1$

Substitute -3.5 for x and 0 for y. Solve for a.

$0 = a((-3.5) + 4)^2 - 1$

$0 = a\left(\frac{1}{2}\right)^2 - 1$

$0 = \frac{a}{4} - 1$

$\frac{a}{4} = 1$

$a = 4$

Substitute 4 for a into the equation $y = a(x + 4)^2 - 1$ to get $y = 4(x + 4)^2 - 1$.

The graph illustrates the equation $y = 4(x + 4)^2 - 1$.

9. C

In general, $(a - b)^2 = a^2 - 2ab + b^2$

Substitute m for a and $\frac{n}{5}$ for b into $a^2 - 2ab + b^2$.

$\left(m - \frac{n}{5}\right)^2 = m^2 - 2(m)\left(\frac{n}{5}\right) + \left(\frac{n}{5}\right)^2$

Simplify.

$m^2 - \frac{2}{5}mn + \frac{n^2}{25}$

The expanded form of the expression is

$m^2 - \frac{2}{5}mn + \frac{n^2}{25}$

10. J

$x^2 + 3x$ factors to $x(x + 3)$.

$x^2 - 9$ factors to $(x + 3)(x - 3)$.

$x^2 + 6x + 9$ factors to $(x + 3)(x + 3) = (x + 3)^2$.

$x^2 + 13x - 30$ factors to $(x + 15)(x - 2)$.

Therefore, $x + 3$ is not a factor of $x^2 + 13x - 30$.

11. A

The polynomial function has zeros of $\frac{3}{5}$ and -6. It follows that $r = \frac{3}{5}$ and $s = -6$.

Substitute $\frac{3}{5}$ for r and -6 for s into the equation $y = a(x - r)(x - s)$, where $a = 1$.

$y = \left(x - \frac{3}{5}\right)(x + 6)$ or $y = (5x - 3)(x + 6)$.

12. G

The graphs of equations (i) and (ii) are plotted:

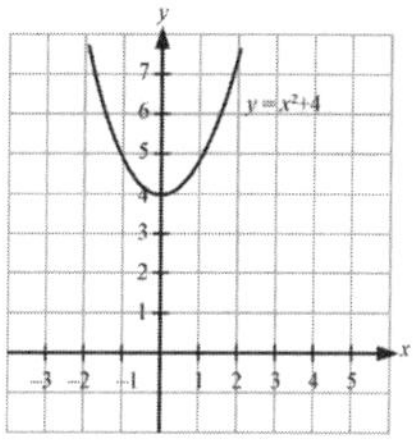

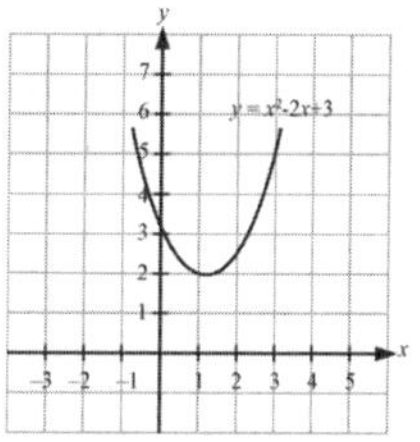

Since neither graph has x-intercepts, the roots of both the given equations are non-real.

13. D

$y = 4(x^2 - x) - 3$	Identify and remove the common factor from the x^2 and x-term of the expression. In this case, the common factor is 4.
$y = 4(x^2 - \underline{x}) - 3$ $\left(\frac{-1}{2}\right)^2 = \frac{1}{4}$	Notice the resulting coefficient for the x-term. Divide this value by 2, and then square it.
$y = 4\left(x^2 - x + \underline{\frac{1}{4} - \frac{1}{4}}\right) - 3$	Both add and subtract this value inside the brackets.
$y = \underline{4}\left(x^2 - x + \frac{1}{4} - \underline{\frac{1}{4}}\right) - 3$ $y = 4\left(x^2 - x + \frac{1}{4}\right)\underline{-1} - 3$	Move the value that will not contribute to a perfect square outside the brackets. [Note: With the distributive property, you have really added -1 and $+1$ to the function, since $4\left(\frac{1}{4}\right) = 1$ and $4\left(-\frac{1}{4}\right) = -1$. To move $-\frac{1}{4}$ outside the brackets, it becomes -1.]
$y = 4\left(x - \frac{1}{2}\right)^2 - 4$	Factor the trinomial inside the brackets to form a perfect square, and collect like terms outside the bracket.

The student's solution matches the given solution; therefore, there is no error.

14. H

Use a graphing calculator to get the following graph of the function $y = -24x^2 + 1\,000x - 3\,250$.

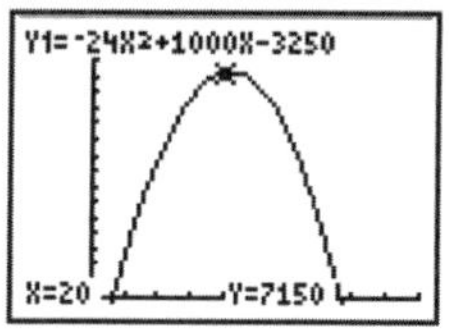

Graph displayed uses the window setting:
x:$[-10, 50, 5]$$y$:$[-200, 8\,500, 500]$
Therefore, the graph in choice H could be a sketch of the quadratic function $y = -24x^2 + 1\,000x - 3\,250$.

15. 1

The roots of the quadratic equation $x^2 + x - 6 = -2(x + 1)$ are found by determining the x-coordinate of each point of intersection of the two graphs. The points of intersection are $(-4,\ 6)$ and $(1,\ -4)$. The roots are -4 and 1; therefore, the largest root is 1.

16. G

Solve $2x^2 + 5x + 1 = 0$ using the quadratic formula.

$$x = \frac{-b \pm \sqrt{b^2 - 4ac}}{2a}$$

Substitute 2 for a, 5 for b, and 1 for c into the quadratic formula.

$$x = \frac{-(5) \pm \sqrt{(5)^2 - 4(2)(1)}}{2(2)}$$

$$x = \frac{-5 \pm \sqrt{25 - 8}}{4}$$

$$x = \frac{-5 \pm \sqrt{17}}{4}$$

17. D

Sergei's procedure will yield the following graphs

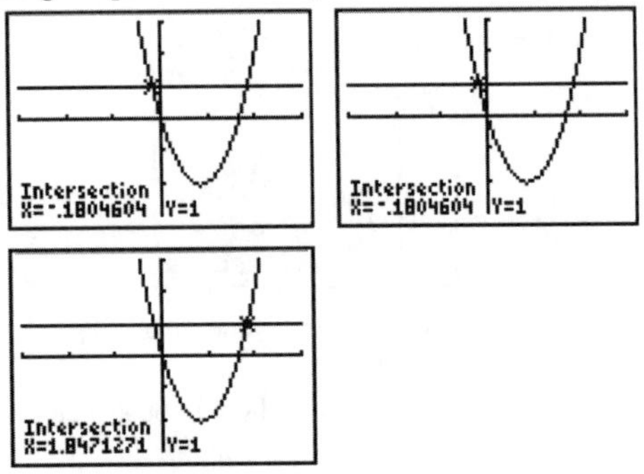

and the solution the equation $3x^2 - 5x = 1$ to the nearest hundredth is $x = -0.18$ or $x = 1.85$.

Jeremy's procedure will yield the following graphs:

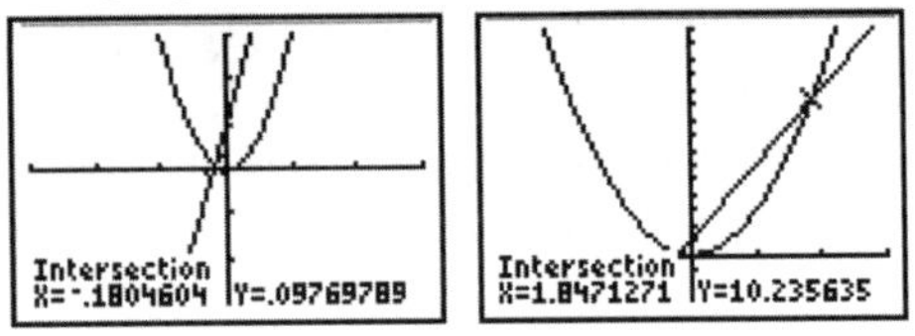

The solution to the equation $3x^2 - 5x = 1$ to the nearest hundredth is $x = -0.18$ or $x = 1.85$.

Alexi's procedure will yield the following graphs:

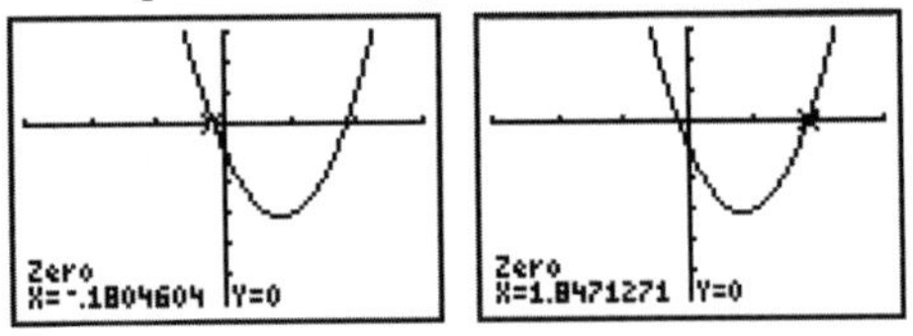

The solution to the equation $3x^2 - 5x = 1$ to the nearest hundredth is $x = -0.18$ or $x = 1.85$.

Beyonce's procedure will yield the following graphs:

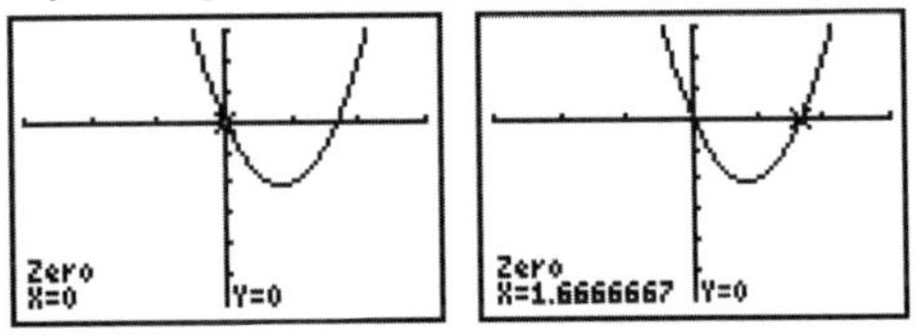

Subtract 1 from each of the zeros. The solution to the equation $3x^2 - 5x = 1$ to the nearest hundredth is $x = -1$ or $x = 0.67$.

Therefore, the student with the incorrect procedure is Beyonce.

18. G

The roots of the equation $ax^2 + bx - 16 = 0$ are 2 and 4.

The x-coordinate of the vertex of the graph of $y = ax^2 + bx - 16$ is halfway between the two roots of the equation $ax^2 + bx - 16 = 0$.

Thus, the x-coordinate of the vertex of the graph of $y = ax^2 + bx - 16$ is $x = \frac{2+4}{2} = 3$.

Insert $x = 3$ into $y = ax^2 + bx - 16$.

$\Rightarrow$ the y (maximum) value $= 9a + 3b - 16$

However, $a(x-2)(x-4) = 0$

Expand this equation.

$\Rightarrow ax^2 - 6ax + 8a = 0$

$\Rightarrow 8a = -16$ (since $c = -16$ in the equation $ax^2 + bx - 16 = 0$

$\Rightarrow a = -2$

$\Rightarrow b = -6a = -6(-2) = 12$ (from the equation $ax^2 - 6ax + 8a = 0$)

Enter the values of a and b into the maximum value $9a + 3b - 16$.

Hence, the maximum value is $9 \times (-2) + 3 \times 12 - 16$
$= -18 + 36 - 16 = 2$

19. B

Determine the maximum height by completing the square.

$y = -2x^2 + 8x + 27$

$y = -2(x^2 - 4x) + 27$

$y = -2(x^2 - \underline{4x}) + 27$

$\left(\frac{-4}{2}\right)^2 = 4$

$y = -2(x^2 - 4x + \underline{4 - 4}) + 27$

$y = \underline{-2}(x^2 - 4x + 4 \underline{- 4}) + 27$

$y = -2(x^2 - 4x + 4)\underline{+8} + 27$

$= -2(x-2)^2 + 35$

Here, the stone describes a parabolic path with vertex $(2, 35)$.

The stone reaches its maximum height in $x = 2s$.

The maximum height attained by the stone is 35 m.

20. H

The point $(K, -3)$ must satisfy both equation.

Substitute K for x and -3 for y in the equation $8x + 3y = -41$.

$8(K) + 3(-3) = -41$

$8K - 9 = -41$

$8K = -32$

$K = -4$

Note: the equation $6x - 5y = -9$ could have been used to determine the value for K.

21. A

To verify a solution to a system of equations, the solution must satisfy both equations. A particular point could satisfy one equation but not the other.

22. G

Let x = the number of tickets sold in sections A to M.
Let y = the number of tickets sold in sections N to Z.
The total number of tickets sold is represented by the equation $x + y = 55\ 300$.
The amount brought in by the sales is represented by tickets sales is represented by the equation
$55x + 85y = 37\ 40\ 500$.
Now, set up a system of equations.
(1) $x + y = 55\ 300$
(2) $55x + 85y = 37\ 40\ 500$
Multiply equation (1) by 55 (method of elimination).
(1) × 55 $\quad 55x + 55y = 30\ 41\ 500$
(2) $\quad \underline{55x + 85y = 37\ 40\ 500}$
Subtract the equations, and solve for y.
$-30y = -699000$
$y = 23\ 300$
Thus, 23 300 tickets were sold in sections N to Z.

23. D

Begin by sketching the parallelogram

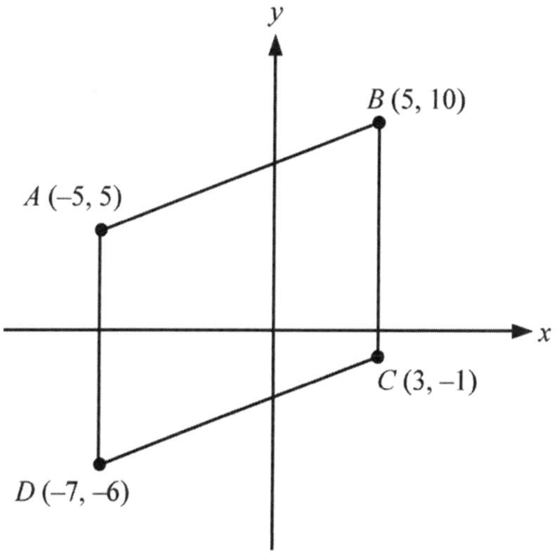

Here, you want the midpoint of diagonals AC and BD.
Using the midpoint formula:

$$M_{AC} = \left(\frac{-5+3}{2}, \frac{5+(-1)}{2}\right) \quad M_{AC} = \left(\frac{-7+5}{2}, \frac{-6+10}{2}\right)$$

$M_{AC} = (-1, 2) \qquad M_{AC} = (-1, 2)$

In both cases, the midpoint is (–1, 2).

24. G

Using the distance formula $d = \sqrt{(x_2 - x_1)^2 + (y_2 - y_1)^2}$, find d_{AC}, d_{AB}, and d_{BC}.

$$\begin{aligned} d_{AC} &= \sqrt{(-2-2)^2 + (2-6)^2} \\ &= \sqrt{(-4)^2 + (-4)^2} \\ &= \sqrt{16+16} \\ &= \sqrt{32} \\ &= \sqrt{16(2)} \\ d_{AC} &= 4\sqrt{2} \end{aligned}$$

$$\begin{aligned} d_{AB} &= \sqrt{(-2-1)^2 + [2-(-4)]^2} \\ &= \sqrt{(-3)^2 + 6^2} \\ &= \sqrt{9+36} \\ &= \sqrt{45} \\ &= \sqrt{9(5)} \\ d_{AB} &= 3\sqrt{5} \end{aligned}$$

$$\begin{aligned} d_{BC} &= \sqrt{(1-2)^2 + (-4-6)^2} \\ &= \sqrt{(-1)^2 + (-10)^2} \\ &= \sqrt{1+100} \\ d_{BC} &= \sqrt{101} \end{aligned}$$

The perimeter is $d_{AC} + d_{AB} + d_{BC} = 4\sqrt{2} + 3\sqrt{5} + \sqrt{101}$.

25. B

Begin by finding the length of the radius using the distance formula.

$$\begin{aligned} d &= \sqrt{(x_2 - x_1)^2 + (y_2 - y_1)^2} \\ &= \sqrt{(5-0)^2 + (-2-0)^2} \\ &= \sqrt{25+4} = \sqrt{29} \end{aligned}$$

Recall that $x^2 + y^2 = r^2$.
Thus, $x^2 + y^2 = (\sqrt{29})^2$
$x^2 + y^2 = 29$
Therefore, the equation $x^2 + y^2 = 29$ describes a circle with centre (0, 0) that passes through the point (5, –2).

26. F

Since the equation $x^2 + y^2 = r^2$ represents a circle with centre (0, 0) and radius r, it follows that in the equation

$x^2 + y^2 = 16$

$r^2 = 16$

$r = \sqrt{16} = 4$

The radius of the circle $x^2 + y^2 = 16$ is 4 units.
Since the diameter represents twice the radius, the diameter of the circle $x^2 + y^2 = 16$ is 8 units.
Jacqueline sketches a circle with a diameter that is twice as long as the diameter of $x^2 + y^2 = 16$, so the diameter of Jacqueline's circle is 16 units.
Since diameter represents twice the radius, the radius of Jacqueline's circle is 8 units. The sketch that represents a circle with a radius of 8 units is shown.

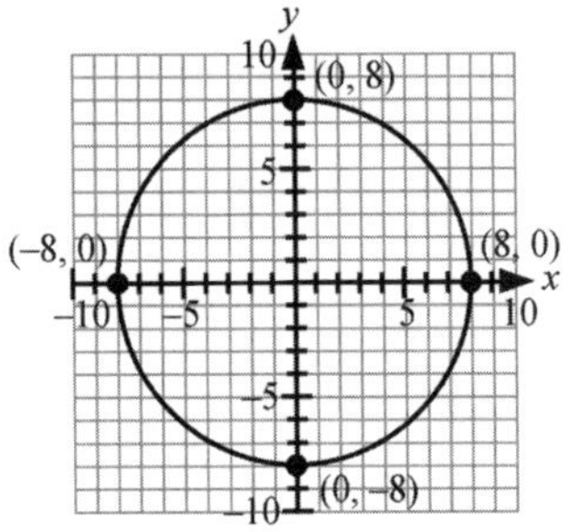

27. B

Use the midpoint formula $M = \left(\frac{x_1 + x_2}{2}, \frac{y_1 + y_2}{2}\right)$:

$M_{AB} = \left(\frac{-5 - 1}{2}, \frac{0 + 4}{2}\right)$

$M_{AB} = (-3, 2)$

Use the distance formula, $d = \sqrt{(x_2 - x_1)^2 + (y_2 - y_1)^2}$ to find the distance from C to the midpoint (−3, 2).

$d = \sqrt{(-3 - 1)^2 + (2 - (-1))^2}$

$d = \sqrt{(-4)^2 + 3^2}$

$d = \sqrt{16 + 9}$

$d = \sqrt{25}$

$d = 5$

The length of the median from point C to line segment AB is 5 units.

28. 15

To determine the value of K, first determine the equation of the right bisector of the line segment with the given endpoints. $m = \frac{y_2 - y_1}{x_2 - x_1} = \frac{-4 - (-6)}{-8 - 2} = \frac{2}{-10} = -\frac{1}{5}$

The right bisector of the line segment with the given endpoints has a slope of 5 since it is perpendicular to the given line segment and the negative reciprocal of $-\frac{1}{5}$ is $\frac{5}{1}$.

Now, determine the midpoint of the line segment using the given points.

$M = \left(\frac{x_1 + x_2}{2}, \frac{y_1 + y_2}{2}\right) = \left(\frac{2 + (-8)}{2}, \frac{-6 + (-4)}{2}\right)$

$= \left(\frac{-6}{2}, \frac{-10}{2}\right) = (-3, -5)$

Finally, use the point-slope form of the equation of a line to determine the equation of the line right bisector:

$y = m(x - x_1) + y_1$

$y = 5(x - (-3)) + (-5)$

$y = 5(x + 3) - 5$

$y = 5x + 15 - 5$

$y = 5x + 10$

Since the ordered pair $(1, K)$ is located on the right bisector defined by the equation $y = 5x + 10$, substitute 1 for x and K for y into the equation and solve for K.

$K = 5(1) + 10$

$K = 15$

This can also be verified graphically.

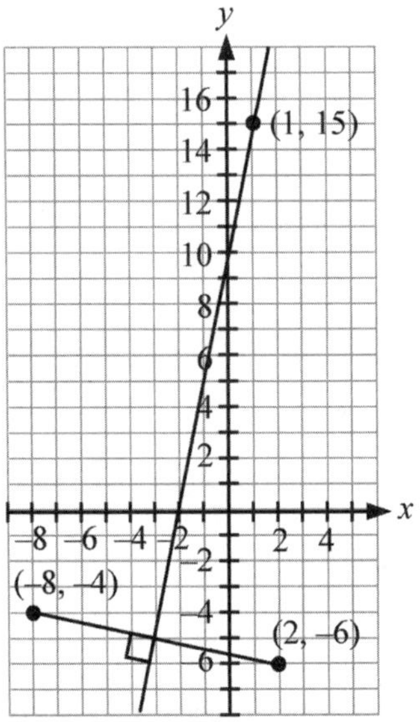

29. C

Two lines are perpendicular if their slopes are negative reciprocals of each other.

$(M_1 \times M_2 = 1)$

Therefore, the perpendicular lines are given by pairs II, III, and V only.

30. J

The circle with chord AB and the perpendicular bisector of AB is shown.

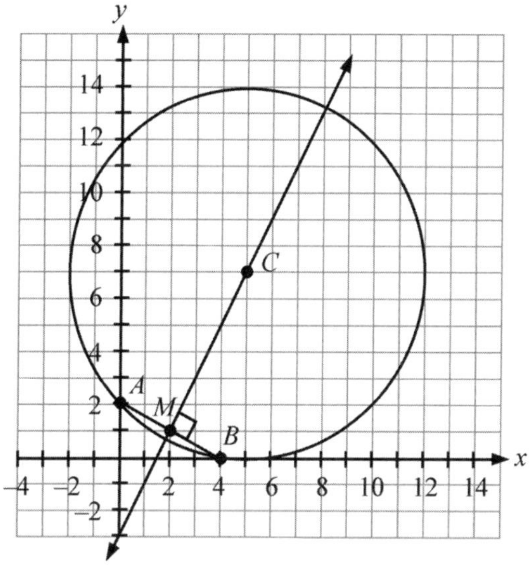

To verify that the perpendicular bisector of a chord of a circle passes through the centre of the circle, determine the equation of the perpendicular bisector of chord AB, and then determine if the point (5, 7) is on this perpendicular bisector.

Step 1: Determine the slope, m, of chord AB.

$m = \dfrac{2-0}{0-4} = -\dfrac{1}{2}$

Step 2: Determine the midpoint, m, of chord AB.

$m = \left(\dfrac{0+4}{2}, \dfrac{2+0}{2}\right) = (2, 1)$

Step 3: Determine the equation of the perpendicular bisector of chord AB by applying the formula $y = m(x - x_1) + y_1$.

Recall that the slope of chord AB is $-\dfrac{1}{2}$; therefore, the slope of the perpendicular bisector must be 2 (since perpendicular slopes are negative reciprocals of each other).

Now, substitute 2 for m and 2 for x_1 and 1 for y_1 into the equation $y = m(x - x_1) + y_1$.

$y = 2(x - 2) + 1$

$y = 2x - 4 + 1$

$y = 2x - 3$

Step 4: Verify that the point (5, 7) is on the line $y = 2x - 3$.

Therefore, Cody's partial solution is incorrect because he made his first error in step 3.

31. B

Since the triangles are similar, the ratio of corresponding sides are equal; therefore,

$\dfrac{x}{1.95\text{ m}} = \dfrac{2.00\text{ m}}{1.50\text{ m}}$

$x = \dfrac{2.00\text{ m} \times 1.95\text{ m}}{1.50\text{ m}}$

$x = 2.6\text{ m}$

32. G

Begin with a diagram for clarity.

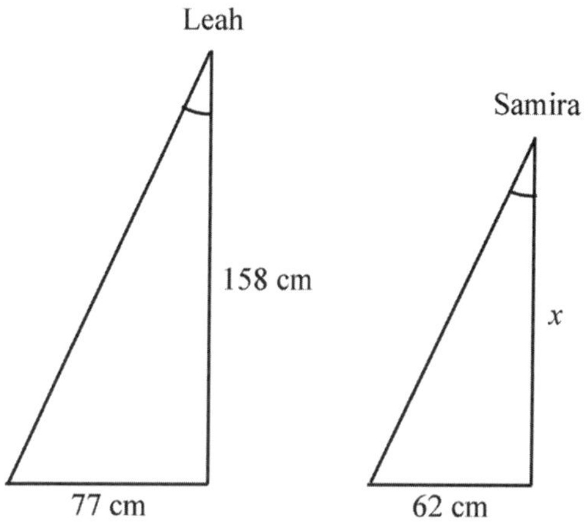

The triangles are similar since they are created using the shadows created by the same angle of the sun at the same point in time, and the remaining corresponding angles are equal. Therefore, corresponding sides will have equal ratios.

$\dfrac{77}{158} = \dfrac{62}{x}$

$x = \dfrac{62 \times 158}{77}$

$x \approx 127\text{cm}$

33. A

To solve, use the Pythagorean theorem $c^2 = a^2 + b^2$. Substitute the values of the hypotenuse, $c = 3x$, and sides, $a = 8$ cm, $b = 12$ cm into the equation.

$(3x)^2 = (8)^2 + (12)^2$

Simplify and solve for x.

$9x^2 = 64 + 144$

$9x^2 = 208$

$x^2 = 23.\bar{1}$

$x = \sqrt{23.\bar{1}}$

$x \approx 4.81$ cm

34. H

Since the cone is made up of two right triangles, the line passing through 36° will bisect that angle as well as the width w of the ice-cream cone's opening. Thus, a given angle in the triangle is 18°. Use that angle to determine half the value of w, labelled as y as shown below.

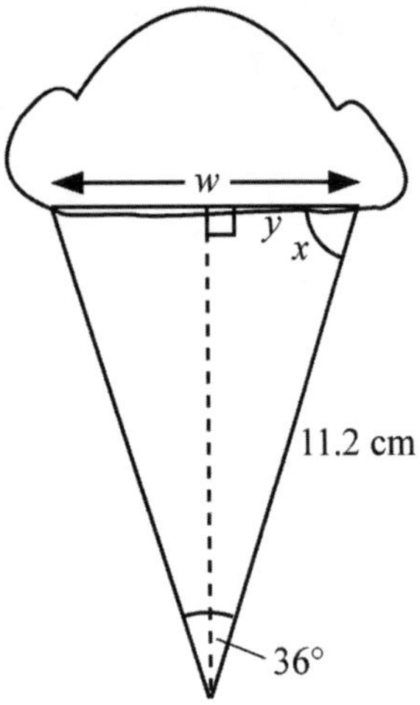

$\sin \theta = \frac{\text{opposite}}{\text{hypotenuse}}$

$\sin 18° = \frac{y}{11.2}$

$y = (11.2)(\sin 18°)$

$y \approx 3.5$ cm

Since $w = 2y$, $w = 2(3.5 \text{ cm}) = 7.0$ cm

35. C

As shown in the diagram, triangle ACD is a right triangle, where AC (the sidewalk) is the hypotenuse, AD is the length of the garden (50 m), CD is the width, and angle A is 32°. Given this information, use the cosine ratio to determine the length, x, of the sidewalk.

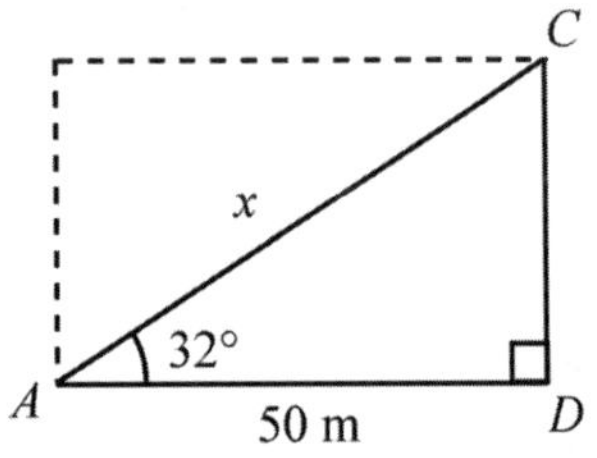

$\cos A = \frac{\text{adjacent}}{\text{hypotenuse}}$

$\cos 32\,° = \frac{50}{x}$

$x(\cos 32°) = 50$

$x = \frac{50}{\cos 32°}$

$x \approx 58.96$ m

To the nearest metre, the length of the sidewalk is 59 m.

36. H

Since the helicopter is at a height of 51 m from sea level, label the diagram as follows:

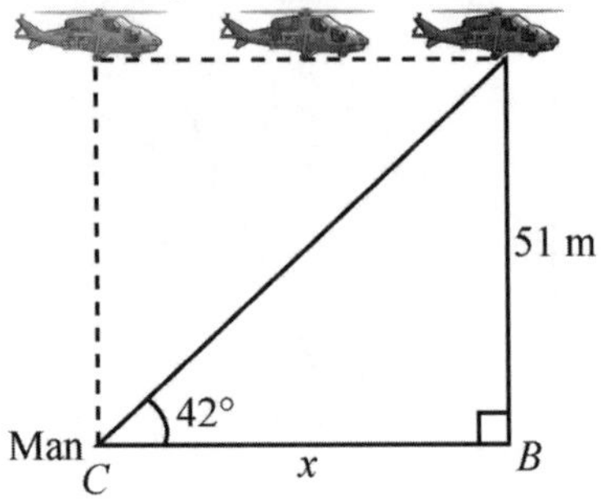

To determine the length from point C to point B, labelled x, use the tangent ratio.

$\tan \theta = \frac{\text{opposite}}{\text{adjacent}} = \tan 42° = \frac{51 \text{ m}}{x}$

$x = \frac{51 \text{ m}}{\tan 42°}$

$x = 56.64$ m

37. 1.9

Begin with a sketch for clarity.

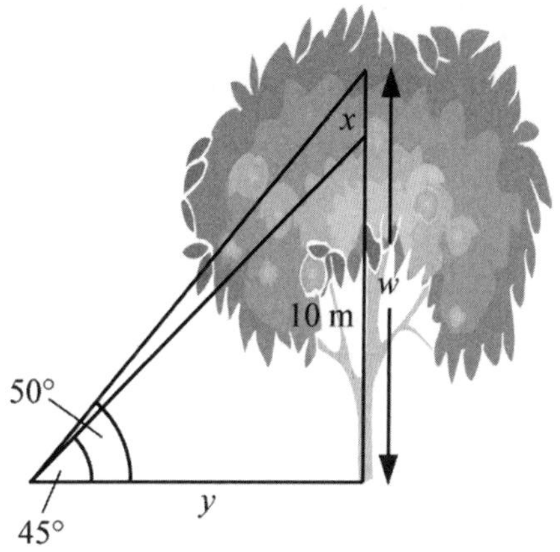

Let x represent the distance between the two apples, y represent the distance from Ted to the base of the tree, and w represent the distance from the ground to the second apple.

Solve for y in the first triangle by using the tangent ratio.

$$\tan\theta = \frac{\text{opposite}}{\text{adjacent}}$$

$$\tan 45° = \frac{10}{y}$$

$$y = \frac{10}{\tan 45°}$$

$$y = 10 \text{ m}$$

Now, solve for w in the second triangle by using the tangent ratio again.

$$\tan\theta = \frac{\text{opposite}}{\text{adjacent}}$$

$$\tan 50° = \frac{w}{10}$$

$$w = 10 \times \tan 50°$$

$$w \approx 11.9 \text{ m}$$

The diagram shows that $w = 10 + x$. Since you are solving for x, it follows that $x = w - 10$.

Therefore, $x = 11.9 \text{ m} - 10 \text{ m} = 1.9 \text{ m}$.

38. H

The ratio $\frac{50}{\sin 40°} = \frac{x}{\sin 58°}$ implies that the side measuring 50 cm is opposite to the 40° angle and the side measuring x cm is opposite to the 58° angle.

39. B

Since $x^2 + h^2 = c^2, h^2 = c^2 - x^2$.

Since $(b - x)^2 + h^2 = a^2, h^2 = a^2 - (b - x)^2$.

Since the value of h is identical in each equation, it follows that $a^2 - (b - x)^2 = c^2 - x^2$.

40. F

Since it is not a side-side-side situation, make use of the law of sines in order to determine the measure of $\angle RTS$ as follows:

$$\frac{RS}{\sin\angle RTS} = \frac{ST}{\sin\angle SRT}$$

Substitute 37 for RS, 28 for ST, and 49° for $\angle SRT$.

$$\frac{37}{\sin\angle RTS} = \frac{28}{\sin 49°}$$

$$28 \times \sin\angle RTS = 37 \times \sin 49°$$

$$\sin\angle RTS = \frac{37 \times \sin 49°}{28}$$

$$\sin\angle RTS \approx 0.9973$$

$$\angle RTS \approx 85.79°$$

The measure of $\angle RTS$ to the nearest tenth is 85.8°.

41. Part A – Open Response

The window setting for the graph shown is x: [0, 7, 1] and y: [0, 50, 5].

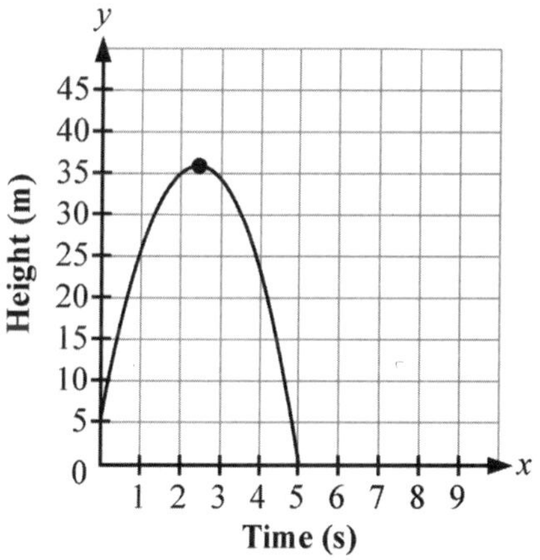

Part B – Open Response

The maximum height of the ball above the ground corresponds to the y-coordinate of the vertex (the highest point on the parabola). The vertex can either be determined graphically (using the maximum key on your calculator) or algebraically by completing the square as follows:

$$y = -4.9x^2 + 24.5x + 6$$

$$y = -4.9(x^2 - 5x) + 6$$

$$y = -4.9(x^2 - 5x + 6.25 - 6.25) + 6$$

$$\rightarrow -\frac{5}{2} = -2.5, (-2.5)^2 = 6.25$$

$$y = -4.9(x^2 - 5x + 6.25) + 30.625 + 6$$

$$y = -4.9(x - 2.5)^2 + 36.625$$

The coordinates of the vertex are (2.5, 36.625). To the nearest tenth, the maximum height of the ball above the ground is 36.6 m.

Part C – Open Response

The maximum height of the ball is 36.6 m, and the minimum height of the ball is 0 m (when the ball lands on the ground). Therefore, the range is $0 < y < 36.6$.

In order to determine the domain, first determine the number of seconds it takes the ball to land on the ground. This can be done by using the zero feature on your graphing calculator or by substituting 0 for y (since the height is 0 m when the ball lands on the ground) in the equation $y = -4.9x^2 + 24.5x + 6$ and then solving for x by using the quadratic formula as follows:

$-4.9x^2 + 24.5x + 6 = 0$

Substitute -4.9 for a, 24.5 for b, and 6 for c.

$$x = \frac{-24.5 \pm \sqrt{(24.5)^2 - 4(-4.9)(6)}}{2(-4.9)}$$

$$x = \frac{-24.5 \pm \sqrt{600.25 + 117.6}}{-9.8}$$

$$x = \frac{-24.5 \pm \sqrt{717.85}}{-9.8}$$

$$x = \frac{-24.5 + \sqrt{717.85}}{-9.8} \quad \text{or} \quad x = \frac{-24.5 - \sqrt{717.85}}{-9.8}$$

$$x \approx -0.234 \qquad x \approx 5.234$$

The time cannot be negative, so to the nearest tenth, $x = 5.2$. Thus, the domain is $0 \le x \le 5.2$.

Part D – Open Response

In order to determine the number of seconds that the ball is more than 25 m above the ground, it is best to use a graphical approach. Choose an appropriate window setting, and then graph $y_1 = -4.9x^2 + 24.5x + 6$ and $y_2 = 25$. Next, find the x-coordinate of each point of intersection of the two graphs. The difference of these two values will be the number of seconds the ball is more than 25 m above the ground. The x-coordinates of the two intersection points are about 4.04 and 0.96.

$4.04 - 0.96 = 3.08$

To the nearest tenth, the ball is more than 25 m above the ground for 3.1 s.

42. Part A – Open Response

The total cost of the popcorn is \$114(\$4.75 × 24).

Part B – Open Response

Let x = the number of adult tickets sold.

Let y = the number of student tickets sold.

Thus, (1) $12.50x + 8y = 2\,280$

(2) $2x = y$

Equation (1) can be rewritten as $125x + 80y = 22\,800$ when each term is multiplied by 10. Equation (2) can be rewritten as $2x - y = 0$.

Equations (1) and (2) can be solved by using the method of elimination as shown:

(1) $125x + 80y = 22\,800$

(2) $2x - y = 0$

$$\begin{aligned} (1)\quad & 125x + 80y = 22\,800 \\ 80 \times (2)\quad & \underline{160x - 80y = 0} \\ (1) + 80 \times (2)\quad & 285x = 22\,800 \\ & x = 80 \end{aligned}$$

The value of y can be determined by substituting 80 for x in either equation (1) or (2). Using equation (2), the result is as follows:

$2x - y = 0$

$2(80) - y = 0$

$160 - y = 0$

$160 = y$

There were 80 adult tickets and 160 student tickets sold.

43. Part A – Open Response

The given diagram can be labelled as shown below.

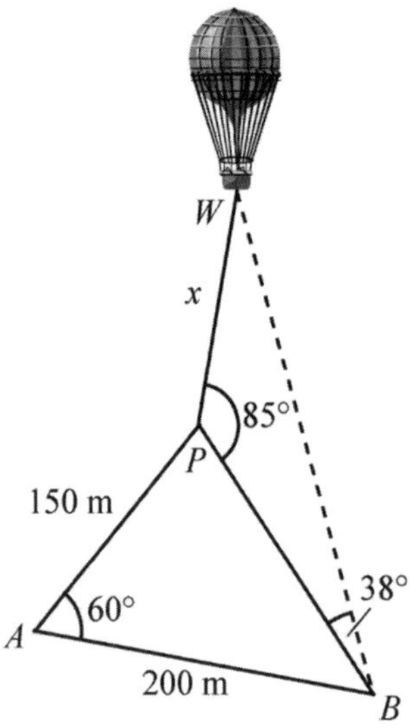

Diagram not to scale

In ΔABP, make use of the law of cosines as follows:

$(PB)^2 = (AP)^2 + (AB)^2 - 2(AP)(AB)\cos A$

Substitute 150 for AP, 200 for AB, and 60° for A.

$(PB)^2 = 150^2 + 200^2 - 2(150)(200)\cos 60°$

$(PB)^2 = 22\,500 + 40\,000 - 30\,000$

$(PB)^2 = 32\,500$

$PB = \sqrt{32\,500}$

$PB \approx 180.28$

To the nearest metre, the distance from anchor point P to point B is 180 m.

Part B – Open Response

The given diagram can be labelled as shown below.

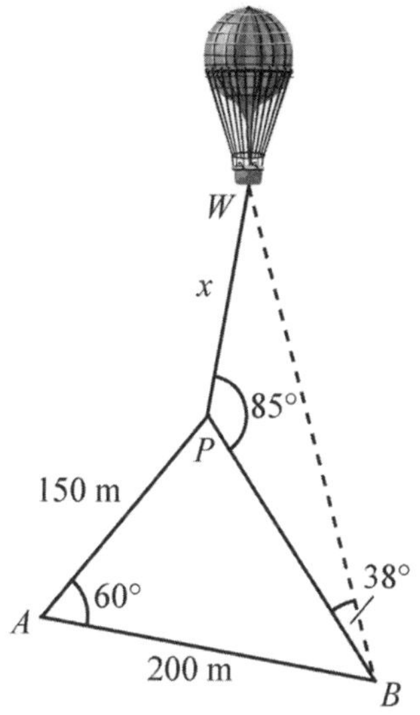

Diagram not to scale

In ΔBPW, make use of the law of sines as follows:

$\angle BWP = 180° - 85° - 38° = 57°$

Therefore, $\frac{PB}{\sin \angle BWP} = \frac{PW}{\sin \angle PBW}$

$\frac{180.28}{\sin 57°} = \frac{x}{\sin 38°}$

$x \times \sin 57° = 180.28 \times \sin 38°$

$x = \frac{180.28 \times \sin 38°}{\sin 57°}$

$x \approx 132.34$

To the nearest metre, the value of x is 132 m.

NOTES

Solutions–Practice Test 2

1. B	**11. C**	**21. 18**	**31. C**	**41.** Part A- **OR**
2. H	**12. H**	**22. H**	**32. G**	Part B- **OR**
3. B	**13. B**	**23. A**	**33. A**	Part C- **OR**
4. J	**14. F**	**24. F**	**34. G**	Part D- **OR**
5. A	**15. B**	**25. B**	**35. A**	**42.** Part A- **OR**
6. H	**16. J**	**26. G**	**36. H**	Part B- **OR**
7. C	**17. 4.2**	**27. B**	**37. D**	Part C- **OR**
8. F	**18. J**	**28. H**	**38. 10**	Part D- **OR**
9. B	**19. B**	**29. C**	**39. C**	**43.** Part A- **OR**
10. G	**20. J**	**30. G**	**40. J**	Part B- **OR**

1. B

The regression equation representing the data (to one decimal) is: $H = -4.8t^2 + 148.5t + 5.9$

Determine the height of the model rocket after 6s by substituting 6 for t in the regression equation

$H = -4.8t^2 + 148.5t + 5.9.$

Thus,

$H = -4.8(6)^2 + 148.5(6) + 5.9$

$H = 724.1$

Therefore, the best estimate of the height of the rocket after 6 s is 725 m.

2. H

Since $a < 0$, the graph of $y = ax^2 - 12x + 7$ must open downward.

Graph two test equations, such as $y = -2x^2 - 12x + 7$ and $y = -\frac{1}{2}x^2 - 12x + 7.$

Therefore, graph H could be the graph of the quadratic function $y = ax^2 - 12x + 7, a < 0.$

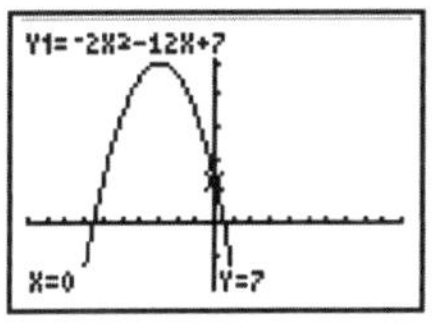

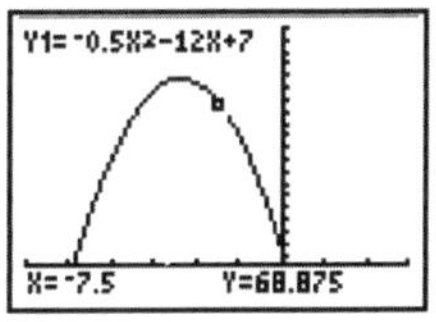

3. B

The domain of the quadratic relation $y = ax^2 + bx + c$, $(a \neq 0)$ will always be $x \in \mathbf{R}$. This is true regardless of the direction of opening.

The zeros are the x-coordinate of each ordered pair where the parabola touches or intersects the x-axis.

The parabola that opens upward has no zeros, whereas the parabola that opens downward will have two zeros.

The axis of symmetry is a vertical line that passes through the vertex of the parabola. Since the two parabolas share the same vertex, they will have the same equation of the axis of symmetry.

A maximum value occurs when the parabola opens down, and a minimum value occurs when the parabola opens up. Since the parabolas each have different directions of opening, one will have a minimum value, and one will have a maximum value.

Therefore, the only correct statements are I and III.

4. J

Any number or variable with an exponent of zero is equal to 1; $x^0 = 1$.

Therefore, $2^0 = 1$. Applying the product rule,

$2^x \times 2^{-x} = 2^{x+(-x)} = 2^0 = 1$

Therefore, the value of a must be $-x$.

5. A

The graph of the new parabola can be obtained by translating the graph of $y = x^2$ left 4 units and down 3 units as shown in the following diagram.

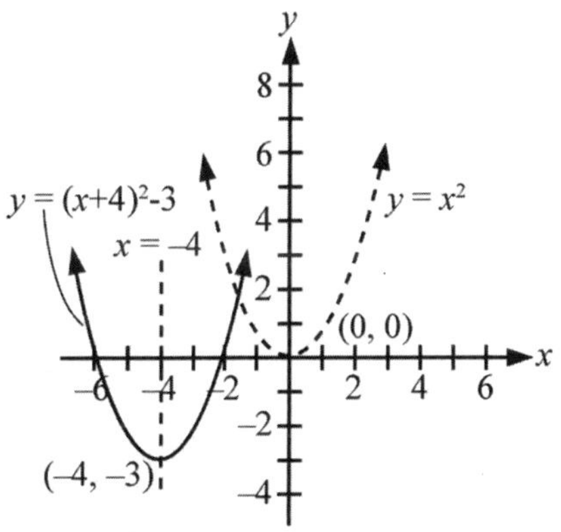

6. H

Since the equation $y = -3(x - h)^2 + k$ is in the form $y = a(x - h)^2 + k$, it follows that:

- The equation of the axis of symmetry is $x = h$.
- The vertex is (h, k).

7. C

Apply the given transformations to the graph of $y = x^2$ to get the following result:

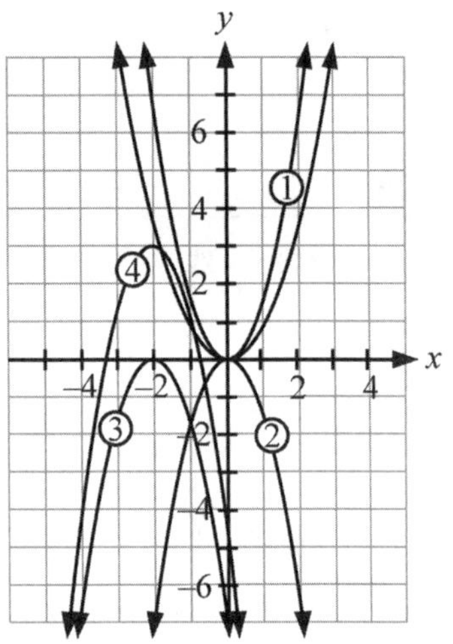

Therefore, graph C best represents the graph of the transformed function.

8. F

The parabola shown can have an equation of the form $y = a(x - h)^2 + k$, where (h, k) is the vertex.

Since the vertex is at $\left(8, \frac{11}{2}\right)$, $h = 8$ and $k = \frac{11}{2}$.

Substitute 8 for h and $\frac{11}{2}$ for k into $y = a(x - h)^2 + k$ to get $y = a(x - 8)^2 + \frac{11}{2}$.

Since the graph opens upward, the value of a is positive. Thus, the required equation of the parabola is

$y = (x - 8)^2 + \frac{11}{2}$.

9. B

Begin by using the perfect square formula $(a + b)^2 = a^2 + 2ab + b^2$, leaving -2 outside the brackets.
In this case, $a = 3x$ and $b = 5$.
Substitute into the formula.

$= -2\left[(3x)^2 + 2(3x)(5) + (5)^2\right]$

$= -2\left(9x^2 + 30x + 25\right)$

Use the distributive property to distribute -2 through the brackets.

$= -18x^2 - 60x - 50$

From the equation, $a = -18$ and $c = -50$; therefore, $a + c = -18 + -50 = -68$.

10. G

In order to factor $9mn^2 - 12mn - 12m$, begin by factoring out the GCF $(3m)$ from each term of the expression.

$3m\left(3n^2 - 4n - 4\right)$

To factor $\left(3n^2 - 4n - 4\right)$, find two numbers that have a product of $-12(a \times c)$ and a sum of -4 (the b–value). In this case, the numbers are 2 and -6. Rewrite the expression by replacing the term $-4n$ with $2n$ and $-6n$.

$= 3m\left[3n^2 + 2n - 6n - 4\right]$

Group the terms inside the brackets.

$= 3m\left[\left(3n^2 + 2n\right) + (-6n - 4)\right]$

Remove the GCF from each group.

$= 3m[n(3n + 2) - 2(3n + 2)]$

Factor out the common binomial.

$= 3m(n - 2)(3n + 2)$

Therefore, one expression that is not a factor is $n - 4$.

11. C

The x-intercepts of the graph shown are 2 and 4. Therefore, substitute 2 for r and 4 for s into the equation $y = a(x - r)(x - s)$ as follows:

$y = a(x - 2)(x - 4)$

The ordered pair $(0, 4)$ is a point on the graph shown. Solve for a in the equation $y = a(x - 2)(x - 4)$ by substituting 0 for x and 4 for y as follows:

$4 = a((0) - 2)((0) - 4)$

$4 = a(-2)(-4)$

$4 = 8a$

$a = \frac{4}{8} = \frac{1}{2}$

Therefore, the equation of the quadratic relation in the form $y = a(x - r)(x - s)$ is $y = \frac{1}{2}(x - 2)(x - 4)$.

12. H

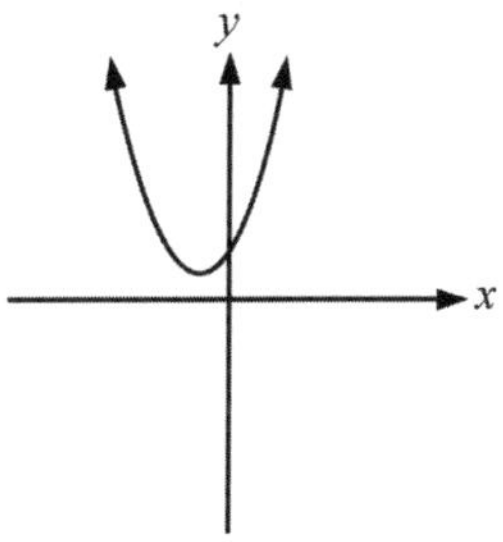

A quadratic equation with no real roots is one that has no x-intercepts. This means the graph of the parabola does not cross the x-axis.

Therefore, graph H illustrates a quadratic equation with no real roots.

13. B

$y = 3(x^2 + 14x) + 142$	Identify and remove the common factor from the x^2-term and x-term of the expression. In this case, the common factor is 3.
$y = 3(x^2 + \underline{14x}) + 142$ $\left(\frac{14}{2}\right)^2 = 49$	Notice the resulting coefficient for the x-term. Divide this value by 2, and then square it.
$y = 3(x^2 + 14x + \underline{49 - 49}) + 142$	Both add and subtract this value inside the brackets.
$y = \underline{3}(x^2 + 14x + 49 \underline{- 49}) + 142$ $y = 3(x^2 + 14x + 49) \underline{- 147} + 142$	Move the value that will not contribute to a perfect square outside the brackets. [**Note**: With the distributive property, you have really added -147 and $+147$ to the function, since $3(-39) = -147$ and $3(39) = 147$. To move -49 outside the brackets, it becomes -147.]
$y = 3(x + 7)^2 - 5$	Factor the trinomial inside the brackets to form a perfect square, and collect like terms outside the bracket.

When the equation $y = 3x^2 + 42x + 142$ is written in the completed square form $y = a(x - h)^2 + k$, it becomes $y = 3(x + 7)^2 - 5$. The k-value is -5.

14. F

Determine the x-intercepts by letting $y = 0$.

$0 = -2(x^2 + 6x + 8)$
$0 = -2(x + 2)(x + 4)$
$x = -2$ or $x = -4$

Find the y-intercept by substituting 0 or x.

$y = -2((0)^2 + 0 + 8)$
$y = -16$

Find the midpoint of the x-intercepts in order to find the equation of the axis of symmetry.

$$M = \left(\frac{x_1 + x_2}{2}\right), \left(\frac{y_1 + y_2}{2}\right)$$
$$= \left(\frac{-2 + (-4)}{2}\right), \left(\frac{0 + 0}{2}\right)$$
$$= (-3, 0)$$

The equation of the axis of symmetry is $x = -3$.

Find the vertex. Substitute -3 for x in the equation $y = -2(x^2 + 6x + 8)$.

$y = -2((-3)^2 + 6(-3) + 8)$
$y = -2(9 - 18 + 8)$
$y = 2$

The vertex is at point $(-3, 2)$.

Therefore, the only correct statements are II and IV.

15. B

To solve by factoring, begin by rearranging the equation $6x^2 - 13x = 5$ to $6x^2 - 13x - 5 = 0$.

Factor by decomposition, and find two numbers that have a product of $-30(axc)$ and a sum of -13 (b-value). In this case, those numbers are 2 and -15.

$6x^2 - 13x - 5 = 0$

$6x^2 + 2x - 15x - 5 = 0$

$2x(3x + 1) - 5(3x + 1) = 0$

$(2x - 5)(3x + 1) = 0$

$x = \frac{5}{2}$ or $x = -\frac{1}{3}$

To solve using the quadratic formula, begin by rearranging the equation $6x^2 - 13x = 5$ to $6x^2 - 13x - 5 = 0$.

$$x = \frac{-b \pm \sqrt{b^2 - 4ac}}{2a}$$

Substitute 6 for a, -13 for b, and -5 for c into the quadratic formula.

$$x = \frac{-(-13) \pm \sqrt{(-13)^2 - 4(6)(-5)}}{2(6)}$$

$$x = \frac{13 \pm \sqrt{169 + 120}}{12}$$

$$x = \frac{13 \pm \sqrt{289}}{12}$$

$$x = \frac{13 \pm 17}{12}$$

$$x = \frac{13 + 17}{12} = \frac{30}{12} = \frac{5}{2} \text{ or } x = \frac{13 - 17}{12} = \frac{-4}{12} = -\frac{1}{3}$$

Since the actual solutions and solutions given by the students do not match, Rhett's work and Vlad's work will each lead to an incorrect solution.

16. J

Change the form of the function by completing the square.

$y = 4(x^2 - 3x) + 15$

$y = 4(x^2 - \underline{3x}) + 15$

$\left(\frac{-3}{2}\right)^2 = \frac{9}{4}$

$y = 4\left(x^2 - 3x + \frac{9}{4} - \frac{9}{4}\right) + 15$

$y = \underline{4}\left(x^2 - 3x + \frac{9}{4} \underline{- \frac{9}{4}}\right) + 15$

$y = 4\left(x^2 - 3x + \frac{9}{4}\right) \underline{- 9} + 15$

$y = 4\left(x - \frac{3}{2}\right)^2 + 6$

This equation is of the form $y = a(x - h)^2 + k$, where $a = 4$, $h = \frac{3}{2}$, and $k = 6$.

Thus, when the graph is drawn, the vertex of the parabola is $\left(\frac{3}{2}, 6\right)$, and the parabola opens upward since $a > 0$.

The minimum value of the given quadratic function is attained at its vertex.

Thus, the minimum value of the function is 6.

17. 4.2

Use a TI-83 Plus graphing calculator to plot the line $y = 200$ and the parabola $y = -7x^2 + 61x + 98$.

Then use the **INTERSECTION** feature to find the intersection points of the two graphs.

The first intersection point is $(2.256, 200)$.

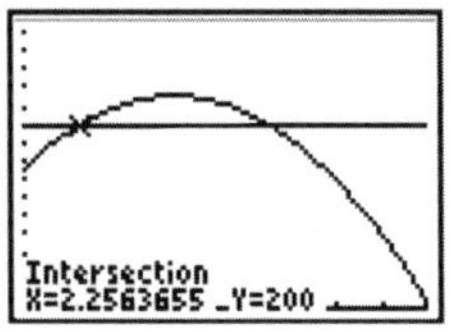

The second intersection point is $(6.458, 200)$.

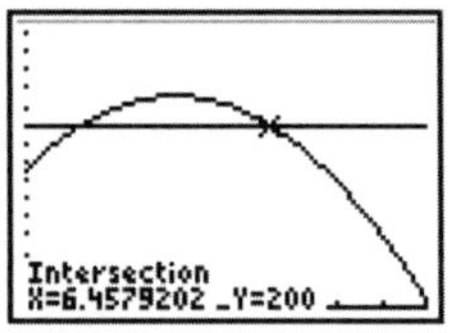

Therefore, the roller coaster car is 200 feet or more above the ground for$6.458 - 2.256 = 4.2$ s to the nearest tenth.

18. J

Using technology, graph the equation $y = 100t - 5t^2$. Then use the **MAXIMUM** feature of a TI-83 Plus graphing calculator and a window setting such as x:[1, 20, 2]y:[0, 600, 50].

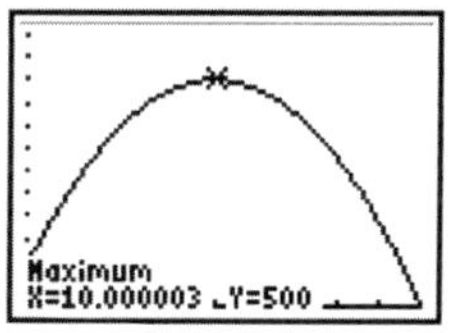

The function's maximum value occurs when $x = 10$; therefore, the maximum height attained by the bullet can be determined as follows.

$h = 100t - 5t$

$h = 100(10) - 5(10)^2$

$h = 500$ m

19. B

When Maj initially kicks the ball, no time has passed, so $x = 0$. Substitute 0 for x into the equation

$y = -4.9x^2 + 13.7x + 0.7$.

$y = -4.9(0)^2 + 13.7(0) + 0.7$

$y = 0.7$

Therefore, Maj was holding the soccer ball 0.7 m above the ground when she kicked it.

20. J

No mistake was made in either solution. Thus, both will yield the same correct answer.

21. 18

Subtract equation (2) from equation (1).

(1) $5x + y = 93$

(2) $\underline{2x + y = 48}$

$3x = 45$

$x = 15$

To find y, substitute 15 for x in one of the equations.

(2) $2(15) + y = 48$

$30 + y = 48$

$y = 18$

22. H

Let H be the cost of 1 hamburger.
Let F be the cost of 1 small french fries.
Create a system representing the two cases.

(1) $2H + F = 7.00$

(2) $H + 2F = 5.75$

Subtract the equations, and solve for H.

(1) × 2 $\quad 4H + 2F = 14.00$

(2) $\quad \underline{-(H + 2F = 5.75)}$

$3H = 8.25$

$H = 2.75$

Thus, one hamburger costs $2.75.

23. A

(1) $x + y = 5\ 000$ (equation showing total amount invested)

$0.04x$ = interest earned on the amount invested at 4%

$0.06y$ = interest earned on the amount invested at 6%

(2) $0.04x = 0.06y + 50$ (equation showing interest earned from the amount invested at 4%, which is $50 more than the interest earned from the amount invested at 6%)

(2) × 100 becomes $4x = 6y + 5\ 000$

The system of equations is $x + y = 5\ 000$ and $4x = 6y + 5\ 000$.

24. F

Using the midpoint formula,

$M = \left(\frac{x_1 + x_2}{2}, \frac{y_1 + y_2}{2}\right)$. Thus,

$M_{AB} = \left(\frac{2 + x}{2}, \frac{1 + 7}{2}\right)$

$M_{AB} = \left(\frac{2 + x}{2}, 4\right)$

$\frac{2 + x}{2} = -3$

$2 + x = -6$

$x = -8$

25. B

First, determine the coordinate of point C by using the midpoint formula $m = \left(\frac{x_1 + x_2}{2}, \frac{y_1 + y_2}{2}\right)$.

$$m_{AC} = \left(\frac{-4 + x}{2}, \frac{12 + y}{2}\right)$$

Thus, $\frac{-4 + x}{2} = -1$

$-4 + x = -2$

$x = 2$

and $\frac{12 + y}{2} = 8$

$12 + y = 16$

$y = 4$

Since point C is at $(2, 4)$, use the distance formula $d = \sqrt{(x_2 - x_1)^2 + (y_2 - y_1)^2}$ to find the distance from point C to point A.

$$d_{AC} = \sqrt{(-4 - 2)^2 + (12 - 4)^2}$$

$$d_{AC} = \sqrt{(-6)^2 + (8)^2}$$

$$d_{AC} = \sqrt{36 + 64}$$

$$d_{AC} = \sqrt{100}$$

$$d_{AC} = 10$$

Thus, the distance from point A to point D must also be 10.

$d_{AD} = \sqrt{(-4 - 2)^2 + (12 - y)^2}$. (Note: D is the point $(2, y)$).

$10 = \sqrt{(-6)^2 + (12 - y)^2}$

$10 = \sqrt{36 + (12 - y)^2}$

Square both sides.

$100 = 36 + (12 - y)^2$

Subtract 36 from both sides.

$64 = (12 - y)^2$

Take the square root of both sides.

$\pm 8 = 12 - y$

Thus, $8 = 12 - y$ or $-8 = 12 - y$.

$-4 = -y$ or $-20 = -y$

Solve for y in both cases.

$4 = y$ or $20 = y$

The value for y is 20, since a y-coordinate of 4 would be the same location as cruise ship C.

26. G

Find the length of the radius using the distance formula.

$d = \sqrt{(x_2 - x_1)^2 + (y_2 - y_1)^2}$

$= \sqrt{(a - 0)^2 + (b - 0)^2}$

$= \sqrt{a^2 + b^2}$

The radius of this circle is given by the expression $\sqrt{a^2 + b^2}$.

27. B

Begin by simplifying the given equation by dividing each term of the equation by the GCF of 4.

$\frac{4x^2}{4} + \frac{4y^2}{4} = \frac{36}{4}$

$x^2 + y^2 = 9$

Since the equation $x^2 + y^2 = r^2$ represents a circle with centre $(0, 0)$ and radius r, it follows that:

$r^2 = 9$

$r = \sqrt{9} = 3$

Thus, the radius of the circle $x^2 + y^2 = 9$ is 3 units.

28. H

Using the slope formula $m = \frac{y_2 - y_1}{x_2 - x_1}$, find the slope of QR.

$m = \frac{8 - 2}{-2 - 6}$

$m = \frac{6}{-8}$

$m = -\frac{3}{4}$

The slope of the perpendicular bisector will be $\frac{4}{3}$, which is the negative reciprocal of $\frac{-3}{4}$.

The midpoint of QR can be found by using the midpoint formula

$M = \left(\frac{x_1 + x_2}{2}, \frac{y_1 + y_2}{2}\right)$

$M_{QR} = \left(\frac{6 + (-2)}{2}, \frac{2 + 8}{2}\right)$

$M_{QR} = (2, 5)$

The perpendicular bisector of QR has a slope of $\frac{4}{3}$ and passes through the point $(2, 5)$.

Using the point-slope form, the equation of this line can be determined as follows:

$y = m(x - x_1) + y_1$

$y = \frac{4}{3}(x - 2) + 5$

$y = \frac{4}{3}x - \frac{8}{3} + 5$

Use a common denominator.

$y = \frac{4}{3}x - \frac{8}{3} + \frac{15}{3}$

$y = \frac{4}{3}x + \frac{7}{3}$

29. C

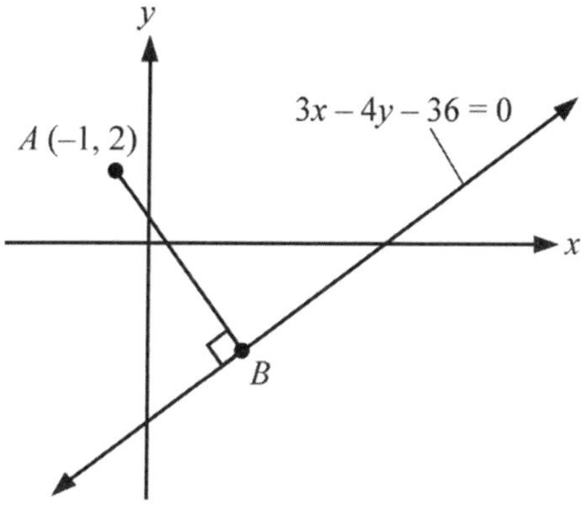

Write $3x - 4y - 36 = 0$ in the slope-intercept form
$y = mx + b$
$3x - 36 = 4y$
$\frac{3x}{4} - \frac{36}{4} = \frac{4y}{4}$
$y = \frac{3}{4}x - 9$

Here, the slope is $m = \frac{3}{4}$ (the coefficient of x).

Thus, the slope of AB (in the diagram) is $-\frac{4}{3}$(the negative reciprocal of $\frac{3}{4}$).

The equation of AB can be determined as follows:
$y = m(x - x_1) + y_1$
$y = -\frac{4}{3}(x - (-1)) + 2$
$y = -\frac{4}{3}(x + 1) + 2$
$y = -\frac{4}{3}x - \frac{4}{3} + 2$
Use a common denominator.
$y = -\frac{4}{3}x - \frac{4}{3} + \frac{6}{3}$
$y = -\frac{4}{3}x + \frac{2}{3}$
Multiply both sides by 3.
$3y = -4x + 2$
Adding $4x$ to both sides.
$4x + 3y = 2$
The intersection point B can be found by solving the system involving of equations
$3x - 4y - 36 = 0$ and $4x + 3y = 2$.
(1) $3x - 4y - 36 = 0 \Rightarrow 3x - 4y = 36$
(2) $4x + 3y = 2$
$12x - 16y = 144$ (1) $\times 4$
$12x + 9y = 6$ (2) $\times 3$
Subtract the equations.
$-25y = 138$
Solve for y.
$y = -5.52$
Substitute $y = -5.52$ into either (1) or (2) to solve for x.

$4x + 3(-5.52) = 2$
$4x - 16.56 = 2$
$4x = 18.56$
$x = 4.64$
Thus, point B (in the diagram) is $(4.64, -5.52)$.
Use the distance formula $d = \sqrt{(x_2 - x_1)^2 + (y_2 - y_1)^2}$ to find the distance from A to B.
$d_{AB} = \sqrt{(-1 - 4.64)^2 + (2 - (-5.52))^2}$
$d_{AB} = \sqrt{(-5.64)^2 + (7.52)^2}$
$d_{AB} = \sqrt{88.36}$
$d_{AB} = 9.4$

30. G

First, use the distance formula
$d = \sqrt{(x_2 - x_1)^2 + (y_2 - y_1)^2}$ to determine the length of side BC.
$d_{BC} = \sqrt{(-3 - 6)^2 + (1 - (-4))^2}$
$d_{BC} = \sqrt{(-9)^2 + 5^2}$
$d_{BC} = \sqrt{106}$
ΔABC is an isosceles triangle (two equal sides).
Note: this is not a right triangle because the three sides will not satisfy the Pythagorean theorem.

31. C

Begin with a diagram for clarity.

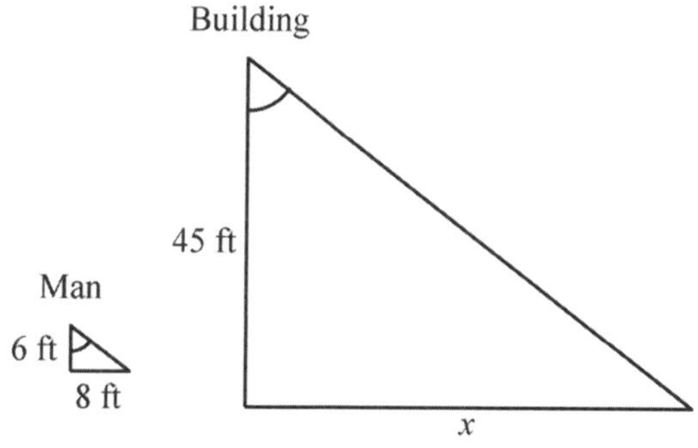

The triangles are similar since they are formed using the shadow created by the same angle of the sun at the same point in time. The remaining corresponding angles are equal. Therefore, corresponding sides will have equal ratios.
$\frac{8}{6} = \frac{x}{45}$
$x = \frac{8 \times 45}{6}$
$x = 60$ ft

32. G

In the diagram, $\angle B = \angle D = 90°$.
Thus, $AB \parallel DE$, and segments AE and DB are transversals. Therefore, $\angle A = \angle E$. It follows that $\angle DCE = \angle BCA$.
Thus ΔABC is similar to ΔEDC.
Draw the two triangles with the same orientation.

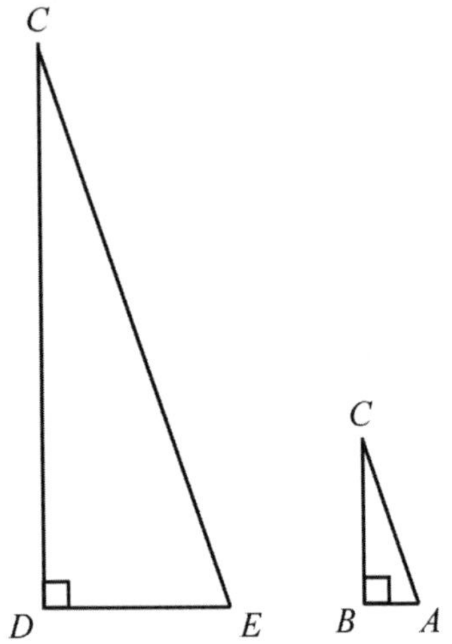

Since ΔABC is similar to ΔEDC, $\frac{BC}{DC} = \frac{AB}{DE}$.
Substitute the given values into this equation.

$\frac{30}{120} = \frac{15}{W}$

$W = \frac{15 \times 120}{30} = 60$

Therefore, the width of the river is 60 m.

33. A

The given triangle is made up of two congruent right triangles. Label the top angle of each right triangle as angle y, as shown below.

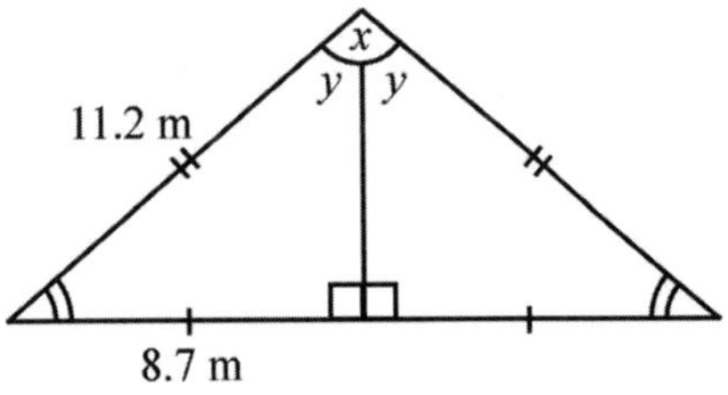

A triangle

Determine the measure of angle y.

$\sin \theta = \frac{\text{opposite}}{\text{hypotenuse}}$

$\sin y = \frac{8.7}{11.2}$

$y = \sin^{-1} = \left(\frac{8.7}{11.2}\right)$

$y \approx 50.97°$

Since $x = 2y$, angle $x \approx 2(51°) \approx 102°$.

34. G

The general form of the law of sines is

$\frac{a}{\sin A} = \frac{b}{\sin B} = \frac{c}{\sin C}$.

This equation implies that side a is opposite to angle A, side b is opposite to angle B, and side C is opposite to angle C.
In the given triangle, NP is opposite to $\angle M$, MN is opposite to $\angle P$, and MP is opposite to $\angle N$.

Thus, $\frac{MN}{\sin P} = \frac{MP}{\sin N}$ correctly represents the law of sines.

35. A

The equation $x^2 = 80^2 + 95^2 - 2(80)(95)\cos 73°$ is a form of the law of cosines and implies that side x is opposite to the 73° angle.

36. H

To begin, determine the length of side BD.

In ΔBAD, $\sin \angle ADB = \frac{AB}{BD}$

Substitute 41° for $\angle ADB$ and 9 for AB.

$\sin 41° = \frac{9}{BD}$

$BD \times \sin 41° = 9$

$BD = \frac{9}{\sin 41°}$

$BD = 13.72$

In ΔBAD, $\angle ABD = 49°$(from $180° - 90° - 41°$); therefore, in ΔCBD, $\angle CBD = 41°$(from $90° - 49°$). Thus, in ΔCBD, $\angle BDC = 61°(180° - 41° - 78°)$.
In ΔCBD, since it is not a side-angle-side situation, solve for x by making use of the law of sines as follows.

$\frac{BC}{\sin \angle BDC} = \frac{BD}{\sin \angle BCD}$

Substitute x for BC, 13.72 for BD, 61° for $\angle BDC$, and 78° for $\angle BCD$.

$\frac{x}{\sin 61°} = \frac{13.72}{\sin 78°}$

$x \times \sin 78° = 13.72 \times \sin 61°$

$x = \frac{13.72 \times \sin 61°}{\sin 78°}$

$x = 12.27$

The length of side x, correct to the nearest tenth, is 12.3 m.

37. D

Begin by determining the length of side AD. In ΔACD, it is a side-angle-side situation, so solve for AD by making use of the law of cosines as follows:

$(AD)^2 = (AC)^2 + (DC)^2 - 2(AC)(DC)\cos C$

Substitute 26.0 for AC, 18.0 for DC, and 32 for C.

$(AD)^2 = 26.0^2 + 18.0^2 - 2(26.0)(18.0)\cos 32°$

$(AD)^2 = 206.227$

$AD = \sqrt{206.27}$

$AD = 14.36$

In ΔABD, since it is not a side-side-side situation, use the law of sines to determine the measure of $\angle ADB$ as follows:

$$\frac{AB}{\sin \angle ADB} = \frac{AD}{\sin \angle ABD}$$

Substitute 19.5 for AB, 14.36 for AD, and 45° for $\angle ABD$.

$$\frac{19.5}{\sin \angle ADB} = \frac{14.36}{\sin \angle 45°}$$

$14.36 \times \sin \angle ADB = 19.5 \times \sin \angle 45°$

$$\sin \angle ADB = \frac{19.5 \times \sin 45°}{14.36}$$

$\sin \angle ADB \approx 0.9602$

$\angle ADB \approx 73.8°$

The measure of $\angle ADB$, correct to the nearest degree, is 74°.

38. 10

The given diagram can be labelled as follows:

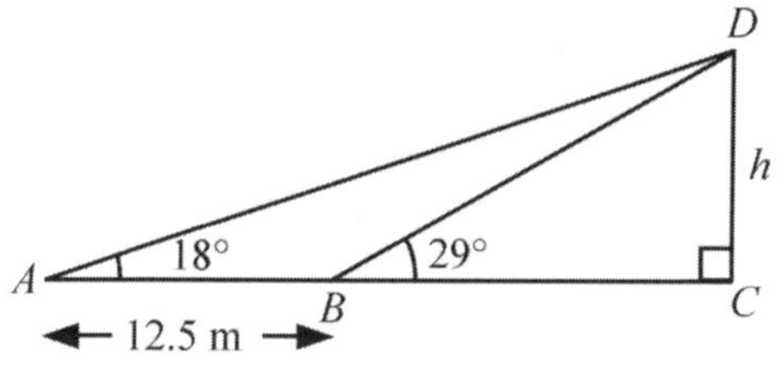

In ΔABD, observe that $\angle ABD = 180° - 29° = 151°$. Now, determine the length of side BD in ΔABD by applying the law of sines as shown:

$$\frac{BD}{\sin \angle DAB} = \frac{AB}{\sin \angle ADB}$$

Substitute 18° for $\angle DAB$, 12.5 for AB, and 11°(180° − 151° − 18°) for $\angle ADB$.

$$\frac{BD}{\sin 18°} = \frac{12.5}{\sin 11°}$$

$BD \times \sin 11° = 12.5 \times \sin 18°$

$$BD = \frac{12.5 \times \sin 18°}{\sin 11°}$$

$BD \approx 20.24$

Next, solve for h in right triangle BCD as follows:

$$\sin \angle DBC = \frac{DC}{BD}$$

$$\sin 29° = \frac{h}{20.24}$$

$h = 20.24 \times \sin 29°$

$h \approx 9.81$

The height of the school, to the nearest metre, is 10 m.

39. C

In ΔABC, it is a side-angle-side situation; therefore, solve for the distance from A to C as follows:

$(AC)^2 = (BA)^2 + (BC)^2 - 2(BA)(BC)\cos \angle ABC$

Substitute 65 for BA, 70 for BC, and 38 degrees for $\angle ABC$.

$(AC)^2 = 65^2 + 70^2 - 2(65)(70)\cos 38°$

$(AC)^2 \approx 4\,225 + 4\,900 - 7\,171.90$

$(AC)^2 \approx 1\,954.10$

$AC \approx \sqrt{1\,954.10}$

$AC \approx 44.21$

To the nearest tenth, the wakeboarders are 44.2 feet apart.

40. J

In ΔBCD, it is a side-angle-side situation; therefore, solve for BD by applying the law of cosines as shown:

$(BD)^2 = (CB)^2 + (CD)^2 - 2(CB)(CD)\cos \angle BCD$

Substitute 3 for CB, 5 for CD, and 68° for $\angle BCD$.

$(BD)^2 = 3^2 + 5^2 - 2(3)(5)\cos 68°$

$BD = \sqrt{3^2 + 5^2 - 2(3)(5)\cos 68°}$

Thus, the equation $BD = \sqrt{3^2 + 5^2 - 2(3)(5)\cos 68°}$ could be used to determine the length of the roadway, BD.

41. Part A – Open Response

Solve for x by substituting \$62 750 for C in the equation $C = 2x^2 - 700x + 92\ 750$ as follows:

$$62\ 750 = 2x^2 - 700x + 92\ 750$$
$$0 = 2x^2 - 700x + 30\ 000$$
$$0 = 2(x^2 - 350x + 15\ 000)$$

The two numbers that have a sum of −350 and a product of 15 000 are −50 and −300.

$0 = 2(x - 50)(x - 300)$

Therefore, $x - 50 = 0$ or $x - 300 = 0$

$x = 50$ or $x = 300$

The equation $2x^2 - 700x + 30\ 000 = 0$ can also be solved by using the quadratic formula $x = \dfrac{-b \pm \sqrt{b^2 - 4ac}}{2a}$ as shown:

Substitute 2 for a, −700 for b, and 30 000 for c.

$$x = \frac{-(-700) \pm \sqrt{(-700)^2 - 4(2)(30\ 000)}}{2(2)}$$
$$x = \frac{700 \pm \sqrt{490\ 000 - 240\ 000}}{4}$$
$$x = \frac{700 \pm \sqrt{250\ 000}}{4}$$
$$x = \frac{700 \pm 500}{4}$$
$$x = \frac{700 + 500}{4} = \frac{1\ 200}{4} = 300$$
$$\text{or } x = \frac{700 - 500}{4} = \frac{200}{4} = 50$$

Part B – Open Response

In order to determine the number of Road Racer bicycles that must be manufactured to minimize the cost, complete the square of the equation $C = 2x^2 - 700x + 92\ 750$, as follows:

$$C = 2x^2 - 700x + 92\ 750$$
$$C = 2(x^2 - 350x) + 92\ 750$$
$$\frac{-350}{2} = -175, (-175)^2 = 30\ 625$$
$$C = 2(x^2 - 350x + 30\ 625 - 30\ 625) + 92\ 750$$
$$C = 2(x^2 - 350x + 30\ 625) - 61\ 250 + 92\ 750$$
$$C = 2(x - 175)^2 + 31\ 500$$

The minimum value of C is 31 500, when $x = 175$. Thus, 175 Road Racer bicycles have to be manufactured to minimize the cost.

Part C – Open Response

The minimum cost of manufacturing the Road Racer bicycles is \$31 500.

Part D – Open Response

First, choose an appropriate window setting on your graphing calculator. Next, graph $y_1 = 2x^2 - 700x + 92{,}750$ and $y_2 = 50\ 000$. Finally, determine the x-coordinate of the first point of intersection of the two graphs. This x-coordinate is about 78.823. Thus, the fewest number of bicycles that can be manufactured for a cost of \$50 000 is 78.

42. Part A – Open Response

Corner post A has the same x-coordinate as corner post B and the same y-coordinate as corner post D. Therefore, the coordinates of A are (139, 89).

Part B – Open Response

Since soccer net EF is centered on the back line AB, begin by determining the midpoint of AB by using the midpoint formula $M = \left(\dfrac{x_1 + x_2}{2}, \dfrac{y_1 + y_2}{2}\right)$.

$$M_{AB} = \left(\frac{139 + 139}{2}, \frac{15 + 89}{2}\right)$$
$$M_{AB} = \left(\frac{278}{2}, \frac{104}{2}\right)$$
$$M_{AB} = (139, 52)$$

Recall that the width of soccer net EF is 8 yards. Therefore, the y-coordinate of point E must be 4 more than the y-coordinate of the midpoint of AB.

The coordinates of point E are (139, 56).

The y-coordinates of point F must be 4 less than the y-coordinate of the midpoint of AB.

The coordinates of point F are (139, 48).

Part C – Open Response

In order to determine the minimum distance the soccer ball must travel from player P to player Q, determine the length of the line segment PQ by applying the distance formula.

$$d = \sqrt{(x_2 - x_1)^2 + (y_2 - y_1)^2}$$
$$d_{PQ} = \sqrt{(83 - 54)^2 + (62 - 41)^2}$$
$$d_{PQ} = \sqrt{(29)^2 + (21)^2}$$
$$d_{PQ} = \sqrt{841 + 441}$$
$$d_{PQ} = \sqrt{1{,}282}$$
$$d_{PQ} \approx 35.81$$

The minimum distance, to the nearest tenth, that the soccer ball must travel from player P to player Q is 35.8 yards.

Part D – Open Response

In order to verify that the diagonals of the playing field bisect each other at the centre mark, M, show that the midpoint of diagonal BD is the same as the midpoint of diagonal AC by making use of the midpoint formula $M = \left(\frac{x_1 + x_2}{2}, \frac{y_1 + y_2}{2}\right)$.

$$M_{BD} = \left(\frac{139 + 19}{2}, \frac{15 + 89}{2}\right)$$

$$M_{AC} = \left(\frac{139 + 19}{2}, \frac{89 + 15}{2}\right)$$

$$M_{BD} = \left(\frac{158}{2}, \frac{104}{2}\right) \qquad M_{AC} = \left(\frac{158}{2}, \frac{104}{2}\right)$$

$$M_{BD} = (79, 52) \qquad M_{AC} = (79, 52)$$

Thus, the diagonals of the playing field bisect each other at $(79, 52)$. This corresponds to the coordinates of the centre mark M.

43. Part A – Open Response

In ΔABC, the distance BC can be determined as follows:

$$\tan 25° = \frac{BC}{AB}$$

Substitute 130 for AB.

$$\tan 25° = \frac{BC}{130}$$

$$BC = 130 \times \tan 25°$$

$$BC \approx 60.62$$

The distance from the sprinkler head at point B to the sprinkler head at point C, to the nearest tenth, is 60.6 m.

Part B – Open Response

In order to determine the distance from the sprinkler head at point D to the sprinkler head at point E, first find the length of AD. This can be done as follows:

In ΔABC, $\cos 25° = \frac{AB}{AC}$.

Substitute 130 for AB.

$$\cos 25° = \frac{130}{AC}$$

$$AC \times \cos 25° = 130$$

$$AC = \frac{130}{\cos 25°}$$

$$AC \approx 143.44$$

In ΔACD, $\cos 15° = \frac{AC}{AD}$

Substitute 143.44 for AC.

$$\cos 15° = \frac{143.44}{AD}$$

$$AD \times \cos 15° = 143.44$$

$$AD = \frac{143.44}{\cos 15°}$$

$$AD \approx 148.50$$

Now use the tangent ratio:

$$\tan(A) = \frac{DE}{AD}$$

$$\tan(22°) = \frac{DE}{148.50}$$

$$DE = 60$$

The distance from the sprinkler head at point D to the sprinkler head at point E, to the nearest metre, is 60 m.

NOTES

Appendices

Formula Sheet

Quadratic Relations

Standard form: $y = a(x-h)^2 + k$

Factored form: $y = a(x-r)(x-s)$

General form: $y = ax^2 + bx + c, \quad a \neq 0$

Quadratic formula: $x = \dfrac{-b \pm \sqrt{b^2 - 4ac}}{2a}$

Factoring Polynomials

Perfect squares: $(a+b)^2 = a^2 + 2ab + b^2$
$(a-b)^2 = a^2 - 2ab + b^2$

Difference of squares: $a^2 - b^2 = (a-b)(a+b)$

Expanding polynomials

Distributive property: $a(x+y) = ax + ay$

Analytic Geometry

Midpoint formula: $M_{AB} = \left(\dfrac{x_1 + x_2}{2}, \dfrac{y_1 + y_2}{2}\right)$

Distance formula: $d = \sqrt{(x_2 - x_1)^2 + (y_2 - y_1)^2}$

Slope: $m = \dfrac{y_2 - y_1}{x_2 - x_1}$

Equation of a circle: $x^2 + y^2 = r^2$

Equation of a line: $y = mx + b$

Trigonometry

Right Triangles

Primary trigonometric ratios:

Sine ratio: $\sin A = \dfrac{\text{opposite}}{\text{hypotenuse}}$

Cosine ratio: $\cos A = \dfrac{\text{adjacent}}{\text{hypotenuse}}$

Tangent ratio: $\tan A = \dfrac{\text{opposite}}{\text{adjacent}}$

Acute Triangles

Law of sines: $\dfrac{a}{\sin \mathrm{A}} = \dfrac{b}{\sin \mathrm{B}} = \dfrac{c}{\sin \mathrm{C}}$

Law of cosines: $a^2 = b^2 + c^2 - 2bc \cos \mathrm{A}$

GLOSSARY

acute angle An angle measuring more than 0° but less than 90°.

acute triangle A triangle with all three angles each measuring less than 90°.

adjacent angle Two angles that share a common vertex and a common side. The sum of their measures is 180°. In the diagram below, angles a and b are adjacent angles as well as angles a and d.

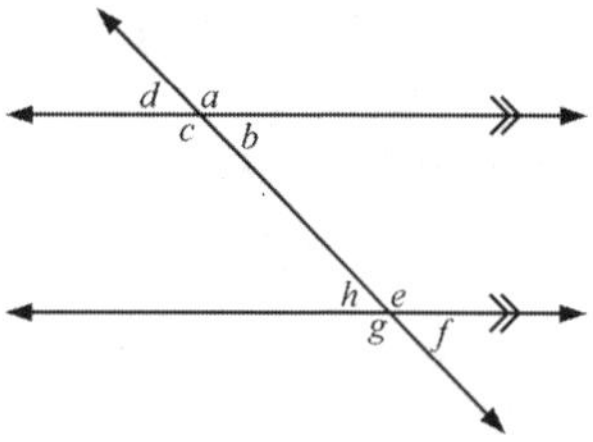

algebraic expression A mathematical phrase made up of numbers and variables that are connected by addition, subtraction, or both (3x, 5x + 6).

algebra tiles Manipulatives used to assist understanding of algebraic expressions and equations.

altitude A perpendicular line segment from the base of a figure to the opposite side or vertex.

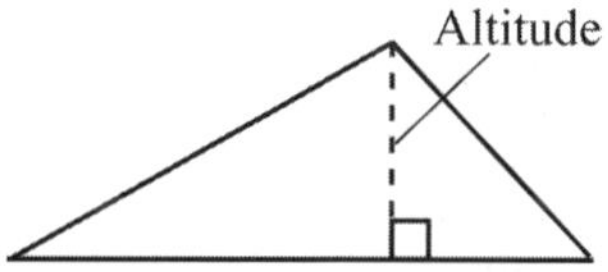

angle of elevation The angle formed between two rays where one of the rays is above the horizontal ray.

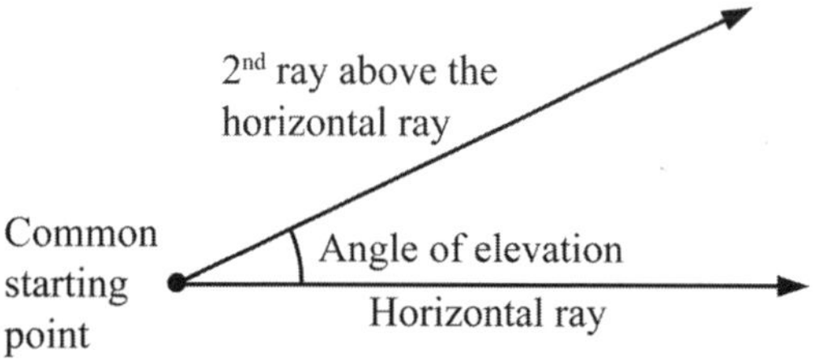

angle of depression The angle formed between two rays where one of the rays is below the horizontal ray.

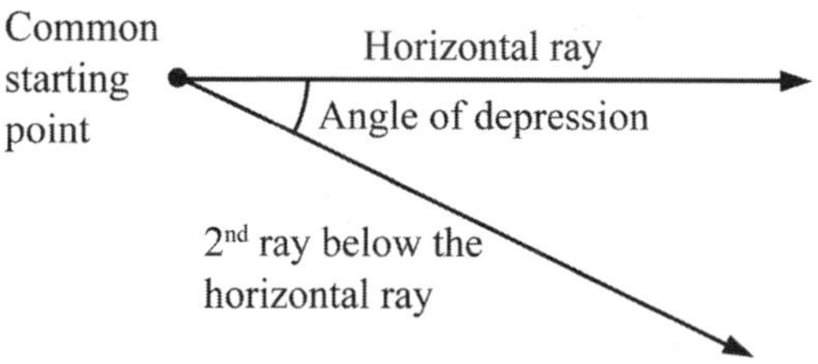

axis of symmetry A vertical line that passes through the vertex of the parabola and divides the parabola into two equal halves each of which is the mirror image of the other.

base (of a power) The number or symbol that is repeatedly multiplied as indicated by the exponent (2^3—2 is the base and is multiplied $2\times2\times2$).

binomial A two-termed polynomial ($2x+3y$).

bisect To cut into equal halves.

circle A collection of points in a plane that are an equal distance from a fixed point (the centre).

coefficient (numerical) The number immediately in front of a variable in a term that determines the factor by which the variable is multiplied. In 13x, the numerical coefficient is 13.

common factor A number that can be evenly divided into each number within a set of given numbers.

completing the square A mathematical process used to change the form of a quadratic function from the general form $y = ax^2 + bx + c$ to the standard form $y = a(x-h)^2 + k$.

conjecture A statement that appears to be true, but has not been proven true using appropriate mathematical logic.

congruent figures Figures of the same shape and size where all corresponding angles are congruent and all corresponding lengths are equal.

constant A term in a polynomial that contains no variables, only a single number.

coordinate plane A two-dimensional surface across which a number line extends horizontally (the x-axis) and is intersected by a number line extending vertically (the y-axis).

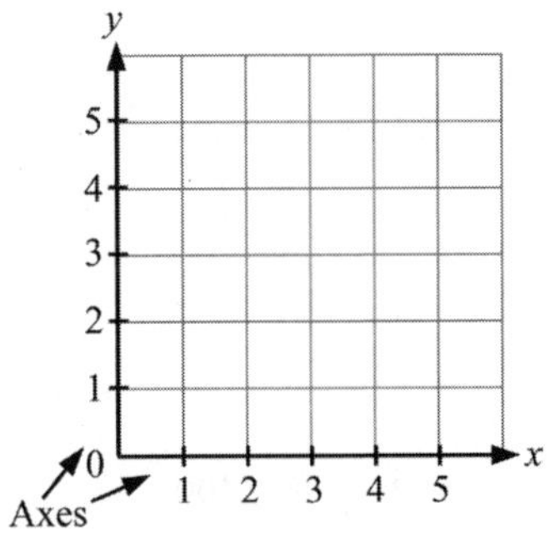

corresponding angles/sides Angles and sides that have the same relative positions in two or more geometric figures.

curve of best fit A curve that passes as close as possible to points plotted on a non-linear graph.

data Facts, statistics, or bits of information.

decomposition A commonly used procedure for factoring trinomials of the form $y = ax^2 + bx + c$, $a \neq 0$, where the middle term (bx) of the trinomial is split into two separate monomials such that the resulting expression can be factored by grouping.

diagonal A line connecting two non-adjacent vertices of a figure.

diameter The longest distance connecting two points on a circle and passing through the origin (see radius).

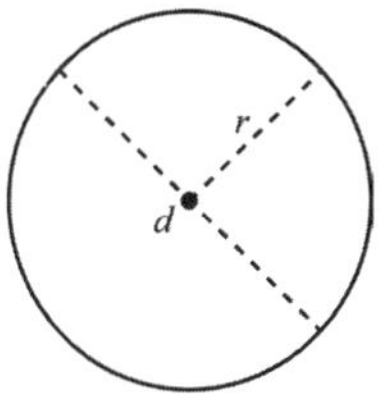

difference of squares A polynomial that can be expressed in the form $a^2 - b^2$, which can be factored into two monomials $(a+b)(a-b)$.

distributive property To multiply out the parts of an expression; $a(x+y) = ax + ay$.

domain The set of input values (usually represented by variable x) of a function.

equilateral triangle A triangle where each side of a triangle is equal in length.

expand To multiply through polynomials using real number properties.

exponent A number or variable, shown in a smaller size and raised, that indicates how many times the base is multiplied by itself before it is used as a factor; for example, 3 is the exponent in the expression 9^3 and x^3 [see base (of a power)].

exponential function A function of the form $y = ab^x$ where the input variable x is located in the exponent position.

expression Terms separated by operators (+, −, ×, ÷) with no equal sign ($2x+3$).

factor To multiply numbers or expressions to form another number or expression (2 and 4 are factors of 8).

factor by grouping A factor method where a polynomial is rewritten with an even number of terms, into smaller groups that contain a common factor.

factoring The process of breaking down a number or polynomial into its factors.

first differences The difference between consecutive y-values with evenly spaced x-values.

general form The equation of a parabola in the form $y = ax^2 + bx + c$, where $a \neq 0$.

greatest common factor (GCF) The largest factor common to two or more numbers.

horizontal translation A transformation that moves the graph of a relation horizontally on a coordinate plane.

hypotenuse The longest side of a right triangle; the side that is directly opposite the right angle.

interior angle The angle on the inside of a closed two-dimensional geometric figure.

intersecting lines Lines with one point in common (see point of intersection).

inverse The operation that cancels the given value (addition and subtraction are inverses; multiplication and division are inverses).

isosceles triangle A triangle where exactly two sides of the triangle are equal in length.

like terms Terms that have the same variables with identical exponents ($2y^2$ and $5y^2$).

linear equation An equation with a degree of 1 and whose graph is a straight line.

line segment All the points including and between two given points.

lowest common denominator (LCD) The lowest of all multiples shared by two or more numbers $\left(\text{LCD of } \frac{1}{2} \text{ and } \frac{1}{3} \text{ is } 6\right)$.

maximum value The y-coordinate of the highest point on the curve.

median (of a triangle) A line segment that joins the vertex to the midpoint of the opposite side.

midpoint The point halfway between two other given points.

minimum value The y-coordinate of the lowest point on the curve.

monomial A polynomial with only one term.

negative reciprocal The reciprocal of a number with the opposite sign added; for $\frac{3}{2}$, the negative reciprocal is $-\frac{2}{3}$.

oblique triangle A triangle that does not contain an angle of 90°.

ordered pair A pair of numbers, (x, y), on a coordinate plane that signify the value of x and the value of y for a given point on the plane.

origin The point of intersection of the horizontal and vertical axes on a graph, defined as (0, 0).

parabola A relation of the form $y = ax^2 + bx + c$, $(a \neq 0)$ will yield a U-shaped graph that either opens upward or downward.

parallel lines Lines in the same plane that are an equal distance apart and never meet. Parallel lines have the same slope and different y-intercepts.

parallelogram A quadrilateral that has two sets of parallel lines.

perimeter The measure of the distance around a closed figure.

perpendicular lines Lines that intersect at a 90° angle, and their slopes are negative reciprocals of each other.

point of intersection The point where two lines intersect and the x-values and the y-values for both lines are equal.

point-slope formula The equation $y - y_1 = m(x - x_1)$ that is used to determine the equation of a line when given one point (x, y) and the slope (m).

polynomial An algebraic expression that consists of one or more terms that are connected with addition or subtraction signs.

product rule for exponents An exponent law that states that when multiplying two powers of the same base, add the exponents.

Pythagorean theorem For any right triangle, the area of the square formed on the longest side is equal to the sum of the areas of the squares formed on the other two sides $(a^2 + b^2 = c^2)$.

quadratic equation An equation in which the variable is squared of the form $ax^2 + bx + c = 0$.

quadratic function An equation of the form $y = ax^2 + bx + c$, $a \neq 0$ and $a, b, c \in \mathbb{R}$.

quadratic regression The process of determining the equation of the curve of best fit for a given set of data.

quadratic relation A relation of the form $y = Ax^2 + Bxy + Cy^2 + Dx + Ey + F$, for the purpose of this course $B, C,$ and $E = 0$; for example, $y = Ax^2 + Dx + F$.

quadrilateral Any polygon with four sides (parallelogram, trapezoid, rhombus, rectangle, and square).

quotient rule for exponents An exponent law that states that when dividing two powers of the same base, subtract the exponents.

radius (plural: radii) The distance from the centre of a circle to any point lying on the circumference of the circle (see diameter).

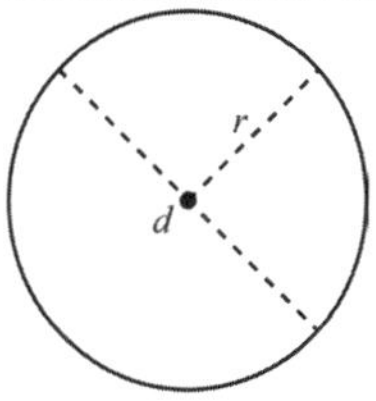

range The set of output values (usually represented by variable y) of a function.

reciprocal The multiplicative inverse of a number that has a product of 1 (the multiplicative inverse or reciprocal of $\frac{1}{3}$ is $\frac{3}{1}$).

rectangle A quadrilateral in which opposite sides are parallel to one another and equal in length, and adjacent sides are perpendicular to one another.

reflection in the *x*-axis A transformation in which all points on a relation that are above the x-axis get reflected to below the x-axis and all points below the x-axis get reflected above the x-axis. This creates a mirror image, using the x-axis as a reflection line.

relation Any set of ordered pairs.

rhombus A parallelogram with four equal sides. The diagonals are perpendicular.

right bisector A line that passes through the midpoint of a line segment and is perpendicular to the line segment (can also be referred to as the perpendicular bisector).

right triangle A triangle that has an interior angle of 90º (a right angle).

roots of an equation The values for the variable that satisfy the equation.

scalene triangle A triangle where each side of a triangle is different in length.

scatter plot A graph used in statistics to display the relationship of the data of two variables. The points are plotted as ordered pairs on a coordinate plane.

similar triangles Triangles with the same shape but not necessarily the same size or orientation.

simplify To find an equivalent expression that is simpler (more reduced) than the original.

slope The rate at which the y-values of a point of a line on a coordinate plane change with respect to a change in the x-values. It is the measure of the steepness of a line.

slope formula The equation $m = \frac{y_2 - y_1}{x_2 - x_1}$ used to find the slope of a line; m is the slope. The numerator represents the rise, and the denominator represents the run of the line.

slope y-intercept form The equation of a line in the form $y = mx + b$, where m is the slope and b is the y-intercept of the line.

square A quadrilateral in which all four sides are equal in length and opposite sides are parallel and adjacent sides are perpendicular.

standard form The equation of a parabola in the form $y = a(x - h)^2 + k$, where $a \neq 0$.

substitution When a specific value is used in place of a variable in an algebraic expression.

sum The value that results from adding numbers.

supplementary angles Two angles that have a sum of exactly 180°.

system of linear equations A set of linear equations involving two or more variables. A solution to this system is a set of points common to both lines.

table of values A table with the ordered pairs of the relation recorded. Typically, the x-value is in the left column, and the y-value is in the right column.

term A value or algebraic expression separated by plus or minus signs.

transformations Any mapping of a figure that results in a change in position, shape, size, or appearance of the figure; for example, translations, reflections, stretches, and compressions are transformations.

transversal A line that intersects two or more parallel lines.

trapezoid A quadrilateral in which the slope of exactly one pair of opposite sides is equal.

trinomial Any polynomial with exactly three terms; for example, $x^2 + 2x + 1$ is a trinomial.

variable A letter or symbol used to represent a value.

vertex of a parabola The ordered pair where the maximum or minimum value of y occurs.

vertical compression A transformation where the graph of a relation vertically flattens.

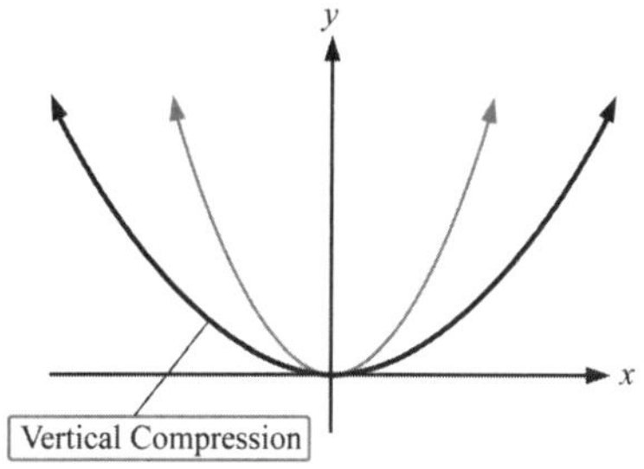

vertical stretch A transformation where the graph of a relation becomes elongated vertically.

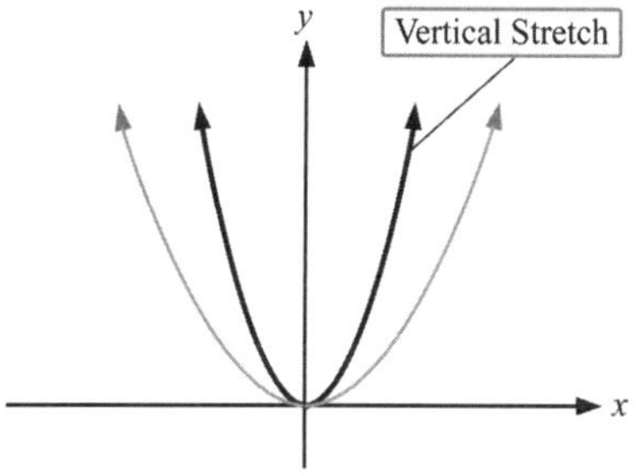

vertical translation A transformation that moves the graph of a relation vertically on a coordinate plane.

vertically-opposite angles Angles across two intersecting lines. These angles have the same measure.

x-axis The horizontal number line on a coordinate plane.

x-intercept The value of x when y is equal to zero or the point where the line crosses the x-axis.

y-axis The vertical number line on a coordinate plane.

y-intercept The value of y when x is equal to zero or the point where the line crosses the y-axis.

zeros Values that make a function equal to 0. These are also known as the x-intercepts of the graph of a function.

CREDITS

Every effort has been made to provide proper acknowledgement of the original source and to comply with copyright law. However, some attempts to establish original copyright ownership may have been unsuccessful. If copyright ownership can be identified, please notify Castle Rock Research Corp so that appropriate corrective action can be taken.

NOTES

NOTES

NOTES

NOTES

NOTES

NOTES

NOTES

RESOURCE INFORMATION *Order online at www.castlerockresearch.com*

SCHOOL ORDERS

Schools are eligible for an education discount. Contact Castle Rock Research Ontario for more information.

THE KEY Study Guides assist in preparing students for course assignments, unit tests, and final or provincial assessments.

***THE KEY* Study Guides** – $29.95 each plus G.S.T.

SECONDARY	ELEMENTARY
Biology 12, University Prep (SBI4U)	Science 8
Canadian and World Politics 12, University Prep (CPW4U)	Math 7
Chemistry 12, University Prep (SCH4U)	Science 7
English 12, University Prep (ENG4U)	Language 6 Reading & Writing
English 12, College Prep (ENG4C)	Math 6
Math 12 Advanced Functions, University Prep (MHF4U)	Science 6
Math 12 Calculus and Vectors, University Prep (MCV4U)	Math 5
Math 12 Data Management, University Prep (MDM4U)	Science 5
Physics 12, University Prep (SPH4U)	Math 4
World History 12, University Prep (CHY4U)	Science 4
Biology 11, University Prep (SBI3U)	Language 3 Reading & Writing
Chemistry 11, University Prep (SCH3U)	Math 3
English 11, University Prep (ENG3U)	Science 3
Math 11, Foundations for College Mathematics (MBF3C)	
Math 11, Functions and Applications, U/C Prep (MCF3M)	
Math 11, Functions, University Prep (MCR3U)	
World History 11, University/College Prep (CHW3M)	
Canadian History 10, Academic (CHC2D)	
Canadian History 10, Applied (CHC2P)	
Civics 10, (CHV2O)	
English 10, Academic (ENG2D)	
Math 10, Academic, Principles of Mathematics (MPM2D)	
Math 10, Applied, Foundations of Mathematics (MFM2P)	
OSSLT, Ontario Secondary School Literacy Test	
Science 10, Academic (SNC2D)	
English 9, Academic (ENG1D)	
Geography of Canada 9, Academic (CGC1D)	
Math 9, Academic, Principles of Mathematics (MPM1D)	
Math 9, Applied, Foundations of Mathematics (MFM1P)	
Science 9, Academic (SNC1D)	

The **Student Notes and Problems (SNAP)** workbooks provide complete lessons for course expectations, detailed explanations of concepts, and exercises with complete solutions.

SNAP Workbooks – $29.95 each plus G.S.T.

SECONDARY
Physics 12, University Preparation (SPH4U)
Physics 11, University Preparation (SPH3U)
Math 10, Academic, Principles of Mathematics (MPM2D)
Math 9, Academic, Principles of Mathematics (MPM1D)
Math 9, Applied, Foundations of Mathematics (MFM1P)

Visit our website for a tour of resource content and features or order online at
www.castlerockresearch.com

5250 Satellite Drive, Unit 11
Mississauga, ON L4W 5G5
E-mail: Ontario@castlerockresearch.com

Phone: 905.625.3332
Fax: 905.625.3390

CASTLE ROCK
RESEARCH CORP